The Software Principles of Design for Data Modeling

Debabrata Samanta
Rochester Institute of Technology, Kosovo

A volume in the Advances in Systems Analysis,
Software Engineering, and High Performance
Computing (ASASEHPC) Book Series

Published in the United States of America by
    IGI Global
    Engineering Science Reference (an imprint of IGI Global)
    701 E. Chocolate Avenue
    Hershey PA, USA 17033
    Tel: 717-533-8845
    Fax: 717-533-8661
    E-mail: cust@igi-global.com
    Web site: http://www.igi-global.com

Library of Congress Cataloging-in-Publication Data

Names: Samanta, Debabrata, 1987- editor.
Title: The software principles of design for data modeling / edited by
  Debabrata Samanta.
Description: Hershey, PA : Engineering Science Reference, [2023] | Includes
  bibliographical references and index. | Summary: "This book covers key
  topics such as gathering requirements, modeling requirements with use
  cases, testing the system, building entity-relationship models, building
  class models in UML with patterns of data modeling and software quality
  attributes, and use case modeling. It also includes case studies of
  relational and object-relational database schema design"-- Provided by
  publisher.
Identifiers: LCCN 2023017270 (print) | LCCN 2023017271 (ebook) | ISBN
  9781668498095 (h/c) | ISBN 9781668498132 (s/c) | ISBN 9781668498101
  (eISBN)
Subjects: LCSH: Computer simulation. | Software engineering.
Classification: LCC QA76.9.C65 S645 2023 (print) | LCC QA76.9.C65 (ebook)
  | DDC 003/.3--dc23/eng/20230906
LC record available at https://lccn.loc.gov/2023017270
LC ebook record available at https://lccn.loc.gov/2023017271

This book is published in the IGI Global book series Advances in Systems Analysis, Software Engineering, and High Performance Computing (ASASEHPC) (ISSN: 2327-3453; eISSN: 2327-3461)

British Cataloguing in Publication Data
A Cataloguing in Publication record for this book is available from the British Library.

For electronic access to this publication, please contact: eresources@igi-global.com.

Advances in Systems Analysis, Software Engineering, and High Performance Computing (ASASEHPC) Book Series

Vijayan Sugumaran
Oakland University, USA

ISSN:2327-3453
EISSN:2327-3461

MISSION

The theory and practice of computing applications and distributed systems has emerged as one of the key areas of research driving innovations in business, engineering, and science. The fields of software engineering, systems analysis, and high performance computing offer a wide range of applications and solutions in solving computational problems for any modern organization.

The **Advances in Systems Analysis, Software Engineering, and High Performance Computing (ASASEHPC) Book Series** brings together research in the areas of distributed computing, systems and software engineering, high performance computing, and service science. This collection of publications is useful for academics, researchers, and practitioners seeking the latest practices and knowledge in this field.

COVERAGE

- Network Management
- Metadata and Semantic Web
- Parallel Architectures
- Storage Systems
- Performance Modelling
- Engineering Environments
- Computer Networking
- Human-Computer Interaction
- Software Engineering
- Virtual Data Systems

IGI Global is currently accepting manuscripts for publication within this series. To submit a proposal for a volume in this series, please contact our Acquisition Editors at Acquisitions@igi-global.com or visit: http://www.igi-global.com/publish/.

Titles in this Series

For a list of additional titles in this series, please visit: www.igi-global.com/book-series

Neuromorphic Computing Systems for Industry 4.0
S. Dhanasekar (Department of ECE, Sree Eshwar Engineering College, India) K. Martin Sagayam (Karunya Institute of Technology and Sciences, India) Surbhi Vijh (KIET Group of Institutions, India) Vipin Tyagi (Jaypee University of Engineering and Technology, India) and Alex Norta (Tallinn University of Technology, Esonia)
Engineering Science Reference • © 2023 • 300pp • H/C (ISBN: 9781668465967) • US $270.00

Business Models and Strategies for Open Source Projects
Francisco José Monaco (Universidade de São Paulo, Bazil)
Business Science Reference • © 2023 • 300pp • H/C (ISBN: 9781668447857) • US $270.00

Principles, Policies, and Applications of Kotlin Programming
Duy Thanh Tran (University of Economics and Law, Ho Chi Minh City, Vietnam & Vietnam National University, Ho Chi Minh City, Vietnam) and Jun-Ho Huh (Korea Maritime and Ocean University, South Korea)
Engineering Science Reference • © 2023 • 457pp • H/C (ISBN: 9781668466872) • US $215.00

Concepts and Techniques of Graph Neural Networks
Vinod Kumar (Koneru Lakshmaiah Education Foundation (Deemed), India) and Dharmendra Singh Rajput (VIT University, India)
Engineering Science Reference • © 2023 • 247pp • H/C (ISBN: 9781668469033) • US $270.00

Cyber-Physical System Solutions for Smart Cities
Vanamoorthy Muthumanikandan (Vellore Institute of Technology, Chennai, India) Anbalagan Bhuvaneswari (Vellore Institute of Technology, Chennai, India) Balamurugan Easwaran (University of Africa, Toru-Orua, Nigeria) and T. Sudarson Rama Perumal (Rohini College of Engineering and Technology, India)
Engineering Science Reference • © 2023 • 300pp • H/C (ISBN: 9781668477564) • US $270.00

Adaptive Security and Cyber Assurance for Risk-Based Decision Making
Tyson T. Brooks (Syracuse University, USA)
Engineering Science Reference • © 2023 • 243pp • H/C (ISBN: 9781668477663) • US $225.00

Novel Research and Development Approaches in Heterogeneous Systems and Algorithms
Santanu Koley (Haldia Institute of Technology, India) Subhabrata Barman (Haldia Institute of Technology, India) and Subhankar Joardar (Haldia Institute of Technology, India)
Engineering Science Reference • © 2023 • 323pp • H/C (ISBN: 9781668475249) • US $270.00

701 East Chocolate Avenue, Hershey, PA 17033, USA
Tel: 717-533-8845 x100 • Fax: 717-533-8661
E-Mail: cust@igi-global.com • www.igi-global.com

To my parents, Mr. Dulal Chandra Samanta, Mrs. Ambujini Samanta; my elder sister, Mrs. Tanusree Samanta; brother-in-law, Mr. Soumendra Jana; and daughter, Ms. Aditri Samanta.

Table of Contents

Detailed Table of Contents

Chapter 1
Muskan Garg, Mayo Clinic, USA

Amid the pandemic, people express the cause and consequences of their mental disturbance on social media platforms with ease. The causal analysis through cause detection, cause inference, and cause classification, and identifying consequences such as loneliness and low self-esteem expedite the interpersonal risk factors. The interpersonal risk factors of thwarted belongingness and perceived burdensomeness trigger clinical depression, which if left untreated advances to suicidal ideation and self-harm. The mental health practitioners are reliable on mental health triaging and motivational interviewing. To this end, this chapter models the evolution of mental disturbance through self-reported texts generated by users suffering with mental disturbance. The clinical psychology theories on interpersonal needs questionnaire (INQ) supporting a theory on thwarted belongingness and perceived burdensomeness is followed by extracting causes and consequences in a given text.

Chapter 2
Olsa Rama, Rochester Institute of Technology, Kosovo

The network of billionaires could be analyzed through their data and information. Python has the capability of taking data and information from many sources and analyzing them from a single database. The idea of the report is to compare databases with all the billionaires in the world at different time frames. By collecting all the needed, such as personal information and integrable data, the program will output them in a table. The program takes datasets in the Comma Separated Values file and gives out the output through the Google Colab platform. The authors give importance to net worth and other publicly sensitive information that will be analyzed by the Python program. The purpose of analyzing billionaires around the world is to find similarities among countries with the potential for greater economic development.

Chapter 3

Diabetes is characterized by either insufficient or inefficient insulin production by the body. High blood glucose levels result from this, which over time can harm a number of tissues and organs in the body. Diabetes can be brought on by a specific age, obesity, inactivity, insufficient physical activity, inherited diabetes, lifestyle, poor diet, hypertension, etc. This chapter explores modeling requirements with diabetes using supervised machine learning techniques.

Chapter 4

Day-to-day life has become smarter and more intertwined with technology in the modern era. We can chat with AI chatbots, and we can play with AI machines. In many cases, AI machines are defeating human players. All age groups are likely to play these games. The computer gaming industry has found Artificial intelligence as a necessary element to make more entertaining and challenging games. This work involves the integration of rock-paper-scissors (RPS) game with artificial intelligence (AI) using OpenCV and MediaPipe. Through collaboration with designers and animators, the framework is designed to be computationally light while also entertaining and visually appealing. To evaluate kinematic hand data in Python, the basic gesture recognition pipeline employs a leap motion device and two distinct machine learning architectures. This proposed system will provide a powerful application for future research into social human-machine interaction.

Chapter 5

Modeling is the designing of software applications before coding according to the object-oriented groups where under the model-based software design and development, software modeling and design are used as an important and mandatory part of the software development process. Software models are methods of expressing a software design. Basically, some sort of abstract language or pictures are used to express the software design under modeling. For object-oriented software, an object modeling language such as UML and many more are used to develop and express the software design. Also, the design model is based on the analysis and architectural essentials of the system. It denotes the application components and determines their appropriate placement and use within the overall architecture.

Microservice architecture (MSA) is a popular software architecture style for developing scalable and resilient applications. However, designing data models for MSA presents unique challenges that require careful consideration. This chapter explores the relationship between MSA and data modeling and provides insights into best practices for designing data models that are optimized for MSA. It defines MSA and its key principles, examines the implications of MSA on data modeling, and discusses strategies for designing data models that are modular, decoupled, and flexible. The chapter also presents several case studies of organizations that have implemented MSA and data modeling strategies and discusses future trends in MSA and data modeling strategy, including the use of artificial intelligence and machine learning to automate data modeling. By following the best practices outlined in this chapter, organizations can realize the benefits of MSA while ensuring data consistency, scalability, and maintainability.

Chapter 7

   Devasis Pradhan, Acharya Institute of Technology, Bangalore, India
   Gnapika Mallavaram, Acharya Institute of Technology, Bangalore, India
   Kumari Priyanka, Acharya Institute of Technology, Bangalore, India
   S. Sneha, Acharya Institute of Technology, Bangalore, India
   Sidhi Jain, Acharya Institute of Technology, Bangalore, India

Boundary detection of foreign objects in airports is a critical safety concern, as debris and other objects can cause significant damage to aircraft and pose a serious risk to passenger safety. This chapter explores the use of Python programming language and computer vision techniques for the detection of objects at airports. The study presents an overview of the detection of objects in airport problems and their significance in aviation safety, followed by a detailed description of the Python-based foreign object detection system architecture. The system incorporates image processing algorithms and deep learning models to identify and classify foreign objects on airport runways and other operational areas. The chapter discusses the advantages and limitations of using Python for detection and highlights the potential for future research in this area. The study concludes by emphasizing the importance of detection in ensuring safe and efficient airport operations and the potential benefits of boundary detection using Python version 3.

Chapter 8

   Fiona Veseli, Rochester Institute of Technology, Kosovo
   Orinda Visoka, Rochester Institute of Technology, Kosovo
   Erudit Jupolli, Rochester Institute of Technology, Kosovo

The music industry generates an enormous amount of data, which makes classifying and organizing that data into a genre a very difficult task. A potential solution to that problem is to cluster the music using machine learning. Machine learning algorithms might enhance personalized suggestions, search engines, and music categorization systems by creating a model which can precisely identify different genres relying on their acoustic and subjective properties. Recent research suggests that even though there is a large overlap across genres, with machine learning algorithms, we can properly categorize music genres by recognizing differences as well as similarities between them. In more general terms, grouping musical styles using machine learning has several uses in the music industry. It can speed up the identification of new musical styles and encourage cross-genre collaborations among musicians.

We might become interested in stock market investment during the course of our lives. But to do that, we first need to have a clear understanding and analysis of the market. We may be unsure of whether to buy or sell stocks; thus, this is vital. It can be challenging to determine whether a stock will rise or decline in value or whether it will be a successful investment. In the event that the stock decreases, we can be unsure about whether to sell or stay on to it. Given the large number of investors who purchase stocks globally and the potential for significant losses, stock market analysis is crucial. The goal is to develop a project that analyzes the stock market and aids in our decision-making when it comes to purchasing and selling stocks.

A one-player game, 2048 is also known as stochastic puzzle. This fascinating and engaging game has gained widespread acclaim and drawn researchers to create gaming software. The game 2048 has evolved into an engaging and difficult platform for assessing the efficacy of machine learning techniques because of its simplicity and complexity. Convolutional neural networks were used to create some computer players, but they performed poorly. In this work, the authors create a 2048 agent based on the reinforcement learning method and neural networks. The authors want to outperform other neural-network-based competitors in terms of results. Additionally, cutting-edge software created using this methodology for 2048 achieves the best performance out of all learning-based algorithms.

Human resource management practices bring all the industrial experts under one umbrella and encourages them to work for common organizational goals. Industrial operations are the combination of technology, innovation, arts, management, and commerce. Industrial HRM practices are changing from time to time with consideration of changing business perspectives, technology, and competition. The principal motive of presenting the research initiative was to identify the changing scenario of industrial HRM practices over the last two decades that represented the use case modeling for the next generation entrepreneurs. The research outcomes are well connected to address the industrial HR issues in the area of engineering, data mining, and analysis for the development of object-oriented business operations.

Chapter 12

Ritwika Das Gupta, CHRIST University (Deemed), India

This chapter focuses on software development principles and discusses each principle thoroughly with diagrammatic representation. It also includes the definition of UML (unified modeling language) modelling with an explanation regarding how UML modelling takes place and a detailed example. It also focuses on software testing methods, with each method definition and diagrams well explained. A simple case study situation is taken to discuss the example of UML model. This chapter's main objective is to focus on all key points of software development testing and model design techniques precisely.

Chapter 13

Rajesh Kanna Rajendran, CHRIST University (Deemed), India
T. Mohana Priya, CHRIST University (Deemed), India

Relational databases are a critical component of modern software applications, providing a reliable and scalable method for storing and managing data. A well-designed database schema can enhance the performance and flexibility of applications, making them more efficient and easier to maintain. Data modeling is an essential process in designing a database schema, and it involves identifying and organizing data entities, attributes, and relationships. In this chapter, the authors discuss the principles of designing an efficient and scalable relational database schema, with a focus on data modeling techniques. They explore the critical aspects of normalization, data types, relationships, indexes, and denormalization, as well as techniques for optimizing database queries and managing scalability challenges. The principles discussed in this chapter can be applied to various database management systems and can be useful for designing a schema that meets the demands of modern data-intensive applications.

Chapter 14

Guri Arianit Sokoli, Rochester Institute of Technology, Kosovo

The number of billionaires in a country gives us significant insights regarding the country's corporate and economic landscape. The number of billionaires indicates the country's economic performance, financial market strength, and amount of support for entrepreneurship and innovation. The presence of a large number of billionaires suggests that the country has a solid business climate that promotes the growth and success of affluent individuals. These people' riches may have been built through creative business methods, technical developments, or savvy investments. However, it is crucial to highlight that the number of billionaires does not always imply a thriving economy. Our project seeks to investigate the global links of billionaires and their commercial specialization tactics.

Chapter 15

Art Hajdari, Rochester Institute of Technology, Kosovo

A relational database schema was designed for the Kosovo Hospital Management System. The objective was to create a platform to store patient information, appointments, billing, and feedback, with the main goal of improving patient care. Eleven unique tables were created, with primary and foreign keys defining the relationships between them. Through the tables it is possible the management of patient and doctor schedules, medical records, allergies, blood donations, medical equipment, and hospital department administration, among others. The management system benefits all healthcare institutions such as hospitals, clinics, and blood banks, as well as medical staff such as doctors and nurses. Patients can also benefit from this by providing better healthcare services, faster appointment scheduling, and more.

Chapter 16

Albana Zejnullahi, Rochester Institute of Technology, Kosovo

It's crucial to thoroughly research the prior history of the cryptocurrency market, in this case Dogecoin, before considering investing in the financial market, especially the cryptocurrency market. The authors want to create a Python project that forecasts Dogecoin's price. To accomplish this, researchers need to gather all available data on Dogecoin's price history and use it to create mathematical formulas that will decide the currency's pricing. In order to help people grasp this data, the authors also create a chart to display it all.

Chapter 17

Saurabh Bhattacharya, Chitkara University, India

The method for researchers to ascertain clients' software needs is requirement gathering. Requirement gathering rarely occurs successfully, and numerous software programs have failed as a result of incorrect or partial knowledge of the needs of users. The requirement-gathering technique is widely considered to be an essential part of development. The chapter will critically discuss why many developments fail due to poor requirements gathering. It is a challenging task to elicit requirements. When requirements are elicited, errors are most common. Addressing the system's needs presents several challenges, and the chapter intends to study these challenges and provide a solution. Professionals face challenges in gathering requirements due to the unavailability of stakeholders, unclear requirements, frequent changes in demand, and lack of skills for analysts. In a variety of contexts and areas, interviews with a preference for framework proved to be among the best gathering approaches.

Chapter 18

Amrit Singh, NIST Institute of Science and Technology (Autonomous), India
Harisankar Mahapatra, NIST Institute of Science and Technology (Autonomous), India
Anil Kumar Biswal, Udayanath College of Science and Technology (Autonomous), India
Milan Samantaray, Trident Academy of Technology, India
Debabrata Singh, Institute of Technical Education and Research, Siksha 'O' Anusandhan
  (Deemed), India

The project focuses on the development of a credit scoring model. Concerns with credit scoring are being raised when developing an empirical model to support the financial decision-making process for financial institutions. This chapter focuses on the development of a credit scoring model using a combination of feature selection and ensemble classifiers. The most relevant features are identified, and an ensemble classifier is used to reduce the risk of overfitting with the aim of improving the classification performance of credit scoring models in the proposed method. Several metrics, including accuracy, precision, recall, F1 score, and AUC-ROC, are used to evaluate the performance of the model. The accuracy and robustness of credit scoring models can potentially be improved by the proposed method, and the evaluation metrics can be used to further enhance it.

Chapter 19

Industrial applications and research studies report that organizations using machine learning (ML) solutions may be at risk of failure or they could fall short of business objectives. One serious issue that is often neglected is meeting the specific requirements of machine learning-driven software systems (MLD-SS). The use of a variety of information technologies, integration methods and tools, and domain-specific processes can add to this complexity. The data-driven and black-box nature of ML may be another great challenge. Therefore, there is a clear need for adopting a stakeholder-centered approach to the requirements engineering (RE) of MLD-SS. Use case modeling (UCM) can make requirements simpler and understandable by all stakeholders, allow better communication of ideas and provide support to testing, validation, and verification processes. In this chapter, a ten-step RE method and a four-step UCM method are proposed for MLD-SS, and then these methods are applied in a real case study of a university hospital.

Chapter 20

5G NR (new radio) coverage tool is a software-based solution that helps network planners and engineers to analyze and optimize the coverage of 5G networks. The tool uses advanced algorithms and models to predict the 5G signal propagation and coverage performance in different environments and scenarios. It takes into account various factors such as the frequency band, the antenna configuration, the terrain, the building materials, and the interference from other sources. It provides a detailed analysis of the signal strength, quality, and throughput in different locations, enabling network operators to identify areas with poor coverage and take appropriate measures to improve it. It also allows network planners to simulate different deployment scenarios and optimize the network design for maximum coverage and capacity. The tool provides real-time feedback and visualization of the coverage performance, allowing engineers to adjust the network parameters and antenna configurations on the fly.

Preface

In this book, use case-driven data modeling is used to cover the *Software Principles of Design for Data Modeling*, including gathering requirements, modeling requirements with use cases, testing the system, building entity-relationship models, building class models in UML with patterns of data modeling and software quality attributes, and use case modeling. The book gives a unified method for creating software architectures for data modeling while outlining the particular problems associated with each category of software concepts. The few case studies presented include Designing an Object-Relational Database Schema and A Relational Database Schema. In this book, several software modeling and design processes that make use of Class Models are explained. The highly iterative approach addresses the requirements, analysis, and development of object-oriented software.

Chapter 1: People easily express the origin and effects of their mental disturbance on social media platforms during an epidemic. The identification of outcomes like loneliness and low self-esteem, as well as causal analysis using cause detection, cause inference, and cause classification, speed up the identification of interpersonal risk factors. Clinical depression is sparked by the interpersonal risk factors of not feeling like you belong and feeling like a burden, which, if untreated, can lead to suicidal thoughts and self-harm. Mental health professionals are trustworthy when it comes to motivational interviewing and mental health triage. In order to achieve this, this book chapter uses user-generated, self-reported texts to model the development of mental illness. Extracting causes and effects from a text is followed by the clinical psychology theories on the Interpersonal Needs Questionnaire (INQ), which support a theory on thwarted belongingness and felt burdensomeness. These cause-and-effect relationships aid in spotting potential signs of loneliness and low self-esteem, which can lead to severe mental health problems like the risk of self-harm or suicide.

Chapter 2: Their data and information could be used to analyze the network of billionaires. Python is capable of processing data and information from several sources using just one database. The purpose of the paper is to examine databases that include all billionaires worldwide during various time periods. A table will be produced by the application after gathering all the necessary data, including integrable and personal information. The software outputs data through the Google Colab platform using datasets in Comma Separated Values files. We definitely consider Net worth and other publicly sensitive data that the Python application will assess. Finding commonalities among nations with the potential for greater economic development is the goal of studying the world's billionaires.

Chapter 3: A chronic illness like diabetes is a diagnosable problem that has an impact on how your body needs glucose, a type of sugar essential for giving your cells the energy and nutrition they need to function. As you eat, your body turns the meal's carbohydrates into glucose, which is then transported to your cells by the blood with the help of the hormone insulin, which the pancreas produces. Diabetes is characterized by the body producing either insufficient or ineffective amounts of insulin. This leads to high blood glucose levels, which over time can damage a number of body tissues and organs. Age, obesity, lack of physical exercise, genetic diabetes, lifestyle, a bad diet, hypertension, etc. can all contribute to the development of diabetes. Numerous factors contribute to diabetes's damaging effects on the kidney, eye, and Age, obesity, lack of physical exercise, genetic diabetes, lifestyle, a bad diet, hypertension, etc. can all contribute to the development of diabetes. Diabetes can harm human organs like the kidney, eye, vision, heart, brain, and toes among others for a variety of reasons. Machine learning is a young field of data science that examines how computers learn via experience. By utilizing the data, this greatly aids in the diagnosis of disorders affecting the eyes, heart, brain, and toes, among other organs. Machine learning is a young field of data science that examines how computers learn via experience. This greatly aids in the prediction of any ailments when using the data.

Chapter 4: In the modern period, daily life has evolved and become increasingly technologically dependent. We can communicate with AI chatbots and play games with AI devices. Artificial intelligence (AI) computers frequently outperforms human players. People of all ages like playing these games. Artificial intelligence has been recognized by the computer gaming industry as a crucial component to making games more engaging and difficult. In this project, OpenCV and MediaPipe are used to integrate the RPS game with artificial intelligence (AI). The framework is created in partnership with designers and animators to be computationally light, engaging, and visually appealing. The fundamental gesture recognition pipeline uses a 1eap motion device and two different machine learning architectures to analyze kinematic hand data in Python. Future studies into social human-machine interaction will find tremendous applications for the proposed approach.

Chapter 5: Software modeling and design are used as a crucial and necessary component of the software development process in model-based software design and development. According to object-oriented classifications, modeling is the process of creating software programs before they are coded. Software models can be used to communicate a software design. In essence, the software design that is being modelled is communicated through some form of abstract language or visuals. The program design for object-oriented software is created and communicated using an object modeling language, such as UML and many others. The system analysis and significant architectural elements also serve as the foundation for the design model. It recognizes the components of the application and decides how and where to use them in connection to the overall architecture. This software's design is broken down into four design models: sequential, design-centered, concurrent, and dynamic. The three levels of design are interface design, architectural design, and detailed design. Today, modeling provides a visual depiction of the systems that will grow and contribute to a successful software organization. Modeling is a tried-and-true method that is widely used in the highly regarded field of software engineering. The four principles of modeling are as follows: The architecture of the system being produced must always be taken into consideration, data design is just as important as processing, and interfaces must be designed. Traceable designs must be created for model requirements. Any physical model is a concrete depiction of the system as opposed to the mathematical and logical models, which are both more abstract. Additionally, the abstract model can be broken down into two groups: analytical (similar to mathematical) and descriptive (comparable to logical). Models are developed, examined, and used to direct the actual development of the system before it is actually put into use. The model-driven architecture, UML, and an overview of software modeling and architectural design are all covered in this chapter. Additionally, object-oriented notations and methods are included. Object-oriented principles are crucial for software analysis and design because they address the core issues of program modifiability, adaptation, and evolution. The fundamental principles of object-oriented approaches are information hiding, classes, and inheritance in this Chapter 5.

Chapter 6: A common software architecture style for creating scalable and resilient applications is microservice architecture (MSA). However, creating data models for MSA has particular difficulties that call for careful thought. This book chapter examines the connection between MSA and data modeling and offers guidance on how to create data models that are effective for MSA. It describes MSA and its core tenets, explores how MSA affects data modeling, and covers techniques for creating modular, decoupled, and adaptable data models. The chapter also includes a number of case studies of businesses that have used MSA and data modeling strategies, as well as discussion of upcoming developments in these fields, such as the automation of data modeling through artificial intelligence and machine learning. Organizations can reap the benefits of MSA while guaranteeing data consistency, scalability, and maintainability by adhering to the recommended practices described in this chapter. This book chapter seeks to give readers a thorough grasp of how MSA and data modeling are related, as well as to arm developers with the information and resources they need to create data models that are tailored for MSA in Chapter 6.

Chapter 7: Airport boundary detection of foreign objects is a crucial safety concern since debris and other items can seriously endanger passenger safety and cause serious damage to aircraft. The usage of the Python programming language and computer vision techniques for the detection of items at airports is explored in this abstract. The study begins with an introduction of object identification in airport issues and their importance to aviation safety. This is followed by a detailed discussion of the architecture of the Python-based foreign object detection system. To recognize and categorize foreign objects on airport runways and other operational zones, the system combines image processing techniques and deep learning models. The study analyzes the benefits and drawbacks of using Python for detection and points out the promise of further investigation in this field. The study's conclusion highlights the value of detection in ensuring safe and effective airport operations as well as the possible advantages of employing Python version 3 for border detection.

Chapter 8: The music industry produces a huge amount of data, making it incredibly challenging to categorize and organize that data into a genre. Using machine learning to cluster the music could be a solution to that issue. By developing a model that can properly identify various genres based on their subjective and acoustic characteristics, machine learning algorithms may help improve personalized suggestions, search engines, and music categorization systems. According to recent study, even if there is significant overlap across genres, machine learning algorithms can effectively classify music genres by identifying both their differences and their similarities. In the music industry, categorizing musical types using machine learning has a variety of applications. It can hasten the discovery of fresh musical genres and promote cross-genre musical collaborations.

Chapter 9: Throughout our lifetimes, we could develop an interest in stock market investments. But in order to do that, we must first clearly grasp and analyze the market. This is important because we can be unclear whether to buy or sell stocks. Determining whether a stock will increase in value or decrease in value, or if it will be a profitable investment, can be difficult. We may be unsure of whether to sell or hold onto the stock if it drops in price. Stock market analysis is essential because of the vast number of investors that buy equities globally and the possibility of substantial losses. Our objective is to create a project that analyzes the stock market and helps us make decisions about buying and selling equities.

Chapter 10: One-player 2048 is another name for a stochastic problem. A lot of people have praised this unique and captivating game, which has inspired academics to make gaming software. Because of its simplicity and complexity, the game 2048 has developed into an interesting and challenging platform for evaluating the effectiveness of machine learning algorithms. Some computer players were made using convolutional neural networks, but they weren't very good. In this work, we build a 2048 agent using neural networks and the reinforcement learning technique. In terms of results, we aspire to outperform other neural network-based rivals. Furthermore, among all learning-based algorithms, a cutting-edge software developed for 2048 utilizing this methodology achieves the best performance.

Chapter 11: Human resource management is a relatively new profession that unites all industrial professionals under one roof and motivates them to collaborate on shared organizational objectives. The intersection of technology, innovation, the arts, management, and commerce is what makes up industrial operations. Industrial HRM procedures occasionally change as a result of evolving corporate perspectives, technological advancements, and competitive pressures. The main goal of presenting the study endeavor was to pinpoint the evolution of industrial HRM methods over the last two decades, which served as use case modeling for the future generation of business owners. The study's findings have a strong connection to industrial HR problems in the fields of engineering, data mining, and analysis for the creation of object-oriented business operations.

Chapter 12: The principles of software development are the main topic of this chapter, which goes into great detail and includes diagrams to illustrate each idea. Additionally, a definition of UML modeling is provided, along with an explanation of how UML modeling works and a thorough example. It also emphasizes software testing techniques, thoroughly describing each technique's concept and flowchart. A straightforward case study scenario is used to demonstrate a UML model example. The major goal of this chapter is to precisely focus on all crucial aspects of software development testing and model creation methodologies.

Chapter 13: Relational databases are an essential part of contemporary software programs because they offer a dependable and scalable way to store and manage data. Applications can perform better and be more flexible with a well-designed database schema, which also makes them easier to maintain and more effective. Data modeling, which involves identifying and arranging data entities, properties, and relationships, is a crucial step in the design of a database schema. With a focus on data modeling strategies, we go over the fundamentals of creating a relational database schema that is effective and scalable in this chapter. We examine the crucial facets of normalization, data types, relationships, indexes, and denormalization as well as strategies for query optimization in databases and handling scalability issues. The techniques covered in this paper can be used to develop a schema that satisfies the requirements of contemporary data-intensive applications and can be beneficial for a variety of database management systems.

Chapter 14: The number of billionaires in a nation provides us with important information about the corporate and economic climate of that nation. The number of billionaires is a good indicator of a nation's financial market strength, entrepreneurship, and innovation support. The presence of several billionaires shows that the nation has a positive business environment that fosters the development and success of wealthy people. These persons may have amassed their wealth as a result of innovative business strategies, technological advancements, or astute financial decisions. It is important to note that a large number of billionaires does not necessarily indicate a booming economy. Our initiative aims to look into the global connections of billionaires and their strategies for commercial specialization. Examining data on billionaires' histories, industries, and investing preferences allows us to spot trends and patterns in their backgrounds, sectors, and investment strategies. Our team will use cutting-edge data visualization tools to present this information in an approachable and educational way, giving people and businesses insights into the practices and strategies of the world's wealthiest people. Future business decisions, investment plans, and policy development may be informed by this.

Chapter 15: The Kosovo Hospital Management System was created with a relational database schema. The main goal was to enhance patient care, so the purpose was to build a platform to store patient data, appointments, billing, and feedback. Primary and foreign keys were used to define the connections between the eleven distinct tables. The management of patient and doctor appointments, medical records, allergies, blood donations, medical equipment, and administration of hospital departments, among other things, is feasible through the tables. All healthcare organizations, including blood banks, hospitals, and clinics, as well as medical personnel like doctors and nurses, profit from the management system. By offering better healthcare services, quicker appointment scheduling, and more, patients can also gain from this in this Chapter 15.

Before considering investing in the financial industry, particularly the cryptocurrency market, it is essential to conduct in-depth study on the prior history of the cryptocurrency market, in this case Dogecoin. A Python project that projects Dogecoin's price is what we want to build. In order to do this, we must compile all information about Dogecoin's past price movements and utilize it to develop mathematical algorithms that will determine the price of the cryptocurrency. We also make a graphic to show all of this data so that others may better understand it. Using a range of visualizations, including head values, price charts, and outputs, we were able to identify substantial differences between the datasets. We found that the most recent data and the appropriate dataset selection are essential for accurate price prediction. We also used the machine learning tool AutoTS to further improve the accuracy of our predictions. This study highlights the importance of careful data collection and analysis for precise price prediction. By utilizing the latest information and cutting-edge tools, investors may make better decisions and earn better returns in Chapter 16.

Chapter 17: Requirements gathering is the process by which researchers identify clients' software needs. Requirement The inability to accurately or completely understand user wants has contributed to the failure of many software products and the rarity of successful data gathering. The approach of gathering requirements is frequently regarded as a crucial component of development. The chapter will critically explore how inadequate requirements gathering contributes to the failure of numerous advancements. The task of eliciting requirements is difficult. Errors are most frequently made when requirements are elicited. The chapter aims to examine these difficulties and offer a solution as they relate to addressing the needs of the system. Due to the absence of stakeholders, ambiguous needs, rapid changes in demand, and a lack of analyst skills, professionals have difficulty obtaining requirements. Interviews with a preference for framework has out to be one of the greatest methods for getting information in a number of situations and fields.

Chapter 18: The project's main goal is to create a credit scoring model. When creating an empirical model to support the financial decision-making process for financial institutions, questions about credit scoring are being highlighted. The creation of a credit scoring model utilizing feature selection and ensemble classifiers is the main topic of this chapter. The most important characteristics are identified in order to improve the classification performance of credit scoring models in the proposed method, and an ensemble classifier is used to reduce the risk of overfitting. The ensemble learning models Bagging, Boosting, and Stacking are a few examples. In order to anticipate defaults and determine people's credit ratings, our credit scoring model, which is depicted in Fig. 1, uses Decision Tree, Random Forest, Gradient Boosting, and Extreme Gradient Boosting approaches. Financial firms utilize statistical analysis known as credit scoring models to determine whether a consumer is creditworthy.

Chapter 19: Research studies and commercial applications indicate that businesses are utilizing machine learning. Meeting the unique requirements of machine learning-driven software systems (MLD-SS) is a critical challenge that is frequently ignored. This complexity may be increased by the use of various information technologies, integration techniques and tools, and domain-specific procedures. Another significant difficulty with ML may be how data-driven and opaque it is. Therefore, it is obvious that the requirements engineering (RE) of MLD-SS must use a stakeholder-centered approach. Use case modeling (UCM) enables better concept communication, simplifies requirements so they are clearer to all parties involved, and supports testing, validation, and verification processes. For MLD-SS, this chapter proposes a nine-step RE method and a four-step UCM approach. These methods are then put to use in an actual case study of a university hospital.

Chapter 20: A software-based tool called 5G NR (New Radio) coverage tool aids network planners and engineers in analyzing and enhancing the coverage of 5G networks. The program forecasts the performance of the 5G signal propagation and coverage in various settings and scenarios using cutting-edge algorithms and models. It takes into account a number of variables, including the frequency band, the antenna set-up, the topography, the construction materials, and outside interference. It gives network operators a thorough study of the signal strength, quality, and throughput in various locations, allowing them to spot weak coverage spots and take the necessary action to fix them. Additionally, it enables network designers to simulate various deployment scenarios and enhance the network architecture for optimal capacity and coverage. Engineers can quickly change the network settings and antenna configurations thanks to the tool's real-time feedback and visualization of the coverage performance. It is a crucial tool for network engineers and planners to deliver a seamless and dependable user experience while ensuring the best performance of 5G networks.

Debabrata Samanta
Rochester Institute of Technology, Kosovo

Acknowledgment

I express our great pleasure, sincere thanks, and gratitude to the people who significantly helped, contributed and supported to the completion of this book entitled with *"The Software Principles of Design for Data Modeling"*. My sincere thanks to Fr. Benny Thomas, Professor, Department of Computer Science and Engineering, CHRIST (Deemed to be University), Bengaluru, Karnataka India, and Siddhartha Bhattacharyya, Principal, Rajnagar Mahavidyalaya, Rajnagar, Birbhum, India for their continuous support, advice and cordial guidance from the beginning to the completion of this book.

I would also like to express our honest appreciation to my colleagues at Department of Computational Information Technology, Rochester Institute of Technology, Kosovo, Europe for their guidance and support.

I also thank all the authors who have contributed some chapters to this book. This book would not have been possible without their contribution.

I am also very thankful to the reviewers for reviewing the book chapters. This book would not have been possible without their continuous support and commitment towards completing the chapters' review on time.

To complete this book, all the publishing team members at IGI Global extended their king cooperation, timely response, expert comments, guidance, and I am very thankful to them.

Finally, I sincerely express our special and heartfelt respect, gratitude, and gratefulness to my family members and parents for their endless support and blessings.

Chapter 1
The Social Media Psyche:
Modeling Mental Disturbance
in the Digital Age

Muskan Garg
Mayo Clinic, USA

ABSTRACT

Amid the pandemic, people express the cause and consequences of their mental disturbance on social media platforms with ease. The causal analysis through cause detection, cause inference, and cause classification, and identifying consequences such as loneliness and low self-esteem expedite the interpersonal risk factors. The interpersonal risk factors of thwarted belongingness and perceived burdensomeness trigger clinical depression, which if left untreated advances to suicidal ideation and self-harm. The mental health practitioners are reliable on mental health triaging and motivational interviewing. To this end, this chapter models the evolution of mental disturbance through self-reported texts generated by users suffering with mental disturbance. The clinical psychology theories on interpersonal needs questionnaire (INQ) supporting a theory on thwarted belongingness and perceived burdensomeness is followed by extracting causes and consequences in a given text.

INTRODUCTION TO SOCIAL MEDIA PSYCHE

With increasing concerns with social and mental wellbeing, *social determinants of health* plays a pivotal role in society now. Social determinants of health (SDOH) refers to the key factors which are responsible for wellbeing of a person and to achieve the SDOH 2030 goals, there is an accelerated growth of both academic and industrial growth to address the impact of human behavior. Social behavior of a person underlying social interactions, induces the need of *interpersonal skills*. The skills and actions that enable people to interact, cooperate, and communicate effectively with others in social or professional settings are known as interpersonal skills. People meet their *interpersonal needs* by honing their ability to connect with others, through enduring relationships, and communicating clearly by developing strong interpersonal skills. Interpersonal needs is the psychological practice for meaningful social interactions

DOI: 10.4018/978-1-6684-9809-5.ch001

and relationships such as social support, intimacy, belongingness, and affection. Presence of these needs (met) contributes to the feelings of happiness, fulfillment, and well-being, and their absence (unmet) arouses the feelings of loneliness, isolation, and distress.

With increasing complexities in life, especially in the post COVID-19 era, increase in the demand of a clinical psychologist/ mental health therapist has revealed the limitation of healthcare supply (Garg *et al.,* 2023). According to the World Health Organization, approximately 280 million people in the world have depression. Mental health problems are considered as a social stigma/ taboo. People with mental health are considered not sick enough to provide healthcare and thus, are often ignored. Amid *social distancing*, people prefer disclosing their thoughts and share their experiences on social media platforms and through other digital media, with ease. As a result, the digital media, despite its ethical issues (Anshari et al., 2022), has become a more reliable and insightful resource to uncover latent mental disturbance which may lead to prospective chronic disease, if left untreated. To this end, it becomes seemingly important to identify the potential resources to extract potential data that is required to solve the elevating problem of severe mental disorders.

SOCIAL BEHAVIOR AND MENTAL HEALTH

The emerging global phenomenon of social media use suggests novel insights about social cognitive processes as it offers latent indicators of processing, remembering, and using contextual information by online users to explain and predict their own behavior and that of others (Meshi et al., 2015). Thus, social cognition, being a part of the psychological aspect, enables the individuals to understand human perspectives and their behavior towards each other. This journey of perception to decision-making follows a three-step process as examined via the lens of cognitive functionality: (i) social perception, (ii) social understanding, (iii) social decision-making (Arioli et al., 2018). Perception is the state of being aware of something through our five senses: vision, auditory, olfactory, gustatory, tactile, and the sixth-one being common sense. Perception plays a vital part in mental health as it determines how individuals understand and respond to diverse situations, experiences, and stimuli which facilitates the development of positive and adaptive perceptions that may lead to improved mental health outcomes. Moreover, mental disturbance affects how we think, feel, and act, thereby determining the stress handling, making healthy choices and highlighting the importance of mental wellbeing. One of the major psychology-grounded theory on evolution of suicide risk from mental disturbance is based on the impact on interpersonal needs of a person.

Interpersonal Risk Factors: Evolution of Suicide Risk

As discussed above, the interpersonal needs of a person, if left unmet, raise serious concerns of loneliness, isolation, and low self-esteem. Such concerns of loneliness and low self-esteem, if left untreated, may elevate to interpersonal risk factors such as thwarted burdensomeness and perceived belongingness (Sommerfeld et al., 2019). A well-established theory in clinical psychology 'Interpersonal Theory of Suicide' was given by Thomas Joiner in 2005 (Joiner et al., 2005), suggests that two factors are critical in the development of suicidal ideation: (i) Thwarted Burdensomeness (TBe), and (ii) Perceived Belongingness (PBu) which are examined using the Interpersonal Needs Questionnaire (INQ).

Thwarted Belongingness is a feeling of disconnection or isolation from others, or a lack of a sense of belongingness arising from a variety of factors, such as social rejection, loneliness, or a lack of meaningful social connections. Indicators of thwarted belongingness in a given text can be identified by examining the language used to describe social connections or lack thereof. For example, the use of words such as "isolated", "alone", "alienated" or "disconnected" may indicate a sense of thwarted belongingness (see Figure 1). Similarly, words describing lack of or problems with social connections or meaningful relationships may also suggest the absence of a sense of belongingness.

Perceived Belongingness is a psychological reference to an individual's perception or hallucination of being a burden to others around them. They may feel that they are being a liability to others and may feel guilty or ashamed about their perceived impact on those around them. Indicators of perceived burdensomeness in a given text can be identified by examining the language used to describe the individual's perceived impact on others. For example, the use of words such as "liability," "burden," or "hindrance" may suggest a sense of perceived burdensomeness (see Figure 1).

Figure 1. Red and purple color illustrate thwarted belongingness (TBe) and perceived belongingness (PBu)

Tonight he has gone to one of our colleagues house parties, I wasn't invited. No one invited me anywhere and I don't blame them. I'm not angry that he went, I am angry at myself. I have no friends, live miles away from any family and at the age of almost 28 have nothing to live for. I try to stay upbeat but I really don't see the point. I've alienated myself from everyone and this is what I get. I just want it all to be over as I am burden for this society.

The Interpersonal Needs Questionnaires

The Interpersonal Needs Questionnaire (INQ) is a self-administered survey that gauges perceived burdensomeness and thwarted belongingness, which are the two principal components of the Interpersonal Theory of Suicide. Developed in 2009 by Thomas Joiner and his associates, the questionnaire comprises 15 questions, including 5 queries about perceived burdensomeness (such as "I feel like I am a burden to others") and 10 questions about thwarted belongingness (such as "I feel disconnected from other people"). Respondents rate each question on a 7-point Likert scale, varying from 1 (not accurate for me) to 7 (very accurate for me). The INQ is widely used in research and clinical practice to evaluate suicide risk and prevention, and has been adapted for various groups, including young adults/ adolescents and college students, and translated into many languages (Iliceto et al., 2021; Arafat et al., 2022; Liu et al., 2022; Pandia et al., 2022).

Interpersonal Theory of Suicide

As discussed above, the interpersonal theory of suicide lies in determining the prospective suicide attempt through intersection of Thwarted Belongingness (TBe), Perceived Belongingness (PBu), and Capacity for suicide as shown in Figure 2. The intersection of TBe and PBu evolves with the willingness to end their own life, and is referred as *desire of suicide*. The extent of *capacity of suicide* derives suicidal ideation to suicide attempt.

Figure 2. Interpersonal theory of suicide

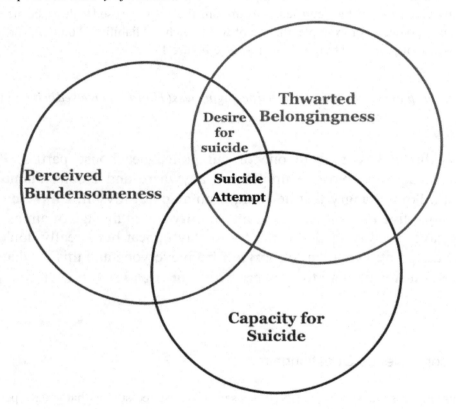

Figure 3. Overview of the evolution of chronic diseases (clinical depression and suicide risk) from mental disturbance

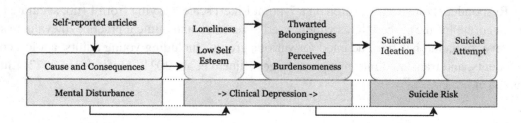

Humans are inherently social whose thought process is influenced by external environment and circumstances. Such circumstances implants the state of confusion and seeds the elements of stress and anxiety. With inappropriate ego development, more complexities in society and career development as compared to personal relations, people are unable to share things among peers, friends and family, resulting in mental disturbance (see Figure 3). Thus, mental disturbance is rooted in cause (reasons) (Garg et al., 2022) and consequence (affect) on mental wellbeing. This mental disturbance is intensified with interpersonal theory of suicide, that leads to suicidal risk (Roy et al., 2020).

Digital Age: Social Media Platforms and Psychology-Grounded Social Theories

Digital data comprises internet blogs, weblogs and social media platforms. As of February 2023, there were 5.3 billion active internet users worldwide, representing 66.25% of the global population[1]. In 2022, 4.9 billion active social media users were reported resulting in 63.2% of the global population[2]. Global Wellness Institute states that the global wellness economy was valued at $4.9 trillion in 2019 downsizing to $4.4 trillion in 2020, due to the widespread impacts of the COVID-19 pandemic. GWI predicts the wellness economy to grow by 9.9% on average annually, resulting in near about $7.0 trillion in 2025[3]. The section focuses on the information acquired from social media platforms and the need of its analyses, followed by the social theories grounded in psychology. *Traditional in-person therapy* sessions (Probst et al., 2021) and other interventions help individuals to identify and address negative perceptions, and develop more positive and adaptive ways of interpreting and responding to their experiences. However, a classic approach of incorporating traditional methods of in-person sessions with mental health practitioners for mental disorders is drifting towards automation through *conversational agents* and *AI chatbots* in the digital age. People express their experiences in self-narrated texts on social media platforms such as Twitter and Reddit, with ease, making it an interesting and reliable resource, despite underlying ethical considerations.

The Social Comparison Theory

Social media users start comparing their emotions, career development and capital within the social circle in digital media which makes them discontented. Thus, people are constantly comparing themselves to others as a way to evaluate their own abilities, achievements, and status, affecting self-esteem and well-being. The *satisfaction of life* is influenced by both *upward comparison* and *downward comparison* in social comparison theory (Olivos et al., 2021) as illustrated in Figure 4.

When an individual compares themselves to someone they believe to be superior or to possess more desired qualities, such as greater intelligence, larger income, or better physical appearance, this is known as an *upward comparison*. Feelings of inspiration, envy, inadequacy, or dissatisfaction with oneself may result from this kind of comparison (Mouris et al., 2022). The method of people's perception and access to their lives, as well as particular spheres and activities within them, is termed as subjective well-being (SWB). The subjective well-being evolves from active and passive usage of the social media platforms (digital data) through social capital/ connectedness and upward social comparison/ envy, respectively (Verduyn et al., 2017). When someone compares themselves to someone they believe to be lesser or to possess less desirable qualities, this is known as a *downward comparison*. Comparisons of this nature can engender sentiments of superiority, fulfillment, or appreciation. The *Social Comparison Theory* also states that the upward comparison and downward comparison influences self- improvement and self-esteem, respectively[4]. The sense of belongingness plays an intermediate role between perceived functions from social media platforms to social attachments (Wang et al., 2021, Yang et al., 2021).

Figure 4. The social comparison theory illustrating the association between the digital age and satisfaction with life

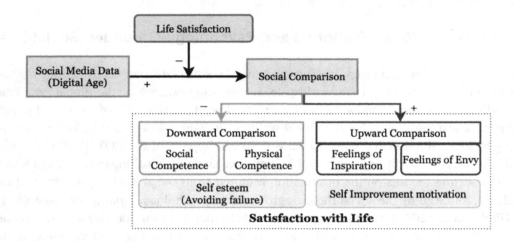

Social Attachment theory

Social Attachment theory suggests that individuals form attachments which influence their behavior and emotional experiences (See Figure 5). The theory suggests that social media platforms may serve as a source of social support, validation, and self-expression, leading to attachment formation. Social media users may also become attached to specific content and can form attachments to other users such as close friends or romantic partners. These attachments to social media can influence users' behavior and emotions, leading to increased engagement with the platform, positive or negative emotional experiences, and a sense of belonging or social connectedness.

Figure 5. Social attachment theory for social attachment through social media platforms

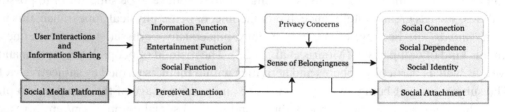

Social attachments are dynamic and can change over time leveraging the social interactions, social support and information sharing which is followed by perceived functions such as information function, entertainment function and social function. Such perceived functions indicate a sense of belongingness, triggering *social attachment*, which is affected by social connection and social dependence. The idea behind using self-reported human writings for determining social attachment roots in a sense of belongingness which is bolstered by ethical and privacy concerns for social media users and other stakeholders. Such ethical considerations and privacy concerns should be accompanied by responsible AI model development through explainable human-like text generation (Saxena et al., 2022; Roy et al., 2022) and other similar mechanisms.

ARCHITECTURE FOR MODELING MENTAL DISTURBANCE

With an established background, modeling mental disturbance through a well defined architecture shall facilitate industrial applications and software development. These softwares, if developed under careful observation of clinical psychologists and mental health practitioners, may help in early risk detection and prevent severe mental disorders (Jia, 2018). Consider an architecture in Figure 6 depicting the modeling of mental disturbance through data analyses and developing computational models.

The data analysis is performed by the research community in social computing in association of mental health practitioners, bolstered with clinical questionnaires for interpersonal needs (INQ, as discussed before). The acquired social media data contains the self-narrated posts about experiences and perception of a social media user depicting the need of its analyses for obtaining useful insights. Such insights may help in better understanding of the evolution of suicidal ideation through given posts, social media user and their metadata, resulting in extensive social computing on multimodal social media data (Jeffers, 2022). Consider corresponding colored texts in Figure 7, illustrating the evolution of mental disorders in longitudinal social media text.

Figure 6. Architecture for modeling mental disturbance for digital data

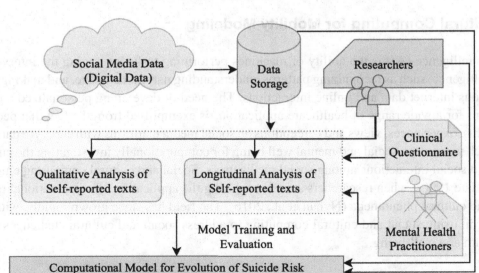

Figure 7. An example of evolution of chronic mental disorders with triggered mental disturbance

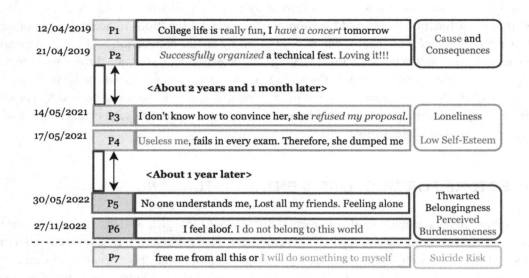

Physical Model: The approach of identifying triggering words in a given self-reported text to determine lonesomeness and low self-esteem illustrates the importance of *domain-specific keyphrase extraction* or *sequence to sequence model* to define the problem of determining the explainable lonesomeness and explainable low self-esteem for interpersonal needs. Such interpersonal risk factors are determined through computational models.

Conceptual Model: The conceptual data model for computing social media data to determine evolution of suicide risk comprises of associations between interpersonal risk factors and cause-and-consequence in a given self-reported text (Kaur et al., 2022; Zirikly et al., 2019). Such associations highlights the elevation of mental disturbance to sub-clinical, followed by clinical depression, which if left untreated, shall lead to chronic mental disorders such as suicidal ideation or self-harm.

Ethnocultural Computing for Mobility Modeling

Artificial Intelligence (AI) is the ability of machines performing tasks leveraging the interventions of human intelligence, such as recognizing patterns, understanding natural language, and making decisions in voluminous internet data and online interactions. The need of developing personalized and cultural interventions for a wide range of healthcare applications is exemplified from the fact that people share their thoughts, experiences, views and perceptions on social media platforms with ease. We narrow down our approach to focus on social and mental well being for computationally investigating the cultural differences and social interactions among social media users. Social and cultural computing emerged as a field in the late 1990s, when researchers started exploring the application of computational techniques to social and cultural phenomena (Nyhan et al., 2016). The field has since grown rapidly, with increasing interest in using social and cultural computing to address social and cultural challenges related to mental health and well-being.

Ethnocomputing is the study of the interactions between computing and culture. It is also termed as Cultural computing or Ethnic computing. Ethnocomputing seeks to develop technologies that are culturally sensitive and that cater to the needs of diverse populations. By doing so, it helps to promote inclusivity and to reduce the digital divide. Many *global challenges, such as climate change and food insecurity*, have cultural dimensions. Ethnocomputing can be used to develop *mental healthcare technologies* that are sensitive to cultural differences and that cater to the needs and values of diverse populations. For example, AI-powered diagnostic tools and AI chatbots/ conversational agents (Virtual Mental Health Agents) must be customized to take into account cultural differences in the presentation of symptoms and addressing the audience, respectively.

Virtual Mental Health Assistants (VMHA)

Online platforms and a recent surge in the inventions of chatbots such as *Virtual Mental Health Assistants (VMHA)*, make therapy more accessible to individuals from diverse cultural backgrounds (Kolenik et al., 2020). VMHA uses computational approaches to provide mental health support and assistance to individuals through virtual platforms. A virtual mental health assistant can be designed to provide personalized and culturally-tailored interventions that address specific mental health concerns (Wibhovo et al., 2021; Deng et al., 2022). Therapy through digital platforms can be delivered remotely as per convenience of a patient having limited access to mental health services due to cultural or geographic barriers. VMHA should not replace professional mental health services, as some mental health conditions may require in-person diagnosis and treatment by a licensed mental health practitioner. Cultural computing can help mental health practitioners to develop a deeper understanding of cultural diversity and to become more culturally competent, thereby increasing the effectiveness of therapy and reducing the risk of cultural misunderstandings.

With increase in globalization, mobility modeling analyzes patterns of movement of people or objects (Kirmayer et al., 2013). In the context of mental disturbance in social media data, ethnocomputing for mobility modeling would involve examining how cultural and social factors influence the patterns of onset of mental decline with the movement of social media users who display symptoms of mental disturbance during their social media use. In order to find patterns of behavior and communication that may point to mental discomfort, this strategy would necessitate the collecting and analysis of significant amounts of social media data. Researchers could learn more about how cultural and societal influences affect mental health and well-being by incorporating cultural and social factors into the analysis.

AVAILABLE TOOLS AND RESOURCES

There are many tools and resources available for modeling mental disturbance in social media data. Researchers use these tools to gain insights from first-hand information generated by social media users and develop interventions to support those who are struggling.

Social Media Data Extraction Tools

An open-source Python framework called Scrapy[5] is used for data extraction and web crawling. Data may be extracted from social media sites like Twitter, Facebook, and Instagram using this method. Custom parsing rules, support for numerous data types, and connection with other Python libraries for data analysis are just a few of the capabilities that Scrapy offers.

Social Networking

There are various tools in Python and R programming languages that can automatically generate networks from social media connections. Additionally, there are many web and window-based applications available online, with many of them being open-source for research purposes. The following network science-based tools are the most commonly used for generating the network of users and their interactions, as they are both reliable and fast. NetworkX (Hagberg et al., 2008) is a Python language package for exploration and analysis of networks and network algorithms. The core package provides data structures for representing many types of networks, or graphs, including simple graphs, directed graphs, and graphs with parallel edges and self loops. The nodes in NetworkX graphs can be any (hashable) Python object, and this flexibility makes NetworkX ideal for representing networks found in many different scientific fields. In addition to the basic data structures, many graph algorithms are implemented for calculating network properties and structure measures: shortest paths, betweenness centrality, clustering, and degree distribution and many more.

Clinical Questionnaires

Other than INQ (Mitchell et al., 2020), there are various clinical questionnaires that can be used to assess interpersonal needs such as Basic Psychological Need Satisfaction and Frustration Scale (BPNSFS): This questionnaire assesses the basic psychological needs of autonomy, competence, and relatedness (Nishimura et al., 2016). It consists of 24 items that measure the extent to which an individual feels satisfied or frustrated in each of these three areas. It's important to note that these questionnaires should be administered and interpreted by a qualified mental health professional. The psychometric properties like INQ have been given for other languages such as Bangla (Arafat et al., 2022), Indonesian (Pandia et al., 2022), and Italian (Iliceto et al., 2021) language, and for other underrepresented groups such as Transgender Women (Liu et al., 2022).

CONCLUSION

In conclusion, social media has become an important platform for people to express their mental health concerns, especially during the pandemic. The analysis of self-reported texts on social media platforms helps in identifying the causes and consequences of mental disturbance, including loneliness, low self-esteem, and interpersonal risk factors such as thwarted belongingness and perceived burdensomeness. Clinical depression triggered by these risk factors can lead to suicidal ideation and self-harm if left untreated. Mental health practitioners rely on mental health triaging and motivational interviewing to address these concerns. The Interpersonal Needs Questionnaire (INQ) supports a theory on the evolution of mental disturbance, and the identification of prospective indicators of loneliness and low self-esteem through the analysis of social media texts can be useful in preventing extreme mental health issues. Therefore, social media offers valuable insights into the psyche of individuals and can serve as an important resource to uncover latent mental disturbance and improve mental wellbeing.

REFERENCES

Anshari, M., Hamdan, M., Ahmad, N., Ali, E., & Haidi, H. (2022). COVID-19, artificial intelligence, ethical challenges and policy implications. *AI & Society*, 1–14. PMID:35607368

Arafat, S. Y., Hussain, F., Zaman, M. S., Tabassum, T., Islam, M. K., Shormi, F. R., Khan, A. R., Islam, M. R., Redwan, A. S. M., Giasuddin, N. A., Mubashir, A., & Khan, M. A. S. (2022). Thwarted belongingness, perceived burdensomeness, and acquired capability for suicide among university students of Bangladesh: Scales validation and status assessment. *Frontiers in Psychiatry*, *13*, 13. doi:10.3389/fpsyt.2022.1025976 PMID:36311516

Deng, M., Zhai, S., Ouyang, X., Liu, Z., & Ross, B. (2022). Factors influencing medication adherence among patients with severe mental disorders from the perspective of mental health professionals. *BMC Psychiatry*, *22*(1), 22. doi:10.118612888-021-03681-6 PMID:34996394

Garg, M. (2023). Mental Health Analysis in Social Media Posts: A Survey. *Archives of Computational Methods in Engineering*, *30*(3), 1–24. doi:10.100711831-022-09863-z PMID:36619138

Garg, M., Saxena, C., Saha, S., Krishnan, V., Joshi, R., & Mago, V. (2022, June). CAMS: An Annotated Corpus for Causal Analysis of Mental Health Issues in Social Media Posts. In *Proceedings of the Thirteenth Language Resources and Evaluation Conference* (pp. 6387-6396). Academic Press.

Hagberg, A., Swart, P., & Chult, S. D. (2008). Exploring network structure, dynamics, and function using NetworkX (No. LA-UR-08-05495; LA-UR-08-5495). Los Alamos National Lab (LANL).

Iliceto, P., D'Antuono, L., Fino, E., Carcione, A., Candilera, G., Silva, C., & Joiner, T. E. (2021). Psychometric properties of the Italian version of the Interpersonal Needs Questionnaire-15 (INQ-15-I). *Journal of Clinical Psychology*, *77*(1), 268–285. doi:10.1002/jclp.23026 PMID:32662083

Jeffers, A. E. (2022). The Field of Computing Needs to Take Care of Its Mental Health. *Computing in Science & Engineering*, *24*(2), 91–94. doi:10.1109/MCSE.2022.3162034

Jia, J. (2018, October). Mental Health Computing via Harvesting Social Media Data. In *Proceedings of the Joint Workshop of the 4th Workshop on Affective Social Multimedia Computing and first Multi-Modal Affective Computing of Large-Scale Multimedia Data* (pp. 70-70). 10.1145/3267935.3267954

Joiner, T. E. (2005). *Why people die by suicide*. Harvard University Press.

Kaur, S., Bhardwaj, R., Jain, A., Garg, M., & Saxena, C. (2022, December). Causal Categorization of Mental Health Posts using Transformers. In *Proceedings of the 14th Annual Meeting of the Forum for Information Retrieval Evaluation* (pp. 43-46). 10.1145/3574318.3574334

Kirmayer, L. J., & Swartz, L. (2013). Culture and global mental health. *Global mental health: Principles and practice*, 41-62.

Kolenik, T., Gjoreski, M., & Gams, M. (2020). PerMEASS-Personal Mental Health Virtual Assistant with Novel Ambient Intelligence Integration. In AAI4H@ ECAI (pp. 8-12). Academic Press.

Liu, Y., Wang, R., Chang, R., Wang, H., Xu, L., Xu, C., Yu, X., Liu, S., Chen, H., Chen, Y., Jin, L., Wang, Y., & Cai, Y. (2022). Perceived Burdensomeness, Thwarted Belongingness, and Social Exclusion in Transgender Women: Psychometric Properties of the Interpersonal Needs Questionnaire. *Frontiers in Psychology, 13*, 787809. doi:10.3389/fpsyg.2022.787809 PMID:35222188

Mitchell, S. M., Brown, S. L., Roush, J. F., Tucker, R. P., Cukrowicz, K. C., & Joiner, T. E. (2020). The Interpersonal Needs Questionnaire: Statistical considerations for improved clinical application. *Assessment, 27*(3), 621–637. doi:10.1177/1073191118824660 PMID:30654631

Mouris, D. J. (2022). *Does Instagram make us feel better or worse?: How Upward Social Comparisons on Instagram Influences Young Adults' Psychological Well-being* [Bachelor's thesis]. University of Twente.

Nishimura, T., & Suzuki, T. (2016). Basic psychological need satisfaction and frustration in J apan: Controlling for the big five personality traits. *The Japanese Psychological Research, 58*(4), 320–331. doi:10.1111/jpr.12131

Nyhan, J., & Flinn, A. (2016). *Computation and the humanities: towards an oral history of digital humanities*. Springer Nature. doi:10.1007/978-3-319-20170-2

Olivos, F., Olivos-Jara, P., & Browne, M. (2021). Asymmetric social comparison and life satisfaction in social networks. *Journal of Happiness Studies, 22*(1), 363–384. doi:10.100710902-020-00234-8

Pandia, V., Fitriana, E., Afriandi, I., Purba, F. D., Danasasmita, F. S., Ichsan, A., & Pradana, K. (2022). Psychometric evaluation of the interpersonal needs questionnaire in the Indonesian language. *PLoS One, 17*(12), e0279272. doi:10.1371/journal.pone.0279272 PMID:36525445

Probst, T., Haid, B., Schimböck, W., Reisinger, A., Gasser, M., Eichberger-Heckmann, H., Stippl, P., Jesser, A., Humer, E., Korecka, N., & Pieh, C. (2021). Therapeutic interventions in in-person and remote psychotherapy: Survey with psychotherapists and patients experiencing in-person and remote psychotherapy during COVID-19. *Clinical Psychology & Psychotherapy, 28*(4), 988–1000. doi:10.1002/cpp.2553 PMID:33448499

Roy, A., Nikolitch, K., McGinn, R., Jinah, S., Klement, W., & Kaminsky, Z. A. (2020). A machine learning approach predicts future risk to suicidal ideation from social media data. *NPJ Digital Medicine, 3*(1), 78. doi:10.103841746-020-0287-6 PMID:32509975

Roy, K., Gaur, M., Zhang, Q., & Sheth, A. (2022). *Process knowledge-infused learning for suicidality assessment on social media*. arXiv preprint arXiv:2204.12560.

Saxena, C., Garg, M., & Saxena, G. (2022). *Explainable causal analysis of mental health on social media data*. arXiv preprint arXiv:2210.08430.

Sommerfeld, E., & Malek, S. (2019). Perfectionism moderates the relationship between thwarted belongingness and perceived burdensomeness and suicide ideation in adolescents. *The Psychiatric Quarterly*, *90*(4), 671–681. doi:10.100711126-019-09639-y PMID:31037588

Verduyn, P., Ybarra, O., Résibois, M., Jonides, J., & Kross, E. (2017). Do social network sites enhance or undermine subjective well-being? A critical review. *Social Issues and Policy Review*, *11*(1), 274–302. doi:10.1111ipr.12033

Wang, Q., Yang, M., & Zhang, W. (2021). Accessing the influence of perceived value on social attachment: Developing country perspective. *Frontiers in Psychology*, *12*, 760774. doi:10.3389/fpsyg.2021.760774 PMID:34721242

Wibhowo, C., & Sanjaya, R. (2021, July). Virtual assistant to suicide prevention in individuals with borderline personality disorder. In *2021 International Conference on Computer & Information Sciences (ICCOINS)* (pp. 234-237). IEEE. 10.1109/ICCOINS49721.2021.9497160

Yang, M., Zhang, W., Ruangkanjanases, A., & Zhang, Y. (2021). Understanding the mechanism of social attachment role in social media: A qualitative analysis. *Frontiers in Psychology*, *12*, 720880. doi:10.3389/fpsyg.2021.720880 PMID:34421773

Zirikly, A., Resnik, P., Uzuner, O., & Hollingshead, K. (2019, June). CLPsych 2019 shared task: Predicting the degree of suicide risk in Reddit posts. In *Proceedings of the sixth workshop on computational linguistics and clinical psychology* (pp. 24-33). 10.18653/v1/W19-3003

ENDNOTES

[1] https://www.statista.com/statistics/273018/number-of-internet-users-worldwide/
[2] https://www.statista.com/statistics/278414/number-of-worldwide-social-network-users/
[3] https://globalwellnessinstitute.org/press-room/statistics-and-facts/
[4] https://is.theorizeit.org/wiki/Social_Comparison_Theory
[5] https://scrapy.org/

Chapter 2
Analyzing Billionaire Databases Using Python

Olsa Rama
Rochester Institute of Technology, Kosovo

ABSTRACT

The network of billionaires could be analyzed through their data and information. Python has the capability of taking data and information from many sources and analyzing them from a single database. The idea of the report is to compare databases with all the billionaires in the world at different time frames. By collecting all the needed, such as personal information and integrable data, the program will output them in a table. The program takes datasets in the Comma Separated Values file and gives out the output through the Google Colab platform. The authors give importance to net worth and other publicly sensitive information that will be analyzed by the Python program. The purpose of analyzing billionaires around the world is to find similarities among countries with the potential for greater economic development.

INTRODUCTION

This report is a comparative analysis that explores the changes between two datasets that contain information on the top billionaires through different points in time (Asif, Muhammad, et al. 2021). The methodology of this research is quantitative; therefore, the conclusion will come from analyzing the statistics. The successful carriers of Billionaires have been linked to larger economic growth and opportunities at the international level (Bart et al. 2016). There has been much debate on what determines Billionaires to rise and remain on the scene. The underlying factor stands on the industries and domains that are prone to be more successful (Dangi et al., 2023; Podder et al., 2023). We will consider other research that has been conducted on this particular topic. The research paper conducted by Eric Neumayer analyzes billionaires from a global perspective, issuing how more economically wealthy countries such as the US appear to dominate in the number of billionaires according to the Forbes lists from 2001-2003 (Guha et al., 2023). There is an observation that there are billionaires emerging from developing countries and there is a correlation between the involvement of the government, the individual, and the circumstances in economic freedom (Banzhaf et al., 2021; Capehart et al., 2014). The analysis estimates models of

DOI: 10.4018/978-1-6684-9809-5.ch002

developed and developing countries. There is a claim that more freedom for individuals with greater qualities to persevere in personal economic growth will reach and impact great successful economic wealth. One of the considerations is additional circumstances, such as the protection rights of private property deducted by an index in economic freedom (Bagchi et al., 2019. Jain et al., 2023). The author hypotheses if an economy is prone to a considerable degree of government involvement, great wealth cannot emerge even when the basic core of economic freedom exists. The conclusion, however, appears to disagree that government involvement has an impact because the differences between estimations are not that significant. The most notable outcome is that developed countries with good privacy protection rights have an advantage in accumulating higher wealth rather than developing countries (Ball et al., 2021).

DATASET DESCRIPTION

The Database consists of Billionaire's information. The collection of the data is displayed on a table in the csv file. The Database from which all the output gets displayed is titled "Billionaires.csv".

- **Size:** 189256
- **Python code:**
  from pathlib import Patho
  sizz = Patho('Billionaire.csv').stat().st_size
  print(sizz)

- **No. of col: 7**
- **No. of row: 2765**

Database Description With All Attributes

The columns of the database are Name, Net Worth, Year, Country, Source, Age, and Industry.

Input

The Python program takes 7 inputs in the order given: Name, Net Worth, Country, Source, Rank, Age, and Industry. The first column is reserved for the First name and the Last name combined. The other column contains the Net Worth value which is denoted in Billion Dollars unit. The Net worth is the most important data and it determines the sequence of the order, to clarify, from highest to lowest (Chesters et al., 201; Althar et al., 2023). The following field is Country, which displays the country where the company of the Billionaire is based on. The source is reserved for the Company that generates the income. The rank is the numbered sequence from 1 to 2765 being directly connected to the Net worth from highest to lowest. The Age input is the age of the Billionaire. The Industry field contains the industry of the billion-dollar company, for example, Technology, Metals Mining, Fashion Retail, Automotive, etc. (Clemente et al., 2021; Gurunath et al., 2023).

Expected Output

The output is expected to display a fulfilled field of all the information given: Full Name, Net Worth, Country of origin, Source of the income, (for instance the company that generates the income in Billion Dollars), the Rank from the ordered sequence ranging from the Highest Net Worth to the Lowest, the age of the Billionaire, and the Industry they belong to. The outcome of this program is for us to be able to analyze the correlation between Industries and Countries that generate the most Billionaires. There is an implied pattern that ties certain countries and industries as more prone to success and we can determine that from the results (outputs) of the dataset (Coupe et al., 2016; Mondal et al., 2023; Garg et al., 2023).

Dataset Description

The collection of the data is from a multi-decade time frame and is displayed in a table in the CSV file. The Database from which all the output gets displayed is originally titled "Billionaire.csv" by Ryan Whitcomb, but for the sake of clarification, it has been changed to "billionaires_database_2" to be differentiated by the first. For the sake of simplification, there have been some alterations in the database that should be mentioned; the name of the columns was changed to accommodate the Python sample code making the execution possible (Flanigan et al., 2022; Cunaku et al., 2023). Initially, there were more columns with additional information that were excluded. There preserved columns are the information are: name, net worth, year, country, source (or company), age, and industry. The original work is credited below:

- **Size:** 163778
- **Python code:**
  from pathlib import Path
  sizz = Path('/content/billionaires_database_2.csv').stat().st_size
  print(sizz)No. of col: 7

- **No. of row: 2616**

Database Description With All Attributes

The columns of the database are Name, Net Worth, Year, Country, Source, Age, and Industry.

Input

The Python program takes 7 inputs in the order given: Name, Net Worth, Year, Country, Source, Age, and Industry. The first column is reserved for the First name and the Last name combined. The other column contains the Net Worth value which is denoted in Billion Dollars unit. The following is the year the company peaked in the ranks then. The following field is Country, which displays where the company of the Billionaire is based on Fuentenebro et al. (2020). The source is reserved for the Company that generates the income. The Age input is the age of the Billionaire. The Industry field contains the industry of the billion-dollar company, for example, Technology, Metals Mining, Fashion Retail, Automotive, etc.

Expected Output

The output is expected to display a fulfilled field of all the information given: Full Name, Net Worth, Year, Country of origin, Source of income, (for instance the company that generates the income in Billion Dollars), the Rank which is taken from the times the billionaire, the age of the Billionaire, and the Industry they belong to. The outcome of this database is directly comparable to the other database.

ALGORITHM AND STEP-BY-STEP SEQUENCE OF PROCESS

The process of analyzing the outputs was done using Google Colab. Colab is an online notebook code editor. It is cloud-based and provided by Google. To start Colab, we can search on Chrome with simply "Colab", and it will take us to the interface website.

- We log in via our Gmail account
- From there we can select the File option on the top left menu.
- That results in opening Python 3 notebook on a new page

There is the option to directly paste the link to the database with the given GitHub project where in that case, Colab directly pulls out the database without needing to store it elsewhere. In the other situation, where we use a CSV database and are required to upload the file directly in the Colab (Haydon et al., 2022; Hooper et al., 1971). There is a disclosure that Colab only temporarily stores the data per session, so any file will need to be saved and stored elsewhere to prevent termination.

To insert our database, we look for the folder icon located on the left. Figure 1 shows the next step is to insert the database through the files option, Figure 2 shows from here we can upload the database from the session storage. Figure 3 presents the next step is to insert the code into the code cells in Colab.

Figure 1. The next step is to insert the database through the files option

Figure 2. From here we can upload the database from the session storage

Figure 3. The next step is to insert the code into the code cells in Colab

```
import pandas as pd
import numpy as np
import seaborn as sns
import matplotlib.pyplot as plot


x = pd.read_csv("")
print(x.head())
```

From this, we need to insert the path to our database (Kavonius et al., 2020). The variable "x" reads the csv file, but it needs the path to the file. We copy the path we took from the content and insert it on the python code line. Figure 4 shows the final step is to run the code and expect the output. Figure 5 Shows the output and Figure 6 shows Flow of execution.

Figure 4. The final step is to run the code and expect the output

```
import pandas as pd
import numpy as np
import seaborn as sns
import matplotlib.pyplot as plot


x = pd.read_csv("/content/billionaires_database_2.csv")
print(x.head())
```

Figure 5. Shows the output

```
import pandas as pd
import numpy as np
import seaborn as sns
import matplotlib.pyplot as plot


x = pd.read_csv("/content/billionaires_database_2.csv")
print(x.head())
```

```
            Name  NetWorth  year Country            Source  Age  \
0     Bill Gates      18.5  1996     USA         Microsoft   40
1     Bill Gates      58.7  2001     USA         Microsoft   45
2     Bill Gates      76.0  2014     USA         Microsoft   58
3  Warren Buffett      15.0  1996     USA  Berkshire Hathaway   65
4  Warren Buffett      32.3  2001     USA  Berkshire Hathaway   70

              Industry
0  Technology-Computer
1  Technology-Computer
2  Technology-Computer
3             Consumer
4             Consumer
```

FLOWCHART

Figure 6. Flow of execution

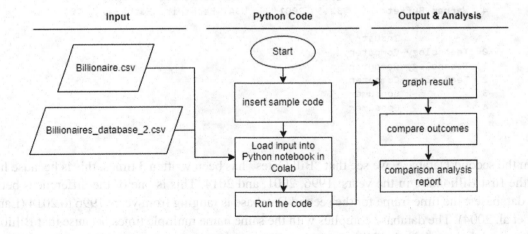

COMPARING THE DATASETS

From the two databases, there are each 5 given outputs. Each output will be briefly described and from there we can compare the outcome and the differences between the outputs. The expected outcome is to see if there are similarities, trends, or patterns of names, states, domains, or industries there are deemed to be more successful (Kriss et al., 2022). From the first database, the raw GitHub set has been used, while from the second database, the file itself was downloaded and refined to fit the code in such a way that the code executes the same as previously mentioned. Figure 7 shows the first Database's first 5 lines as an output and Figure 8 shows the second Database's first 5 lines as an output.

Figure 7. The first database's first 5 lines as an output

```
                      Name NetWorth        Country        Source  Rank  \
0              Jeff Bezos   $177 B  United States        Amazon     1
1              Elon Musk   $151 B  United States  Tesla, SpaceX     2
2  Bernard Arnault & family  $150 B         France          LVMH     3
3              Bill Gates   $124 B  United States     Microsoft     4
4        Mark Zuckerberg    $97 B  United States      Facebook     5

    Age          Industry
0  57.0        Technology
1  49.0        Automotive
2  72.0  Fashion & Retail
3  65.0        Technology
4  36.0        Technology
```

Figure 8. The second database's first 5 lines as an output

```
            Name  NetWorth  year Country            Source  Age  \
0     Bill Gates      18.5  1996     USA         Microsoft   40
1     Bill Gates      58.7  2001     USA         Microsoft   45
2     Bill Gates      76.0  2014     USA         Microsoft   58
3  Warren Buffett     15.0  1996     USA  Berkshire Hathaway   65
4  Warren Buffett     32.3  2001     USA  Berkshire Hathaway   70

              Industry
0  Technology-Computer
1  Technology-Computer
2  Technology-Computer
3             Consumer
4             Consumer
```

From the second Database, we see that "Bill Gates" has been written 3 times, this is because he has ranked the first Billionaire in the years: 1996, 2001, and 2014. This is one of the differences between the two databases: the time frame for the second Database is ranging from years 1996 to 2014 (Lansley, Stewart et al. 2004). The database complies with the same name multiple times because that Billionaire has maintained their rank in the Billionaires list. Figure 9 shows this Output is from the first Database showing the highest Net Worth from the list. Figure 10 projects Output is from the second Database showing the highest Net Worth from the list.

Figure 9. This output is from the first database showing the highest net worth from the list

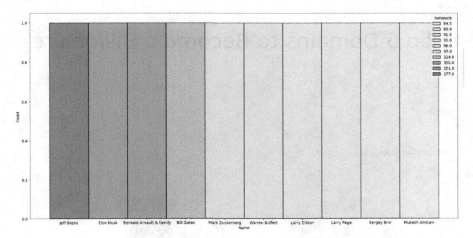

Figure 10. This output is from the second database showing the highest net worth from the list

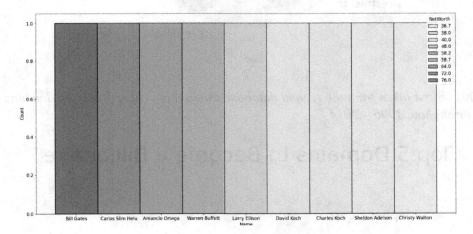

These graphs are the output that displays the amount of Net Worth in Billions. The two Datasets have some underlining similarities and differences in the names and Net Worth they are displaying. For example, the first Database has Jeff Bezos on top with the highest wealth of 177 Billion Dollars. The second Database has Bill Gates leading the graph with 76 Billion Dollars. Both Datasets Feature Bill Gates, however in his position on the output poll is no longer the first (Njangang et al., 2022). We point out that his wealth has significantly increased, the initial 76 Billion Dollars has risen to 124 Billion Dollars. There are common names mentioned such as Warren Buffet, and Larry Ellison. We can see that their wealth has significantly increased from 48 Billion to 93. From this observation, we can see that the Net worth in Billions of Dollars has some gaps between the two. The first database doesn't include Bill Gates as the highest-ranking Billionaire. After further research, there are notable absences of well-known names (Ogada et al., 2023; Kharaba et al., 2022). Figure 11 shows output is taken from the first Database shows a pie chart of the top domains with the most Billionaires. Figure 12 projects output taken from the second Database shows a pie chart of the top domains that have been the top throughout 1996 – 2014.

Figure 11. This output is taken from the first database shows a pie chart of the top domains with the most billionaires

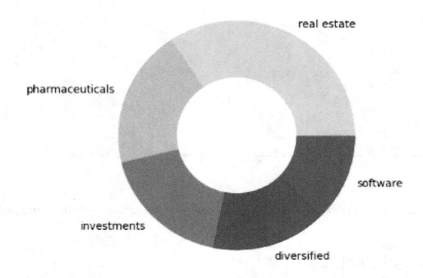

Figure 12. This output taken from the second database shows a pie chart of the top domains that have been the top throughout 1996 – 2014

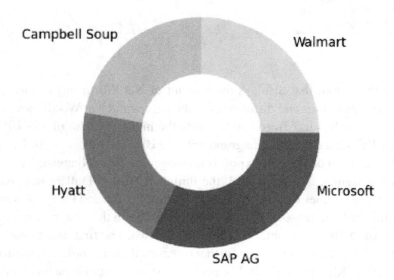

The results of the outputs from the two databases differ in results as shown in domains to become a Billionaire. The dominating domains in the second database are companies such as Microsoft, Walmart, Campbell Soup Hyatt, and SAP AG. The output of this pie chart shows the Names of Companies instead of the domains they belong to, for example, Microsoft and SAP AG both belong to the software domain. Hyatt offers Hospitality services in the real estate domain, whilst Walmart and Campbell Soup belong to the consumer domain. If we compare the results from the first chart, we see that the software domain remains at the top, while the others have changed. The rising domains in recent times are investments, pharmaceuticals, and the dominating real estate. Lastly, it is estimated that the rest belong to a diversified range of domains. Figure 13 shows a pie chart of the Top 5 Industries with the most Billionaires taken from the first database. Figure 14 shows a pie chart of the Top 5 Industries with the most Billionaires taken from the second database. Figure 15 shows a pie chart that is taken from the first database of the top 5 countries with the most billionaires. Figure 16 shows a pie chart that is taken from the second database of the top 5 countries with the most billionaires.

Figure 13. Shows a pie chart of the top 5 industries with the most billionaires taken from the first database

Top 5 Industries with Most Number of Billionaires

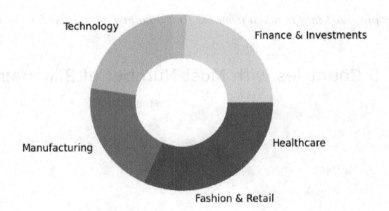

The top industries from 2022 are Technology, Manufacturing, Fashion & Retail, Healthcare, and Finance & investments. These industries correlate to the recent trends in the economy and events. I.E. The rise of the healthcare industry is not surprising considering the recent COVID-19 pandemic. Technology, Finance & Investments have been apparent in recent years, hence they have the most billionaires. The second database shows that the dominating domains through decades have been Consumer, Retail & Restaurant, Real Estate, Money Management, and Media. Considering the larger time frame of the second Database there are differences in the previous demands, however, it gives a broader idea of the overall most successful industries.

Figure 14. Shows a pie chart of the top 5 industries with the most billionaires taken from the second database

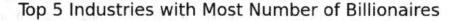

Top 5 Industries with Most Number of Billionaires

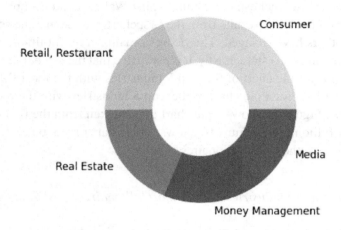

Figure 15. Shows a pie chart that is taken from the first database of the top 5 countries with the most billionaires

Top 5 Countries with Most Number of Billionaires

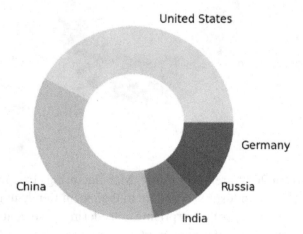

If we analyze the countries with the most Billionaires we see that throughout the decades but as well in recent years, the country with the most billionaires is the United States. When it comes to the number of Billionaires coming from said countries, the said countries remain the same but with the difference of India replacing Japan. The relation between the pie charts of the two databases concludes that there is a bipolarity of Billionaires rising as China is competing closely with the US.

Figure 16. Shows a pie chart that is taken from the second database of the top 5 countries with the most billionaires

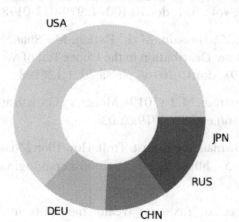

Top 5 Countries with Most Number of Billionaires

CONCLUSION

The Databases have a range of data, namely, Name, Net Worth, and Country of origin. The report provides a comparison of databases that have different time frames. The first database has listed the recent Billionaires and their information in the year 2022. The second database provides data throughout the 1996 –2014 time frame. The outcome of analyzing and comparing the outputs directly tells the differences and gives insight into the underlying question about Billionaires and the countries that have greater economic development. The results of the report seek the pattern between the highest domains to become a Billionaire and the industries that are the most successful. After analyzing the two datasets, we saw that the countries at the top of the list have relatively remained the same, however, with shifts in the number of percentages between each other. These countries that have billionaires have the opportunity to develop their own country's economies. It has shown that the demand in the software industry has remained throughout years in decades and in recent years as well. The other implied change is that certain domains in recent years correlate to events and trends, for example, the healthcare domain received a higher income only recently, as implied by COVID-19. We concluded that certain Billionaires are still standing relevant at the highest rankings among the top positions. Namely, their name and status are still at the top and their Net Worth and wealth have exponentially increased in amount. Therefore, there is a connection between the number of billionaires and their countries because the majority of them come from highly economically developed states and provide services to industries in high demand. come from highly economically developed states and provide services to industries in high demand.

REFERENCES

Althar, R. R., Samanta, D., Purushotham, S., Sengar, S. S., & Hewage, C. (2023). Design and Development of Artificial Intelligence Knowledge Processing System for Optimizing Security of Software System. *SN Computer Science, 4*(4), 331. doi:10.100742979-023-01785-2

Asif, M., Hussain, Z., Asghar, Z., Hussain, M. I., Raftab, M., Shah, S. F., & Khan, A. A. (2021). A Statistical Evidence of Power Law Distribution in the Upper Tail of World Billionaires' Data 2010–20. *Physica A, 581*(126198), 126198. doi:10.1016/j.physa.2021.126198

Bagchi, S., Curran, M., & Fagerstrom, M. J. (2019). Monetary Growth and Wealth Inequality. *Economics Letters, 182*, 23–25. doi:10.1016/j.econlet.2019.05.036

Ball, M. (2021). Visionary. Showman. Iconoclast. Troll. How Elon Musk Is Reshaping Our World—And Beyond. *Time, 198*(23/24), 36–57. https://search.ebscohost.com/login.aspx?direct=true&db=afh&AN=154157240&site=ehost-live

Banzhaf, W. (2021). The Effects of Taxes on Wealth Inequality in Artificial Chemistry Models of Economic Activity. *PLoS One, 16*(8), e0255719. doi:10.1371/journal.pone.0255719 PMID:34379658

Bart, A. C., Whitcomb, R., Riddle, J., & Saleem, O. (2016). *CORGIS Datasets Project.* https://corgis-edu.github.io/corgis/csv/billionaires/

Capehart, K. W. (2014). Is the Wealth of the World's Billionaires Not Paretian? *Physica A, 395*, 255–260. doi:10.1016/j.physa.2013.09.026

Chesters, J. (2013). Wealth Inequality and Stratification in the World Capitalist Economy. *Perspectives on Global Development and Technology, 12*(1–2), 246–265. doi:10.1163/15691497-12341253

Clemente, F., & Collins, C. (2021). Coronavirus Suller Bowl 2021: Billionaires Win. *USA Today, 149*(2912), 54–56. https://search.ebscohost.com/login.aspx?direct=true&db=afh&AN=152114296&site=ehost-live

Coupe, T., & Monteiro, C. (2016). The Charity of the Extremely Wealthy: Charity of the Extremely Wealthy. *Economic Inquiry, 54*(2), 751–761. doi:10.1111/ecin.12311

Cunaku, E., Ndrecaj, J., Berisha, S., Samanta, D., Dutta, S., & Bhattacharya, A. (2023). An Approach for Digital-Social Network Analysis Using Twitter API. In *Innovations in Data Analytics: Selected Papers of ICIDA 2022* (pp. 625–636). Springer. 10.1007/978-981-99-0550-8_49

Dangi, P., Jain, A., Samanta, D., Dutta, S., & Bhattacharya, A. (2023). 3D Modelling and Rendering Using Autodesk 3ds Max. In *2023 11th International Conference on Internet of Everything, Microwave Engineering, Communication and Networks (IEMECON)* (pp. 1–5). IEEE.

Flanigan, J., & Freiman, C. (2022). Wealth without Limits: In Defense of Billionaires. *Ethical Theory and Moral Practice: An International Forum, 25*(5), 755–775. 10.100710677-022-10327-3

Fuentenebro, P. (2020). Will Philanthropy Save Us All? Rethinking Urban Philanthropy in a Time of Crisis. *Geoforum, 117*, 304–307. doi:10.1016/j.geoforum.2020.07.005 PMID:32981949

GargM.SaxenaC.SamantaD.DorrB. J. (2023). *LonXplain: Lonesomeness as a Consequence of Mental Disturbance in Reddit Posts.* doi:10.1007/978-3-031-35320-8_27

Guha, A., Samanta, D., & Sengar, S. S. (2023). Computer Vision Based Automatic Margin Computation Model for Digital Document Images. *SN Computer Science, 4*(3), 253. doi:10.100742979-023-01693-5

Gurunath, R., & Samanta, D. (2023). A New 3-Bit Hiding Covert Channel Algorithm for Public Data and Medical Data Security Using Format-Based Text Steganography. *Journal of Database Management, 34*(2), 1–22. doi:10.4018/JDM.324076

Haydon, S. (2022). Book Review: The Business of Changing the World: How Billionaires, Tech Disrupters, and Social Entrepreneurs Are Transforming the Global Aid Industry by Kumar, R. and The Enlightened Capitalists: Cautionary Tales of Business Pioneers Who Tried to Do Well by Doing Good by O'Toole. *J. Nonprofit and Voluntary Sector Quarterly, 51*(4), 928–932. doi:10.1177/08997640211022745

Hooper, R. (2021). A Trillion Dollars to Fix the World. *New Scientist, 249*(3323), 38–44. https://search.ebscohost.com/login.aspx?direct=true&db=afh&AN=148952434&site=ehost-live

Jain, A., Dangi, P., Samanta, D., Dutta, S., Bhattacharya, A., & Joseph, N. P. (2023). Creation of Bookshelf Using Autodesk 3ds Max: 3D Modelling and Rendering. *In 2023 11th International Conference on Internet of Everything, Microwave Engineering, Communication and Networks (IEMECON)* (pp. 1–4). IEEE.

Kavonius, I. K. (2020). Is Wealth Driving the Income Distribution? An Analysis of the Link between Income and Wealth between 1995 and 2016 in Finland. *Statistical Journal of the IAOS, 36*(2), 483–494. doi:10.3233/SJI-200649

Kharaba, Z., Moutraji, S. A., Al Khawaldeh, R. A., Alfoteih, Y., & Al Meslamani, A. Z. (2022). *What has changed in the pharmaceutical care after COVID-19: Pharmacists' perspective.* https://www.ncbi.nlm.nih.gov/pmc/articles/PMC9296094/

Kriss, S. (2022). The Truth about Bill Gates. *First Things (New York, N.Y.)*, 41–49. https://search.ebscohost.com/login.aspx?direct=true&db=afh&AN=160204806&site=ehost-live

Lansley, S. (2004). Britain Is Now Back to Levels of Gross Income Inequality. *New Statesman (London, England), 133*(4708), 27–29. https://search.ebscohost.com/login.aspx?direct=true&db=afh&AN=14587893&site=ehost-live

Mondal, S., Pal, A. K., Islam, S. K. H., & Samanta, D. (2023). Objectionable Image Content Classification Using CNN-Based Semi-supervised Learning. *Advances in Smart Vehicular Technology, Transportation, Communication and Applications Proceedings of VTCA, 2022*, 311–320.

Njangang, H., Beleck, A., Tadadjeu, S., & Kamguia, B. (2022). Do ICTs Drive Wealth Inequality? Evidence from a Dynamic Panel Analysis. *Telecommunications Policy, 46*(2), 102246. doi:10.1016/j.telpol.2021.102246

Ogada, R. (2022). *Exploratory-Data-Analysis*. Jill Canon Associates. https://github.com/ertgrulyksk/Billionaires-Analysis-with-Python/blob/main/Billionaires_Analysis_with_Python.ipynb

Podder, S. K., Samanta, D., Thomas, B., Dutta, S., & Bhattacharya, A. (2023). Impact of blended education system on outcome-based learning and sector skills development. In *2023 11th International Conference on Internet of Everything, Microwave Engineering, Communication and Networks (IEMECON)* (pp. 1–6). IEEE.

Chapter 3
Modeling Requirements With Diabetes Using Supervised Machine Learning Techniques

Priyal Dangi
CHRIST University (Deemed), India

ABSTRACT

Diabetes is characterized by either insufficient or inefficient insulin production by the body. High blood glucose levels result from this, which over time can harm a number of tissues and organs in the body. Diabetes can be brought on by a specific age, obesity, inactivity, insufficient physical activity, inherited diabetes, lifestyle, poor diet, hypertension, etc. This chapter explores modeling requirements with diabetes using supervised machine learning techniques.

INTRODUCTION

Diabetes is a widespread medical disorder that significantly actually harms wellbeing. Diabetes is characterized by levels of glucose in the blood which seem to be extraordinarily high and therefore are driven by inadequate secretion, inadequate physiologic consequences of glucose, maybe all in case. If diabetes is not treated, there are severe complications then. In the healthcare area, So, instead employing a single classifier, a classification or categorization techniques are usually used to segregate information into numerous groups in line with predefined criteria. Stated below are the different diabetes diagnoses:

Type 1 diabetes: An auto immune disease in which the immune system of the human body targets and damages insulin-producing pancreatic cells, type 1 diabetes is the most common form of the disease. Type 1 diabetics must inject themselves with insulin or use an insulin injection to stabilize their sugar levels in the blood.

DOI: 10.4018/978-1-6684-9809-5.ch003

Type 2 diabetes: The most typical diabetic condition, type 2, is brought on when the body develops a glucose intolerance or is unable to produce enough insulin to control the amount of sugar in the blood. Hypertension, obesity, a inactive lifestyle, and bad eating habits are frequently linked to type 2 diabetes. (Jain et al., 2023).

In order to gather information and forecast, prediction model utilises multiple approaches to machine learning, methods of statistics and data mining are two closely related disciplines. Significant conclusions and predictions can be made by using predictive analysis on healthcare data. Here approaches for learning algorithms such as SVM, Logistic regression, Naïve bayes, Decision tree, k-nearest neighbours (Knn), Random Forest, can be used for data modelling and prediction model. prediction model strives to improve healthcare outcomes by increasing patient care, optimizing resource use, and making the best possible disease diagnosis. Where Knn is giving the greater accuracy of i.e. (81%) among all the other models we have opted (Dangi et al., 2023).

Related Work

Nongyao et al. implemented a classification method for diabetic patients' risk. The author used the four well-known machine learning categorization methods Naive Bayes, Decision Tree (DT), Artificial Neural Networks (ANN), Naive Bayes, and Logistic Regression for the achievement of the specified objective. The proposed model's power is enhanced by using boosting and bagging strategies. Therefore, Random Forest method, out of all the algorithms used, produces the best outcomes, according to experiment results (Watkins et al., 2002).

Orabi et al. employed the system for predicting the diabetes disorder or disease, with the highly defined objective of predicting the presence of diabetes in an individual at a set age. By using decision trees, the proposed system can be developed using the principle of machine learning. Results were favourable since the system's architecture is good at forecasting diabetes prevalence rate at a specific age (Razavian et al., 2015).

A strategy for the analysis and the assessment of diabetic and insulin statistics was implemented using data and the Hadoop Map reduce technology and programming. The lifestyle factors and form of diabetes are anticipated by this strategy. The technology has been shown affordable for any healthcare business (Lipton et al., 2014).

Georga et al. centred on the glucose and, as a multivariate regression problem, used support vector regression (SVR) to forecast diabetes. Also, to increase the accuracy, more and more studies have been using ensemble approaches (Park et al., 2017).

K. Rajesh and V. Sangeetha (2012) a classification and categorization strategy was utilized. They have been using the C4.5 decision tree model to derive and detect the specific underlying patterns from the collection in order to perform effective and appropriate categorization (Svetnik et al., 2015).

Sajida et al. shows how Boost and Bagging cluster strategies are utilized for machine learning techniques through using the decision tree as the core effect in the detection of the people with diabetes and those without it based on factors that increase the likelihood of the condition (Li et al., 2017).

The Simple K-means algorithm called is included in the suggested combination prediction model, which then applies a classification algorithm to the outcomes of the classification method. Using the C4.5 decision tree approach, classifiers are created (Yue et al., 2008).

About the Dataset

Where this dataset or the collection have been found from The National Institute of Diabetes and Digestive and Kidney Diseases. Based on signs and symptoms criteria, it is intended to determine if a patient has diabetes or not (Rajagopalan et al., n.d.).

The Pima Indian Diabetes dataset is one of the most frequently utilized datasets for diabetes research among the several freely accessible diabetes datasets. Information on 768 female Pima Indians over the age of 21 was gathered for this dataset between 1988 and 1990 (Bengio et al., 2005).

Eight medical predictor factors and one target variable are included in the dataset:

1. **Pregnancies:** This variable represents the total number of pregnancies for the patient.
2. **Glucose:** In an oral tolerance test to glucose, this variable represents the plasma glucose concentration. The sugar glucose gives the cells in the body energy. High blood sugar levels might be a sign of diabetes or pre-diabetes (American Diabetes Association, 2012).
3. **Blood Pressure:** In mm Hg, this factor describes the blood pressure at the systolic level. The pressure exerted by blood on the artery walls is known as the name blood pressure (BP). Therefore, heart disease can result from high blood pressure (Podder et al., 2023).
4. **Skin Thickness:** The value of this parameter represents the mm-thickness of the forearm skinfold. It is possible to calculate body fat using skin thickness, a measure of fatty tissue.
5. **Insulin:** This measure indicates the micro-units per millilitre (mu U/ml) 2-hour serum insulin level. The pancreas secretes the hormone insulin, which aids in controlling blood sugar levels.
6. **BMI:** This field contains the measure of body mass, which then has been determined by splitting the given weights in kg by having the square of the height in form inches. There BMI test, which calculates body fat based on height and weight, is frequently used to check for weight categories that could cause health issues (Deng et al., 2019).
7. **Diabetes Pedigree Function:** This measure, which is based on family history, calculates the hereditary risk for diabetes.
8. **Age:** The patient's age in years is indicated by this variable.
9. **Outcome:** The patient has diabetes (1) or not, according to this variable, which is the goal variable (0).Although there are no null data in the dataset, certain values are entered as 0, which is not practical (for example, a zero value for glucose is not possible). Hence, prior to using the dataset for analysis or modelling, some preparation may be required. Figure 1 represents the count of the outcome variable.

Figure 1. Count of the outcome variable

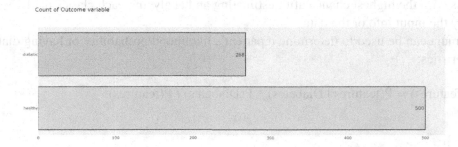

- Wherein, according to the dataset there are 268 people who are having diabetes disease and 500.

METHODS EMPLOYED

Supervised Learning/Predictive Models

Prediction models are built using algorithms that are supervised during learning. A prediction model generalises the value of a new item from other values contained in the data set. A model is developed by a supervised algorithm for learning using a set of data as input and as output in order to generate precise prediction about the performance of new datasets. Wherein, supervised approaches include decision trees, the Bayes or probabilistic approach, neural networks with artificial intelligence, instantiation training, and the interaction between the system. Such machine learning approaches then are in the high demand (Ye et al., n.d.).

1. **KNN:**

Prediction of diabetes can be done using the K-nearest neighbour (KNN) method. In order to categorise a new data point according to the vast majority among its k-nearest/immediate neighbors, where the method first determines the specific k nearest data points to it. KNN has been used to predict diabetes in a number of papers and instances, including comparisons to other machine learning algorithms and actual implementation. Number of times neighbours will be considered when making a prediction depends on the value of K. A minor K-value can result in the model being overfit, whereas a huge number can result in the model being underfit (Althar et al., 2023). It is best to experiment with various values to see which one fits better on the testing dataset before choosing on any one. You must estimate the distance between the new patient and each of the patients in the testing phase in to generate a prediction using the KNN algorithm. Depending on the type of data, you can utilise several distance metrics, such as Distance metric, Manhattan distance or Euclidean distance. Choose the K nearest neighbours after the distances have been obtained. After that, if you know the K closest neighbours, you can predict that whatever the new patient will perceive. The new patients will be categorized as diabetic if the majority of the K neighbours have that diabetes disease; otherwise, the new patients will be categorized as not diabetic (Gong et al., 2019).

2. **Naive Bayes:**

The Naive Bayes method can be used to predict diabetes. A probabilistic algorithm called Naive Bayes picks the class with the highest chance after estimating and analyzing each class's likely or probability determined by the input info or the data.

Given formula can be used to determine a patient's likelihood/probability of having diabetes given their characteristics:

P(Diabetes | features) = P(features | Diabetes) * P(Diabetes) / P(features)

In this equation, P(Diabetes | features) represents the posterior distribution of the patient having diabetes disease given their characteristics, P(features | Diabetes) represents the likelihood of the patient having the similar phenomenon given they have diabetes, P(Diabetes) represents the prior distribution of a patient having diabetes, and P(features) represents the relatively modest probability of analysing the features (Guha et al., 2023).

The approach uses the conditional probabilities and prior probabilities to determine the posterior probability of each class when a new patient with features is introduced to the model. The predicted class for such patient represents the one that has the greatest likelihood. For instance, if the patient is anticipated to have diabetes if the posterior probability of the diabetic class is larger than the non-diabetic class (Alghamdi et al., 2017).

3. SVM:

The Support Vector Machines (SVM) algorithm is another tool for predicting diabetes. The supervised machine learning technique that may be applied to both tasks involving regression and classification. SVM looks for the optimum hyperplane to divide the data into various classes and categories with utmost margin. It determines the new patient's distance from the hyperplane and then assigns them to the class on the other side of the plane. Then to enhance the model's performance, adjust its hyperparameters. The selection of the kernel function is one of the hyperparameters (Pal et al., 2005).

Consequently, while using SVM for diabetes prediction, it is crucial to choose significant predictor parameters that correspond to the specific dataset and project topic.

4. Decision Tree:

The Decision tree method may also be utilised to predict diabetes. A supervised machine learning approach called Decision Tree can be applied to both regression analysis and categorization. In order to generate a tree-like model that can be used for prediction, it looks for the optimal split in the data depending on the input attribute values.

Choose a splitting criteria that evaluates the effectiveness of a divide. There are a number of splitting criteria possible, including classification algorithm, entropy, and Gini impure. The type of data will dictate which split factor is used. As measured by the distance between the impurity of the parent node and the balanced impurity of the child nodes, the objective is to increase information gain at every split. When a specific preventing requirement is attained, such as reaching a maximum extent or having a minimum sample count per leaf node, splitting should stop. Reduce the complexity and simplify the structure of the decision tree to reduce the number of features, which happens when the tree tries to fit the noise in the dataset (Cunaku et al., 2023).

In order to determine a new patient's likelihood of having diabetes depending on their characteristics. Using the patient's features, move through the decision tree from the node to its root to a node to its leaf, and then assign to the specified patient to the leaf node's majority class.

5. Random Forest:

Where the number of decision trees are combined and merged in method called Random Forest, a group learning approach for boosting the precision and reduce overfit criteria. To determine whether a person is susceptible to developing diabetes or not, Random Forest can be trained on a dataset containing variables such as age, insulin and glucose levels, blood pressure, etc.For categorizing problems or solving regression problems, the predictions are combined by calculating the mean or the clear majority (Ishaq et al., 2020).

When the model is complete, use it to determine from a patient's features whether they have diabetes or not. Use the majority support for classification problems or the average for regression tasks for prediction purposes to combine all decision tree predictions in the Random Forest (Mondal et al., 2023).

6. Logistic Regression:

Diabetes can be predicted using the logistic regression approach. An approach for supervised machine learning that can be applied to classifying analyses is logistic regression. The purpose of logistic regression is to locate the line that fits the data the finest and divides the information into multiple classes. To determine whether a person is susceptible to developing diabetes or not, Logistic Regression can be trained on a set of extracted features in the instance of diabetes prediction.

This feature's definition reads:

$$p (y=1|x) = \frac{1}{1+e^{-z}}$$

where x is the vector of input features, z is the weighted sum of the attributes from the taken input, where y is indeed the goal variable (if the person is diabetic or not diabetic).

The parameters are iteratively changed to optimize a loss function, such as the cross-entropy function, in order to train the logistic regression model. Gradient descent, a method that involvement of the derivative of the weights with respect to the loss and error function and then adjusting the parameters to minimize the loss and error, is commonly used to make weight adjustments (Ajmalahamed et al., 2014).

It is use to determine a new patient's likelihood of having diabetes depending on their characteristics in the test dataset. The logistic stored procedure input features are input in to produce the predicted probabilities. The patient is categorised as having diabetes if the estimated likelihood exceeds a particular threshold (often 0.5); otherwise, the patient is characterized as not having diabetes (Asadi et al., 2014).

THE STEPS IN PREDICTING DIABETES

Data Collection: Collecting a dataset of historical patient data that includes features such as age, BMI, blood pressure, glucose levels, family history, and other relevant medical information. Data Pre-processing: Cleaning and pre-processing the dataset by removing missing values, handling outliers, and scaling or normalizing the features.

Feature Selection: Selecting the most relevant features that contribute the most to the prediction of diabetes. This is performed to render the dataset lower detailed and even to strengthen the model's functioning.

Splitting the Data: Partitioning the datasets into the sets for training and testing in order to educate the model and assess the extent to which it behaves (Razavian et al., 2015).

Model Selection: Choosing an appropriate machine learning algorithm that can accurately predict the likelihood of diabetes based on the available features. Some popular algorithms for diabetes prediction include SVM, Logistic regression, Naïve bayes, Decision tree, KNN, Random Forest.

Model Training: For training the selected algorithm using the training of dataset and tuning the parameter settings to enhance and strengthen the effectiveness of the algorithm.

Model Evaluation: For assessing the model's performance using the testing dataset and calculating metrics such as recall, F1 score, accuracy, precision (Garg et al., 2023).

Model Deployment: In order for deploying the given trained model in a real-world environment for prediction of diabetes in new patients.

Model Maintenance: Monitoring the performance of the model and updating it with new data periodically to ensure that it continues to perform accurately over time.

Figure 2 depicts the phases involved in predicting Diabetes.

Figure 2. Phases in diabetes prediction

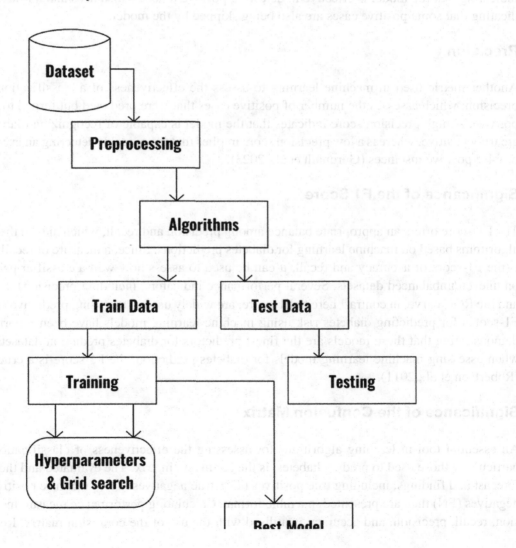

ACCURACY MEASURES

It's crucial to remember that the accuracy metric you choose will rely on the user's particular needs and the problem you're attempting to solve. For instance, in some circumstances, decreasing false negatives—that is, forecasting someone doesn't have diabetes if they really could be more crucial than minimizing false positives—that is, forecasting somebody has diabetes when they don't have be. Hence, based on the particular requirements of the application, the suitable necessary qualifications and accuracy measures must be selected.

Recall

Recall is a measure used in learning algorithms to assess how well a categorization model is performing. Recall estimates the percentage of actual positive diabetes outcomes that the model properly recognized in the context of diabetes forecasting. Recall values vary from high to low, with just a high recall score indicating that the model is effective in detecting positive diabetes instances and a low recall score indicating that some positive cases are also being skipped by the model.

Precision

Another metric used in machine learning to assess the effectiveness of a classification algorithm is precision, which assesses the number of positive cases that were predicted but turned to turn out to be positive. A high precision score indicates that the model is capable of recognizing diabetes cases that are truly positive, whereas a low precision score implies that the model is detecting an excessive number of false positive instances (Gurunath et al., 2023).

Significance of the F1 Score

The F1-score offers an appropriate balance among precision and recall, which aids in the evaluation of algorithms based on machine learning for diabetes predictions. Since, a measure of recall and precision is the F1-score of accuracy and recall, it can be used to assess how well a classifier performs overall on uneven/unbalanced datasets. Several performance indicators, including precision, recall, accuracy, and the ROC curve, in contrast here to F1-score, are widely used in assessing predictive accuracy. High F1-scores for predicting diabetes risk using machine learning models have been reported in studies, demonstrating that these models are the finest predictors for diabetes prediction datasets. As a result, when assessing machine learning models for diabetes prediction, the F1-score is a crucial parameter (Robertson et al., 2011).

Significance of the Confusion Matrix

An essential tool in learning algorithms for assessing the effectiveness of classification algorithms, particularly those used to predict diabetes, is the confusion matrix. The evaluated and the results of the forecast and findings, including true positives (TP), true negatives (TN), and false positives (FP), false negatives (FN) then are presented in a table format. Calculating performance measurements like precision, recall, precision, and accuracy is utilised with the use of the confusion matrix. Recall measures the extent to which the actual positive occurrences were predicted as positive by the algorithm, whereas precision evaluates how many of the projected positive cases are clearly positive. The level of specificity indicates the extent to which a model can spot negative occurrences. In order to evaluate machine learning models for predicting the diabetes and estimate their overall effectiveness, the confusion matrix is a useful factor.

ACCURACY OF METHODS

Table 1 represents the various algorithms with its accuracy.

Table 1. Models with its accuracy

Models	Accuracy
SVM	80%
Logistic regression	75%
Naïve bayes	77%
Decision tree	79%
k-nearest neighbours	81%
Random forest	79%

Need of Hyperparameters Using Grid Search for Fitting the Models

The procedure for identifying the ideal collection of hyperparameters or model parameters for a models and algorithms based on machine learning is recognized as hyperparameter tuning. Before the model is put through training, set variables called hyperparameters are selected, and they have a substantial impact on the performance of any model. After that the hyperparameters that provide the best result are chosen after the model's performance is assessed using a validated model. There are a multitude of methods for fine-tuning hyperparameters, such as Grid Search, which basically compares the performance of each configuration of all the provided hyperparameters and their values before choosing the optimal one.

PROPOSED METHOD

(K-Nearest Neighbours)

Knn is giving the greater accuracy of 81% among all the other models we have opted. So, we have selected it as the best model to work with and to make diabetic predictions. Because of its non-linearity, know how to adapt, resilience to outliers, and scalability, KNN is a good option for diabetes prediction. Table 2 depicts the precision, recall, f1-score, accuracy of the selected k-nearest neighbours.

Table 2. Precision, recall, f1-score, accuracy of KNN

Method	Precision	Recall	F1-Score	Accuracy
K-Nearest Neighbours	0.72	0.57	0.64	0.81

Confusion matrix

Table 3 shows confusion matrix of k-nearest neighbours algorithm.

Table 3. Confusion matrix of KNN

		Predicted	
Negative			Positive
Actual	Negative	97	10
	Positive	20	27

CONCLUSION WITH FUTURE SCOPE

With advancements and improvements in data processing and machine learning analytics, there are now more opportunities than ever before for the precise prediction and prevention of diabetes. These are some relevant directions for additional study and advancement in diabetes forecasting. n general, diabetes prediction has a broad and diverse future, with prospects for the integration of numerous datasets, tailored medication, timely prevention and detection, real-time feedback and tracking, and understandable AI. The accuracy and predictability of diabetes forecast models will keep growing as methods using machine learning develop, improving the results for diabetes patients.

REFERENCES

Ajmalahamed, A., Nandhini, K. M., & Anand, S. K. (2014). Designing a rule based fuzzy expert controller for early detection and diagnosis of diabetes. *ARPN J Eng Appl Sci.*, *9*(5), 21–322.

Alghamdi, M., Al-Mallah, M., Keteyian, S., Brawner, C., Ehrman, J., & Sakr, S. (2017). Predicting diabetes mellitus using SMOTE and ensemble machine learning approach: The henry ford exercise testing (FIT) project. *PLoS One*, *12*(7), e0179805. doi:10.1371/journal.pone.0179805 PMID:28738059

Althar, R. R., Samanta, D., Purushotham, S., Sengar, S. S., & Hewage, C. (2023). Design and Development of Artificial Intelligence Knowledge Processing System for Optimizing Security of Software System. *SN Computer Science*, *4*(4), 331. doi:10.100742979-023-01785-2

American Diabetes Association. (2012). Diagnosis and classification of diabetes mellitus. *Diabetes Care*, *35*(Suppl. 1), S64–S71. doi:10.2337/dc12-s064 PMID:22187472

Asadi, H., Dowling, R., Yan, B., & Mitchell, P. (2014). Machine learning for outcome prediction of acute ischemic stroke post intra-arterial therapy. *PLoS One*, *9*(2), 2. doi:10.1371/journal.pone.0088225 PMID:24520356

Bengio, Y., & Grandvalet, Y. (2005). *Bias in Estimating the Variance of K -Fold Cross-Validation.* Springer. doi:10.1007/0-387-24555-3_5

Cunaku, E., Ndrecaj, J., Berisha, S., Samanta, D., Dutta, S., & Bhattacharya, A. (2023). An Approach for Digital-Social Network Analysis Using Twitter API. In *Innovations in Data Analytics: Selected Papers of ICIDA 2022* (pp. 625–636). Springer. 10.1007/978-981-99-0550-8_49

Dangi, P., Jain, A., Samanta, D., Dutta, S., & Bhattacharya, A. (2023). 3D Modelling and Rendering Using Autodesk 3ds Max. In *2023 11th International Conference on Internet of Everything, Microwave Engineering, Communication and Networks (IEMECON)* (pp. 1–5). IEEE.

Deng, W., Guo, Y., Liu, J., Li, Y., Liu, D., & Zhu, L. (2019). A missing power data filling method based on improved random forest algorithm. *Chin J Electr Eng.*, *5*(4), 33–39. doi:10.23919/CJEE.2019.000025

GargM.SaxenaC.SamantaD.DorrB. J. (2023). LonXplain: Lonesomeness as a Consequence of Mental Disturbance in Reddit Posts. doi:10.1007/978-3-031-35320-8_27

Gong, Z., Zhong, P., & Hu, W. (2019). Diversity in machine learning. *IEEE Access : Practical Innovations, Open Solutions*, *7*, 64323–64350. doi:10.1109/ACCESS.2019.2917620

Guha, A., Samanta, D., & Sengar, S. S. (2023). Computer Vision Based Automatic Margin Computation Model for Digital Document Images. *SN Computer Science*, *4*(3), 253. doi:10.100742979-023-01693-5

Gurunath, R., & Samanta, D. (2023). A New 3-Bit Hiding Covert Channel Algorithm for Public Data and Medical Data Security Using Format-Based Text Steganography. *Journal of Database Management*, *34*(2), 1–22. doi:10.4018/JDM.324076

Ishaq, F. S., Muhammad, L. J., & Yahaya, B. Z. (2020). Fuzzy based expert system for diagnosis of diabetes mellitus. *Int J Adv Sci Technol.*, *136*, 39–50. doi:10.33832/ijast.2020.136.04

Jain, A., Dangi, P., Samanta, D., Dutta, S., Bhattacharya, A., & Joseph, N. P. (2023). Creation of Bookshelf Using Autodesk 3ds Max: 3D Modelling and Rendering. In *2023 11th International Conference on Internet of Everything, Microwave Engineering, Communication and Networks (IEMECON)* (pp. 1–4). IEEE.

Li, J., & Arandjelovic, O. (2017). Glycaemic index prediction: a pilot study of data linkage challenges and the application of machine learning. *IEEE EMBS Int. Conf. on Biomed. & Health Informat. (BHI)*, 357–360. 10.1109/BHI.2017.7897279

Lipton, Z. C., Elkan, C., & Naryanaswamy, B. (2014). Optimal thresholding of classifiers to maximize F1 measure. In *Joint European Conference on Machine Learning and Knowledge Discovery in Databases.* Springer. 10.1007/978-3-662-44851-9_15

Mondal, S., Pal, A. K., Islam, S. K. H., & Samanta, D. (2023). Objectionable Image Content Classification Using CNN-Based Semi-supervised Learning. *Advances in Smart Vehicular Technology, Transportation, Communication and Applications Proceedings of VTCA*, *2022*, 311–320.

Pal, M. (2005). Random forest classifier for remote sensing classification. *International Journal of Remote Sensing*, *26*(1), 217–222. doi:10.1080/01431160412331269698

Park, S., Choi, D., Kim, M., Cha, W., Kim, C., & Moon, I. C. (2017). Identifying prescription patterns with a topic model of diseases and medications. *Journal of Biomedical Informatics*, *75*, 35–47. doi:10.1016/j.jbi.2017.09.003 PMID:28958484

Podder, S. K., Samanta, D., Thomas, B., Dutta, S., & Bhattacharya, A. (2023). Impact of blended education system on outcome-based learning and sector skills development. In *2023 11th International Conference on Internet of Everything, Microwave Engineering, Communication and Networks (IEMECON)* (pp. 1–6). IEEE.

Razavian, N., Blecker, S., Schmidt, A. M., Smith-McLallen, A., Nigam, S., & Sontag, D. (2015). Population-level prediction of type 2 diabetes from claims data and analysis of risk factors. *Big Data*, *3*(4), 277–287. doi:10.1089/big.2015.0020 PMID:27441408

Robertson, G., Lehmann, E. D., Sandham, W., & Hamilton, D. (2011). Blood glucose prediction using artificial neural networks trained with the AIDA diabetes simulator: A proof-of-concept pilot study. *Journal of Electrical and Computer Engineering*, *681786*, 1–11. Advance online publication. doi:10.1155/2011/681786

Svetnik, V., Liaw, A., Tong, C., Culberson, J. C., Sheridan, R. P., & Feuston, B. P. (2015). Random forest: A classification and regression tool for compound classification and QSAR modeling. *Journal of Chemical Information and Computer Sciences*, *43*(6), 1947–1958. doi:10.1021/ci034160g PMID:14632445

Watkins, A. B., & Boggess, L. (2002). A resource limited artificial immune classifier. In *Proceedings of the 2002 Congress on Evolutionary Computation (CEC2002)*. IEEE Press. 10.1109/CEC.2002.1007049

Ye, Q., Qin, L., Forgues, M., He, P., Kim, J. W., Peng, A. C., Simon, R., Li, Y., Robles, A. I., Chen, Y., Ma, Z.-C., Wu, Z.-Q., Ye, S.-L., Liu, Y.-K., Tang, Z.-Y., & Wang, X. W. (2003). Predicting hepatitis B virus–positive metastatic hepatocellular carcinomas using gene expression profiling and supervised machine learning. *Nature Medicine*, *9*(4), 416–423. doi:10.1038/nm843 PMID:12640447

Yue, C., Xin, L., Kewen, X., & Chang, S. (2008). An intelligent diagnosis to type 2 diabetes based on QPSO algorithm and WLS-SVM. *Proceedings of the 2008 IEEE International Symposium on Intelligent Information Technology Application Workshops*. 10.1109/IITA.Workshops.2008.36

Chapter 4
Playing Rock–Paper–Scissors Using AI Through OpenCV

Narendra Kumar Rao Bangole
Mohan Babu University, India

S. Ranjana
Sai Ram Engineering College, Chennai, India

ABSTRACT

Day-to-day life has become smarter and more intertwined with technology in the modern era. We can chat with AI chatbots, and we can play with AI machines. In many cases, AI machines are defeating human players. All age groups are likely to play these games. The computer gaming industry has found Artificial intelligence as a necessary element to make more entertaining and challenging games. This work involves the integration of rock-paper-scissors (RPS) game with artificial intelligence (AI) using OpenCV and MediaPipe. Through collaboration with designers and animators, the framework is designed to be computationally light while also entertaining and visually appealing. To evaluate kinematic hand data in Python, the basic gesture recognition pipeline employs a leap motion device and two distinct machine learning architectures. This proposed system will provide a powerful application for future research into social human-machine interaction.

INTRODUCTION

Artificial intelligence (AI) embedded systems that can establish interaction between human-machine via voice, gestures, facial expressions, etc. are gaining popularity now. Using hands as an input is an appealing method for establishing natural Human Computer Interaction among the various interaction techniques. Hand gestures allow users to communicate more information in less time. As a result, in order to improve the interface between users and computers. Human-computer interaction (HCI) technology is widely used. To implement real time computer vision we can use OpenCV (Open Source Computer Vision Library). In the types of interaction between human-machine, it is one of the most researched and popular, because in this type of interaction machine itself train the machine to understand natural human language.

DOI: 10.4018/978-1-6684-9809-5.ch004

Rock- Paper- Scissors (RPS) is a game which is least studied but with a fascinating tactic which is decidedly not for the faint of heart. Its simplicity differentiates it from other well-known games although its influential underlying principles can be applicable in many aspects and have intriguing repercussions. The RPS game is a simple engagement of action and response which has long piqued the interest of researchers among various disciplines. In Sociology, to study the dynamic behavior of collaborative activities and In Biology, to study the evolution of ecosystems RPS patterns are used. And this RPS patterns also helpful in psychology to analyze the various gestures (Filho, 2018) that one can make and will help in revealing theirs patterns of making gestures in a play or will help in understanding human decision making. As discussed RPS is a game that exchanges information between an AI system and a human player and this provided the foundation for two most important studies in engineering and robotics. In Engineering, it is about the enhancement of basic technology and In Robotics, it is about its use in developing interaction between human and robots.

The following are the key principles to remember when playing Human-Human RPS:

1)   Non-Randomness (Unpredictability)
2)   Sansukumi

Non-Randomness (Unpredictability)

As we all think RPS contains random making of gestures from one of three hand gestures, but that's wrong RPS does not contain any random movements. The next move is totally influenced by the opponent's actions. Because of this RPS is performed within a time constraint:

- If there is no time limit for playing RPS or played very slowly then the players will have enough time to make a random gesture or perhaps to analyze the movements of their own and their opponents. Both of these will lead to the same outcome that may be random moves or having equal chance to win.
- If the RPS is performed fast or in a rhythm, players will not get time to make random gestures or to analyze the opponent moves. Hence the triumph depends on one's ability to make quick decisions, understanding the moves that may lead to failure and assess opponent's conduct.

Players play the RPS game in various ways among various regions. But among all those there is a common thing, i.e., players will countdown or chant something or sets timer for some particular time. During 1990s in some parts of Japan, RPS was popularly played to gain money and the game play will be like choosing the best among three and it will be completed in 4 or 5 seconds.

Sansukumi

Sansukumi is a Japanese term that refers to three opposing forces that keep each other in check. This phrase comes from China, although it first occurs in Japanese literature, where it has been related with both games and a range of enlightening philosophical concepts. The citizens obey the emperor's orders, the slaves obey the citizenry's directives, and the emperor fears that slaves may revolt against him, for example.

Sansukumi is often used to balance computer games; for example, in war games, the Infantry/Cavalry/Artillery sansukumi is widespread.

Historical and Contextual Information

Games that are played based on gestures are wide group of games which are found at various times throughout the history. A plethora of both modern and historical gesture games are offered by East Asia and among all of them RPS is the most popular and successful.

RPS belongs to the family of games which are found only in Japan. RPS is known in Japan as 'janken.' From the game called mushi-ken, the janken game has originated as in Figure 1.

Figure 1. Mushi-hand ken's movements

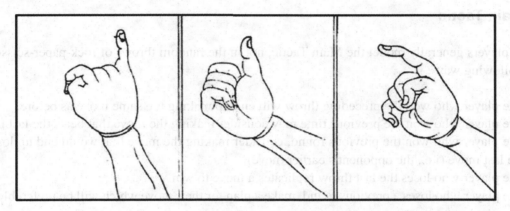

In RPS we will have three options, similar to mushi-ken. So it can be called three option Sansukumi. Also there are many other sansukumi gesture games in Asia that will have 5 or even 4 alternatives. Japan is rich in varients of games that incorporate a broad meta game, based on main sansukumi. One among them is a yakyuuken (in Japanese), the speciality of this game is both the players should sing songs and even they have to dance for those in between the throws!

The gesture games which are not based on the sansukumi will have odd or even results as common, including odds and evens as well as more complicated varieties. It is a fascinating concept to research on does these odd or even games are fully similar to sansukumi games or not.

In the history of gesture games, especially Asian sanukumi games are fascinating. The most interesting thing about the RPS is, it contains practically all of the fascinating notions of the whole group of family games that to in very less number of rules. This could be a reason to gain this much popularity.

Janken (a game in japan) has spread throughout the world since the mid-twentieth century but in several names such as Paper, Scissors, Stone, Roshambo, etc. and each one of these will have its types and rules. Janken game gained much seriousness during the 1980s and many extensive kinds of research are done on the strategies used and also several large-scale tournaments are conducted in China and Japan. Regrettably, the game's popularity is gradually reduced over the last 20 years. But still, there are some other large-scale games same as this game, although there are no powerful regulations in Japan or anywhere. Simultaneously, Playing RPS with AI challenge has been expanded.

Tactic

A game plan for RPS is a much more complicated concept that is not impossible to comprehend completely by a single person. We can partition the tactic into three subcategories:

- **The Main Tactic:** The crucial strategy or tactic revolves around working to develop a fast and mostly an automatic attitude and behavior in which one can adapt their throws against their opponent without taking much time for thinking in order to be successful more than half the time.
- **A Tactic for the Periphery:** In this, we have to cover timing, strategy for team play, and psychology of opponents
- **The Meta-Game:** Events that may occur around the game area but not depending on the game also have an effect on the final result or achievement

The Main Tactic

Serious players generally model the Main Tactic, not in the random throws of rock-paper-scissors, but in the following ways:

1. The player who won the preceding throw will end up making the same move as before.
2. The player who won the previous time may consider making the move that beats the last move.
3. The player who won the previous round, consider making the move that would end up losing for the last move (i.e., the opponent's earlier move).
4. The player who loses the last throw replicates a move to win.
5. The player who loses a previous round, make a plan for their move which will be preferable to win the round.
6. The player who loses a previous round, make a plan for their move to beat a winning move.

The actual symbols of rock-paper-scissors would not have the same level of resonance as concepts such as "if a player wins then the player cannot continue with the same move" or "if a player loses then there is no surety that the player will lose every time with the same move". The above 6 listed options are the building blocks for the RPS game.

A Tactic for the Periphery

A Tactic for the periphery is a main aspect of the game. In general, a Tactic for the periphery depends on the timing of the gameplay which is about the flow of the game and the ability to handle the draws. And the other one is team play. RPS relies heavily on timing. If the RPS is performed faster there is more chance to make default throws (choosing a throw more often which may lead them to win). Playing RPS faster provides an equal winning rate for both the players. This type of variation is also seen in Japanese and American chants. The difference is,

In Japanese chants, they use "Jan, ken, pon!" and throwing when the third syllable occurred and In American chants, they use "one, two, three, go" and throwing when the fourth syllable occurred.

RPS gains a new dimension with team play. Some people perform worse than others for unknown reasons. Mainly the games that are played as a team will have a huge impact when there is a change in the order of play or swapping the team members.

The thoroughness of the RPS rules is crucial. Rules should not be extremely strict or looser because if the rules are strict, the players who may lose will have few options. If the rules are looser, the players who may lose may divert the opponent by changing hands or making gestures after watching the opponent hence there will be a high chance of breaking the rules.

Hence, common estimation rules have a magnificent impact. In most cases, RPS is played as best of three sets but not every time. We have to consider the following questions, how many times a player can make a move before the given time is up? What is the frequency of winning of a dominant player? The RPS game is played seriously when there is a time constraint and played as three or five best of three games and there should be no gap in-between. If the RPS is performed as mentioned then players will get enough time to understand the behavior of their opponent and analyse their throws to win in the game.

Metagame

RPS game tactic will not be completed without mentioning the "meta-game". To understand this let's consider the thing that RPS is oddly the same as golf. The meta-game is nothing but the events or actions that may not be part of the game or depends on some other aspects but this still has a huge impact on the gameplay. Consider the following vital finds:

- Experienced players play with more random moves when compared to the serious players, making them both more difficult to win and more difficult to lose.
- Players of RPS game are susceptible to "tilt" in poker. It is a proclivity for error that may be caused because of an unfair RPS game. The players who are known as tilted will frequently change their moves or repeat the same patterns unnecessarily since they believe they "ought to" win. These players will take a rest and takes time to restart in team play.
- **Money:** RPS was played for large sums of money as betting or tournament in the last 20 years. Managing money is critical when playing a game and will be added extra worries to all of the players. To avoid an emotional impact on players when they are playing to gain money, money will be handled by the ones who are organized as leaders in a team or players' friends.
- **Alcohol:** This is unfortunate yet correct that not all of the players are strong physically, and if the game is played in pubs or bars, alcohol is very common. Some analysts, for instance, believe that most of the losing throws are repeated by the RPS players who consumed alcohol.
- **Bluffing and Mind-Games:** The player approaches their attacker and says, "Planning on throwing out the rock again?" then "will be ready in a minute". Tolerance for this type of tactic varies by location, just as it does in poker.

Statement of the Problem

Designing a game interface between a human and a system that uses OpenCV techniques and the Python programming language to recognise a person's hand gesture and play against the person by selecting one of three hand gestures.

Objectives

- To build a framework for reading human inputs.
- To detect the presence of human hands in a given frame.
- To classify whether the hand gesture is a paper, rock, or scissors based on human input.
- To select the victor by using winning criteria.
- To determine the final winner, who first reaches a score of 3.

Scope

This framework for playing Rock, Paper, Scissors (RPS) game with AI embedded system, which let users play with the computer and the future scope of this is really vast as everything getting digital. With little equipment, this can be implemented easily. Additional features can be added like linking this game with robotics and letting robots learn to make hand gestures and this project can be incorporated into many institutions.

Applications

- Entertainment purposes for Children, adults, etc. RPS with AI can attract more people than normal RPS.
- Can be used in training Robots.
- Can be made into a commercialized product for the children.
- Can construct images using gestures.

Limitations

Works only on Desktop.
 Clarity depends on the camera resolution and the lighting.

LITERATURE SURVEY

Numerous studies have been done that have focus on human motion recognition. They have applied different techniques for analysis and achieved different probabilities for different methods.

The implementation of the Rock-Paper-Scissors game interaction with a computer is presented. With the teamwork of both designers and animators, this game is designed to the final stage. Software is designed to be light to run (Heike Brock, 2020), as well as good-looking animations were integrated (Gomez &Szapiro, 2018). To guess the random pattern in the hand data on the fly, the gesture detection pipeline (Lugaresi, 2019) uses a leap motion device and two different machine learning architectures. Human motion is detected by the first architecture and makes RPS play. Whereas second architecture detects the hand symbol as Rock, paper, or scissor. The tabletop robot will make its choice to win or lose and also draw states to different animated gestures and vocalizations created by animators (Gomez, 2020). Both learning architectures are trained with different feature and classifier types, and the performance of both architectures is thoroughly examined for accuracy, reliability, and speed. We calculate the approach during a collaborative RPS game between a robot and a human. The system will analyze the user play pattern in the real world. It's a great window to a new way of interaction between a human and a machine.

The hand gesture recognition system is created by Leap motion to train the machine learning architecture for user hand gesture recognition (Brock, 2020). The existing system will activate based on the speed of the user's hand and movement of the index finger, and with an early detection scheme, it labels the detected movements. The system can recognize gestures without movement limits by combining multiple gestures labels. The system is evaluated using data from simulations of real-world human-robot interactions, we do investigate the behaviour of the system with help of the performance variables like the pattern of movement, timing, and posture (Bradski, 1998; Bowden et al., 2003).

A novel technique for automatically detecting words within sentence expressions in Sign language of Japan from 3-dimensional body joint positions, was introduced. First, the spaces between line segments of inter-joint pairs are used to determine the flow of the sentence data in sign language within a temporal neighborhood. Using the extracted space and time features, a frame-wise binary random classifier is trained to differentiate between words and non-words frames. The classifier's output is used to propose an automatic word generation method that achieves reliable and very accurate sentence formation with a good average frame-wise F1 score of 0.89. The system approach can also be easily adapted to differentiate between motion transitions and motion primitives for a harsh domain, according to the evaluation of the baseline data set (Cao et al., 2003; Chai et al., 1998).

They created applications to perceive the world around them even though it's difficult. Developers must select and develop similar machine learning algorithms and models, create some prototypes and demos, maintain a balance between resource consumption and solution quality, and identify and make no severe issues for complex cases. All of these are maintained by the Media-Pipe framework. Developers can use Media-Pipe to make prototypes by combining existing components, then upgrade them to optimize in multi-platform applications while measuring system behavior in performance and resource consumption on different platforms. We give demos on how all these features. Make a developer focus on algorithm or model making while using Media-Pipe as an environment for exponentially developing their application with results that are reliable and reproducible on multiple platforms and devices (Conci et al., 2007; Cui et al., 1995; Cutler et al., 1998).

The method of training fine-grained detectors for key points that are prone to blocking, such as hand joint bones, using a multi-camera system (Simon, 2017). A key point detector is used to generate noisy labels in different aspects of the hand. The noisy detections are then eliminated by triangulation in three dimensions using multiview geometry or marked as different objects as detached from the main subject. Finally, the projected triangulations are used to improve the detector as new labeled training data. This process is repeated, with each iteration producing more labeled data. We derive an analytical result relating the least number of aspects required to achieve target true and false-positive rates for a particular detector. For single images.

The key point detector operates in real-time on color images and has accuracy comparable to depth sensor methods. The single view detector is triangulated in multiple views which allows for 3D markerless hand motion capture with some difficult object interactions (Farag, 2019).

The human hand's motion is dynamic so it must be tracked at high-speed and images with no blur in them, in order to achieve reliable and exact recognition. For natural recognition, a large area of recognition is required. To accomplish these goals, they built a new advanced sensing system which can track and also recognize the human hand gesture using a system with high-speed vision (Rautaray, 2015). The rock-paper-scissors game between a human and a machine requires high-speed recognition, and they focused on this task to demonstrate the concluded system. In this case, we track a human hand at high speed and correctly detect its sign (rock, paper, or scissors) in each frame. Our tests revealed that the robot.

A Robot is made to play the game "rock paper scissors". The game is played by a robot and a human facing each other. To recognize the shape of the user's hand, they created the image processing system. They also programmed the robot to express human-like emotions through its voice, body gestures, and facial expressions that changed depending on the result of the game.

ANALYSIS

The goal is to investigate the specific requirements for hardware, software, design, and its functions.

Specific Requirements

Google Collaboratory or Jupyter Notebook that supports (Python version 3.7) as we are using Machine Learning and Data Analysis. Google Collaboratory and Jupyter Notebook are more flexible environments for executing these '.ipynb' files. We can even use Python IDLE for executing this.

Functional Requirements

- Accurate hand detection
- Accurate Finger detection using Landmarks
- Perform mathematical computation
- Approximate coordinate calculation
- Real-time tracking
- Display of result

Non-Functional Requirements

- Scalability
- Accuracy
- Robustness
- Performance
- Reliability
- Response Time
- Maintainability

Design

Logical Design

Representing the flow of data, inputs, and outputs of a system conceptually are known as the Logical design of a system. Logical design can be applied through modeling and this helps to design the model of the existing system. There is also a discussion about the implementation of system design. In the implementation of logical design UML diagrams are used.

Physical Design

Compared with Logical design, Physical design is not about the flow but, it is about how the inputs and outputs are processed. It can also be defined as the processing of output from the inputs given to the machine or system.

EXISTING SYSTEM

Python is a multifunctional language that may be used for almost anything. Python can also be used to create video games. Implementation of the Rock-Paper-Scissor game Without utilizing any external game libraries such as PyGame or OpenCV. The player in this game has the first chance to select amongst Rock, Paper, and Scissors. The winner is then selected in accordance with the regulations when the computer chooses (at random) one of the final two possibilities.

The following are the winning rules:

Consider Human Player as the user and the computer as AI.

- If the user makes a paper gesture and AI selects Scissors then AI will win in that throw.
- If the user makes a rock gesture and AI selects Scissors then the user will win in that throw.
- If the AI selects rock and the user makes a paper gesture then the user will win in that throw.
- If AI selects rock and the user also makes the same gesture –rock then it will be tied in that throw.
- If AI selects paper and the user also makes a paper gesture then this will also lead to a tie.
- If AI selects scissors and the user also makes a scissors gesture then it will also be considered a tie.

In this game, the inbuilt function randint() is used to generate random integer values within the given range. The main aspect here is how we provide the computer input or make a choice. It may be selecting one of the three pictures displayed by clicking on it or entering the spelling or number of our choice. However, gamers will find this monotonous because it is merely a simple technique of providing input and there will be very little interaction between both the player and the computer as in Figure-2.

Figure 2. players can select from the three images displayed

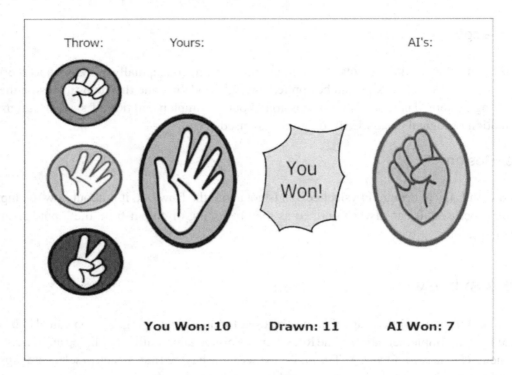

PROPOSED SYSTEM

Rock, Paper, and Scissors (RPS) becomes a lot more intriguing thanks to computer vision. It will be a two-way conversation between a computer and a human. Winning Rock, Paper, and Scissors (RPS) is based on random moves, so it is not a model of a winning AI system as no strategy is used. The system's only intelligence would be in the visual recognition of hand signs. To implement real-time computer vision then we can use a library called OpenCV (Open Source Computer Vision Library). OpenCV is compatible with Windows, Linux, macOS, FreeBSD, NetBSD, and OpenBSD. The library contains over 2400 of the top algorithms, including a comprehensive collection of classic and Advanced computer vision and algorithms used in ML (Machine Learning). These algorithms and methods are widely used to distinguish and in the detection of faces, objects, or things and categorize the actions of humans in a video, monitor the movements in the camera, and implement 3D from them. MediaPipe library provides effective hand tracking and finger tracking systems, with a higher resolution. With the help of Machine learning (ML) which is a part of AI (Artificial Intelligence), one can point out 21 3D landmarks from the palm in one shot. Related to the Hands module in MediaPipe as in Figure 3, the palm detection model and Hand Landmark model are present. The researchers created a new model to detect the objects in the frame, which is an optimized model for mobile real-time purposes comparable to the model implemented in MediaPipe to detect faces using Face Mesh, to detect initial palm placements. The diagram below describes the detection of a hand over the complete image and will point out all of the 21 3D coordinates in the detected palm which is a direct coordinate prognostication.

Figure 3. Recognizing hand gesture using MediaPipe

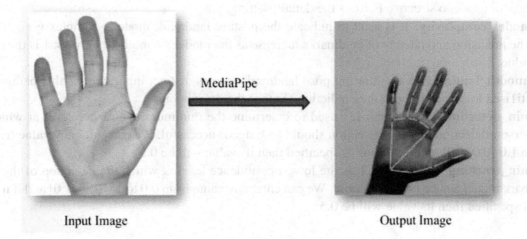

Input Image   Output Image

OpenCV

A sizable open-source library for image processing, machine learning, and computer vision is called OpenCV. Python, C++, Java, and many other programming languages are supported by OpenCV. It can analyse pictures and movies to find faces, objects, and even human handwriting. When it is integrated with a variety of libraries, such as when you use the very effective numerical operations library Numpy.

Because all of the operations that we can do using NumPy will be more powerful when it is integrated with OpenCV.

Applications

- Color palette with trackbars for OpenCV BGR.
- Using OpenCV we can convert an image to a pencil sketch.
- With OpenCV, we can display the points on which we clicked from the image.
- OpenCV can be used to give objects as input and extract from them.

MediaPipe

High-resolution hand and finger tracking programme is called Hands by MediaPipe. From a single image, machine learning (ML) is used to infer 21 3D properties of a hand. Our method offers real-time performance on a mobile device and even scales to several hands, in contrast to current cutting-edge systems that mostly rely on robust desktop environments for inference. We believe that opening out these hand perception skills to the larger research and development community would encourage the development of new studies and applications as in Figure 4.

The landmarks present on each finger can be used to track the position of the finger. It can converted to necessary coordinate values in the given image frame.

- **static_image_mode:** It specifies whether the supplied images should be processed as static images or as video streams. False is the default setting.
- **model_complexity:** It is used to indicate the posture landmark model's complexity: 0, 1, or 2. The precision and latency of landmarks increase as the model's complexity grows. 1 is the default value.
- **smooth_landmarks:** By filtering pose landmarks across distinct input photos, this parameter is utilised to reduce jitter in the prediction. True is the default value.
- **min_detection_confidence:** It's used to determine the minimum confidence level at which the person-detection model's detection should be judged successful. We can enter any value from 0.0 to 1.0 [0.0, 1.0] and if nothing is specified then its value will be 0.5.
- **min_tracking_confidence:** It is the lowest confidence level at which the detection of the landmark model can be treated as valid. We can enter any value from 0.0 to 1.0 [0.0, 1.0] and if nothing is specified then its value will be 0.5.

Figure 4. Recognizing hand gesture using MediaPipe

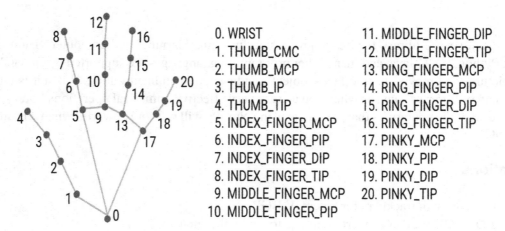

Few Design Specific details:
Use Case Diagram:

Figure 5. Use case diagram

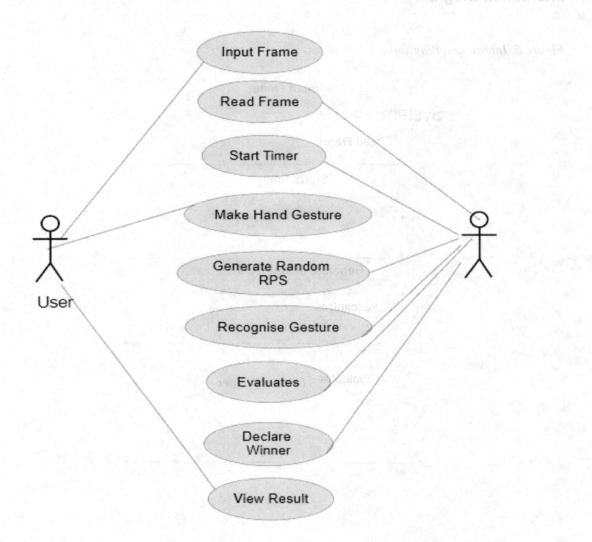

Interaction Diagram

Figure 6. Interaction diagram

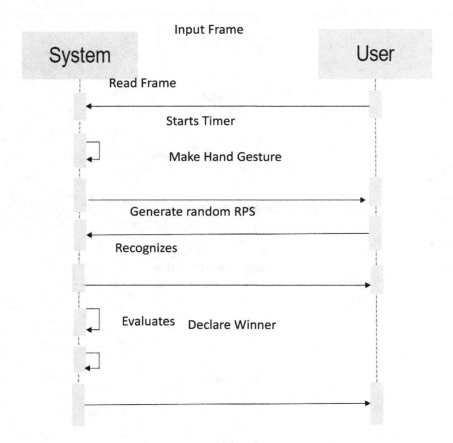

Collaboration Diagram

Figure 7. Collaboration diagram

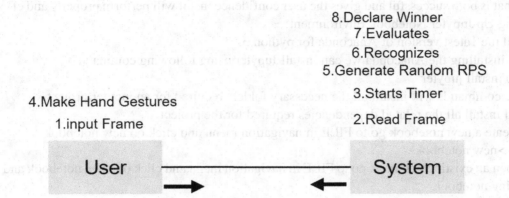

Figure 8. Activity diagram

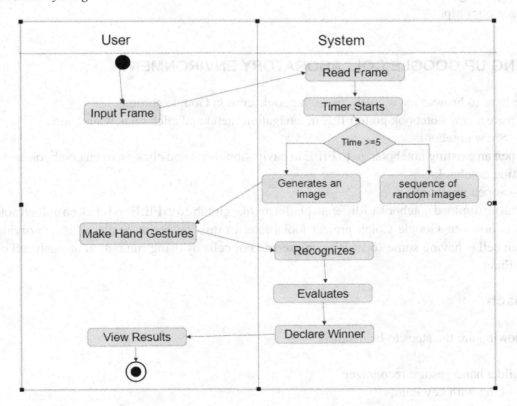

IMPLEMENTATION

The suggested system design is turned into a working system during the project's implementation stage. As a result, it might be considered the most important stage in achieving a successful output, a new system that is both successful and gives the user confidence that it will perform properly and effectively.

Setting Up Jupyter Notebook Environment:

Install the latest version of Anaconda for python 3.

After installing the Anaconda we can install Jupyter using following command

->pip install jupyter

These commands will install all the necessary folders required for an jupyter project.

It will install all the related dependencies required for the project

To create a new notebook go to FILE in navigation menu and click on new notebook.

File-->new notebook

To open an existing notebook go to FILE in navigation menu and click on open notebook and choose the existing notebook.

File-->open notebook

In this the entire notebook is sub divided into cells each cell is having some code. We can execute our cells by using run button on each cell or Press CTRL+Enter. Once all the cells executed successfully we can see our output.

SETTING UP GOOGLE COLLABORATORY ENVIRONMENT

First we have to browse www.colab.research.google.com in Google chrome.

To create a new notebook go to FILE in navigation menu and click on new notebook

File-->new notebook

To open an existing notebook go to FILE in navigation menu and click on open notebook and choose the existing notebook.

File-->open notebook

We can also upload notebook to different platforms like github go to FILE and click on upload notebook.

This is how our Google Colab project looks like. In this the entire notebook is sub divided into cells each cell is having some code. We can execute our cells by using run button on each cell or Press CTRL+Enter.

Approach

The following are the steps to be detailed:

- Build a hand gesture recognizer
- Working with key Points
- Defining Gestures

Build a Hand Gesture Recognizer

The primary issue in creating a RPS game is to recognise the three hand gestures inside a camera picture ✊ ✌.

The initial step is to determine whether or not a hand is visible within the camera image.

We estimate the position of all finger joints to trace the hand skeleton if a hand is observed as in Figure 9.

Figure 9. Hand recognizer

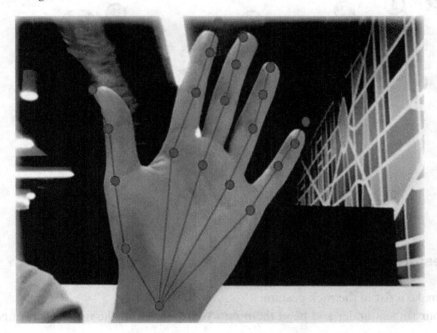

Working With Key Points

The hand skeleton detector returns the following 21 key locations (sometimes known as "landmarks"): Each finger has four joints, plus the wrist.

The key points are 2D coordinates that inform us where each skeletal point in the image is located.

It is not a very helpful way to describe a hand gesture because it is so difficult to compare two hand movements based on joint position.

A hand can be present in any location in the image, it can be rotated, and people can be left-handed or right-handed as in Figure 10.

Figure 10. Key points

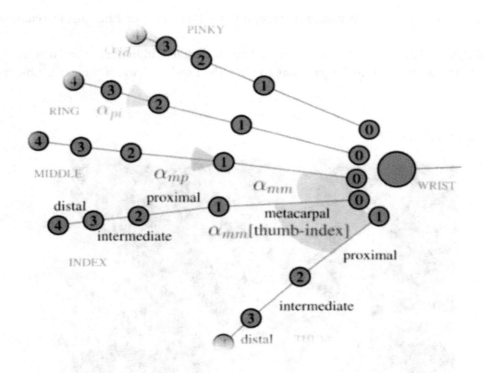

Defining Gestures

You basically make a fist in the rock gesture:

You curl your fingers under and bend them into your palm until the tip of each finger reaches its matching base.

The thumb is next bent down and placed across the top parts of the index and middle fingers.

A "rock" gesture is defined as follows in this rule:

All of our fingers are fully curled.

Gesture for Paper

You must spread out all of your fingers and your thumb to produce a "paper" motion.

Gesture for Scissors

The "scissors" sign looks a lot like a "winning" sign. The index and middle fingers are extended. The ring and pinky should be curled in half or completely.

SYSTEM ARCHITECTURE

Figure 11. System architecture

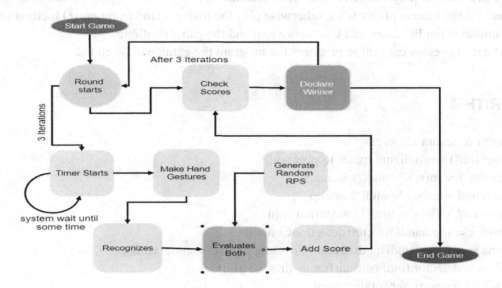

Explanation of Architecture Figure 11

1. Import the necessary modules required. The modules imported are PyGame, Cvzone, NumPy, MediaPipe, OpenCV.
2. Create a module named Hand_Tracking and initialize the instance variables.
3. Define a function for locating the hands in the frame and sketching their landmarks.
4. Define another function for determining hand position and their key points and rendering them as circles in the window frame.
5. Now, Create a new module called Play to carry out the main activity.
6. Initialize the mixer which is imported from pygame to play sounds using mixer.init().
7. Create variable to store video using VideoCapture() function. Pass parameter 1 in VideoCapture(1) to access webcam.
8. Store the folder path for hand images (Rock, Paper and Scissors) in a variable and store all the images in that folder in a array using cv2.imread() method.
9. In a variable store the HandDetector class from Hand_Tracking module to use the functions.
10. Start a loop and run it till a desired key is pressed. In the loop, read each frame that is being recorded. Frames per second varies from webcam to webcam.
11. Display PC score and User score using a method "putText" in OpenCV library as
12. cv2.putText(). Start a timer and display random images from the images array until timer reaches 5.
13. Count the number of fingers opened by the user using the findHands and findPosition
14. function.

15. Generate random image from the images stored in the array using random library.
16. Evaluate both the human gesture and image generated by system, and increment the Score of the particular player who wins that round.
17. Declare the first player to reach a score of 3 as the final winner, and play the winning
18. Sound if the human player wins, otherwise play the losing sound using play() method in mixer.
19. Reinitialize the PC score and User score to 0 and the game continues.
20. If the user presses esc button or closes the program the game will be ended.

ALGORITHM

1. import Relevant Packages
2. mixer.init() #initializing mixer to play audio
3. winsound = mixer.Sound('win.mp3')
4. losesound = mixer.Sound('lose.mp3')
5. cap = cv2.VideoCapture(1) #external cam
6. detector = mp.handDetector(detectionCon=0)
7. frame = detector.findHands(frame) #reading inputs from the camera
8. lmList = detector.findPosition(frame, draw=False)
9. totalFingers=getUserTotalFingers()
10. if totalFingers = 5 then
    a. frame = cvzone.overlayPNG(frame, overlayList[0], [0, 0]) #to display paper
11. if totalFingers == 0 then
    a. frame = cvzone.overlayPNG(frame, overlayList[1], [0, 0]) # to display rock
12. if totalFingers == 2 then
    a. frame = cvzone.overlayPNG(frame, overlayList[2], [0, 0]) #to display scissors
13. else display "Try Again"
14. if time >=5 then result=evaluate()
15. if pc_score>user_score then
    a. play(losesound)
    b. display "you lost the game"
16. else
    a. play(winsound)

display "you win the game"

EXECUTION PROCEDURE AND TESTING

We'll need some tools, and a server to complete the job. The following are the requirements and procedures:
   To complete the project, we can also use Google co1ab.
   Google Co1ab is a free cloud-based service that now includes free GPU support! Setting up an environment with Anaconda in a computer is time-consuming although it has a GPU and troubleshooting the issues of installation is also tough. But this will be resolved by using Colaboratory which is a free

Jupyter notebook developed by Google. Working with Google Colab is easy, first, we need to sign in to a Google account and then navigate to the website https://colab.research.google.com.

RESULTS

This application enables the user to construct images in air using their fingers. The landmarks of the hand are detected and images are constructed by keeping track of the position of the finger. The various gestures for the game are as in Figure 12 to Figure 14.

When the Hand_tracking_module.py is run or opened:

Figure 12. Paper

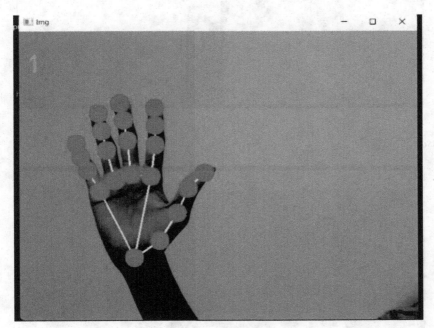

PERFORMANCE EVALUATION

On both desktop and mobile devices, MediaPipe provides models with high accuracy and low latency. It gives a 3D Hand Landmark model that uses machine learning techniques to predict 21 points from a single picture and can be used on desktops, mobile devices, and browsers, among other platforms. The palm detection model has a precision of 95.7 percent on average.

Figure 13. Rock

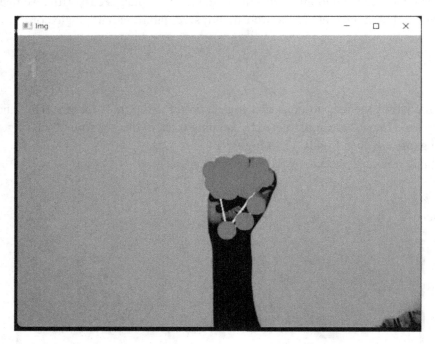

Figure 14. Scissor

CONCLUSION AND FUTURE WORK

Conclusion

An OpenCV and MediaPipe based Virtual Paint application is proposed in this paper. The palm detection model and hand landmark model were used to identify the hand and its landmarks. OpenCV has in-built image processing algorithms which preprocesses the frames captured and displays output as required by the user. Therefore, the application provides interactive environment between human player and AI (computer).

Future Work

Future work based on this project has a much broader scope. A few are listed here:

- This application can be converted into a mobile application.
- This can be enhanced by linking this software with the Robotic Hand to play against the user.
- This will be helpful in training the Robots to make relevant Hand Gestures.
- In this we can include Machine Learning models to predict the user and generate hand gestures according to that, other than making random gestures.

REFERENCES

Bowden, R., Zisserman, A., Kadir, T., & Brady, M. (2003). Vision based interpretation of natural sign languages. In *Exhibition at ICVS03: the 3rd international conference on computer vision systems*. ACM Press.

Bradski, G. (1998). Real time face and object tracking as a component of a perceptual user interface. IEEE Workshop on Applications of Computer Vision, 214–219. doi:10.1109/ACV.1998.732882

Brock, H., Sabanovic, S., Nakamura, K., & Gomez, R. (2020). Robust real-time hand gestural recognition for non-verbal communication with tabletop robot haru. *Proc. 29th IEEE Int. Conf. Robot Human Interact. Commun. (RO-MAN)*, 891–898.

Cao, X., & Balakrishnan, R. (2003). Visionwand: interaction techniques for large displays using a passive wand tracked in 3d. In *UIST '03: proceedings of the 16th annual ACM symposium on User Interface software and technology*. ACM Press.

Chai, D., & Ngan, K. (1998). Locating the facial region of a head and-shoulders color image. IEEE international conference on automatic face and gesture recognition, 124–129. doi:10.1109/AFGR.1998.670936

Cohen, P. R., Johnston, M., McGee, D., Oviatt, S., Pittman, J., Smith, I., Chen, L., & Clow, J. (1997). Quickset: multimodal interaction for distributed applications. In *Proceedings of the fifth ACM international conference on Multimedia*. ACM Press. 10.1145/266180.266328

Conci, N., Ceresato, P., & De Natale, F. G. B. (2007). Natural human–machine interface using an interactive virtual blackboard. IEEE international conference on image processing, 181–184. doi:10.1109/ICIP.2007.4379795

Cui, Y., Swets, D., & Weng, J. (1995). Learning-based hand sign recognition using shoslf-m. *International workshop on automatic face and gesture recognition*, 201–206.

Cutler, R., & Turk, M. (1998). View-based interpretation of real-time optical flow for gesture recognition. In *Proceedings of the international conference on face and gesture recognition*. IEEE Computer Society. 10.1109/AFGR.1998.670984

Farag, I., & Brock, H. (2019). Learning motion disfluencies for automatic sign language segmentation. *Proc. IEEE Int. Conf. Acoust. Speech Signal Process. (ICASSP)*, 7360–7364.

Filho, I. A. S., Chen, E. N., da Silva, J. M. Jr, & da Silva Barboza, R. (2018). Gesture recognition using leap motion: A comparison between machine learning algorithms. *Proc. ACM SIGGRAPH Posters*, 1–2. 10.1145/3230744.3230750

Gomez, R., Nakamura, K., Szapiro, D., & Merino, L. (2020). A holistic approach in designing tabletop robot's expressivity. *Proc. IEEE Int. Conf. Robot. Automat. (ICRA)*, 1970–1976.

Gomez, R., Szapiro, D., Galindo, K., & Nakamura, K. (2018). Hardware design of an experimental tabletop robot assistant. *Proc. ACM/IEEE Int. Conf. Human-Robot Interact.*, 233–240. 10.1145/3171221.3171288

LugaresiC.TangJ.NashH.McClanahanC.UbowejaE.HaysM.ZhangF.ChangC.-L.Guang YongM.LeeJ.ChangW.-T.HuaW.GeorgM.GrundmannM. (2019). MediaPipe: A framework for building perception pipelines. Available: https://arxiv.org/abs/1906.08172

Rautaray, S., & Agrawal, A. (2015, January). Vision based hand gesture recognition for human computer interaction: A survey. *Artificial Intelligence Review*, *43*(1), 1–54. doi:10.100710462-012-9356-9

Simon, T., Joo, H., Matthews, I., & Sheikh, Y. (2017). Hand keypoint detection in single images using multiview bootstrapping. *Proc. IEEE Conf. Comput. Vis. Pattern Recognit. (CVPR)*, 1145–1153.

Chapter 5
Software Modeling and Design Process

Smrity Dwivedi
Indian Institute of Technology (BHU), Varanasi, India

ABSTRACT

Modeling is the designing of software applications before coding according to the object-oriented groups where under the model-based software design and development, software modeling and design are used as an important and mandatory part of the software development process. Software models are methods of expressing a software design. Basically, some sort of abstract language or pictures are used to express the software design under modeling. For object-oriented software, an object modeling language such as UML and many more are used to develop and express the software design. Also, the design model is based on the analysis and architectural essentials of the system. It denotes the application components and determines their appropriate placement and use within the overall architecture.

INTRODUCTION

Here, view of external system, their connection with system and their needs like what it provides and what its requirements are very important. Always before giving the design, quality has to be checked of the software, just because of requirements of software like security, performance and maintainability, which should have fulfilled before in use. Software design architecture is having high level as well as low level design, but high level is important to check the every point in well before as functional and non functional. It is all about to start the program. Also there are few notations to represent the figure and text for software design. The best way that is being used. UML and its notation to presents the design and modeling with different class and object as UML is object oriented software and used for many applications. Also these notations are used to perform a design but it is not used for develop the design. As software design architecture is a fundamental approach like security of information, that is why, design is perform with proper strategy, planning and way to direct towards the best results under overall design. Software strategy is like object oriented discrimination. Structuring is also important

DOI: 10.4018/978-1-6684-9809-5.ch005

while designing to provide the help to designer with proper steps to create the design as per applications. Structuring helps a designer and design team identify the design decisions. Under the design sequence and structuring, proper concepts, one and more than strategy, documentation are employed, in which collaborative object modeling and design, UML notation are used. Here, collaborative concepts are used for information hiding, classes, concurrent woks and inheritance, which address the active and passive objects and its interconnection. Also, under this structuring criteria during analysis of design and some additional criteria to get the information regarding subsystems and its tasks during the design. Each part given above will be discussed in this chapter with explanations and case analysis (Erl, 2006, 2008, 2009). By using modeling in software, it does not mean, to express any scientific theory or algorithm in software. But it is something that scientists traditionally call a software model and also software modeling is larger than an algorithm used or a single method. Software modeling should represent the entire software design including all interfaces, all interactions with other software being used, and all the software methods used.

Thinking of designing of software is like to design a house where rough sketch of the floor plan and layout of rooms and floors are decided first. Sketching is like modeling language and resulting view of overall thinking process is design. Modification is possible in the sketching to get final approved design to meet the requirements. Then start with, cutting and writing the code is the final touch. Also, in this design, any time, problems can be discovered and corrected with its code (Gomaa, 2011).

Now, the Software design is the process of defining software methods, functions, objects, and also the overall structure and interaction of code that is discussed above so that the results obtained will be satisfy to the users. According to requirements of users, code can be written. In the designing, there are so many methods to design the software with all initial design and modify it as necessary. Different software designers prefer different types of design while processing and during implementation phase (Friedenthal et al., 2009). Before, start the implementation, reviewing it again necessary. It is important and even easy to try out different designs first and also discover the problems initially in the development cycle to move on final design.

Software design should include all description of the overall architecture. This will cover the hardware, databases, and third-party frameworks so that designed software could interact with other software.

SOFTWARE DESIGN ARCHITECTURE

A software architecture separates the overall system structure from the underlying specifics of each individual component in a number of ways, including the components and how they are connected. According to Gamma et al. (1995), programming in the large (PITL) and programming in the small (PITS) are terms used to describe the main emphasis on components and their interconnections, respectively. It can provide a high-level description of the division of the software system into subsystems. According to H. Gomaa (2011), it can specify the breakdown of subsystems into modules or components at a lower level. In each instance, the interfaces, demands, and connections with other subsystems and components serve as the primary points of focus for the external picture of the subsystem or component. When creating the software architecture, it is important to take into account the system's software quality attributes. These characteristics show how crucial nonfunctional needs like performance, security, and maintainability are addressed by the architectural design. Another effective method for expressing design graphically, visually, or both is a software design architectural notation (Gomaa, 1994, 1986, 1989a, 1989b).

Pseudocode is a textual design notation, while diagrams for the class are a graphical design notation. Another graphical notation for object-oriented software programs is UML, which is mentioned above. A design notation suggests a specific approach to the designer when creating a design. It follows that it does not offer a methodical way for creating a necessary design. A fundamental concept called software design architecture can be used to design a system according to its needs. One type of software design is information concealing. An overall strategy and the approach for creating a design are both included in an architectural software design idea. An illustration of a software architecture design concept is an object-oriented tool. construction of Software is planned thinking that designers use to organize a software system into its various parts. Rules for breaking the system down into objects, for instance, are provided by object structuring. A software architecture design process is a foolproof strategy that outlines all the actions to take in order to improve the design in accordance with the application's needs. This approach helps the designer, or possibly the entire design team, recognize the design first and make the necessary decisions to produce methodical and effective results. The ultimate output of this method is documented using a design notation and is based on a set of design rules that are connected to one or more design strategies. This approach may provide design criteria for structuring the software as well as provide the designer with a number of clear guidelines for breaking the system down into its component parts. Evaluation of UML based design: Initially, only UML based design is set as modeling language and its notation for developing the object oriented design architecture. Kobryn has given the full description of UML and before him, Booch and Jacobson has introduced UML 9.0 and then Rumbaugh also added few terms in it. UML 9.0 has developed on the basis of standard and effective effort along with the additional features of a diverse mix of vendors and system integrators as per requirement. The stand and effective works complied and submit to get initial UML 1.0. Then final UML 1.1 has come a year later with enhance quality. Final and the last version of UML 1,3 has come with advance features but some errors which is removed and introduce the next UML 1.3 and UML 1.4. Again revision has been done and UML 2.0 has come with collaboration of Booch, Rumbaugh and Jacobson. Many more researchers have given their effort to make revision and generate new version (Gomaa, 2011).

There are two types of UML one is platform independent and other is platform specific where platform independent is a precise model for software architecture design before doing final task. For platform independent development, it is necessary to develop first, because it is mapped with other useful software like COM, CORBA, .NET, J2EE, Web Services and another Web platform in between the process (Gomaa, 2011).

Other important aspects of software architecture: There is different perspective to see the software architecture design which is given by many researchers as per their theory. 4+1 model of design is given by Kruchten in which the case view is unifying view and also these views are logical which is actually in other words static modeling view and the development view which is the sub system and component design view (Brooks, 1995). Industrial perspective on applied software design architecture has also four views like previous one in which conceptual view, code view, module view and execution view are important and it is given by (Hofmeister et al. 2000). All views having their own specific task like define main design elements, organizing source code into object code, libraries and directories, consists of subsystems and modules and the last one is concurrent and distributed execution perspective. Further, these views are classified as per their task and requirements. Case view is a functional view of requirements which is useful as an input to develop the design, where every time, all interaction between one and more than users and the systems are fully described. Static view is useful in terms of classes and relationships which is important during association like composition, aggregation, generalization and specialization and all are verified by UML (Gomaa, 2011). Dynamic interaction view denotes the architecture of objects and message and also the communication set up between these points (Brown, 2000; Budgen, 2003). It is also predict the machine view, control component view and state chart diagram on the UML platform. Structural component view is used to develop the interface to support other important interfaces again the UML platform. Dynamic concurrent view is actually software design architecture to check the concurrent components and execute all the diverse nodes and deliver the message. Deployment view is used to develop the specific configuration foe diverse architecture along with components as per assign hardware instruction and it is working on UML based diagrams.

First view of software architecture design and modeling: Few decades ago, when there were no UML platform then without having systematic requirements, program were written and implemented using graphical notations under the effect of flowcharts gain with less knowledge and with the help of documentation tool as well as design tool before doing the final coding for design and analysis. During that time, subroutines are made to construct the blocks of code and it was called in other program as per requirements. After few years of generation of this technique, construction of modular system is adopted as tool for project. Under this process, programs were divided into small module and each module had given to each person, then they developed the subroutines for the program (Buhr et al., 1996). Thereafter, during seventies, this type of programming has been taken as prominent too for program writing and design with structured method. One of the scientists has design first design method with some new operating system with the use of hierarchical architecture and that was first design to address the concurrent system which is called as operating system. After seventies, again two other software design have developed with flow and data based design (Buschmann et al., 1996). Flow based design methods is used to write the structured program which is well documented and comprehensive methods that evolved. For better understanding, this design of system is flow of data. It is consisted of flow diagram and mapping of the system. It is basically divided into small modules and interfaces with other modules. It is also useful to decide the quality of design in terms of coupling. After that it is extended for structural analysis. Apart from that there is alternative approach which is similar to first one, is data structural programming. So, as per discussion, this view is of full understanding to get the best structures as per consideration of data structures. Under this, there are two programming methods, one is Jackson and other is Warnier. Both are very famous in their concept of logical and physical separations to develop the data base management system. For logical contribution, there are several databases with entity relationship which made useful help to hide the actual data with good results. Initially, there were the major problem is the use of global data which gives error and also difficult to change to remove the error. So, this new approach of security like hide is great to reduce that error (Gomaa, 2011). After that there are few more methods are generated like MASCOT which is great in design the system and also easy to write the program to understand and to interface. This method gives the freedom to communicate to each other by using channels or pools in real time system without eliminating the use of global data. This type data design is secure by calling it using function with the help of procedure given in channels. Also it is well maintained in synchronization by using technique known as semaphores to hide during calling. In eighties, again new methods are evolved with matured design. Again there were many researchers who were involved and gave new methods with the help of Naval research lab to generate the high security at large scale with reduction of cost and that is known as cost reduction software design methods. Then working with structural analysis and design in real time developed the real time structured analysis and design. Few more methods are developed using Jackson method which is extended version of that known as system development (Cheesman et al., 2001). This is one of the best ways to use secure data analysis with hiding and to interface with other software without exposing and easy calling is possible and this is actually a modern object oriented development programming.

Evaluation of new method of programming: During eighties, there were many methods including booch, Wirf, Wilkerson, Wiener, Rumbaugh, Shlaer has developed which was first introduction of object oriented programming. They were developed and highly secured system. There are two ways to define object oriented programming, one is design and other is analysis. Booch has introduced the design which was later used to hiding the data and information and then others have added new features in it. They have given approach for the smoother transition between designs to analysis to design. Analysis part is used to check the life cycle of software, in which finding the real world object and mapping them with others are important. Under this system, entity relationship module is used to modeling of object which is logical modeling in other words. Under this modeling, identifying the entity which is an intensive object is used. There are several entities in which creating the relationship is main task and this is actually taken from entity relationship diagram (Gomaa, 2011). Then it is mapped with data base during the design. Under this new programming method, objects are identified and then modeled to form software classes with their relation with other classes. Entity and class are different in their module scheme like first one is used under entity relationship and other one is used under static modeling.

Use of UML: This is the first which is developed on the basis of notation as a language with several versions over the years which can be seen from the given Figure 1. This is very famous diagram having with several instructions, which is why it is mentioned as UML diagrams. There are so many things like activity, class, case, object, sequence, state machine, communication, composite structure, deployment diagrams can be seen.

Figure 1. According to cases, UML notation

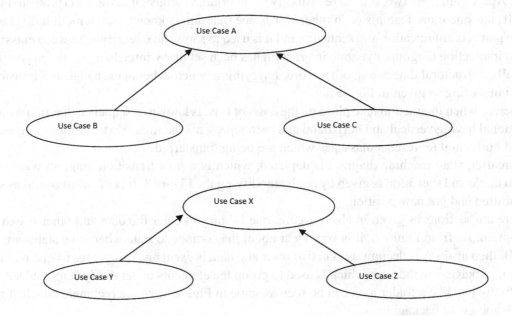

Here, the cases are set of instructions between system and main part, where main part is the most important and stick figure on this diagram. Here system is whole box, inside it all the others are associated and created a interaction as well as set relationship between then by using include and extend methods. Again under this box, there are classes and objects which define the UML notations. This class is very important because to hold the name with attributes and operation. This is given in Figure 2.

Figure 2. Notation for class and object

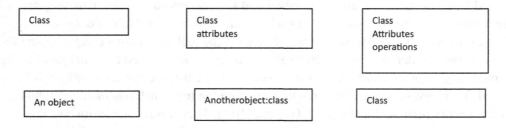

Class diagram is used as box in above figure which creates a permanent relationship between all other boxes. There are three relationship is majorly important such as association, part and specialization and apart from it one more is there, which is known as dependency. Now under this class, there is several associations which is structural relationship between all the classes. As per connection between two classes under association, this is known as binary association which is a line connecting two classes.

One more term is important under the class is visibility which is being used to check the visibility from outside of box dedicated to class. It is an optional diagram and classified into categories like public and private, where public defines the visibility from outside and private defines the visibility from within. Apart from these two, one more visibility is important to protect it is known is protected visibility.

UML has one more features or in other words one diagram is known as interaction diagram which has two parts communication and sequence and it is used to show the interaction between classes. Under the first interaction diagram, dynamic interaction has been set up by interchanging the massages which is actually a structural diagram in other word. Everything which is being exchange and transferred has proper numbering as given in Figure 3.

Whereas when interaction take place on the basis of time is known as sequence diagram which is two dimensional having vertical and horizontal and both represents the time. Vertical lines represent the life line and horizontal represents massages which are being transferred.

Thereafter, state machine diagram is depicted, which is a state transition diagram where states as given in circle and transition is given by arc by modifying the Figure 3. It is the most useful as states are being shifted and got new position.

There are sections as given in above figure, one is entry to enter the data and other is exit to close the program. As from Figure 8, it is very clear about the composite state where two states are given as A and B. then again A is decomposed in two parts and data is exchange using lines as given in Figure 4.

Then, packages are the term which is used to group the elements under the systems and subsystems. It is actually just like a folder icon can be seen as same in Figure 4, where rectangle attached represent the each and every packaging.

Figure 3. Communication link using UML notation

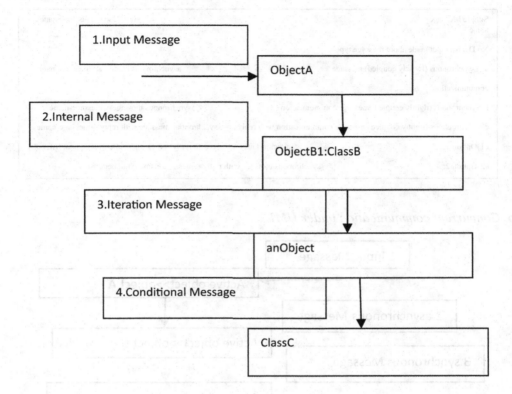

Figure 4. Composite state under state chart using UML notation

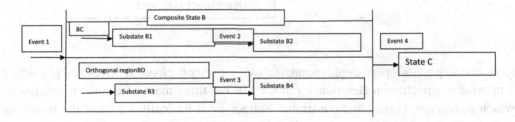

Now, one more diagram is very useful known as concurrent communication, represents object, process, thread, task in concurrent form as rectangular box with two vertical lines towards left and right hand side. This object is in form of active object and passive object where active object has own control and passive object has no control as shown in Figure 4.

As mentioned above, massage is in form asynchronous and syncrhronous form in concurrent mode, where asynchronous is loosely coupled and synchronous is tightly coupled object. UML notation for these objects are represented by Figure 5, where everything is given with their specific code. Also in Figure 6, represents only active object in form thread, task, process and communication between them through massages.

Figure 5. Massages under UML notations

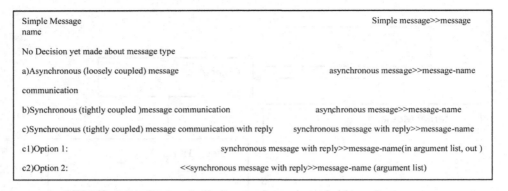

Simple Message name	Simple message>>message
No Decision yet made about message type	
a)Asynchronous (loosely coupled) message communication	asynchronous message>>message-name
b)Synchronous (tightly coupled)message communication	asynchronous message>>message-name
c)Synchrounous (tightly coupled) message communication with reply	synchronous message with reply>>message-name
c1)Option 1:	synchronous message with reply>>message-name(in argument list, out)
c2)Option 2:	<<synchronous message with reply>>message-name (argument list)

Figure 6. Concurrent communication under UML

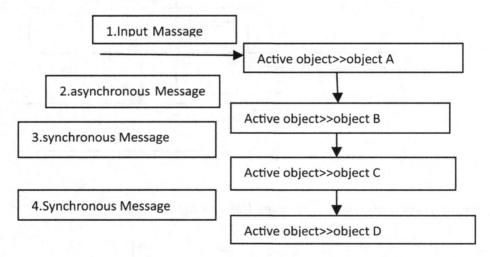

As mentioned in previous part, deployment diagram represents physical nodes and physical connections like network connection in electrical circuit. UML has three main mechanisms to show the notation, in which stereotype, tagged and constraint. Stereotype is basically a root of the modeling which is derived from existing module but once again it is tailored to identify the main the problem. As far as tagged is concern, it is extended to get the properties of UML basic block by adding new information. Whereas, under the constraint, it sets the conditions like in flow chart, and that should be true for successful results. Notation for deployment diagram is given in Figure 7. About all types of mechanism Figure 7 is dedicated.

Basics for modeling: There are many terms which is denoted in different notations with different names and even in figure as well text, that must be specified before use it. These are like requirement modeling, analysis modeling where in requirement modeling figure and text are represents in form uppercase initial letter and spaces and in analysis modeling, naming conventions have been used as classes and object. Under the first one such as classes, uppercase initial letter is used with proper space like open account. Also attributes are in lowercase initial letter like Account and when multi words are being used then there is no spacing. Now the second category, such as object, there are various ways to represent it. Individual named object and individual named object and again these are discriminated by its letter which is being used here. Individual named object has first lowercase letter followed uppercase letter and figure, object show like aSavingAccount or anotherSavingAccount. Under the individual named object, there is no object name, So, these are few things which is very important when UML notation is used to developed the program for design through perfect model. Now the massage is also playing an important role like simple massage without having decision over it. Statecharts is also being used to state, event, condition, action, activities in both figure and text. Again uppercase initial letter is used for single and spaces for multiword names. Then, design modeling is also very useful to design the model. Design modeling has four parts one is active and passive class and other one is active and passive object, massages and operations and both active and passive type class and object are same as discussed above under analysis modeling, whereas massage and operation are used to show the figure and text under given format so that it can easily readable and transfer to other under the same domain.

Figure 7. Deployment under UML

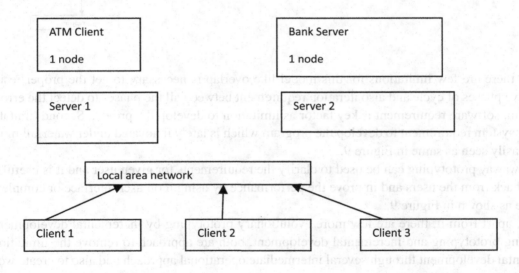

Figure 8. Tagged and constraint for UML

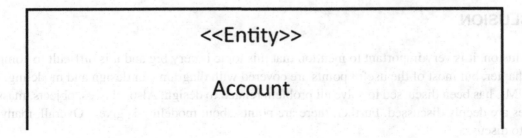

Types of software model: This is the part of design and without it nothing can be one as with the help specific software, the deliverables is prepared and setting milestones within the system. There are several types of model which is used to generate the software model. Few decades ago, waterfall model used and this was the basic of next coming software model (Gomaa, 2011).

Figure 9. Waterfall model

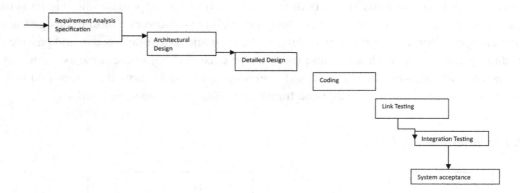

Now there are few limitations for this model like overlap is necessary to get the proper results in successive phases of cycle and also iteration requirement between all the phases to detect the errors. As a problem, software requirement is key factor as limitation to develop the project. Second limitation is working system requirement to develop the program which is lately innovated under waterfall model. It can be easily seen as same in Figure 9.

Throwaway prototyping can be used to clarify the requirements for given user and it is useful to get the feedback from the users and improve the performance by using it on user interface or complex user interface as shown in Figure 9.

Now, apart from it, there are few more evolutionary prototyping by incremental development and combining prototyping and incremental development, both are approach to remove the limitations by incremental development through several intermediate operational approach and also to create working systems in form evolutionary prototype.

CONCLUSION

As conclusion, it is very important to mention that this topic is very big and it is difficult to compile in single chapter, but most of the useful points are covered with diagrams for design and modeling. Especially, UML has been discussed to solve all problem related to design. Also, classes, objects, massages, attributes are deeply discussed. Further, there are points about modeling is given. Overall, many parts remain to discuss.

REFERENCES

Brooks, F. (1995). TheMythicalMan-Month: Essays on Software Engineering. Boston: Addison-Wesley.

Brown, A. (2000). *Large-Scale, Component-Based Development*. Prentice Hall.

Budgen, D. (2003). *Software Design* (2nd ed.). Addison-Wesley.

Buhr, R. J. A., & Casselman, R. S. (1996). *Use Case Maps for Object-Oriented Systems*. Prentice Hall.

Buschmann, F., Meunier, R., & Rohnert, H. (1996). *Pattern-Oriented Software Architecture: A System of Patterns*. Wiley.

Cheesman, J., & Daniels, J. (2001). *UML Components*. Addison-Wesley.

Erl, T. (2006). *Service-Oriented Architecture (SOA): Concepts, Technology, and Design*. Prentice Hall.

Erl, T. (2008). *SOA Principles of Service Design*. Prentice Hall.

Erl, T. (2009). *SOA Design Patterns*. Prentice Hall.

Espinoza, Cancila, Selic, & Gerard. (2009). *Challenges in Combining SysML and MARTE for Model-Based Design of Embedded Systems*. Berlin: Springer.

Freeman, P. (1983). The Nature of Design. In Tutorial on Software Design Techniques (4th ed.). IEEE Computer Society Press.

Freeman, P., & Wasserman, A. I. (Eds.). (1983). *Tutorial on Software Design Techniques* (4th ed.). IEEE Computer Society Press.

Friedenthal, Moore, & Steiner. (2009). *A Practical Guide to SysML: The Systems Modeling Language*. Burlington, MA: Morgan Kaufmann.

Gamma, E., Helm, R., & Johnson, R. (1995). *Design Patterns: Elements of Reusable Object-Oriented Software*. Addison-Wesley.

Gomaa, H. (1984). A Software Design Method for Real Time Systems. *Communications of the ACM*, 27(9), 938–949. doi:10.1145/358234.358262

Gomaa, H. (1986). Software Development of Real Time Systems. *Communications of the ACM*, 29(7), 657–668. doi:10.1145/6138.6150

Gomaa, H. (1989a). A Software Design Method for Distributed Real-Time Applications. *Journal of Systems and Software*, 9(2), 81–94. doi:10.1016/0164-1212(89)90012-5

Gomaa, H. (1989b). Structuring Criteria for Real Time System Design. In *Proceedings of the 11th International Conference on Software Engineering,* May 15–18, 1989, Pittsburgh, PA, USA (pp. 290–301). Los Alamitos, CA: IEEE Computer Society Press. 10.1109/ICSE.1989.714436

Gomaa, H. (2011). *Software modeling and design*. Cambridge University Press.

Chapter 6
The Art of Breaking Down:
Mastering Microservice Architecture and Data Modeling Strategy

Tapan Kumar Behera

 https://orcid.org/0000-0003-2524-9171

Department of Technology Management, Forrester Research, USA

ABSTRACT

Microservice architecture (MSA) is a popular software architecture style for developing scalable and resilient applications. However, designing data models for MSA presents unique challenges that require careful consideration. This chapter explores the relationship between MSA and data modeling and provides insights into best practices for designing data models that are optimized for MSA. It defines MSA and its key principles, examines the implications of MSA on data modeling, and discusses strategies for designing data models that are modular, decoupled, and flexible. The chapter also presents several case studies of organizations that have implemented MSA and data modeling strategies and discusses future trends in MSA and data modeling strategy, including the use of artificial intelligence and machine learning to automate data modeling. By following the best practices outlined in this chapter, organizations can realize the benefits of MSA while ensuring data consistency, scalability, and maintainability.

INTRODUCTION

In today's world of software design and development data modeling plays an important role. There are several factors that affect the design of a data model, such as the type and volume of data as well as the specific requirements of the application or system being developed. The type of data refers to its structure and format, such as whether it is structured or unstructured, or whether it requires complex relationships or hierarchies. For example, a data model for a relational database would typically be structured differently than a data model for a document-oriented NoSQL database.

DOI: 10.4018/978-1-6684-9809-5.ch006

Data models are also determined by the volume of data. In the case of large datasets, it may be necessary to store and process the data in a distributed manner, which may affect the design of the data model. Finally, the specific requirements of the application or system can influence the data model. For example, an e-commerce application may require a data model that is optimized for fast retrieval and processing of customer transactions, while a scientific research application may require a data model that supports complex data analysis and visualization.

Data modeling is an important aspect of developing applications using Microservice Architecture (MSA). MSA is a software development approach that involves building a system as a set of small, independent services that can be deployed and scaled independently (Behera, 2023). Here are some factors to consider when designing data models for MSA:

1. **Decoupling of Data Models:** In MSA, each microservice is responsible for its own data storage, which means that data models should be designed to be decoupled from each other. This allows for greater flexibility and scalability, as each microservice can evolve its own data model independently.
2. **Modular Design:** Data models should be designed to support a modular architecture, with each microservice having its own data model that is focused on the specific needs of that service. This allows for greater flexibility and makes it easier to make changes to the system over time.
3. **Data Consistency:** In a distributed system like MSA, maintaining data consistency across microservices can be challenging. Data models should be designed to ensure consistency across microservices, either using distributed transactions or other techniques such as eventual consistency.
4. **Data Partitioning:** In MSA, it is common for data to be partitioned across multiple microservices. Data models should be designed to support this partitioning, with each microservice responsible for its own partition of the data.
5. **API Design:** The design of the API that exposes the data should be considered when designing data models. The API should be designed to be simple and easy to use, with clear documentation and well-defined contracts between microservices.

MICROSERVICE ARCHITECTURE (MSA)

Microservice Architecture (MSA) is a software development approach that involves building a system as a collection of small, independent services that can be deployed and scaled independently. In MSA, each service is designed to perform a specific business function and can communicate with other services through well-defined APIs (Fresno et al., 2023). This approach contrasts with traditional monolithic architectures, where the entire system is built as a single, tightly-coupled application.

Monolithic vs. Microservices Architecture

The monolithic and microservices architectures are two different approaches to developing software applications. In a monolithic architecture, the entire application is designed as a single, tightly coupled unit, with all of its components running within the same process and on the same hardware. In this architecture, a single codebase, a single database, and a single user interface are typically used. A Monolithic Architecture requires the entire application to be modified and re-deployed to make changes to the system.

On the other hand, in a Microservices Architecture, the application is constructed as a collection of small, independent services that can be deployed and scaled independently. The services are designed to perform specific business functions, and each has its own data storage, processing, and business logic. Through well-defined APIs, these services communicate with one another. A Microservices Architecture allows individual services to be modified and re-deployed without modifying the entire system.

The following are some key differences between monolithic and microservices architectures:

1. **Scalability:** When a monolithic architecture is used, scaling the entire application requires scaling the entire system, which can lead to performance and scalability problems. As a result of a Microservices Architecture, individual services are able to scale independently, enabling the system to handle increased workloads and traffic without overloading itself.
2. **Flexibility:** In a monolithic architecture, making changes to the system can be time-consuming and complex, since all system components must be modified. With a Microservice Architecture, individual services can be modified and re-deployed independently, allowing for easier adaptation to changing business requirements as well as the introduction of new functionality in a timely manner.
3. **Resilience:** The failure of a monolithic architecture can result in a decrease in availability and downtime for the entire system. Using a Microservices Architecture, each service is designed to be autonomous and resilient to failure, so failures can be handled without affecting the entire system.
4. **Technology Diversity:** The monolithic architecture requires all components of the system to use the same technology stack. An organization can choose the best tool for each specific task when implementing a Microservices Architecture, as individual services can be developed using different technologies.

Figure 1. Shows the monolithic to microservice breakdown

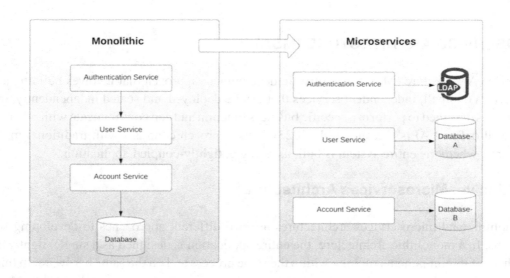

MICROSERVICE ARCHITECTURE DESIGN PRINCIPLES

A microservice architecture (MSA) is an approach to software development that emphasizes the development and deployment of small, independent services. A microservices architecture should be designed and implemented in accordance with several principles (Rademacher et al., 2020). The following are some key principles of microservices architecture design:

Domain-Driven Design

Microservices should be designed based on the domain of the business problem they solve, with each service having a specific business capability. The microservice architecture consists of a set of loosely coupled, independently deployable services, each with its own domain model and data store. As a result, greater flexibility and scalability is now possible, but this also introduces new challenges in terms of service boundaries, data consistency, and the communication between services.

In order to address these challenges, DDD can provide a clear and shared understanding of the problem domain and its boundaries. By defining bounded contexts for each microservice, you can ensure that each service has a clear set of responsibilities and a clearly defined domain model that is closely aligned with the problem it is solving. A domain-driven design approach involves the collaboration between domain experts and software developers so that they can capture the essence of the domain and create a software model that is easy to understand, maintain, and extend. Many complex business applications are based on this method since the domain of the problem is not well understood or changes frequently within the context of the application.

There are many patterns and practices associated with DDD, including ubiquitous language, bounded contexts, aggregates, entities, value objects, and domain events. Using these patterns, DDD allows developers to build software that is both well-designed and well-aligned with the domain of the problem they are trying to solve.

Service Isolation

Microservices should be isolated from each other, with each service having its own data storage, processing, and business logic. The purpose of service isolation is to minimize dependencies between services and reduce the risk of cascading failures when one service fails or experiences performance problems (Cambell, 2015). As a result of isolating services, you can also increase the scalability and maintainability of your application, as each service can be deployed, tested, and updated independently of the others.

Several best practices can be followed in order to achieve service isolation:

1. **Define Clear Service Boundaries:** There should be a clear boundary separating each service from the others and a clearly defined set of responsibilities for each. As described in Domain-Driven Design, this can be accomplished by defining bounded contexts for each service.
2. **Use API Gateways:** The API gateway provides a unified entry point for all requests between the clients and the microservices. The API gateways can handle tasks such as authentication, routing, load balancing, and caching while also enforcing service isolation and keeping the implementation details of the services underlying them hidden from the end user.

3. **Use Asynchronous Communication:** Instead of using synchronous communication methods (e.g., REST APIs) between services, consider using asynchronous communication methods, such as messaging or event-driven architecture. As a result, services can be decoupled and scalability can be improved, as each service can process requests independently and in parallel.
4. **Separate Data Stores:** There should be a separate data store for each service that is optimized to meet its specific requirements. By allowing each service to scale its data store independently, you can reduce the risk of data inconsistencies and improve the scalability of the system.

API-First Design

The API-First Design approach emphasizes the development of APIs (Application Programming Interfaces) before creating any other part of the software application. This approach focuses on the API as the core of the application, around which all other components are based (Roda et al., 2023). There are several reasons why API-First Design may be beneficial. Firstly, it allows developers to focus on the API's functionality and usability, which is often one of the most important characteristics of the software for external users. As a second benefit, it promotes a modular architecture, which can make the application more flexible and easier to maintain. Thirdly, the API facilitates collaboration among different teams and stakeholders, as it serves as a common language and interface.

An API-First Design approach involves creating a detailed specification of the API, including endpoints, data structures, authentication mechanisms, and error handling. This specification can be created using tools such as OpenAPI or Swagger. Upon completion of the specification, developers can use it to generate code stubs, which can then be used to build the actual API (Khan & Hassan, 2023). Finally, the rest of the application can be developed using the API as a foundation. In microservice architectures, where each microservice has its own API, API-First Design is particularly useful. The developers can ensure that each microservice is well-defined and that it works seamlessly together by designing each API first.

Database per Service

A database per service is a design pattern used in software architecture in which each microservice has its own database. Each microservice is responsible for managing its own data and database schema, and the data is not shared between them. A database per service approach offers the advantage of greater scalability and resilience in large, complex systems. It is possible for each microservice to scale its database independently without impacting other services or causing performance bottlenecks. Moreover, if one service fails or has database issues, the rest of the system will continue to function normally.

Database per service, however, poses some challenges as well. This can increase the complexity of the system as each service must manage its own database schema and ensure that data is consistent across multiple databases. In addition, it can lead to data duplication, as some data may be required by multiple services, but stored separately in the databases of each service (Fritzsch et al., 2023). In order to address these challenges, some teams use a hybrid approach, in which some data is shared between services, while other data is stored in separate databases. The database per service approach can reduce complexity while maintaining the benefits of scalability and resilience. The decision to use a database per service approach will ultimately depend on the specific requirements of the system and the tradeoffs between complexity and scalability.

Autonomous Services

In software architecture, autonomous services are microservices that are designed to be self-contained and independently deployable. By using this approach, each microservice is responsible for a specific business capability and may operate independently of the others. In large, complex systems, autonomous services provide greater scalability and flexibility. As each microservice is independently developed, deployed, and scaled, other services are not impacted or performance bottlenecks are not created. Moreover, if one service fails or needs to be updated, the rest of the system will continue to function as usual.

Infrastructure Automation

An infrastructure automation process involves the use of software tools and techniques to automate the provisioning, configuration, and management of IT infrastructure. An application or service may require servers, networks, storage, and other hardware and software resources. Infrastructure automation aims to streamline and standardize the deployment and management of infrastructure, resulting in faster, more efficient, and less error-prone operations. The automation of routine tasks, such as provisioning new servers or updating software configurations, allows IT teams to devote more time and resources to more strategic initiatives.

As part of infrastructure automation, specialized tools and platforms are typically used, including configuration management tools (such as Chef, Puppet, Ansible), containerization platforms (such as Docker, Kubernetes), and cloud orchestration platforms (such as Azure Resource Manager, AWS Cloud-Formation). IT teams can now define and manage infrastructure resources as code, allowing them to version control, test, and deploy infrastructure changes with the same rigor as application code.

Fault Tolerance

Microservices should be designed with fault tolerance in mind, with each service able to operate independently and continue to function in the event of a failure (Bushong et al., 2021). The concept of fault tolerance in software architecture refers to a system's ability to continue functioning despite a failure or error. A fault-tolerant system can withstand and recover from unexpected events or errors without causing a complete system failure.

It is particularly important to ensure fault tolerance in distributed systems, where failures can occur in any part of the system, including hardware, software, and network components. Typically, distributed systems are designed to be fault-tolerant through the use of a variety of techniques, such as redundancy, replication, and automated recovery.

The following are some common techniques for achieving fault tolerance:

1. **Redundancy:** This refers to creating multiple copies of critical components, such as servers and databases, so that, in the event of one failing, the others will continue to operate.
2. **Replication:** The process of replicating data or services across multiple servers or data centers so that if one fails, another can take over without interruption.
3. **Automated Recovery:** The use of automated processes to detect and recover from failures, such as automatically switching over a database or restarting a service after a failure.

4. **Load Balancing:** This involves spreading workload across multiple servers or instances so that if one fails or becomes overloaded, others can take over.
5. **Graceful Degradation:** In the event of a failure or error, systems should continue to function at a reduced level of performance or functionality.

Event-Driven Architecture

Microservices should be designed using an event-driven architecture, with each service able to consume and produce events that trigger other services.

In event-driven architecture (EDA), events are emphasized as the primary method of communication between components or services within a software system. It is common practice in EDA for components to publish events when certain actions occur or state changes occur, and other components or services can subscribe to these events and react accordingly.

EDA consists of the following characteristics:

1. **Asynchronous Messaging:** Events are communicated between components or services asynchronously, meaning that components do not have to wait for a response before proceeding.
2. **Loose Coupling:** A loosely coupled system includes components or services that are independent of one another and do not need to be aware of one another's internal workings.
3. **Scalability:** EDA components are loosely coupled, so they can be scaled independently of one another, making it easier to manage performance and scale the system as needed.
4. **Flexibility:** Due to the fact that the components of an EDA system are independent of each other, it is easier to modify or replace individual components without affecting the overall system.
5. **Resilience:** EDA systems are often designed to be highly resilient, with components automatically recovering from failures or being replaced with new ones as needed.

Overall, these design principles enable organizations to build scalable, resilient, and flexible systems that can quickly adapt to changing business requirements and handle increased workload and traffic.

ADVANTAGES AND DISADVANTAGES OF MICROSERVICE ARCHITECTURE

The microservice architecture offers a number of advantages that make it an attractive option for modern software development. The key advantage of microservices is their scalability, as they can be scaled up or down independently to meet changing demands (Daraghmi et al., 2022). As a result of this approach, each microservice can be developed and deployed independently utilizing a variety of different technologies and development processes. Furthermore, microservices provide fault isolation and resilience, which can reduce the downtime of systems and improve their overall reliability. As well, microservices promote cross-functional collaboration, improve communication, and enhance the efficiency of teams.

Microservice architecture, however, also has some disadvantages that need to be considered. Due to the complexity of the architecture, it can be challenging to coordinate and communicate between the various services. Complexity can increase development time, and distributed systems can make monitoring and management more challenging. The maintenance and management of multiple microservices can also be more complex and time-consuming than the maintenance and management of a single monolithic application. Due to the distributed nature of the system, testing and debugging can be more challenging. In spite of these potential disadvantages, microservice architecture has been found to be a highly effective method for building modern, scalable, and resilient software systems.

Real-World Examples of Microservice Architecture Implementations

Many organizations across a variety of industries have implemented microservice architecture. Here are a few examples of real-world implementations:

1. **Netflix:**

Netflix is a popular video streaming service that utilizes a microservice architecture in order to provide personalized recommendations to its users. It is the responsibility of each microservice to carry out a specific business function, such as content discovery, playback, and user authentication. As a result of this approach, Netflix has been able to improve its scalability and reliability, while also allowing rapid experimentation and deployment of new capabilities.

2. **Uber:**

Uber is a transportation network company that provides its customers with a seamless experience by leveraging microservices. Each microservice is responsible for a particular business function, such as managing trips, processing payments, and managing drivers. As a result of this approach, Uber has been able to scale its business rapidly, while also improving its reliability and resilience.

3. **Amazon:**

Amazon is a leading online retailer that offers personalized shopping experiences to its customers through a microservice architecture. Each microservice performs a specific business function, such as search, recommendations, and order processing. As a result of this approach, Amazon has been able to improve its scalability and efficiency, while also enabling it to introduce new features and services in a timely manner.

4. **PayPal:**

PayPal is an online payment system that uses a microservice architecture to process transactions and provide a seamless payment experience for its customers. The microservices are each responsible for a specific business function, such as fraud detection, payment processing, and transaction tracking. Through this approach, PayPal has been able to improve its scalability and reliability, as well as respond rapidly to changing market conditions and customer demands.

5. **SoundCloud:**

Music streaming service SoundCloud uses microservice architecture to provide seamless listening experiences to its users. Each microservice performs a specific business function, such as audio transcoding, content delivery, and user management. As a result of this approach, SoundCloud has been able to increase its scalability and reliability, as well as introduce new features and services rapidly.

DATA MODELING IN MICROSERVICE ARCHITECTURE

Data modeling is crucial in microservice architecture as it enables the efficient management and storage of data across multiple services. As microservices are developed and deployed independently of each other, they must be able to work seamlessly together, sharing data and functionality (Yussupov et al., 2020). A well-designed data model helps to ensure that data is stored and accessed consistently across all services, which is critical for maintaining the integrity and accuracy of the data. Another important aspect of data modeling in microservice architecture is that it enables independent development and scaling of services. As each service can have its own data model optimized for its specific requirements, it can be easier to add new features or modify existing ones without affecting the rest of the system.

There are several data modeling techniques that can be used in a microservices architecture. Here are some of the most common ones:

Entity-Relationship Modeling (ER)

The entity-relationship model identifies the entities in a system and their relationships. It can be useful for developing a conceptual model of the system as well as for identifying the data entities and their relationships between microservices. Entity-Relationship Modeling (ER) is a useful technique for designing data models in a microservices architecture (Behera et al., 2023). By using ER modeling, it is possible to identify the data entities and their relationships between microservices, which is crucial for the development of data structures that enable each service to perform its functions.

In a microservices architecture, each service has its own data store, which contains data related to a specific business capability. An ER model can be used to identify the entities and relationships that are required to support each business capability, and to guide the design of data stores related to each microservice. The first step to using ER modeling in a microservices architecture is to identify the business capabilities that each microservice will support. Once the business capabilities have been identified, the data entities and their relationships can be identified using ER modeling. The resulting data model can be used to guide the design of the data stores for each microservice. Microservices architectures are characterized by frequent changes in the data entities and their relationships as new services are added or existing services are modified. ER modeling should be used to guide the initial design of the data model, but the model should also be flexible enough to accommodate changing requirements over time.

ER modeling typically involves creating a graphical representation of the data entities and their relationships. Diagrams typically include entities, attributes of entities, and relationships between entities. The entities are represented by rectangles, and the relationships are represented by diamonds or lines connecting the entities. An entity's attributes are represented by ovals. ER modeling is the process of creating a conceptual model of the system that captures the relationships between the data entities. Using this model, the microservices architecture and the data structures required to support each microservice are designed.

As part of a microservices architecture, ER modeling is useful for identifying the data entities and their relationships between microservices. Through the use of ER modeling, organizations can design a data architecture that is flexible, scalable, and supports the flow of data between microservices.

Data Flow Diagrams (DFD)

DFD represents the flow of data through a system graphically. Identifying the data flow between microservices and designing the data architecture that supports it is useful. A DFD represents a system as a set of processes, data stores, and data flows. Processes represent operations performed on the data, data stores represent the locations where the data is stored, and data flows represent the movement of data between processes and data stores.

In order to design a data architecture for supporting the data flow, DFDs are useful in identifying the data flow between microservices. Through the use of DFDs, organizations can gain a better understanding of how data is processed, stored, and transmitted between microservices. Understanding the data flow can assist in identifying potential bottlenecks or inefficiencies, as well as guiding the design of the data architecture in order to ensure that it supports the required data flow between microservices. DFDs can also be used to identify the inputs and outputs of each microservice, which can aid in the design of the interfaces between microservices. Based on this understanding, APIs that connect microservices can be designed to ensure that the APIs support the required data flow between the microservices.

NoSQL Data Modeling

NoSQL data modeling is a technique for designing data models for NoSQL databases that are used in microservices architecture. A NoSQL database can handle large volumes of data that may have a high degree of variability or complexity, and it can be used to store the data that is required by microservices. NoSQL data modeling focuses on designing data models that can support the data requirements of microservices. There is typically no fixed schema in NoSQL databases (Behera et al., 2022), which makes them more flexible than traditional relational databases. Due to this flexibility, different types of data can be stored and the data model can be modified as the requirements of the microservices evolve over time.

Microservices typically require a document or key-value store that is optimized for the data access patterns required by NoSQL data modeling. As the data is stored in a denormalized format, complex joins are not required as in traditional relational databases. It simplifies the data access process and can improve the performance of the microservices (González et al., 2023). NoSQL data modeling can also support the development of microservices that are highly available and fault-tolerant. Data replicated across multiple nodes in the network can be achieved using NoSQL databases, which are designed to support distributed architectures. Using replication can improve the availability of the microservices and ensure that data is accessible even if a node fails.

Agile Data Modeling

Agile data modeling is a technique for designing data models that is aligned with the principles of Agile software development (Cerny et al., 2022). The goal of agile data modeling is to design data models that can be rapidly adapted in response to changing business needs and evolving software features. In agile data modeling, developers, stakeholders, and data architects collaborate in iterative and incremental design processes. Agile data modeling is focused on delivering working software that meets business needs and can be continuously improved.

As part of Agile data modeling, the data model is designed to support the minimum viable product (MVP) and is continuously refined based on feedback from stakeholders and users (Rios et al., 2022). In Agile data modeling, simple and flexible data models are designed so that changes can be made quickly and efficiently. The agile data modeling process also involves the creation of user stories that describe the data requirements of the microservices. Using user stories, you can capture the requirements of the microservices in a format that is easily understood by developers and stakeholders alike. The user stories can be used to guide the design of the data model and can be used as a basis for testing the microservices.

Polyglot Persistence

Polyglot Persistence is an approach to data storage in which different types of databases are used for different parts of an application, based on the specific data storage requirements of each component. In a Microservices architecture, Polyglot Persistence can be used to design data models that are optimized for the data storage requirements of the microservices (Behera et al., 2022). The Polyglot Persistence framework recognizes that no single database can meet the needs of all use cases. Choosing the right database for each use case can result in a more efficient and scalable system. As an example, a document database such as MongoDB may be a good choice for storing unstructured data, while a relational database such as MySQL may be a better choice for storing structured data.

Each microservice can use a different database that is optimized for its specific data storage requirements in a microservices architecture. As an example, a microservice that handles user authentication and authorization may use a relational database such as PostgreSQL, and a microservice that handles image storage and retrieval may use an object storage service such as Amazon S3. Different databases can be used for different microservices in order to make the system more flexible and scalable (Esas et al., 2022). Using Polyglot Persistence, microservices can also be deployed independently and managed by separate teams, simplifying deployment and maintenance. However, using multiple databases can also introduce complexity and require an additional level of effort for data synchronization and consistency. Polyglot Persistence also requires careful consideration of the trade-offs between consistency, availability, and partition tolerance in a distributed system.

Data Mesh

Data Mesh is an emerging approach to data architecture that emphasizes the separation of data into self-contained domains and treats it as a product (Hübener et al., 2022). In a Microservices architecture, Data Mesh can be used to design data models that are aligned with the business domain and can support the business needs of the microservices. The Data Mesh team recognizes that data is a strategic asset which should be owned and managed by the teams that create and use it. In treating data as a product, Data Mesh enables data teams to focus on delivering high-quality data that aligns with the organization's business needs.

The Data Mesh approach also emphasizes the organization of data into self-contained domains, with each domain managed by a dedicated team. This can facilitate better data governance and support the development of data-driven applications. In a Microservices architecture, Data Mesh can be used to design data models that are aligned with the business domain and can support the data storage requirements of the microservices. Each microservice has access to the data it needs from the appropriate domain without requiring knowledge of the underlying data storage technology.

Data Mesh also encourages the use of data platforms that provide standardized tools and services for managing data across domains. Using a standardized set of tools and services to access and manage data can simplify the development and deployment of microservices. In spite of this, implementing a Data Mesh architecture can require significant organizational and cultural changes. A shift in mindset is required from a centralized approach to data management to a decentralized approach. A commitment to standardization and collaboration across teams is also required.

Event Sourcing

Event Sourcing is a pattern that involves storing changes to an application's state as a sequence of events. In Microservices architecture, Event Sourcing can be used to design data models that capture the history of changes made to the application's state. As a result, better auditing can be performed and applications that require time-based queries can be developed. As these events are immutable and append-only, they cannot be modified or deleted once they have been stored.

With Event Sourcing, the state of the application can be reconstructed at any point in time by replaying the events from the beginning. The use of this approach allows developers to implement features such as temporal queries and rewind and replay capabilities. In Event Sourcing, events are the source of truth and can be viewed as a log of all system activities. A database or message queue can be used to store events, and different services can subscribe to them and act upon them as necessary.

Even though Event Sourcing is useful in many types of systems, it is especially well-suited to complex domains where business rules and requirements change frequently. Event Sourcing allows developers to track the history of the application's state by capturing every change as an event. This can be useful for debugging, auditing, and complying with regulations.

DATA INTEGRATION IN MICROSERVICE ARCHITECTURE

Data integration is an important aspect of microservice architecture as it involves combining data from multiple microservices into a unified view. In the context of a microservice architecture, the following considerations should be taken into account:

1. **Use APIs:** APIs are the primary way that microservices communicate with each other. By designing and implementing APIs with a consistent schema and protocol, data integration can be simplified.
2. **Use Event-Driven Architectures:** In an event-driven architecture, microservices communicate with each other by publishing and subscribing to events. By publishing events when data changes, other microservices can update their own data to maintain consistency.
3. **Use a Message Bus:** A message bus can be used to facilitate communication between microservices. When a microservice updates its data, it can publish a message to the message bus, which can then be consumed by other microservices to update their own data.
4. **Use a Data Lake:** A data lake is a centralized repository that stores all data, regardless of its structure or format. Data can be extracted from multiple microservices and stored in the data lake, where it can be processed and analyzed.

5.   **Use ETL Tools:** Extract, transform, load (ETL) tools can be used to extract data from multiple sources, transform it into a consistent format, and load it into a target system.

6.   **Use a Data Virtualization Layer:** A data virtualization layer provides a unified view of data from multiple sources, without the need for data to be physically integrated. This can be useful when data needs to be accessed across multiple microservices, but integrating the data physically would be difficult or impossible.

IMPORTANCE OF DATA INTEGRATION IN MICROSERVICE ARCHITECTURE

In microservice architectures, large, monolithic applications are broken down into smaller, independent services that work together to provide a complete solution. A microservice is responsible for a specific business capability and manages its own data. In spite of the fact that this approach has many benefits, it does present some challenges when it comes to the integration of data (Ahmed et al., 2022). To ensure that each microservice has access to the data it needs to perform its functions, and to provide a unified view of data across the entire system, data integration is crucial in microservice architectures. Data integration in microservice architecture has the advantage of providing a unified view of data. It can be difficult to obtain a comprehensive view of business operations when data is distributed across multiple microservices. Integrating data from multiple microservices provides a unified view of business operations by combining data from multiple microservices. The information can be used for reporting, analysis, and decision-making purposes. A unified view of data allows organizations to gain insight into business operations that would otherwise be difficult to obtain.

Data integration in microservice architecture has the additional advantage of enabling real-time data access. Data integration can ensure that data is updated in real-time across multiple microservices, providing up-to-date information that can be utilized to support business activities (Raj et al., 2022). The ability to access data in real-time is crucial in today's fast-paced business environment, where decisions must be made quickly and based on the latest information available. The integration of data also facilitates business agility. By leveraging data from multiple microservices, organizations can quickly adapt to changing business needs. As a result, organizations may be able to respond more quickly to changes in market conditions and customer demands, thereby improving business agility and responsiveness. Lastly, data integration can simplify the process of managing data across multiple microservices. Data integration reduces complexity and improves data governance by consolidating data into a single view. In this way, it can be ensured that data is accurate and consistent across multiple microservices, reducing the risk of errors or inconsistencies in business operations.

FUTURE TRENDS IN MICROSERVICE ARCHITECTURE AND DATA MODELING STRATEGY

Microservice architecture and data modeling strategy are fields that are constantly evolving, and there are several future trends to keep an eye out for. The following are a few examples:

1.   An increase in the adoption of serverless computing:

Serverless computing is one of the newest trends in cloud computing, whereby organizations can run applications without worrying about the underlying infrastructure. Organizations can reduce costs and improve scalability by using this approach, which is highly compatible with microservice architecture.

2.   Further use of machine learning and AI:

With the increasing volume of data generated by microservices, organizations are exploring the use of machine learning and artificial intelligence to extract insights and improve decision-making. Microservices can be enabled to learn and adapt in real time by integrating machine learning models.

3.   Greater focus on event-driven architecture:

The event-driven architecture is becoming more and more popular in microservice architecture due to its ability to enable services to communicate with one another through a publish-subscribe model. By adopting this approach, organizations are able to handle large volumes of data with greater scalability and fault tolerance.

4.   Continued emphasis on DevOps and automation:

A successful microservice architecture and data modeling strategy depends on DevOps and automation. Automation, testing, and continuous integration and deployment will become increasingly important as organizations adopt these strategies.

CONCLUSION

Microservice architecture and data modeling strategy are critical components of modern software development, enabling organizations to build scalable, resilient, and agile systems. By adopting a microservice architecture, organizations can break down large monolithic applications into smaller, more manageable services, each with their own data model. Data modeling plays a critical role in ensuring that these services can communicate with each other and share data effectively, while maintaining data consistency and integrity.

Throughout this book chapter, we have explored various aspects of microservice architecture and data modeling strategy, including their advantages and disadvantages, popular data modeling methodologies, best practices, and challenges faced by organizations. We have also looked at real-world examples of organizations that have successfully implemented microservice architecture and data modeling strategies.

Despite the challenges, microservice architecture and data modeling strategy continue to evolve, with new technologies and approaches emerging to address current and future needs. As organizations continue to adopt microservice architecture and data modeling strategies, they must remain vigilant in their approach to ensure that they are building scalable, reliable, and secure systems that can keep up with changing business requirements.

REFERENCES

Behera, T. (2022). *How Blockchain Solves the Supply Chain Problems Using RFID Techniques*. Academic Press.

Behera, T., & Panda, B. S. (2023). *Master Data Management using Machine Learning Techniques: MDM Bot*. doi:10.36227/techrxiv.21818040.v1

Behera, T., & Tripathi, K. (2022): Root Cause Analysis Bot using Machine Learning Techniques. TechRxiv. Preprint. doi:10.36227/techrxiv.21588159.v3

Bushong, V. (2021). Using static analysis to address microservice architecture reconstruction. In *2021 36th IEEE/ACM International Conference on Automated Software Engineering (ASE)*. IEEE. 10.1109/ASE51524.2021.9678749

Cerny, T., & ... Microservice architecture reconstruction and visualization techniques: A review. In *2022 IEEE International Conference on Service-Oriented System Engineering (SOSE)*. IEEE. 10.1109/SOSE55356.2022.00011

Daraghmi, Zhang, & Yuan. (2022). Enhancing Saga Pattern for Distributed Transactions within a Microservices Architecture. *Applied Sciences, 12*(12), 6242.

Esas, O. (2022). *Design patterns and anti-patterns in microservices architecture: a classification proposal and study on open source projects*. Academic Press.

Fresno–Aranda, R. (2023). Semi-automated capacity analysis of limitation-aware microservices architectures. In *Economics of Grids, Clouds, Systems, and Services: 19th International Conference, GECON 2022, Izola, Slovenia, September 13–15, 2022, Proceedings*. Cham: Springer Nature Switzerland. 10.1007/978-3-031-29315-3_7

Fritzsch, J., Bogner, J., Haug, M., Franco da Silva, A. C., Rubner, C., Saft, M., Sauer, H., & Wagner, S. (2023). Adopting microservices and DevOps in the cyber-physical systems domain: A rapid review and case study. *Software, Practice & Experience, 53*(3), 790–810. doi:10.1002pe.3169

González-Aparicio, M. T., Younas, M., Tuya, J., & Casado, R. (2023). A transaction platform for microservices-based big data systems. *Simulation Modelling Practice and Theory, 123*, 102709. doi:10.1016/j.simpat.2022.102709

Hübener, T., & ... Automatic anti-pattern detection in microservice architectures based on distributed tracing. *Proceedings of the 44th International Conference on Software Engineering: Software Engineering in Practice*. 10.1109/ICSE-SEIP55303.2022.9794000

Khan, M. R. H. (2023). *Toward an Automated Real-Time Anomaly Detection Engine in Microservice Architectures* [Diss.]. Carleton University.

Kumar, B. T. (2023). Architecture Principles for Enterprise Software and Mobile Application Development. In *Designing and Developing Innovative Mobile Applications*. IGI Global. doi:10.4018/978-1-6684-8582-8

Rademacher, F., Sachweh, S., & Zündorf, A. (2020). A modeling method for systematic architecture reconstruction of microservice-based software systems. In *Enterprise, Business-Process and Information Systems Modeling: 21st International Conference, BPMDS 2020, 25th International Conference, EMMSAD 2020, Held at CAiSE 2020, Grenoble, France, June 8–9, 2020, Proceedings 21*. Springer International Publishing. 10.1007/978-3-030-49418-6_21

Raj, V., & Srinivasa Reddy, K. (2022). Best Practices and Strategy for the Migration of Service-Oriented Architecture-Based Applications to Microservices Architecture. In *Proceedings of Second International Conference on Advances in Computer Engineering and Communication Systems: ICACECS 2021*. Singapore: Springer Nature Singapore. 10.1007/978-981-16-7389-4_43

Rios, J., Jha, S., & Shwartz, L. (2022). Localizing and Explaining Faults in Microservices Using Distributed Tracing. In *2022 IEEE 15th International Conference on Cloud Computing (CLOUD)*. IEEE. 10.1109/CLOUD55607.2022.00072

Roda-Sanchez, L. (2023). Cloud-edge microservices architecture and service orchestration: An integral solution for a real-world deployment experience. *Internet of Things*.

Shaikh. (2022). Microservices Design Patterns. *Azure Kubernetes Services with Microservices: Understanding Its Patterns and Architecture*, 61-101.

Yussupov, V. (2020). Pattern-based modelling, integration, and deployment of microservice architectures. In *2020 IEEE 24th International Enterprise Distributed Object Computing Conference (EDOC)*. IEEE. 10.1109/EDOC49727.2020.00015

KEY TERMS AND DEFINITIONS

Data Modeling: The process of creating a conceptual representation of data objects and their relationships to each other, as well as their attributes and constraints. Data modeling is a critical step in software development as it provides a foundation for database design, application development, and data analysis.

Data Modeling Strategy: The approach or plan for creating a data model that meets the requirements of the application being developed. A data modeling strategy should consider the characteristics of the data, the business rules governing the data, and the constraints of the technology and architecture being used. In the context of microservices, a data modeling strategy should consider the need for data consistency across services, the impact of service boundaries on data access, and the trade-offs between data duplication and data sharing.

Microservice Architecture (MSA): A software architectural style that structures an application as a collection of loosely coupled services, each running in its own process and communicating with other services through lightweight mechanisms such as HTTP APIs. Microservices allow for greater flexibility, scalability, and resilience compared to traditional monolithic architectures.

Chapter 7
Designing for Boundary Detection of Foreign Objects in Airports Using Python 3

Devasis Pradhan
Acharya Institute of Technology, Bangalore, India

Gnapika Mallavaram
Acharya Institute of Technology, Bangalore, India

Kumari Priyanka
Acharya Institute of Technology, Bangalore, India

S. Sneha
Acharya Institute of Technology, Bangalore, India

Sidhi Jain
Acharya Institute of Technology, Bangalore, India

ABSTRACT

Boundary detection of foreign objects in airports is a critical safety concern, as debris and other objects can cause significant damage to aircraft and pose a serious risk to passenger safety. This chapter explores the use of Python programming language and computer vision techniques for the detection of objects at airports. The study presents an overview of the detection of objects in airport problems and their significance in aviation safety, followed by a detailed description of the Python-based foreign object detection system architecture. The system incorporates image processing algorithms and deep learning models to identify and classify foreign objects on airport runways and other operational areas. The chapter discusses the advantages and limitations of using Python for detection and highlights the potential for future research in this area. The study concludes by emphasizing the importance of detection in ensuring safe and efficient airport operations and the potential benefits of boundary detection using Python version 3.

DOI: 10.4018/978-1-6684-9809-5.ch007

INTRODUCTION

This paper enables individuals to effortlessly recognize and distinguish objects within an image, a task that the human visual system is capable of performing with speed and precision. The human visual system can also execute intricate undertakings such as identifying multiple objects and detecting obstacles with minimal conscious effort. In this project, we will work on object detection, and optimize the same with the help of modern convolutional techniques. Foreign object detection in airports is a security measure that involves using specialized equipment to scan for and locate any objects that do not belong in a designated area, such as an airport. The goal of foreign object detection is to ensure the safety and security of passengers and personnel by identifying and removing any potential threats before they can cause harm. There are several different types of equipment that can be used for foreign object detection, including x-ray machines, metal detectors, and bomb-sniffing dogs. These measures are typically implemented in high-traffic areas such as security checkpoints and boarding gates. In object detection, a boundary box, also known as a bounding box, is a graphical representation of the location and size of an object in an image or video. It is typically represented as a rectangular box drawn around the object, with the dimensions of the box indicating the size of the object and the position of the box indicating the location of the object within the image or video. Boundary boxes are commonly used in computer vision tasks such as object recognition, tracking, and classification. Traditional Boundary detection methods involve manual inspections by airport staff, which can be time-consuming and error-prone. To address this challenge, several automated Boundary detection systems have been developed using computer vision techniques and machine learning algorithms. In recent years, Python has emerged as a popular programming language for developing Boundary detection systems due to its ease of use, flexibility, and extensive library support. Python-based Boundary detection systems can process live video feeds from airport cameras and identify any foreign objects present in the footage. Python also provides a range of machine learning libraries, including TensorFlow, Keras, and PyTorch, which can be used to develop deep learning models for Boundary detection. This paper presents a Python-based Boundary detection system that utilizes deep learning techniques for object detection and classification. The system also includes a user-friendly interface that allows airport staff to monitor Boundary detections in real time and take appropriate action to remove any foreign objects. It also aims to demonstrate the feasibility and effectiveness of using Python and deep learning techniques for Boundary detection in airports. The proposed system can significantly improve airport safety and efficiency by reducing the risk of aircraft damage and downtime caused by foreign objects. The paper also serves as a valuable contribution to the field of aviation safety and provides a framework for future research in this area.

LITERATURE REVIEW

Wang et al. (2022) describes the concept of a "trainable bag-of-freebies" and how it contributes to YOLOv7's success. The authors also discuss the technical details of YOLOv7 and compare its performance to other object detectors. This extension reduces the number of identities switches and allows objects to be tracked through longer periods of occlusion. The implementation runs in real-time and is computationally efficient. The paper provides details on the methodology, experimental results, and code availability for further research experimentation and practical application development. In Muayer et al. (2018), the use of artificial intelligence to find foreign object debris (FOD) on airport runways is covered in this PDF document. FOD must be found and removed because it might be hazardous for aircraft during takeoff and landing. The study describes how real-time monitoring of airport runway photographs and FOD identification can be accomplished using computer vision techniques. The study's findings suggest that artificial intelligence technology has enormous promise for FOD identification. In Girshick et al. (2017), current two-stage object detection algorithms, like R-CNN, achieve excellent accuracy by applying a classifier to a sparse set of object locations. One-stage detectors, which more intensively sample potential object locations, have the potential to be simpler and faster, but they haven't been as accurate as two-stage detectors. The high foreground-background class imbalance experienced during the training of dense detectors, according to the report, is what primarily accounts for this disparity. The Focused Loss, which modifies the common cross-entropy loss so that the loss assigned to well-classified samples is down-weighted, is proposed as a fix to this class imbalance. RetinaNet, the proposed dense detector, is demonstrated to match the speed of earlier one-stage detectors after being trained using the Fo-cal Loss (Wang et al., 2023). To automate repetitive procedures and streamline the da-taset creation workflow, customized Python scripts were created. The conclusion of the dataset production process is a crucial step in realizing our objective of creating a powerful boundary detection system that can improve airport security and safety and contribute to the global advancement of aviation security.

In Cheng et al. (2021), due to their lengthy methods for producing oriented suggestions, current two-stage oriented object detectors experience a computational bottleneck, which lowers their speed. orientated R-CNN, a universal two-stage orientated detector with promising accuracy and efficiency, is a new framework that is proposed in this research. The framework is made up of a first-stage oriented region proposal network (oriented RPN) that creates high-quality oriented suggestions for essentially little cost, and a second-stage oriented R-CNN head that identifies and recognizes oriented regions of interest (oriented RoIs). On two widely used datasets for oriented object detection, including DOTA (75.87% mAP) and HRSC 2016 (96.50% mAP), the suggested method achieves state-of-the-art detection accuracy without the use of any tricks. On a single RTX 2080 Ti, Oriented R-CNN with ResNet50 runs at a speed of 15.1 FPS with an image size of 1024x1024 (Wojke et al., 2017).

METHODOLOGY

The dataset generation comprises two major steps.

Data Collection

The practice of gathering photos and videos of debris or foreign items on airport runways, taxiways, and aprons is known as the collection of foreign object debris (FOD) datasets. This dataset is used to train computer vision models to detect and classify FOD in real-time, which helps improve safety and prevent damage to an aircraft as it is taking off or landing (Bao et al., 2009). FOD can be made up of various types of debris including Cutter, Luggage Tag, Nail, Hammer, Luggage Part, Rock, Pen, Pliers, Battery, Paint Chip, Screw, Screwdriver, Wire, Wood, Tape, Wrench, Bolt Washer, Bolt Nut Set, Hose etc. Capturing images of this debris in airport environments is a difficult assignment because of things like the lighting, the climate, and the quick-moving nature of airport activities. These images and videos are then annotated with labels indicating the type of FOD present, its location on the runway, and other relevant information. FOD detection systems are typically based on computer vision algorithms that use cameras or other sensors to detect and classify debris on the runway. Several organizations and research institutions have conducted FOD dataset collection campaigns at airports around the world (Munyer et al., 2021).

Data Annotation

It is advisable to add as many examples of FOD objects as you can to build a strong dataset. As a result, a quick and effective annotation procedure was used. The FOD-A (foreign object debris annotation) image annotation process can be done using various tools, and one of the more popular tools is CVAT (Computer Vision Annotation Tool). CVAT's video annotation set of rules calls for every ten frames to be annotated, with guide modifications as necessary. The two handwritten annotations are used to generate the annotations for various frames mathematically (Tian et al., 2020). The in-between frames nonetheless want to be tested to make certain accuracy; however, we discovered that this simplest call for minor modifications. The annotations are then exported in a well-known XML format (i.e., Pascal VOC). Once exported, we sincerely locate annotations in the applicable folder created through the growth tool. The dataset was too big once the annotation procedure was finished for convenient storage. The photographs ranged in resolution from 2K to 4K, resulting in a dataset with a total size of more than 100 terabytes. The photos and annotations are downsized, and the dataset storage is substantially decreased to just 5 gigabytes to solve this problem. All of the photos, together with their bounding boxes and labels, may be seen in the resize tool (Lin et al., 2017).

ADVANTAGES OF USING PYTHON FOR BOUNDARY DETECTION OF FOREIGN OBJECTS IN AIRPORTS

There are several advantages of using Python for foreign object detection (FOD) in airports. Here are some of them:

- **Ease of Use:** Python has a simple syntax and intuitive structure that makes it easy to write, read, and debug code. This makes it an ideal language for developers with limited programming experience who want to develop FOD detection systems.
- **Flexibility:** Python is a versatile language that can be used for various applications, including FOD detection. It provides a range of libraries and tools that can be used for image processing, machine learning, and deep learning, making it an ideal choice for developing FOD detection systems.
- **Large and Active Community:** Python has a large and active community that regularly develops and maintains open-source libraries. This makes it easy to access and use a wide range of tools for FOD detection.
- **Efficiency:** Python-based FOD detection systems can process live video feeds from airport cameras and detect any foreign objects present in the footage in real-time. This helps reduce the risk of aircraft damage and downtime caused by foreign objects.
- **Accuracy:** Deep learning models developed in Python, such as YOLOv4 and EfficientDet, have demonstrated high accuracy and efficiency in detecting foreign objects of various sizes and shapes in airport footage. This helps improve the reliability of FOD detection systems.

- Python is a cost-effective option for creating FOD detection systems because it is a free and open-source language.

Hence, Python offers several advantages for developing FOD detection systems in airports, including ease of use, flexibility, efficiency, accuracy, and cost-effectiveness. These advantages make Python a popular choice for developers who want to improve airport safety and efficiency by detecting foreign objects in airport footage (Xie et al., 2021).

LIMITATIONS OF USING PYTHON FOR BOUNDARY DETECTION OF FOREIGN OBJECTS IN AIRPORTS

One of the potential disadvantages of using Python for foreign object detection (FOD) in airports is that it may require a significant amount of computational power and resources. Another potential disadvantage is that the accuracy of the FOD detection system may be affected by environmental factors such as lighting conditions, weather conditions, and camera placement (Wan et al., 2014).

Additionally, the detection system may also produce false positives or false negatives, leading to unnecessary delays or potential safety risks. False positives may occur when the system detects a foreign object that is actually harmless debris, while false negatives may occur when the system fails to detect a foreign object that poses a risk to aircraft safety. Therefore, the implementation of FOD detection systems using Python may require significant expertise in machine learning and computer vision, making it challenging for some airports to adopt this technology (Zhao et al., 2019). This can lead to higher costs and longer implementation times for airports that do not have the necessary expertise in-house.

RESULTS AND DISCUSSION

In this paper, we have generated the dataset required to train our model. The FOD-A collection comprises of pictures of typical Foreign Object Debris (FOD) against a background of a runway or taxiway. FOD-A contains distinct light-level and weather classification annotations in addition to the core bounding box annotation style. Here we have generated boundary boxes for those objects with respect to the YOLO format (Ren et al., 2015). We have extracted 31 classes of images which are in different shapes and sizes. A number of classes: 31

```
Classes: {'Hose', 'Label', 'AdjustableClamp', 'BoltWasher', 'FuelCap', 'Nail',
'LuggagePart', 'Screw', 'Wood', 'Ta pe', 'MetalSheet', 'Nut', 'ClampPart',
'Cutter', 'SodaCan', 'AdjustableWrench', 'Rock', 'Pen', 'Hammer', 'MetalPart',
'Screwdriver', 'PlasticPart', 'Washer', 'Wrench', 'PaintChip', 'Pliers',
'Wire', 'LuggageTag', 'Bolt', 'Battery', 'BoltNutSet'}.
```

The samples are shown in Figure 1

Figure 1. Sample output of boundary detected object with dimension

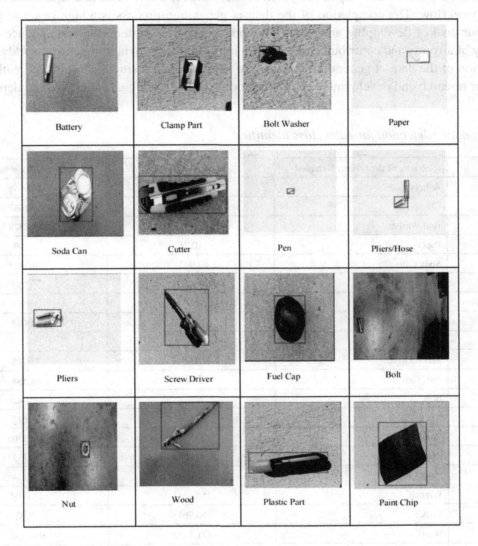

CONCLUSION

After extensive data collection and preprocessing, we have successfully concluded the dataset generation process for foreign object detection in airports using Python. The dataset consists of a large and diverse set of images or sensor data, which includes different types of foreign objects that may be encountered in airport security scenarios, such as luggage tags, metal parts, cutter, etc. The dataset was carefully curated to include a wide range of scenarios, lighting conditions, perspectives, and object placements, to ensure that the resulting model is robust and can accurately detect foreign objects in various real-world situations. Python was used extensively throughout the dataset generation process, including for data collection, data preprocessing, data augmentation, and annotation tasks. Python libraries such as OpenCV, NumPy, and Pandas were utilized for image processing, data manipulation, and annotation tasks. Custom scripts were developed in Python to automate repetitive tasks and streamline the dataset generation workflow. The completion of the dataset generation process is a significant step towards achieving our goal of developing an effective boundary detection system that can enhance the safety and security of airports and contribute to the overall improvement of aviation security worldwide. With the conclusion of the dataset generation process, we are now well-positioned to proceed with the next phase of our research and development efforts, including model training, evaluation, and deployment.

Table 1. Boundary detection for each class identified

Sl No.	Name of the Object Detected	Length (in mm)	Breadth (in mm)
1.	Battery	13.2187	44.0638
2.	Clamp Part	26.8781	55.3667
3.	Bolt Washer	58.7138	41.2329
4.	Paper	10.78	12.89
5.	Soda Can	67.9431	103.893
6.	Cutter	95.432	207.98
7.	Pen	57.918	239.08
8.	Hose	135.97	118.88
9.	Pliers	41.1038	236.169
10.	Screw Driver	169.1314	221.75
11.	Fuel Cap	32.8197	48.588
12.	Bolt	42.67	121.408
13.	Nut	97.059	58.612
14.	Wood	172.8297	192.3305
15.	Plastic Part	118.0224	216.7133
16.	Paint Chip	77.9	43.134
17.	Wrench	255.3611	43.1204
18.	Rock	56.764	67.32
19.	Wire	171.1542	96.3305
20.	Metal Sheet	160.39	249.695
21.	Adjustable clamp	72.64	111.134
22.	Bolt Nut Set	344.57	87.81
23.	Washer	106.36	191.99
24.	Hammer	73.83	155.641
25.	Adjustable Wrench	206.32	118.883
26.	Paper	231.45	54.99
27.	Label	97.059	58.6129
28.	Metal Part	40.421	78.333
29.	Nail	37.303	51.337
30.	Luggage Tag	17.56	62.45
31.	Luggage Part	260.63	43.4401

REFERENCES

Bao, Y., Zhao, E., Gan, X., Luo, D., & Han, Z. (2009, August). A review on cutting-edge techniques in evolutionary algorithms. In *2009 Fifth International Conference on Natural Computation* (Vol. 5, pp. 347-351). IEEE. 10.1109/ICNC.2009.459

Lin, T. Y., Goyal, P., Girshick, R., He, K., & Dollár, P. (2017). Focal loss for dense object detection. In *Proceedings of the IEEE international conference on computer vision* (pp. 2980-2988). IEEE.

Munyer, T., Huang, P. C., Huang, C., & Zhong, X. (2021). *Fod-a: A dataset for foreign object debris in airports.* arXiv preprint arXiv:2110.03072.

Ren, S., He, K., Girshick, R., & Sun, J. (2015). Faster r-cnn: Towards real-time object detection with region proposal networks. *Advances in Neural Information Processing Systems*, 28.

Tian, H., Zheng, Y., & Jin, Z. (2020, October). Improved RetinaNet model for the application of small target detection in the aerial images. *IOP Conference Series. Earth and Environmental Science*, *585*(1), 012142. doi:10.1088/1755-1315/585/1/012142

Wan, J., Wang, D., Hoi, S. C. H., Wu, P., Zhu, J., Zhang, Y., & Li, J. (2014, November). Deep learning for content-based image retrieval: A comprehensive study. In *Proceedings of the 22nd ACM international conference on Multimedia* (pp. 157-166). 10.1145/2647868.2654948

Wang, C. Y., Bochkovskiy, A., & Liao, H. Y. M. (2023). YOLOv7: Trainable bag-of-freebies sets new state-of-the-art for real-time object detectors. In *Proceedings of the IEEE/CVF Conference on Computer Vision and Pattern Recognition* (pp. 7464-7475). IEEE.

WojkeN.BewleyA.PaulusD. (2017, September). Simple online and realtime tracking with a deep association metric. In *2017 IEEE international conference on image processing (ICIP)* (pp. 3645-3649). IEEE.

Xie, X., Cheng, G., Wang, J., Yao, X., & Han, J. (2021). Oriented R-CNN for object detection. In *Proceedings of the IEEE/CVF International Conference on Computer Vision* (pp. 3520-3529). IEEE.

Zhao, Z. Q., Zheng, P., Xu, S. T., & Wu, X. (2019). Object detection with deep learning: A review. *IEEE Transactions on Neural Networks and Learning Systems*, *30*(11), 3212–3232. doi:10.1109/TNNLS.2018.2876865 PMID:30703038

Chapter 8
Discovering Intersections of Music Genres With Machine Learning

Fiona Veseli
Rochester Institute of Technology, Kosovo

Orinda Visoka
Rochester Institute of Technology, Kosovo

Erudit Jupolli
Rochester Institute of Technology, Kosovo

ABSTRACT

The music industry generates an enormous amount of data, which makes classifying and organizing that data into a genre a very difficult task. A potential solution to that problem is to cluster the music using machine learning. Machine learning algorithms might enhance personalized suggestions, search engines, and music categorization systems by creating a model which can precisely identify different genres relying on their acoustic and subjective properties. Recent research suggests that even though there is a large overlap across genres, with machine learning algorithms, we can properly categorize music genres by recognizing differences as well as similarities between them. In more general terms, grouping musical styles using machine learning has several uses in the music industry. It can speed up the identification of new musical styles and encourage cross-genre collaborations among musicians.

INTRODUCTION

As music passionates we and the general public often have this dilemma on what to listen to next. Spending more time browsing my playlist for that one song than actually listening to music is a modern-day problem, especially for students. We can also try the shuffle method on our music players but that also poses a problem because no one wants to listen to a sad song after a hype one. We decided on this project

DOI: 10.4018/978-1-6684-9809-5.ch008

because we like music and want to have a program to solve this issue for us and maybe everyone we share this project with (Zhang et al., 1999).

For most people I know they use music as a free therapy, as it calms them down or makes changes in their mood. It has also been a way for people to connect cultures, since people listen to music from people that come from different parts of the world. The most important thing in this industry is that it is expanding more every day. Since this industry is growing the genres are starting to merge with one another and they are overlapping, what we are trying to do with our project is trying to differentiate these genres with each other. This machine learning might be used in the future so that it is easier to personalize music. And in the future, we can hope that music applications, such as Spotify or YouTube and others, might use this machine learning as a feature to make it easier for people to discover new music (Lu et al., 2001; Mondal et al., 2023).

We all listen to music on a daily basis, and use it as a universal language that connects us with people from different countries. There are around 1000 music genres and sub-genres, and each are unique. The music industry is growing every day, and there is the need to sort and order the music, and personalize it for every user (Althar et al., 2023). Our goal is to cluster the music genres with great precision and accuracy. One of the main problems is the similarity between some genres (Advances in Automatic Text Summarization, 1999). This might make it more difficult for us to classify the genres. Solving this problem will help 'music lovers' find new music they have never heard (Cunaku et al., 2023). This machine learning can be very applicable worldwide, especially in music apps. As a result, tailored suggestions and music search engines get better, new music genres may be discovered, and cross-genre partnerships between artists are encouraged (Ren et al., 1998). Machine learning-based music genre clustering has enormous ramifications for the music business and can improve our listening experience as a whole. Accepting the importance of music throughout history and its impact on civilization itself. Every member of our group being constant music listeners, seeing this project title sparked inspiration. With this Python program, we will group different songs and melodies into different music "playlists" so that if a user likes one song the probability of them liking the next one in that specific group or, linking two groups with similar attributes, will be high (Garg et al., 2023). We will compare factual aspects of songs, such as beats per minute, loudness, acoustics, valence and length, and social aspects, danceability, popularity, energy, etc. (Koumpis et al., 1998). By using to different but similar datasets we will select a bigger sample population and comparing these two by running them on with the same program gives us a variety of data to work with. We will present all this data visually so that the user can better understand and visualize what they are doing with our program. Also, we will present our algorithm and logic with a flowchart so that other developers can follow in our footsteps and use this program confidently (Gurunath et al., 2023). By employing different machine learning algorithms, the authors of the study "Music Genre Classification using Machine Learning Techniques" hope to increase the precision of music genre classification. The research investigates how to train machine learning models that can categorize songs into various genres using audio parameters like pitch, tempo, and timbre (Hori et al., 1998; Jain et al., 2023).

A number of algorithms, including Decision Tree, Random Forest, Naive Bayes, and Support Vector Machines (SVMs), were tested by the authors, and their performance was assessed using parameters including accuracy, precision, recall, and F1 score. According to the study's findings, SVMs performed better than other algorithms in terms of accuracy and F1 score, classifying six different musical genres with an overall accuracy of 91.25% (Guha et al., 2023). The research also emphasizes how crucial it is to use the right audio characteristics for classification tasks and to use the right assessment strategy to gauge the effectiveness of machine learning models (Gong et al., 2001).

This project presents an opportunity to explore the overlap of music genres with one another, and to explore the intersection between music and machine learning; also, what can be done when these two are used together. In this research, we have used to datasets that contain most popular songs of 2000s and songs from 2010 to 2019 (Yahiaoui et al., 2001; Chew et al., 2001). This research analyzes the most frequently used words and their typical pace throughout the years. This way, we could also analyze what genre was listened to mostly during the years, and in a way if we pay attention to these statistics we came up with, we might even predict what will be preferred to be listened a few years from now (Dangi et al., 2023).

Personally, I listen to music all the time, even when I study or code. This means I focus a lot in the frequencies of some songs, and ones with higher frequencies help me focus more and make work faster and more efficiently, the songs that have lower frequencies make me more chill and sleepier. I try to divide songs in two albums, ones that I can work with and the ones that make me feel les focused (Kraft et al., 2001). Ever since I learned machine learning in university, I was thinking of places where people could implement machine learning for something used in daily life (Podder et al., 2023). I came up with a question; What if I could divide songs in those two albums using machine learning, and I didn't have the need to listen to these songs one by one and focus on the way they are making me feel, when a code snippet can do that for me easily in just a few seconds?

To get the snippet of code for the question I answered, I found that I had to do much more research, and at first, I had to learn how to categorize songs into genres, which is what we did in our project. Later on, with even more research, I can create a code that divides songs into frequencies and not genres.

Database Description With All Attributes

Figure 1 shows First Dataset and Figure 2 shows Second Dataset. First Dataset Description:

- Size: 169917
- Python code:
  ```
  #shows the size
  size = Path('Spotify-2000.csv').stat().st_size
  print(size)
  pd.read_csv("/content/Spotify-2000.csv").shape
  ```

- **No. of the column:** 15
- **No. of rows:** 1994

Input: Index, Title, Artist, Top Genre, Year, Beats Per Minute, Energy, Danceability, Loudness, Liveness, Valence, Length (Duration), Acousticness, Speechiness, Popularity.

Excepted Output: This is a way we can use Python to do machine learning based to cluster music genres. The task of categorizing musical genres based on their shared aural characteristics is known as "clustering." The object of this music clustering is to create groups that contain similar energy, loudness, valence, length, etc(B. Logan et al.2000).

Figure 1. First dataset

Index	Title	Artist	Top Genre	Year	Beats Per Minute	Energy	Danceability	Loudness	Liveness	Valence	Length (Duration)	Acousticness	Speechiness	Popularity
1	Sunrise	Norah Jon	adult stand	2004	157	30	53	-14	11	68	201	94	3	71
2	Black Nigh	Deep Purp	album rock	2000	135	79	50	-11	17	81	207	17	7	39
3	Clint Eastw	Gorillaz	alternative	2001	168	69	66	-9	7	52	341	2	17	69
4	The Preter	Foo Fighte	alternative	2007	173	96	43	-4	3	37	269	0	4	76
5	Waitin' On	Bruce Spri	classic roc	2002	106	82	58	-5	10	87	256	1	3	59
6	The Road,	City To Cit	alternative	2004	99	46	54	-9	14	14	247	0	2	45
7	She Will Be	Maroon 5	pop	2002	102	71	71	-6	13	54	257	6	3	74
8	Knights of	Muse	modern ro	2006	137	96	37	-5	12	21	366	0	14	69
9	Mr. Bright:	The Killers	modern ro	2004	148	92	36	-4	10	23	223	0	8	77
10	Without M	Eminem	detroit hip	2002	112	67	91	-3	24	66	290	0	7	82
11	Love Me T	Elvis Presle	adult stand	2002	109	5	44	-16	11	31	162	88	4	49
12	Seven Nati	The White	alternative	2003	124	46	74	-8	26	32	232	1	8	74
13	Als Het Go	De Dijk	dutch indie	2000	102	88	54	-6	53	59	214	2	3	34
14	I'm going t	Ten Years	album rock	2005	117	93	38	-2	81	40	639	18	10	26

Second Dataset Description:

- Size: 49,074 bytes
- Python Code:

```
#shows the size
size = Path('Spotify-2000.csv').stat().st_size
print(size)
pd.read_csv("/content/Spotify-2000.csv").shape
```

- **No. of columns: 15**
- **No. of rows: 603**

Figure 2. Second dataset

Index	Title	Artist	Top Genre	Year	Beats Per Minute	Energy	Danceability	Loudness	Liveness	Valence	Length (Duration)	Acousticness	Speechiness	Popularity
1	Hey, Soul S	Train	neo mellow	2010	97	89	67	-4	8	80	217	19	4	83
2	Love The V	Eminem	detroit hip	2010	87	93	75	-5	52	64	263	24	23	82
3	TiK ToK	Kesha	dance pop	2010	120	84	76	-3	29	71	200	10	14	80
4	Bad Roma	Lady Gaga	dance pop	2010	119	92	70	-4	8	71	295	0	4	79
5	Just the W	Bruno Mar	pop	2010	109	84	64	-5	9	43	221	2	4	78
6	Baby	Justin Bieb	canadian p	2010	65	86	73	-5	11	54	214	4	14	77
7	Dynamite	Taio Cruz	dance pop	2010	120	78	75	-4	4	82	203	0	9	77
8	Secrets	OneRepub	dance pop	2010	148	76	52	-6	12	38	225	7	4	77
9	Empire Sta	Alicia Keys	hip pop	2010	93	37	48	-8	12	11	216	74	3	76
10	Only Girl (I	Rihanna	barbadian	2010	126	72	79	-4	7	61	235	13	4	73
11	Club Can't	Flo Rida	dance pop	2010	128	87	62	-4	6	47	235	3	3	73
12	Marry You	Bruno Mar	pop	2010	145	83	62	-5	10	48	230	33	4	73
13	Cooler Tha	Mike Posn	dance pop	2010	130	82	77	-5	70	63	213	18	5	73
14	Telephone	Lady Gaga	dance pop	2010	122	83	83	-6	11	71	221	1	4	73
15	Like A G6	Far East M	dance pop	2010	125	84	44	-8	13	79	217	1	45	73

Input: Index, Title, Artist, Top Genre, Year, Beats Per Minute, Energy, Danceability, Loudness, Liveness, Valence, Length (Duration), Acousticness, Speechiness, Popularity.

Expected output: This is a method for clustering musical genres using machine learning and Python. Clustering is the process of classifying musical genres according to their shared auditory characteristics. This music is clustered in order to make groups with comparable intensity, loudness, valence, duration, etc.

THE ALGORITHM OF THE PROJECT

At first, we had to choose what dataset we can use during our research from 'plainenglish.io' web page. There were 114 data science projects we could choose from, and we went with Clustering Music Genres with Machine Learning. After choosing our favorite topic, we had to analyze the dataset in detail to understand its structure, variables, and connections between them. Download the dataset from this source and check that it is appropriate for our platforms and tools for analysis. Upload the dataset to a collaborative platform that enables team members to collaborate on the same project at the same time, such Google Colab (Cooper et al., 2002; Peeters et al., 2002). When you go to Google Colab's web page, at first you are introduced to a page that gives instructions for what this website is needed for. Google Colab is a notebook platform that is web-based; this notebook allows users to write Python code for free in a collaborative way. To run this you do not need a local environment. This is the reason why Google Colab makes it easier for everyone who wants to start coding and machine learning without having to install or set up anything. In order to start using Google Colab, what you need to do is open a web browser and search for it. When you open the website, you have to sign in with a Google account, which is free to open if you don't already have one (Rabiner et al., 1993). When you open that website, to start a new notebook, in which you can write code, you have to press the "New Notebook" button. The page it opens is the place where you can write and execute Python code snippets. Upload the dataset that we downloaded from the plainenglish.io web page. That can be done in the left side of the page, where the files are, the last one is to upload files from local files. We have to copy files and put it in the code before we run it. Include the given code in the project and test it on the chosen dataset to make sure it functions properly and accurately. To test the code, we have to run each line of code. We do that by pressing the 'play' button on the left side of the code. You have to do this one by one so it doesn't create conflict between any code and we know where any error can be found. Create a Word Document where we have to report every step we took to create this project (Deller et al., 1999). Describe the main traits, context, and importance of the dataset in a thorough dataset abstract that is included in the project documentation. Analyze each line of code in detail, outlining its functionality, purpose, and relationship to the project's goals and objectives. Compile all the information into a thorough project report that details every step of the process, from choosing the data to analyzing and interpreting it (Joachims et al., 1998).

Step 1: Imported libraries: panda, numpy and, sklearn
Step 2: Load the dataset from a CSV file "Spotify-2000.csv" into a panda data-frame we called "data"
Step 3: Print the first few rows of the data-frame to verify the data using 'head()' method
Step 4: We deleted the index column since it is redundant
Step 5: Calculate the correlation between the other columns
Step 6: Import MinMaxScaler from sklearn and create a loop to iterate each column of the data-set.
Step 7: Import KMeans algorithm and initializes it with 10 clusters.
Step 8: Create a new "data" called Music Segments and assign the cluster labels.
Step 9: Rename the cluster names to be readable by the mass population.
Step 10: Initialize a new plot object named "PLOT" with the 'import plotlu.graph_objects'
Step 11: Create a loop to add a dot into a 3D scatter plot for each cluster by using the value in the "Music Segments"
Step 12: Update the axes of the plot to display three values: Beats per minute, energy and, danceability.

FLOWCHART OF OPERATIONS

Figure 3 shows the flowchart of the process, Figure 4 projects the tabular data representation of the first dataset. Figure 5 explains Correlation of the first Dataset. Figure 6 shows the tabular data representation of the first dataset including the clustering analysis. Figure 7 shows Cluster graph of the first dataset. Figure 8 shows Size of the dataset. Figure 9. No. Rows and Columns of the dataset.

Figure 3. The flowchart of the process

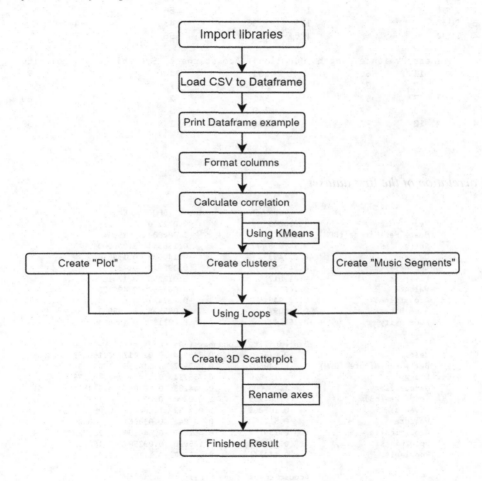

This figure shows the first five lines of the 'Spotify-2000.csv' dataset, containing the title, artist, top genre, the year the song was released, Beats Per Minute (BPM), etc.

This image shows the correlation matrix, which is between different variables in the dataset, the values in this matrix range from -1 to 1.

This output is the same as in Figure 3. But this figure shows another column "Music Segments" which is the result of the cluster analysis.

Figure 4. The tabular data representation of the first dataset

```
    Index                    Title          Artist           Top Genre  \
0      1                   Sunrise      Norah Jones      adult standards
1      2               Black Night      Deep Purple           album rock
2      3            Clint Eastwood         Gorillaz   alternative hip hop
3      4             The Pretender     Foo Fighters     alternative metal
4      5   Waitin' On A Sunny Day  Bruce Springsteen          classic rock

    Year  Beats Per Minute (BPM)  Energy  Danceability  Loudness (dB)  \
0   2004                     157      30            53            -14
1   2000                     135      79            50            -11
2   2001                     168      69            66             -9
3   2007                     173      96            43             -4
4   2002                     106      82            58             -5

    Liveness  Valence  Length (Duration)  Acousticness  Speechiness  Popularity
0        11       68                201            94            3          71
1        17       81                207            17            7          39
2         7       52                341             2           17          69
3         3       37                269             0            4          76
4        10       87                256             1            3          59
```

Figure 5. Correlation of the first dataset

```
                           Year  Beats Per Minute (BPM)    Energy  \
Year                   1.000000                0.012570  0.147235
Beats Per Minute (BPM) 0.012570                1.000000  0.156644
Energy                 0.147235                0.156644  1.000000
Danceability           0.077493               -0.140602  0.139616
Loudness (dB)          0.343764                0.092927  0.735711
Liveness               0.019017                0.016256  0.174118
Valence               -0.166163                0.059653  0.405175
Acousticness          -0.132946               -0.122472 -0.665156
Speechiness            0.054097                0.085598  0.205865
Popularity            -0.158962               -0.003181  0.103393

                       Danceability  Loudness (dB)  Liveness   Valence  \
Year                       0.077493       0.343764  0.019017 -0.166163
Beats Per Minute (BPM)    -0.140602       0.092927  0.016256  0.059653
Energy                     0.139616       0.735711  0.174118  0.405175
Danceability               1.000000       0.044235 -0.103063  0.514564
Loudness (dB)              0.044235       1.000000  0.098257  0.147041
Liveness                  -0.103063       0.098257  1.000000  0.050667
Valence                    0.514564       0.147041  0.050667  1.000000
Acousticness              -0.135769      -0.451635 -0.046206 -0.239729
Speechiness                0.125229       0.125090  0.092594  0.107102
Popularity                 0.144344       0.165527 -0.111978  0.095911

                       Acousticness  Speechiness  Popularity
Year                      -0.132946     0.054097   -0.158962
Beats Per Minute (BPM)    -0.122472     0.085598   -0.003181
Energy                    -0.665156     0.205865    0.103393
Danceability              -0.135769     0.125229    0.144344
Loudness (dB)             -0.451635     0.125090    0.165527
Liveness                  -0.046206     0.092594   -0.111978
Valence                   -0.239729     0.107102    0.095911
Acousticness               1.000000    -0.098256   -0.087604
Speechiness               -0.098256     1.000000    0.111689
Popularity                -0.087604     0.111689    1.000000
```

Figure 6. The tabular data representation of the first dataset including the clustering analysis

```
                      Title              Artist          Top Genre  Year  \
0                   Sunrise         Norah Jones     adult standards  2004
1               Black Night         Deep Purple          album rock  2000
2            Clint Eastwood            Gorillaz  alternative hip hop  2001
3             The Pretender         Foo Fighters   alternative metal  2007
4  Waitin' On A Sunny Day  Bruce Springsteen         classic rock  2002

   Beats Per Minute (BPM)  Energy  Danceability  Loudness (dB)  Liveness  \
0                     157      30            53            -14        11
1                     135      79            50            -11        17
2                     168      69            66             -9         7
3                     173      96            43             -4         3
4                     106      82            58             -5        10

   Valence Length (Duration)  Acousticness  Speechiness  Popularity  \
0       68              201            94            3          71
1       81              207            17            7          39
2       52              341             2           17          69
3       37              269             0            4          76
4       87              256             1            3          59

  Music Segments
0            NaN
1      Cluster 1
2      Cluster 4
3      Cluster 4
4      Cluster 9
```

Figure 7. Cluster graph of the first dataset

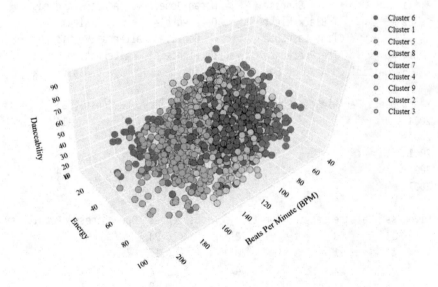

This shows the 3D scatterplot and all values in "Music Segments" are plotted as a distinct trace. The "Beats Per Minute (BPM)" data, "Energy" data, and "Danceability" data are displayed on the x, y, and z axes, and visualizes the relationship between them.

Size of the dataset: 169917

In this figure, it is shown the size of the file.

No. rows and columns of the dataset: (1994, 15)

This output shows the number of rows and columns in the dataset.

RESULT AND DISCUSSION

Figure 8 shows First five lines of the first dataset, Figure 9 projects First five lines of the second dataset. Figure 10 shows the correlation of the first dataset. Figure 11 projects the correlation of the second dataset. Figure 12 shows Cluster analysis of the first dataset. Figure 13 projects luster analysis of the second dataset. Figure 14 shows 3D cluster graph of the first dataset. Figure 15 projects 3D cluster graph of the second dataset.

Figure 8. First five lines of the first dataset

```
  Index                 Title          Artist         Top Genre  \
0     1                Sunrise     Norah Jones    adult standards
1     2            Black Night     Deep Purple         album rock
2     3         Clint Eastwood        Gorillaz  alternative hip hop
3     4          The Pretender    Foo Fighters  alternative metal
4     5  Waitin' On A Sunny Day  Bruce Springsteen       classic rock

   Year  Beats Per Minute (BPM)  Energy  Danceability  Loudness (dB)  \
0  2004                     157      30            53            -14
1  2000                     135      79            50            -11
2  2001                     168      69            66             -9
3  2007                     173      96            43             -4
4  2002                     106      82            58             -5

   Liveness  Valence  Length (Duration)  Acousticness  Speechiness  Popularity
0        11       68                201            94            3          71
1        17       81                207            17            7          39
2         7       52                341             2           17          69
3         3       37                269             0            4          76
4        10       87                256             1            3          59
```

Figure 9. First five lines of the second dataset

	Index	Title	Artist	Top Genre	Year \
0	1	Hey, Soul Sister	Train	neo mellow	2010
1	2	Love The Way You Lie	Eminem	detroit hip hop	2010
2	3	TiK ToK	Kesha	dance pop	2010
3	4	Bad Romance	Lady Gaga	dance pop	2010
4	5	Just the Way You Are	Bruno Mars	pop	2010

	Beats Per Minute (BPM)	Energy	Danceability	Loudness (dB)	Liveness \
0	97	89	67	-4	8
1	87	93	75	-5	52
2	120	84	76	-3	29
3	119	92	70	-4	8
4	109	84	64	-5	9

	Valence	Length (Duration)	Acousticness	Speechiness	Popularity
0	80	217	19	4	83
1	64	263	24	23	82
2	71	200	10	14	80
3	71	295	0	4	79
4	43	221	2	4	78

In these two figures, we see that the 'Spotify-2000.csv' dataset, which contains details on various music tracks including their title, artist, beats per minute, energy, danceability, and popularity is displayed in the first five rows in the first output. While, in the second output, the first five rows of a separate dataset with comparable columns are displayed. This dataset contains music tracks from various time periods and genres.

Comparing these two outputs we can notice that even though both of them have the same range of variables, they do not have the same values. In Figure 11 we can see that we have another column which is "Length (Duration)", which differs the outputs between the two different datasets.

In Figures 12 and 13 except for the given data, we can see that the values are different and the songs are parted on different clusters.

In Figures 14 and 15 the difference between them is visible where we can see that the songs were separated in different clusters. Both graphs have 9 clusters and the reason that the first graph is more crowded since it received more data than the second dataset, which accounts for this.

Figure 10. The correlation of the first dataset

	Year	Beats Per Minute (BPM)	Energy \
Year	1.000000	0.012570	0.147235
Beats Per Minute (BPM)	0.012570	1.000000	0.156644
Energy	0.147235	0.156644	1.000000
Danceability	0.077493	-0.140602	0.139616
Loudness (dB)	0.343764	0.092927	0.735711
Liveness	0.019017	0.016256	0.174118
Valence	-0.166163	0.059653	0.405175
Acousticness	-0.132946	-0.122472	-0.665156
Speechiness	0.054097	0.085598	0.205865
Popularity	-0.158962	-0.003181	0.103393

	Danceability	Loudness (dB)	Liveness	Valence
Year	0.077493	0.343764	0.019017	-0.166163
Beats Per Minute (BPM)	-0.140602	0.092927	0.016256	0.059653
Energy	0.139616	0.735711	0.174118	0.405175
Danceability	1.000000	0.044235	-0.103063	0.514564
Loudness (dB)	0.044235	1.000000	0.098257	0.147041
Liveness	-0.103063	0.098257	1.000000	0.050667
Valence	0.514564	0.147041	0.050667	1.000000
Acousticness	-0.135769	-0.451635	-0.046206	-0.239729
Speechiness	0.125229	0.125090	0.092594	0.107102
Popularity	0.144344	0.165527	-0.111978	0.095911

	Acousticness	Speechiness	Popularity
Year	-0.132946	0.054097	-0.158962
Beats Per Minute (BPM)	-0.122472	0.085598	-0.003181
Energy	-0.665156	0.205865	0.103393
Danceability	-0.135769	0.125229	0.144344
Loudness (dB)	-0.451635	0.125090	0.165527
Liveness	-0.046206	0.092594	-0.111978
Valence	-0.239729	0.107102	0.095911
Acousticness	1.000000	-0.098256	-0.087604
Speechiness	-0.098256	1.000000	0.111689
Popularity	-0.087604	0.111689	1.000000

Size of the first dataset: 169917
Size of the second dataset: 49074

In these two figures, we can clearly see the difference in the dataset size.

No. rows and columns of the first dataset: (1994, 15)
No. rows and columns of the second dataset: (603, 15)

These two figures show that the first dataset received significantly more data than the second dataset. which provides us with more precise outcomes.

Figure 11. The correlation of the second dataset

```
                             Year  Beats Per Minute (BPM)      Energy  \
Year                     1.000000               -0.104247  -0.225596
Beats Per Minute (BPM)  -0.104247                1.000000   0.126170
Energy                  -0.225596                0.126170   1.000000
Danceability             0.079269               -0.131301   0.167209
Loudness (dB)           -0.126471                0.183870   0.537528
Liveness                -0.136331                0.081579   0.186738
Valence                 -0.122025                0.016021   0.409577
Length (Duration)       -0.215344               -0.029359  -0.143610
Acousticness             0.101725               -0.113257  -0.562287
Speechiness              0.004778                0.058999   0.107313
Popularity               0.241261                0.018983  -0.057645

                        Danceability  Loudness (dB)  Liveness   Valence  \
Year                        0.079269      -0.126471 -0.136331 -0.122025
Beats Per Minute (BPM)     -0.131301       0.183870  0.081579  0.016021
Energy                      0.167209       0.537528  0.186738  0.409577
Danceability                1.000000       0.233170 -0.028801  0.501696
Loudness (dB)               0.233170       1.000000  0.081934  0.282922
Liveness                   -0.028801       0.081934  1.000000  0.020226
Valence                     0.501696       0.282922  0.020226  1.000000
Length (Duration)          -0.176841      -0.104723  0.098339 -0.262256
Acousticness               -0.240064      -0.190401 -0.098167 -0.249038
Speechiness                -0.028041      -0.001110  0.144103  0.122013
Popularity                  0.116054       0.156897 -0.075749  0.038953

                        Length (Duration)  Acousticness  Speechiness  \
Year                            -0.215344      0.101725     0.004778
Beats Per Minute (BPM)          -0.029359     -0.113257     0.058999
Energy                          -0.143610     -0.562287     0.107313
Danceability                    -0.176841     -0.240064    -0.028041
Loudness (dB)                   -0.104723     -0.190401    -0.001110
Liveness                         0.098339     -0.098167     0.144103
Valence                         -0.262256     -0.249038     0.122013
Length (Duration)                1.000000      0.091802     0.054564
Acousticness                     0.091802      1.000000     0.002763
Speechiness                      0.054564      0.002763     1.000000
Popularity                      -0.104363      0.026704    -0.041490

                        Popularity
Year                      0.241261
Beats Per Minute (BPM)    0.018983
Energy                   -0.057645
Danceability              0.116054
Loudness (dB)             0.156897
Liveness                 -0.075749
Valence                   0.038953
Length (Duration)        -0.104363
Acousticness              0.026704
Speechiness              -0.041490
Popularity                1.000000
```

Figure 12. Cluster analysis of the first dataset

	Title	Artist	Top Genre	Year	\
0	Sunrise	Norah Jones	adult standards	2004	
1	Black Night	Deep Purple	album rock	2000	
2	Clint Eastwood	Gorillaz	alternative hip hop	2001	
3	The Pretender	Foo Fighters	alternative metal	2007	
4	Waitin' On A Sunny Day	Bruce Springsteen	classic rock	2002	

	Beats Per Minute (BPM)	Energy	Danceability	Loudness (dB)	Liveness	\
0	157	30	53	-14	11	
1	135	79	50	-11	17	
2	168	69	66	-9	7	
3	173	96	43	-4	3	
4	106	82	58	-5	10	

	Valence	Length (Duration)	Acousticness	Speechiness	Popularity	\
0	68	201	94	3	71	
1	81	207	17	7	39	
2	52	341	2	17	69	
3	37	269	0	4	76	
4	87	256	1	3	59	

	Music Segments
0	NaN
1	Cluster 1
2	Cluster 4
3	Cluster 4
4	Cluster 9

Figure 13. Cluster analysis of the second dataset

	Title	Artist	Top Genre	Year	\
0	Hey, Soul Sister	Train	neo mellow	2010	
1	Love The Way You Lie	Eminem	detroit hip hop	2010	
2	TiK ToK	Kesha	dance pop	2010	
3	Bad Romance	Lady Gaga	dance pop	2010	
4	Just the Way You Are	Bruno Mars	pop	2010	

	Beats Per Minute (BPM)	Energy	Danceability	Loudness (dB)	Liveness	\
0	97	89	67	-4	8	
1	87	93	75	-5	52	
2	120	84	76	-3	29	
3	119	92	70	-4	8	
4	109	84	64	-5	9	

	Valence	Length (Duration)	Acousticness	Speechiness	Popularity	\
0	80	217	19	4	83	
1	64	263	24	23	82	
2	71	200	10	14	80	
3	71	295	0	4	79	
4	43	221	2	4	78	

	Music Segments
0	Cluster 3
1	NaN
2	NaN
3	Cluster 4
4	Cluster 9

Figure 14. 3D cluster graph of the first dataset

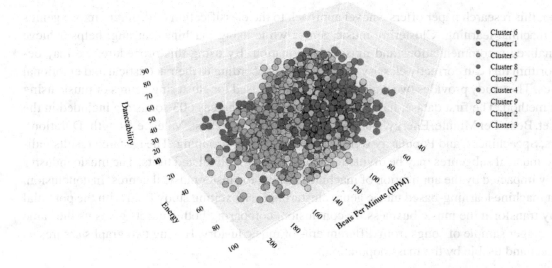

Figure 15. 3D cluster graph of the second dataset

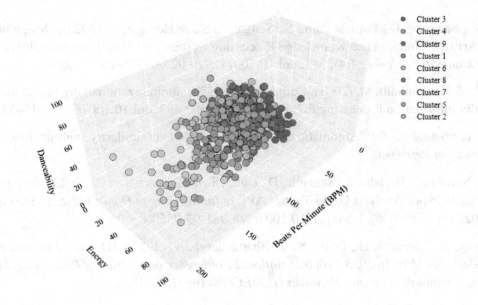

CONCLUSION

In conclusion, this research paper offers a novel approach to the classification of different music genres while using machine learning. Clustering music genres while using machine learning, helps achieve better-personalized recommendations and music classification. By using this procedure, we may develop an algorithm that can correctly classify various genres according to their acoustical and emotional characteristics. This study provides two datasets and the codes used for clustering genres of music using the KMeans method. The first dataset has 1994 songs included, whereas 603 songs are included in the second dataset. Beats Per Minute, Energy, Danceability, Loudness, Liveness, Valence, Length (Duration), Acousticness, Speechiness, and Popularity were used as criteria for grouping. The research results indicated that the musical subgenres may be divided into ten clusters with related traits. The music industry will be greatly impacted by the application of machine learning to cluster musical genres. In conclusion, we think that machine learning-based music genre clustering is an exciting study field with the potential to completely transform the music business. In conclusion, comparing both datasets gives us the same graph with a bigger sample of songs from different eras of music history. Having two graphs assures us that it is correct and usable by the mass population.

REFERENCES

Althar, R. R., Samanta, D., Purushotham, S., Sengar, S. S., & Hewage, C. (2023). Design and Development of Artificial Intelligence Knowledge Processing System for Optimizing Security of Software System. *SN Computer Science*, 4(4), 331. doi:10.100742979-023-01785-2

Chew, C. M., & Kankanhalli, M. (2001). Compressed domain summarization of digital video. Advances in Multimedia Information Processing PCM 2001, 2195, 490-497. doi:10.1007/3-540-45453-5_63

Cooper, M., & Foote, J. (2002). Automatic music summarization via similarity analysis. *Proc. Int. Conf. Music Information Retrieval*.

Cunaku, E., Ndrecaj, J., Berisha, S., Samanta, D., Dutta, S., & Bhattacharya, A. (2023). An Approach for Digital-Social Network Analysis Using Twitter API. In *Innovations in Data Analytics: Selected Papers of ICIDA 2022* (pp. 625–636). Springer. 10.1007/978-981-99-0550-8_49

Dangi, P., Jain, A., Samanta, D., Dutta, S., & Bhattacharya, A. (2023). 3D Modelling and Rendering Using Autodesk 3ds Max. In *2023 11th International Conference on Internet of Everything, Microwave Engineering, Communication and Networks (IEMECON)* (pp. 1–5). IEEE.

Deller, J. R., Hansen, J. H. L., & Proakis, J. G. (1999). *Discrete-Time Processing of Speech Signals*. Wiley. doi:10.1109/9780470544402

El-Maleh, K., Klein, M., Petrucci, G., & Kabal, P. (2000). Speech/music discrimination for multimedia application. *Proc. ICASSP00*.

Garg, M., Saxena, C., Samanta, D., & Dorr, B. J. (2023). *LonXplain: Lonesomeness as a Consequence of Mental Disturbance in Reddit Posts*. doi:10.1007/978-3-031-35320-8_27

Gong, Y., & Liu, X. (2001). Summarizing video by minimizing visual content redundancies. *Proc. IEEE Int. Conf. Multimedia and Expo*, 788-791.

Guha, A., Samanta, D., & Sengar, S. S. (2023). Computer Vision Based Automatic Margin Computation Model for Digital Document Images. *SN Computer Science, 4*(3), 253. doi:10.100742979-023-01693-5

Gurunath, R., & Samanta, D. (2023). A New 3-Bit Hiding Covert Channel Algorithm for Public Data and Medical Data Security Using Format-Based Text Steganography. *Journal of Database Management, 34*(2), 1–22. doi:10.4018/JDM.324076

Hori, C., & Furui, S. (1998). Improvements in automatic speech summarization and evaluation methods. *Proc. Int. Conf. Spoken Language Processing.*

Jain, A., Dangi, P., Samanta, D., Dutta, S., Bhattacharya, A., & Joseph, N. P. (2023). Creation of Bookshelf Using Autodesk 3ds Max: 3D Modelling and Rendering. In *2023 11th International Conference on Internet of Everything, Microwave Engineering, Communication and Networks (IEMECON)* (pp. 1–4). IEEE.

Joachims, T. (1998). Text categorization with support vector machines. *Proc. European Conf. Machine Learning.*

Kimber, D., & Wilcox, L. (1996). Acoustic segmentation for audio browsers. *Proc. Interface Conf.*

Koumpis, K., & Renals, S. (1998). Transcription and summarization of voicemail speech. *Proc. Int. Conf. Spoken Language Processing.*

Kraft, Lu, & Teng. (2001). *Method and Apparatus for Music Summarization and Creation of Audio Summaries.* Academic Press.

Logan, B., & Chu, S. (2000). Music summarization using key phrases. *Proc. IEEE Int. Conf. Audio Speech and Signal Processing.*

Lu, L., Jiang, H., & Zhang, H. J. (2001). A robust audio classification and segmentation method. *Proc. ACM Multimedia 2001.* 10.1145/500141.500173

Mondal, S., Pal, A. K., Islam, S. K. H., & Samanta, D. (2023). Objectionable Image Content Classification Using CNN-Based Semi-supervised Learning. *Advances in Smart Vehicular Technology, Transportation, Communication and Applications Proceedings of VTCA, 2022*, 311–320.

Peeters, G., Burthe, A., & Rodet, X. (2002). Toward automatic music audio summary generation from signal analysis. *Proc. Int. Conf. Music Information Retrieval.*

Podder, S. K., Samanta, D., Thomas, B., Dutta, S., & Bhattacharya, A. (2023). Impact of blended education system on outcome-based learning and sector skills development. In *2023 11th International Conference on Internet of Everything, Microwave Engineering, Communication and Networks (IEMECON)* (pp. 1–6). IEEE.

Rabiner, L. R., & Juang, B. H. (1993). *Fundamentals of Speech Recognition.* Prentice-Hall.

Ren, F., & Sadanaga, Y. (1998). An Automatic Extraction of Important Sentences Using Statistical Information and Structure Feature (Vol. NL98). Academic Press.

Scheirer, E., & Slaney, M. (1997). Construction and evaluation of a robust multifeature music/speech discriminator. *Proc. ICASSP97,* 2, 1331-1334. 10.1109/ICASSP.1997.596192

Sounders, J. (1996). Real-time discrimination of broadcast speech/music. *Proc. ICASSP96,* 2, 993-996.

Yahiaoui, I., Merialdo, B., & Huet, B. (2001). Generating summaries of multi-episode video. *Proc. IEEE Int. Conf. Multimedia and Expo,* 792-795.

Zhang, T., & Kuo, C.-C. (1999). Video content parsing based on combined audio and visual information. Proc. SPIE 1999, 4, 78-89.

Chapter 9
Python–Powered Stock Market Analysis Leveraging Data Science Techniques for Informed Investment Decisions

Arta Zejnullahi
Rochester Institute of Technology, Kosovo

ABSTRACT

We might become interested in stock market investment during the course of our lives. But to do that, we first need to have a clear understanding and analysis of the market. We may be unsure of whether to buy or sell stocks; thus, this is vital. It can be challenging to determine whether a stock will rise or decline in value or whether it will be a successful investment. In the event that the stock decreases, we can be unsure about whether to sell or stay on to it. Given the large number of investors who purchase stocks globally and the potential for significant losses, stock market analysis is crucial. The goal is to develop a project that analyzes the stock market and aids in our decision-making when it comes to purchasing and selling stocks.

INTRODUCTION

Understanding the Stock Market is very important in this modern age. With the high inflation and the war happening in Ukraine, it is important to understand how investments work (NeuralNine et al., n.d.; Ahmad Bazzi et al., 2020). By choosing this project we will have an insight investment decision making, by informing the investors the current market trends, and performance on companies or corporates (Abdar et al., 2019; Alippi et al., 2019). By this, investors can identify the investments opportunities and the risks associated with it. The project's goal is to conduct a stock market analysis to assist investors in making purchase and sell choices (Macarty et al., 2021). We have mentioned a dataset with 251 rows and 7 columns that contains information on Tesla's stock values in addition to giving a brief introduction

DOI: 10.4018/978-1-6684-9809-5.ch009

to why understanding the stock market is crucial in the present era (Kuznetsov et al., 2018; Qin et al., 2020; Raza et al.,2019). We have provided a 20-step algorithm that downloads and examines historical Tesla stock price data using a variety of libraries and modules, including plotly.graph_objects, plotly. express, datetime, timedelta, and pandas. A flowchart showing the algorithm's steps was also provided. Last but not least, we provide sample code for the algorithm's first stage, which collects data on Tesla's historical stock price and shows it as a Candlestick chart (Algovibes et al., 2021; Kharwal et al., 2022; James et al., 2017).

DATASET DESCRIPTION

- **Size**: 18974
- **Python code**:
  from pathlib import Path
  sz = Path("/content/TSLA.csv").stat().st_size
  print(sz)

- **No. of col.**: 7 **& No. of row**: 251
  # import module
  import pandas as pd
  # read the csv file
  results = pd.read_csv("/content/TSLA.csv")
  # display dataset
  print(results)

Figure 1 shows Values of Tesla Stock. Figure 2 shows Flowchart of Algorithm from Step all steps.

Input: This project focus on the analysis of the stock market therefore, the input will be different stocks, in order to make a buying or selling decision (Shah et al., 2018; Yoo et al., 2018; Chen et al., 2013).

Excepted Output: The expected output of this will be for us to analyze the stock based on historical data therefore it will be outputting the date and time, the amount it opened, the peak high value and low value of the stock, the time it closed and the volume it was traded (Huang et al.,2019). As well as it will output historical charts to make a better buying or selling decision (Brownlee et al., 2018; Chollet et al., 2018; Fawcett et al., 2018).

ALGORITHM

Step 1. Importing the essential libraries and modules, such as plotly.graph_objects, plotly.express, datetime, timedelta, and pandas.

Step 2. Obtaining the current date using the date.today() method, converting it to a string format (YYYY-MM-DD), and then assigning it to the end_date variable.

Step 3. Subtracting 365 days (1 year) from the current date using the timedelta method, translating the result to the string format YYYY-MM-DD, and assigning it to the variable start_date (Chen et al., 2021; Cheng et al., 2016; De Lima Silva et al., 2020).

Figure 1. Values of Tesla stock

```
            Date        Open        High         Low       Close   Adj Close  \
0     2022-04-07  350.796661  358.863342  340.513336  352.420013  352.420013
1     2022-04-08  347.736664  349.480011  340.813324  341.829987  341.829987
2     2022-04-11  326.799988  336.156677  324.880005  325.309998  325.309998
3     2022-04-12  332.546661  340.396667  325.533325  328.983337  328.983337
4     2022-04-13  327.026672  342.079987  324.366669  340.790009  340.790009
..           ...         ...         ...         ...         ...         ...
246   2023-03-31  197.529999  207.789993  197.199997  207.460007  207.460007
247   2023-04-03  199.910004  202.690002  192.199997  194.770004  194.770004
248   2023-04-04  197.320007  198.740005  190.320007  192.580002  192.580002
249   2023-04-05  190.520004  190.679993  183.759995  185.520004  185.520004
250   2023-04-06  183.080002  186.389999  179.740005  185.059998  185.059998

          Volume
0       79447200
1       55013700
2       59357100
3       65976000
4       55121100
..           ...
246    169638500
247    169545900
248    126463800
249    133882500
250    123583100

[251 rows x 7 columns]
```

Step 4. Downloading historical stock price information for Tesla for the start_date and end_date ranges using the yf.download method and assigning it to the variable data.

Step 5. Creating a new column in the data DataFrame called "Date" to carry the index value, or the dates.

Step 6. Resetting the index after only the essential Date, Open, High, Low, Close, Adj Close, and Volume columns have been chosen in the data DataFrame.

Step 7. Using the plotly.graph_objects module, making a Candlestick chart and adding it to the variable Figure 1.

Step 8. Adjusting Figure 1's layout to display the title and conceal the x-axis range variable.

Step 9. Using the Figure 1 object's show() function to display the Candlestick chart.

Step 10. Using the plotly.express module, making a bar chart and assigning it to the variable figure 2.

Step 11. Using the Figure 2 object's show() method to display the bar chart.

Step 12. Using the plotly.express module to create a line graph and adding it to the variable figure3.

Step 13. Modifying Figure 3's x-axis to include a range slider and change the title.

Step 14. Using the Figure 3 object's show() function to display the line graph.

Step 15. Using the plotly.express module, make a second line graph and add it to the variable Figure 4.

Step 16. Adding preset time period pickers and changing the title on the x-axis of Figure 4.

Step 17. Using the Figure 4 object's show() method to display the line graph.

Step 18. Using the plotly.express module, producing a scatter plot and assigning it to the variable Figure 5.

Step 19. Changing Figure 5's x-axis to hide the weekend gaps and set the title.

Step 20. Using the show() function of the Figure 5 object to display the scatter plot.

FLOWCHART

Figure 2. Flowchart of algorithm from Step 1 to Step 20

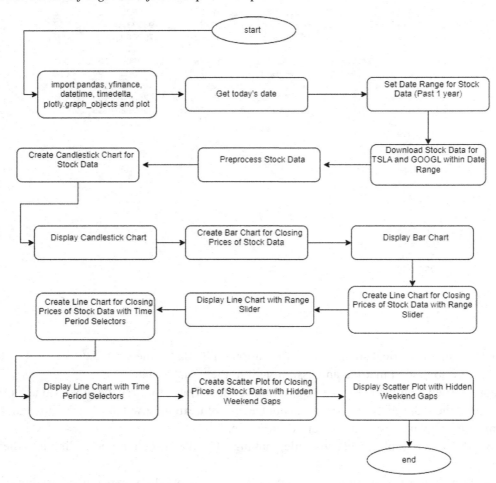

EXPERIMENT RESULTS

Figure 3 shows Head Values of Tesla Stock. Figure 4 projects Price Chart of Tesla Price. Figure 5 shows Candle Stick Price Chart of Tesla Stock Price. Figure 6 projects Rangeslider Price Chart for Tesla Stock. Figure 7 shows Time Period Selectors for Tesla Stock Price. Figure 9 shows Head Values of the dataset of Tesla Stock price (Egrioglu et al., 2010, 2011, 2016).

We have got the head values of Tesla Stock price including Date, Open, High Price, Low Price, Closed Price, adj close, and volume.

This is a candlestick Price Chart for Tesla Stock so analysts can better analyze and predict the tesla stock price.

In Figure 11 we see a better visualization of the Stock price so we can have a better look at the price history of the Tesla Price.

Figure 3. Head values of Tesla stock

	Date	Open	High	Low	Close	Adj Close	\
0	2022-05-02	286.923340	302.119995	282.676666	300.980011	300.980011	
1	2022-05-03	301.059998	308.026672	296.196655	303.083344	303.083344	
2	2022-05-04	301.313324	318.500000	295.093323	317.540009	317.540009	
3	2022-05-05	313.006653	315.200012	285.899994	291.093323	291.093323	
4	2022-05-06	295.666656	296.000000	281.036682	288.549988	288.549988	

	Volume
0	75781500
1	63709500
2	81643800
3	92519100
4	72903000

Figure 4. Price chart of Tesla price

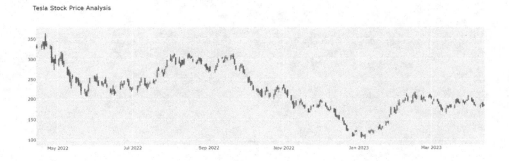

Figure 5. Candle stick price chart of Tesla stock price

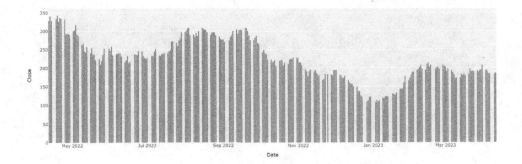

In Figure 12 we use a range slider to analyze Tesla Stock, this gives a better understanding of the price analysis of the stock market (Garg et al., 2016; Ghosh et al., 2016; Gupta et al., 2019).

We use Period Selectors, so we can analyze how the price of the Tesla Stock has changed during that period of time and that leads us to better predictions (Guha et al., 2023).

Figure 6. Rangeslider price chart for Tesla stock

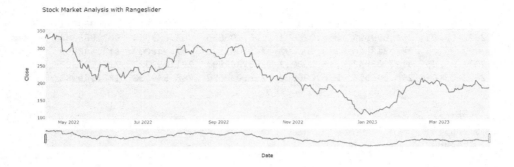

Figure 7. Time period selectors for Tesla stock price

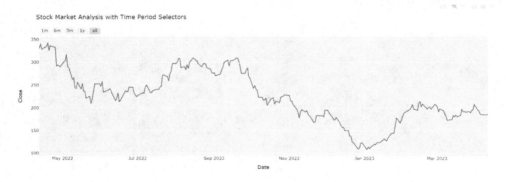

Figure 8. Price chart hiding weekend gaps for Tesla stock price

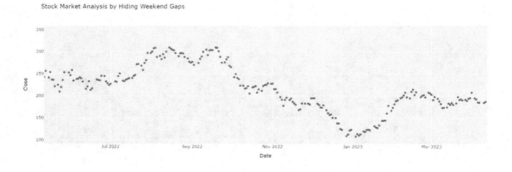

In Figure 14 we have included a chart that doesn't include the weekend, and so we understand how the price of Tesla Stock is affected (Huarng et al., 2001; Huarng et al., 2006; Kuo et al., 2009).

Figure 9. Head values of the dataset of Tesla stock price

```
        Date        Open        High         Low       Close   Adj Close  \
0 2022-05-02  286.923340  302.119995  282.676666  300.980011  300.980011
1 2022-05-03  301.059998  308.026672  296.196655  303.083344  303.083344
2 2022-05-04  301.313324  318.500000  295.093323  317.540009  317.540009
3 2022-05-05  313.006653  315.200012  285.899994  291.093323  291.093323
4 2022-05-06  295.666656  296.000000  281.036682  288.549988  288.549988

     Volume
0  75781500
1  63709500
2  81643800
3  92519100
4  72903000
```

Figure 10. Candlestick chart for Google stock price analysis

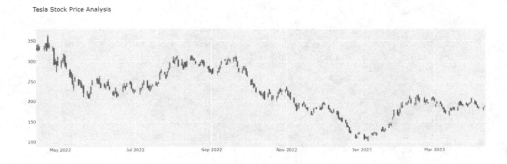

Figure 11. A bar plot visualization to analyze the stock price

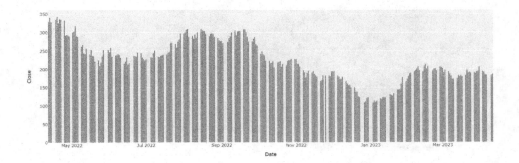

Figure 12. A range slider stock market analysis for Tesla stock

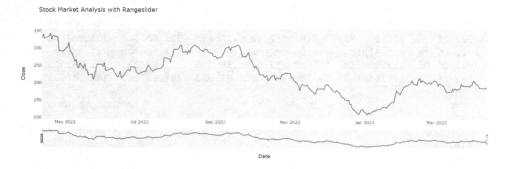

Figure 13. This figure shows a market analysis with period selectors

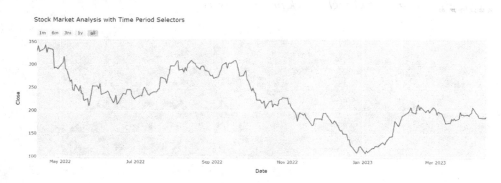

Figure 14. This figure shows a chart where the weekends are not included since the stock market is closed

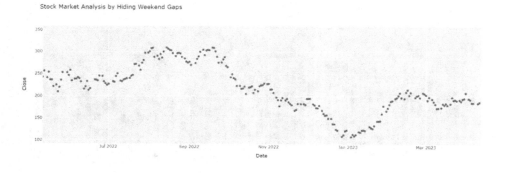

COMPARE TWO DATASETS WITH ALL OUTPUTS

1)   Dataset 1 for Google Stock Price and Tesla stock price
     a)   Dataset description

We have used the dataset of Google Stock price, and it shows the history of Google stock price throughout the year and as well as Tesla.

     b)   Output of Dataset - Google and Tesla

Figure 15. Value of the dataset of Google stock price

```
        Date        Open        High         Low       Close   Adj Close  \
0  2022-05-02  113.404999  116.745499  112.599998  116.583000  116.583000
1  2022-05-03  116.430496  118.442001  116.034500  117.334000  117.334000
2  2022-05-04  117.031502  122.854500  115.115997  122.261002  122.261002
3  2022-05-05  120.204002  121.039001  115.005501  116.505501  116.505501
4  2022-05-06  115.184502  117.571503  114.015503  115.746498  115.746498

       Volume
0    35534000
1    24968000
2    49916000
3    45840000
4    39710000
```

Figure 16. Value of the dataset of Tesla stock price

```
        Date        Open        High         Low       Close   Adj Close  \
0  2022-05-02  286.923340  302.119995  282.676666  300.980011  300.980011
1  2022-05-03  301.059998  308.026672  296.196655  303.083344  303.083344
2  2022-05-04  301.313324  318.500000  295.093323  317.540009  317.540009
3  2022-05-05  313.006653  315.200012  285.899994  291.093323  291.093323
4  2022-05-06  295.666656  296.000000  281.036682  288.549988  288.549988

       Volume
0    75781500
1    63709500
2    81643800
3    92519100
4    72903000
```

In Figure 15 and Figure 16 we observe the difference of the two data set is price and volume that the stock is traded (Jain et al., 2023).

Based on Figure 17 and in Figure 18 we can see that the price is changing throughout the year. In the X-axis it is shown the years of the stock that was traded and Y-axis the price of the stock. They are two different Stocks, and we can observe that in November 2022 Google Stock has done worse than Tesla where it was doing very well however, by end of March they closed almost same price (Dangi et al., 2023).

Figure 17. This figure shows a candlestick chart for Google stock price analysis

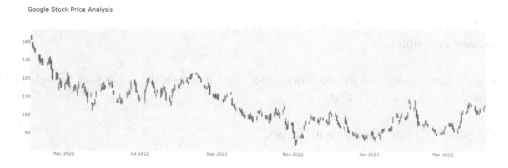

Figure 18. This figure shows a candlestick chart for Google stock price analysis

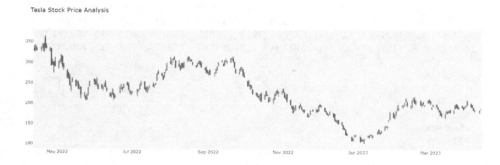

Figure 19. This figure shows a bar plot visualization to analyze the stock price

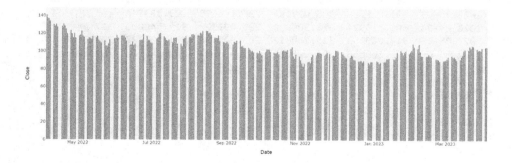

In Figure 19 and in Figure 20 figure we are using a different price charts which is a bar plot visualization and we can see the price differences. In the X-axis it is shown the years of the stock that was traded and Y-axis the price of the stock Example May 2022 we see a slightly more increase in price than Tesla in the bar plot visualization (Podder et al., 2023).

Figure 20. This figure shows a bar plot visualization to analyze the stock price

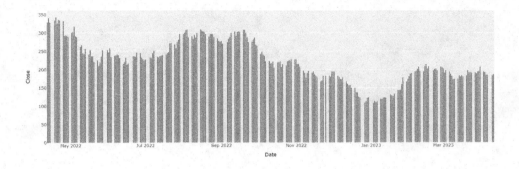

Figure 21. This figure shows a range slider stock market analysis for Google stock

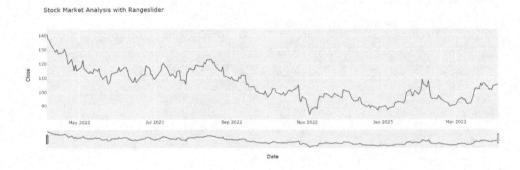

Figure 22. This figure shows a range slider stock market analysis for Tesla stock

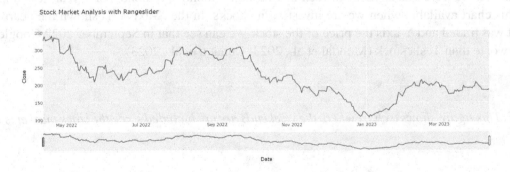

In Figure 21 and in Figure 22 we have used a range slider for the Stock Market analysis of these two Stocks to better analyze the stocks throughout the year, which is called technical analysis. In the X-axis it is shown the years of the stock that was traded and Y-axis the price of the stock. As we see in this chart both stocks in January 2023, we see a decrease in price (Althar et al., 2023).

Figure 23. This figure shows a market analysis with period selectors

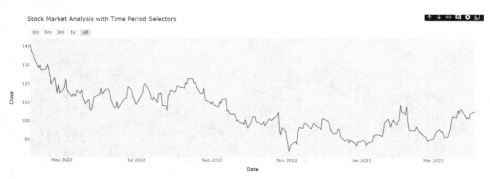

Figure 24. This figure shows a market analysis with period selectors

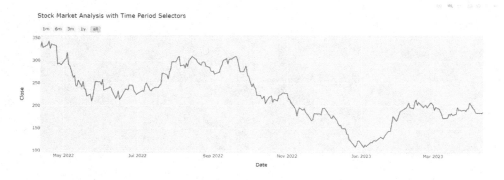

In Figure 23 and in Figure 24 for Google and Tesla Stock analysis we have used Period Selectors due to the reason if we have to analyze the Stock in 1 month, 3 months, 6 months or 1 year. It is important to have this chart available when we are investing in stocks. In the X-axis it is shown the years of the stock that was traded and Y-axis the price of the stock We can see that in September 2022 Google stock has done worse than Tesla stock (Mondal et al., 2023; Cunaku et al., 2023).

Figure 25. This figure shows a chart where the weekends are not included since the stock market is closed

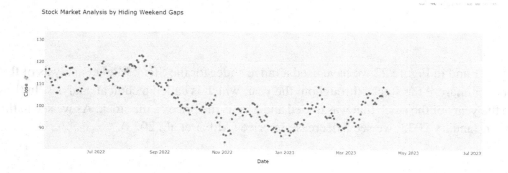

Figure 26. This figure shows a chart where the weekends are not included since the stock market is closed

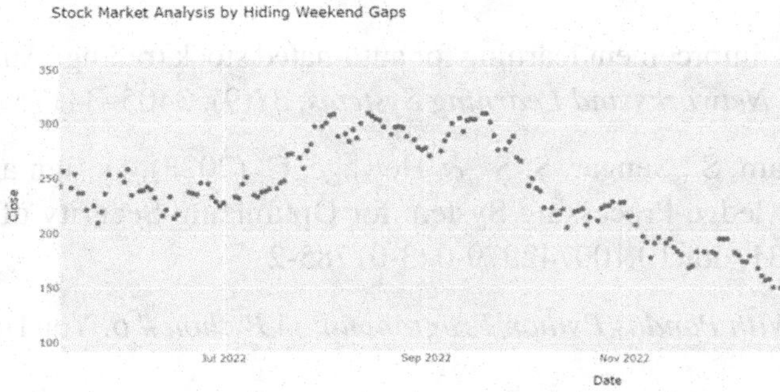

In Figure 25 and in Figure 26 we have used a chart where the weekends are not included. In the X-axis it is shown the years of the stock that was traded and Y-axis the price of the stock.In these two price charts we have used a chart where the weekends are not included to better analyze the charts and the price difference between the two Stocks (Garg et al., 2023; Gurunath et al., 2023). Because the market is closed during weekend, and that makes a big difference when we are trading stocks, because the market is closed. When the market opens again, it gives us a better opportunity to analyze it.

CONCLUSION

We could deduce from this that an analysis of the stock market included an analysis of the price of Tesla's stock over a year's time. Numerous visualizations, including candlestick charts, bar charts, line charts, and scatter plots, are used in the analysis. These visualizations were produced using the interactive, adaptable plots provided by the Python plotly package. The bar chart displays the closing price of the stock over time, whilst the candlestick chart shows the price changes of Tesla's stock over the last year. The viewer can zoom in on a particular time period of interest using the range slider included in the line chart, and the fourth visualization adds additional time period choices so they can choose a specified range. The stock's closing price is shown over time in a scatter plot, with weekend gaps covered up. For investors and financial professionals, this stock market research offers a thorough look into Tesla's stock price changes during the previous year. It is crucial to keep in mind that stock market analysis is a dynamic and complex topic that necessitates thorough evaluation of numerous aspects in addition to previous price data. In order to make informed investment decisions, this research should be used in connection with other data and analysis.

REFERENCES

Abdar, M., & Hosseini, M. (2019). A deep learning approach for stock market prediction using Python. *Journal of Financial Engineering and Management*, *4*(2), 11–26.

Algovibes. (2021). *Fundamental Analysis of Stocks With Python*. YouTube. www.youtube.com/watch?v=ZUQEd22oNek

Alippi, C., & Roveri, M. (2019). Deep reinforcement learning for automated stock trading: An empirical analysis. *IEEE Transactions on Neural Networks and Learning Systems*, *31*(9), 3405–3417.

Althar, R. R., Samanta, D., Purushotham, S., Sengar, S. S., & Hewage, C. (2023). Design and Development of Artificial Intelligence Knowledge Processing System for Optimizing Security of Software System. *SN Computer Science*, *4*(4), 331. doi:10.100742979-023-01785-2

Bazzi. (2020). *Stock Market Analysis With Pandas Python Programming | Python # 6*. YouTube. www.youtube.com/watch?v=57qAxRV577c

Brownlee, J. (2018). *Machine learning for algorithmic trading: Predictive models to extract signals from market and alternative data for systematic trading strategies with Python*. Machine Learning Mastery.

Chen, L. S., Chen, M. Y., Chang, J. R., & Yu, P. Y. (2021). An intuitionistic fuzzy time series model based on new data transformation method. *Int J Comput Intell Syst*, *14*(1), 550–559. doi:10.2991/ijcis.d.210106.002

Chen, S. M., & Kao, P. Y. (2013). Taifex forecasting based on fuzzy time series particle swarm optimization techniques and support vector machines. *Information Sciences*, *247*, 62–71. doi:10.1016/j.ins.2013.06.005

Cheng, S. H., Chen, S. M., & Jian, W. S. (2016). Fuzzy time series forecasting based on fuzzy logical relationships and similarity measures. *Information Sciences*, *327*, 272–287. doi:10.1016/j.ins.2015.08.024

Chollet, F. (2018). *Deep learning with Python*. Manning Publications.

Cunaku, E., Ndrecaj, J., Berisha, S., Samanta, D., Dutta, S., & Bhattacharya, A. (2023). An Approach for Digital-Social Network Analysis Using Twitter API. In *Innovations in Data Analytics: Selected Papers of ICIDA 2022* (pp. 625–636). Springer. 10.1007/978-981-99-0550-8_49

De Lima Silva, P. C., Sadaei, H. J., Ballini, R., & Guimarães, F. G. (2020). Probabilistic forecasting with fuzzy time series. *IEEE Transactions on Fuzzy Systems*, *28*(8), 1771–1784. doi:10.1109/TFUZZ.2019.2922152

Egrioglu, E., Aladag, C. H., Yolcu, U., Uslu, V. R., & Basaran, M. A. (2010). Finding an optimal interval length in high order fuzzy time series. *Expert Systems with Applications*, *37*(7), 5052–5055. doi:10.1016/j.eswa.2009.12.006

Egrioglu, E., Aladag, C. H., Yolcu, U., Uslu, V. R., & Erilli, N. A. (2011). Fuzzy time series forecasting method based on Gustafson-Kessel fuzzy clustering. *Expert Systems with Applications*, *38*(8), 10355–10357. doi:10.1016/j.eswa.2011.02.052

Egrioglu, V., Bas, E., Aladag, C. H., & Yolcu, U. (2016). Probabilistic fuzzy time series method based on artificial neural network. *Am J Intell Syst*, *62*, 42–47.

Fawcett, T. (2018). *Practical machine learning for computer vision: Learn the techniques and tools needed to build computer vision applications with Python and OpenCV*. Packt Publishing Ltd.

Garg, B., & Garg, R. (2016). Enhanced accuracy of fuzzy time series model using ordered weighted aggregation. *Applied Soft Computing*, *48*, 265–280. doi:10.1016/j.asoc.2016.07.002

GargM.SaxenaC.SamantaD.DorrB. J. (2023). *LonXplain: Lonesomeness as a Consequence of Mental Disturbance in Reddit Posts*. doi:10.1007/978-3-031-35320-8_27

Géron, A. (2019). *Hands-on machine learning with Scikit-Learn, Keras, and TensorFlow: Concepts, tools, and techniques to build intelligent systems*. O'Reilly Media, Inc.

Ghosh, H., Chowdhury, S., & Prajneshu, S. (2016). An improved fuzzy time-series method of forecasting based on L-R fuzzy sets and its application. *Journal of Applied Statistics*, *43*(6), 1128–1139. doi:10.1080/02664763.2015.1092111

Goh, G., & Zhou, Y. (2019). Stock prediction using recurrent neural networks with convolutional feature extraction. In *2019 IEEE 16th International Conference on Machine Learning and Applications (ICMLA)* (pp. 1528-1533). IEEE.

Guha, A., Samanta, D., & Sengar, S. S. (2023). Computer Vision Based Automatic Margin Computation Model for Digital Document Images. *SN Computer Science*, *4*(3), 253. doi:10.100742979-023-01693-5

Gupta, K. K., & Kumar, S. (2019). A novel high-order fuzzy time series forecasting method based on probabilistic fuzzy sets. *Granul Comput*, *4*(4), 699–713. doi:10.100741066-019-00168-4

Gurunath, R., & Samanta, D. (2023). A New 3-Bit Hiding Covert Channel Algorithm for Public Data and Medical Data Security Using Format-Based Text Steganography. *Journal of Database Management*, *34*(2), 1–22. doi:10.4018/JDM.324076

Han, L., & Qi, Y. (2020). Deep learning for stock prediction: A comparative study. *Journal of Computational Science*, *44*, 101147.

Huang, T., & Huang, S. (2019). Predicting stock prices with a combined method of sentiment analysis and machine learning. *Applied Sciences (Basel, Switzerland)*, *9*(7), 1374.

Huarng, K. (2001). Heuristic models of fuzzy time series for forecasting. *Fuzzy Sets and Systems*, *123*(3), 369–386. doi:10.1016/S0165-0114(00)00093-2

Huarng, K., & Yu, T. H. K. (2006). Ratio-based lengths of intervals to improve fuzzy time series forecasting. *IEEE Transactions on Systems, Man, and Cybernetics. Part B, Cybernetics*, *36*(2), 328–340. doi:10.1109/TSMCB.2005.857093 PMID:16602593

Jain, A., Dangi, P., Samanta, D., Dutta, S., Bhattacharya, A., & Joseph, N. P. (2023). Creation of Bookshelf Using Autodesk 3ds Max: 3D Modelling and Rendering. In *2023 11th International Conference on Internet of Everything, Microwave Engineering, Communication and Networks (IEMECON)* (pp. 1–4). IEEE.

James, G., Witten, D., Hastie, T., & Tibshirani, R. (2017). *An introduction to statistical learning: with applications in R*. Springer.

Kharwal, A. (2022). *Stock Market Analysis Using Python*. Thecleverprogrammer. thecleverprogrammer.com/2022/07/12/stock-market-analysis-using-python.

Kuo, I. H., Horng, S. J., Kao, T. W., Lin, T. L., Lee, C. L., & Pan, Y. (2009). An improved method for forecasting enrollments based on fuzzy time series and particle swarm optimization. *Expert Systems with Applications*, *36*(3), 6108–6117. doi:10.1016/j.eswa.2008.07.043

Kuznetsov, M., & Kuznetsova, O. (2018). Using deep learning algorithms for stock price prediction. In *Proceedings of the 2018 12th International Conference on Computer Science and Information Technologies (CSIT)* (pp. 239-243). IEEE.

Macarty. (2021). *Quantitative Stock Price Analysis With Python, Pandas, NumPy Matplotlib and SciPy*. YouTube. www.youtube.com/watch?v=PkzVU7Klic0

Mondal, S., Pal, A. K., Islam, S. K. H., & Samanta, D. (2023). Objectionable Image Content Classification Using CNN-Based Semi-supervised Learning. *Advances in Smart Vehicular Technology, Transportation, Communication and Applications Proceedings of VTCA, 2022*, 311–320.

NeuralNine. (2022). *Technical Stock Analysis Made Easy in Python*. YouTube. www.youtube.com/watch?v=N9NqTp_D_bw

Podder, S. K., Samanta, D., Thomas, B., Dutta, S., & Bhattacharya, A. (2023). Impact of blended education system on outcome-based learning and sector skills development. In *2023 11th International Conference on Internet of Everything, Microwave Engineering, Communication and Networks (IEMECON)* (pp. 1–6). IEEE.

Qin, T., & Zhang, Y. (2020). Deep learning for stock price prediction using a long short-term memory network. *Mathematical Problems in Engineering*, *2020*, 1–10.

Raza, K., Amin, M. B., & Keshavjee, K. (2019). An evaluation of machine learning algorithms for stock market prediction. In *2019 IEEE 15th International Conference on e-Science (e-Science)* (pp. 118-127). IEEE.

Shah, V. (2018). Machine learning for financial prediction: experimentation with stock market prediction using various machine learning algorithms. In *Proceedings of the 2nd International Conference on Advances in Electronics, Computers and Communications* (pp. 51-56). ACM.

Yoo, J. S., Kim, D. H., & Jung, Y. J. (2018). Stock price prediction using a hybrid machine learning approach. *Journal of Computational and Applied Mathematics*, *330*, 1109–1118.

Chapter 10
Game Playing (2048) Using Deep Neural Networks

Narendra Kumar Rao Bangole
Mohan Babu University, India

R. B. Moulya
MB University, India

R. Pranthi
Mohan Babu University, India

Sreelekha Reddy
Mohan Babu University, India

R. Namratha
Mohan Babu University, India

ABSTRACT

A one-player game, 2048 is also known as stochastic puzzle. This fascinating and engaging game has gained widespread acclaim and drawn researchers to create gaming software. The game 2048 has evolved into an engaging and difficult platform for assessing the efficacy of machine learning techniques because of its simplicity and complexity. Convolutional neural networks were used to create some computer players, but they performed poorly. In this work, the authors create a 2048 agent based on the reinforcement learning method and neural networks. The authors want to outperform other neural-network-based competitors in terms of results. Additionally, cutting-edge software created using this methodology for 2048 achieves the best performance out of all learning-based algorithms.

DOI: 10.4018/978-1-6684-9809-5.ch010

INTRODUCTION

A 4 × 4 grid is used for the game 2048. It is simple to learn yet challenging to master. To get to a 2048 tile in the original Game 2048, move and merge the tiles on the board in accordance with the regulations. In the initial state, two tiles bearing the numbers 2 or 4 are randomly arranged. The player chooses one of four directions—up, right, down, or left—and all the tiles travel in that direction after that. A tile with the sum value is created when two identically numbered tiles collide, and the player receives the sum as their score. Newly formed tiles do not merge once more in the same move since the merger happens from the opposite side. Additionally, the player is not able to choose a route in which no tiles merge or travel. The game finishes when the player is not able to move any more tiles, which happens when a new tile arrives at random in a cell with the numbers 2 or 4.

In the 2048 game, a straightforward puzzle game, the player joins tiles with the same number to produce a tile with a greater number. Making the appropriate actions at the right moments will help you get to the 2048 tile, which is the game's goal. The software must include a reinforcement learning algorithm, a neural network architecture to calculate the probable reward for performing a particular action in a specific state, and a game environment simulation or emulator to give the agent a way to interact with and learn from other players in the 2048 game. The software must also have a user interface, which can either be a simple API for automated interaction or GUI for human players.

The software can learn to play the 2048 game optimally, maximizing the game score and win rate, by training the agent via reinforcement learning.(Shilun Li et al.) The agent may be educated on a lot of data, which enables it to gain knowledge from a variety of situations and gaming scenarios. An agent created using this method may be more effective and efficient than one created using conventional game-playing algorithms. In this work, the objective is to develop an agent that can master the game on its own and get a high score. The agent will be trained using a reinforcement learning algorithm, where it will be rewarded for actions that increase its score and penalized for those that decrease it. Here the agent will be trained by watching how the game is played, making decisions based on its policy, and being rewarded for acts that increase the score. The agent will be able to learn intricate patterns in the game and adapt to various game situations by the usage of deep neural networks. The work not only sheds light on how deep reinforcement learning can be used to gaming, but it also advances the discipline by offering a fresh approach to the game 2048.By using reinforcement learning we can increase efficiency also when compared with convolutional neural networks. By using convolutional neural networks that performance might be slow and not efficient. So this deep reinforcement learning algorithm plays a major role while the agent is playing games. This reinforcement learning is a sort of machine learning that focuses on instructing an agent to make decisions by rewarding or penalizing its activities. Reinforcement learning algorithms are used in artificial intelligence for various purposes like game playing where this learning is used to train agents and play games like chess, etc., and also this is mainly used in robotics, in controlling robots, allowing them to learn how to perform tasks and navigate their environment.

This reinforcement learning is used in autonomous vehicles and is applied in developing self-driving cars, allowing them to make decisions on their own and navigate roads and avoid obstacles. In addition to operating complex systems like power grids and water distribution networks, this algorithm also aids in system performance optimization and the reduction of energy usage. In these ways, the reinforcement learning algorithm is used in various domains in artificial intelligence. (Nathaniel G et al., Sutton R. S)

LITERATURE SURVEY

A literature survey of developing an agent to play the 2048 game using deep reinforcement learning algorithm would entail researching and reviewing previous studies and works in the field. Some key areas to consider in your literature survey are as follows:

Several studies have applied reinforcement learning to a variety of games, including chess, Go, and Atari games. These studies can shed light on how reinforcement learning can be applied to game play and the difficulties that come with training agents to play games. The use of deep neural networks in reinforcement learning has grown in popularity in recent years, several studies have shown that deep reinforcement learning can outperform traditional reinforcement learning methods. This research can help with the design and training of deep reinforcement learning agents. And also a few studies have used reinforcement learning to play the game 2048, and these studies can provide insight into how to design an agent specifically for this game as well as the challenges involved in training an agent to play 2048 effectively. It is critical to consider how to evaluate your agent's performance and compare it to that of other agents. Game-playing agents can be evaluated using a variety of metrics, including game score and game length.

Some of the studies include:

Taichung performed experiments and claimed that it works with three or more convolution layers excelled those with just two convolution layers in terms of performance.(Naoki K et al.)

They conducted a white box analysis of CNNs' internal workings in order to determine the causes of the performance. Their investigations include filter visualization in the first layers and network back-tracking for a few particular game stages. For the game 2048, they published a number of findings into the inner workings of CNNs.

Allik K. Used AlphaGo Zero(AGZ) solution,applied it for 2048. They trained the neural network that takes the 2048 game state s as inputs and outputs with the use of Monte-Carlo tree Search, used Python Programming language and Keras neural network framework. (David, O.E et al.)

Szubert recently used TD learning and n-tuple networks to successfully play the game 2048. They were able to achieve better results by first altering the n-tuple networks. However, they observed a condition where large tiles, like 32768-tiles, are still difficult for TD learning-based programmes to cover (the tiles with value 32768). To improve performance, they recommended a cutting-edge teaching technique called multi-stage TD learning, especially for the top scores and the ratio of 32768-tiles attained. After implementing shallow expectimax search, the 2048 programme can reach 32768 tiles with a likelihood of 10.9%, as well as the highest score of 605752 and the average score of 328946.(Marcin Szubert et al.)

Chabin T. obtained a fitness value, a generic Linear Genetic Programming open-source tool used to directly write a Java class, which is then corrected, compiled within the provided framework, and run. (Silver D et al.)

Here,Samir M. Georgwiese has used Deep Q-Learning algorithm to train datasets and play 2048 game, used Tensorflow framework, TensorBoard to monitor their Network training.(Boris, T et al.)

Varun kaundinya [6] proposed a method for mastering the game of 2048 using the principles of re-inforcement learning. The strategy is based on the most well-known reinforcement learning algorithms, State Action Reward State Action (SARSA) and Q learning. Neural networks are used in the design as a function approximation technique. The reward function is the brain of any reinforcement learning agent, much like it is in most deep Q learning models. To help the model learn the best playing techniques, they created reward functions. They made an effort to offer a solution to the problem of 2048's built-in randomness. (Hoang, L.N)According to this method, which is based on prioritized experience replay, the model is trained to learn the optimum way to play a game from the experiences amassed. However, using this strategy, we maximized the tile value of 512. (Varun K et al., Kiminori et al.)

REQUIREMENTS SPECIFICATION

Functional Requirements

Functional requirements are the particular characteristics and functions that a software system must have in order to achieve its intended goals. They lay out the system's intended functions and offer precise, quantifiable objectives for the software development process.

Examples of Functional Requirements

Game Environment: A simulation or emulation of 2048 game should be offered by the software, acting both the agents environment and a source of learning for it.

Reinforcement Learning Algorithm: For training the agent to play the game based on the observed rewards for taking different actions, the programme should include a RL algorithm.

Neural Network Architecture: A neural network architecture should be included in the software to estimate the expected reward for performing a specific action in a specific state.

Training Data: To effectively train the agent, the software should be able to generate or use training data.

Game Play: The software should allow the agent to play the 2048 game and make moves based on the policies it has learned.

User Interface: To interact with the agent and play the game, the software should provide a user interface, which could include a GUI for human players or a simple API for programmatic interaction.

Non-Functional Requirements

These are requirements or characteristics, not specific features, that the software must have. Instead of specifying what the system must accomplish, they describe how it must act.

They basically deal with issues like Performance, Reliability, Security, Maintainability, Scalability and Compatibility.

Examples of Non-Functional Requirements

Performance: The game play should be quick and effective, with a minimum acceptable game score and victory percentage provided by the software.

Reliability: The programme must be dependable and able to run continuously without crashing or making mistakes.

Usability: The programme should have a user-friendly interface, clear game play instructions, and be simple to use and comprehend.

Security: Sensitive information, such as training data and learnt policies, should be protected by the software's security measures.

Scalability: If the amount of training data or the complexity of the reinforcement learning algorithm increase, the software should be scalable and capable of handling the change.

Compatibility: The software needs to work with a variety of hardware setups and operating systems.

IMPLEMENTATION AND ALGORITHM

A feedback-based machine learning technique called reinforcement learning teaches an agent how to react in a certain environment by allowing it to take actions and then observe what happens as a result. Each positive activity results in positive feedback for the agent, and each negative action results in negative feedback or a punishment. Reward learning, as opposed to supervised learning, employs feedback to autonomously direct the agent's learning. The agent can only learn by doing as there is no labeled data. In a particular class of problems, such as those in gaming, robotics, and other long-term efforts, RL provides a solution as in Figure-1. The agent investigates and engages with the environment by itself. An agent's main objective in reinforcement learning is to maximize rewards in order to perform better. Trial and error is how the agent learns, and with experience it becomes more adept at completing the task. Since an intelligent agent (computer programme) engages with the environment and learns to react within it, "reinforcement learning" is classified as "a form of machine learning method" in this way. A robotic dog learning to move his arms is an example of reinforcement learning in action.

Figure 1. Reinforcement learning

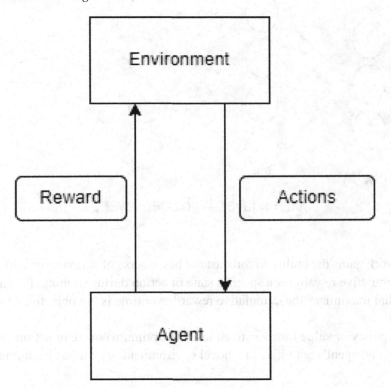

Reinforcement Learning Characteristics

- In real life, the agent is neither informed of the environment nor the necessary activities.
- It is built on the hit-and-trial principle.
- In response to feedback from the previous action, the agent takes the subsequent action and modifies its states.
- The agent may be rewarded later.
- To maximise rewards, the agent must explore the stochastic environment.

Neural Network Model

- Reinforcement learning and neural networks are two potent machine learning approaches that are combined in a neural network model as in Figure-2
- In this kind of model, an agent's policy or value function in a context of reinforcement learning is represented by a neural network. The value function calculates the predicted cumulative reward for a specific condition or action, while the policy function converts an agent's observations into actions.

Figure 2. NN model

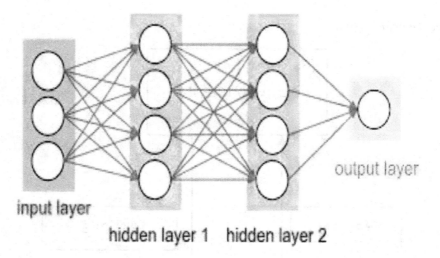

The neural network gains the ability to forecast the best course of action to take in various situations or the predicted cumulative reward for a specific state or action during training. Finding the best policy or value function that maximizes the cumulative reward over time is the objective of the reinforcement learning algorithm.

Using its learnt policy or value function to choose the optimum course of action, the neural network can be used to direct an agent's activities in a novel environment once it has been trained.

Robotics, gaming, and autonomous vehicles are just a few examples of the many uses of reinforcement learning using neural network models. They can perform better than conventional rule-based or manually created models in many tasks and have been proved to be efficient at learning complex rules and value functions.

RELU Activation Function

Deep neural networks and multi-layer neural networks both use the non-linear activation function called RELU. This function can increase the training speed of deep neural networks. It can be represented as,

$$RELU\left(x\right) = \begin{cases} 0 \; if \; x < 0 \\ x \; if \; x >= 0 \end{cases}$$

RMSprop Optimizer

Similar to the gradient descent approach, the RMSprop optimizer uses momentum. The RMSprop optimizer controls the vertical oscillations. As a result, we can speed up conversion and boost learning rate, allowing the algorithm to take larger horizontal leaps.

METHODOLOGY

The "Add Random Tile" method makes the game's random element readily clear as we choose a random square to add the tile to and a random value for the tile as in Figure-3.

Figure 3. Flowchart of gameplay

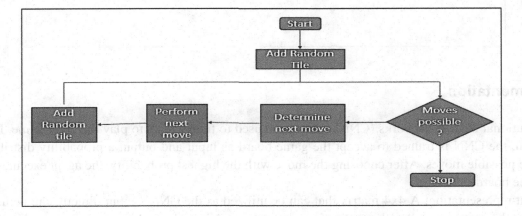

Making a decision for the "Determine Next Move" phase is the challenge. This is the strategy we use to participate in the game as in Figure-4.

Figure 4. Overflow

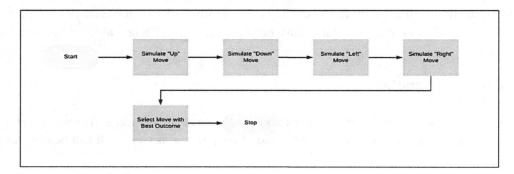

All that is need to do is to simulate every conceivable move, find the one that yields the best outcomes, and apply that. In order to replicate any move and produce a score depending on the results, we have streamlined the algorithm. There are two steps to this process. First, the move is tested to see if it is even feasible; if it is not, the move is abandoned early with a score of "0" as in Figure-5. The real algorithm, which will evaluate how effective the move is, will be used if the move is technically possible:

Figure 5. Simulating the move

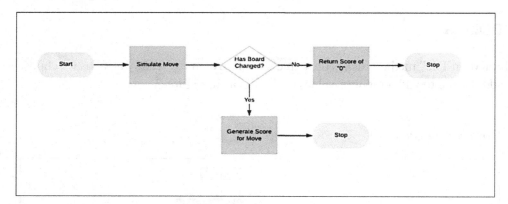

Implementation

Convolutional Neural Networks (CNNs) have been used to train agents to play the 2048 game. In this situation, the CNN is trained to accept the game board as input and output a probability distribution over the possible moves. After choosing the move with the highest probability, the agent executes it on the game board.

Input representation: A 4x4 matrix that can be utilized as the CNN's input directly can be used to represent the game board. Another option is to preprocess the input by making each tile value into a one-hot vector, which creates a 4x4x12 tensor (because the highest tile value in the game is $2^{11} = 2048$).

Convolutional layers: The CNN can have one or more convolutional layers, which are trained to take input's spatial information and extract them. Little filters (such as 3x3 or 5x5) are frequently used in these layers, which can be followed by non-linear activation techniques like ReLU.

Pooling layers: By using pooling layers, the spatial dimensions of the feature maps produced by the convolutional layers can be reduced. Max pooling and average pooling are two popular types of pooling. Convolutional and pooling layer output can be flattened and sent through one or more fully-connected layers, which train to map the extracted features to the output probabilities.

Loss function: Using a reinforcement learning strategy, the model is trained to minimize a loss function. The CNN model's weights are adjusted to minimize the loss function as new game boards and target moves are provided to it during training. After training, the model can be used to play the game by deciding which move has the highest probability on a certain game board.

RESULTS

When the get 2048 tile on moving other numbered tiles then the game is completed as in Figure-6. The graph of various game plays with different outcomes is shown in Figure 7, for the single game graph of moves between agent and player is shown in Figure 8.

Figure 6. Reached max tile

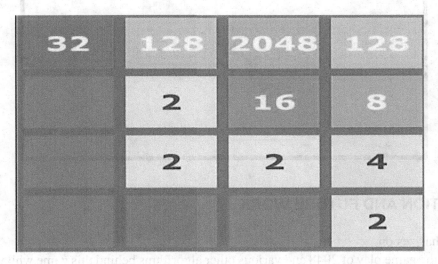

Score graph is a visual representation of the performance of a proposed method or model. It typically shows the scores obtained by the method at different levels of evaluation or experimentation. Score graphs can be used in several ways to understand the performance of the model.

Score graph in Figure 8 shows the performance of the model increases with iterations.

Figure 7. Scores graph

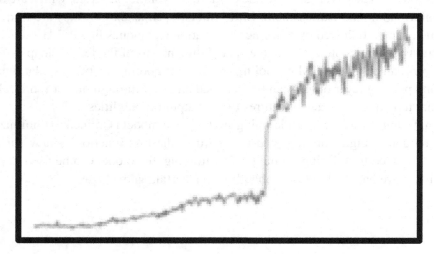

Figure 8. Score graph

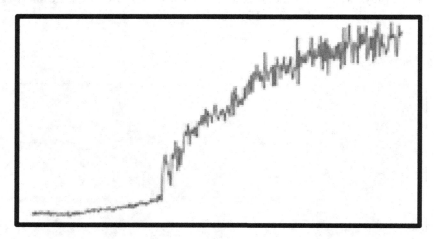

CONTRIBUTION AND FUTURE WORK

The work emphasizes on

Discussing the game play of 2048 and various other algorithms behind this game while playing with humans.

Learn the process done in reinforcement learning and used it in this work.

Observe different kinds of output while using different algorithms like Convolutional Neural Network(CNN) and other whose output were less efficient than RL .

Implemented the efficient 2048 simulator in Python language.

A neural network was trained to play 2048 using a multiprocess reinforcement learning pipeline. Reinforcement learning with High Performance was used to deploy the game.

Used the information to train the residual network to play 2048 with a success rate of over 90% completing the 2048 tile.

The system mostly achieved the objectives, succeeded in developing an agent to play game 2048 with maximum efficiency by using Deep reinforcement learning.

CONCLUSION

In conclusion, creating an agent to play the game 2048 using deep reinforcement learning is an exciting and difficult task in the field of artificial intelligence. We hope to demonstrate the feasibility of using reinforcement learning to train an agent to play 2048 and achieve a high score through the research. The research builds on previous research in the field by employing deep neural networks to learn complex patterns in the game and make informed decisions. The findings of the work show that deep reinforcement learning can be an effective method for teaching agents to play 2048 and achieve high scores, shedding new light on the application of reinforcement learning to game play.

Overall, the work has significant implications for the field of artificial intelligence and adds to the growing body of research on reinforcement learning. We hope to demonstrate the potential of this approach for a wide range of tasks and domains by training an agent to play 2048 using Deep reinforcement learning, and to inspire future research in this area.

REFERENCES

2048 Game. (2016). *2048 game*. https://gabrielecirulli.github.io/2048/

Boris, T. & Goran, S. (2016). Evolving Neural Network to Play Game2048. *Proc. 24th Telecommunications forum (TELFOR 2016)*. IEEE.

David, O. E., Netanyahu, N. S., & Wolf, L. (2016). DeepChess: End-to- End Deep Neural Network for Automatic Learning in Chess. *International Conference on Artificial Neural Networks and Machine Learn- ing (ICANN 2016)*, (pp.88-96). Springer.

Hoang, L. N. (2014). The addictive mathematics of the 2048 tile game. *Science for All*. http://www. science4all.org/article/2048-game/

Kondo, N., & Matsuzaki, K. (2019, April). Playing Game 2048 with Deep Convolutional Neural Networks Trained by Supervised Learning. *Journal of Information Processing*, *27*(0), 340–347. doi:10.2197/ipsjjip.27.340

Li, S., & Peng, V. (2018). Playing 2048 With Reinforcement Learning. *Conference on Neural Information Processing Systems(NeurIPS)*. Springer.

Szubert, M. & Jaskowski, W. (2014). Mathematical Analysis of 2048. *The Game 7*. IEEE.

Matsuzaki, K. (2016). *Systematic selection of N-tuple networks with consideration of interinfluence for game 2048*. TAAI. IEEE.

G., N., Tao, S., & Wu, K. (2020). *What's in a Game: Solving 2048 with Reinforcement Learning*. Stanford University.

Stack Exchange. (2017). Probability that random moves in the game 2048 will win. *Stack Exchange*. https://math.stackexchange.com/questions/727076/probability-that-randommoves-in-the-game-2048-will-win

Silver, D., Schrittwieser, J., Simonyan, K., Antonoglou, L., Huang, A., Guez, A., Hubert, T., Baker, L., Lai, M., Bolton, A., Chen, Y., Lillicrap, T., Hui, F., Sifre, L., van den Driessche, G., Graepel, T., & Hassabis, D. (2017). Mastering the game of Go without human knowledge. *Nature*, *550*(7676), 354–359. doi:10.1038/nature24270 PMID:29052630

Sutton, R. S., & Barto, A. G. (1998). *Reinforcement Learning: An Introduction*. MIT press.

Szubert, M., & Jaskowski, W. (2014). Temporal difference learning of N-tuple networks for the game 2048. *Conference on Computational Intelligence and Games*. IEEE. 10.1109/CIG.2014.6932907

Varun, K., & Vanamala, C. K., Jain, S., & Saligram, S. (2018). Game Playing Agent for 2048 using Deep Reinforcement Learning, NCICCNDA 2018. *AIJR Proceedings 1*, (pp. 363-370). Research gate.

Chapter 11
Use Case Modeling for Industrial Human Resource Management Practices

Suplab Kanti Podder

Dayananda Sagar Institutions, India

ABSTRACT

Human resource management practices bring all the industrial experts under one umbrella and encourages them to work for common organizational goals. Industrial operations are the combination of technology, innovation, arts, management, and commerce. Industrial HRM practices are changing from time to time with consideration of changing business perspectives, technology, and competition. The principal motive of presenting the research initiative was to identify the changing scenario of industrial HRM practices over the last two decades that represented the use case modeling for the next generation entrepreneurs. The research outcomes are well connected to address the industrial HR issues in the area of engineering, data mining, and analysis for the development of object-oriented business operations.

INTRODUCTION

Industrial human resource management is the concept that developed time to time with reference to changing scenario of corporate world. The HRM practices are the dynamic in nature that responses outcome-based business operations in the competitive market. Use case modelling opens up the new vistas for industrial practices and advantages for competitive environment (Janaka S. and Xu Zhang, 2018)). The present study describes the effective use case modelling for futuristic industrial human resource management practices. The research outcomes of effective use case modelling will create the road map for successful entrepreneurs. The following Fig. 1 shows the conceptual framework related to Industrial Human Resource Management Practices.

DOI: 10.4018/978-1-6684-9809-5.ch011

Figure 1. The conceptual framework related to industrial human resource management practices

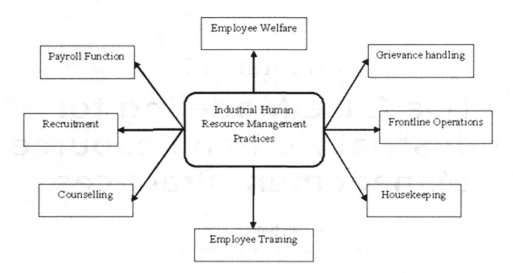

The important industrial human resource management practices include payroll functions, recruitment of the desired candidates, counselling of employees, providing employee welfare, employee training, grievance handling, frontline operations and housekeeping functions. Performing of HRM practices is the art that require cooperation and expert involvement to experience best outcomes (Lee Dyer & Todd Reeves (1995)). Modern organizations demand challenging work environment that develops the employees' performance ability and prepare for future competition. Industrial human resource management department plays important role for procuring and developing human resource skills into the global standards so that the industry can enjoy the competitive advantages (Charbel J., and Fernando Almada (2019)).

Related Works

Frederick L., and Tara S. Behrend (2020) describe the trends of modern industrial human resource management functions that facilitates the business growth and advantages over competitors. David and Kenneth (2019) examine the use case modelling in human resource practices. They have identified the major issues of traditional HRM functions in the competitive world that need to be upgraded with information system. Janaka S. and Xu Zhang (2018) elaborate the green human resource practices in the organization that facilitates for the business ecosystem and reduction of carbon footprint. Naveen and Prabhudesai (2021) describe the impact of use case modelling on industrial functioning. They identified the positive impact of use case modelling that ensure the better working environment and improvement of work efficiency.

Objectives and the Scope the Research

With the consideration of time, space and situation of industrial operations, the researcher listed the principal objectives of identifying common industrial human resource management practices, to find out the elements of use case modeling for industrial human resource management practices, and to analyse the impact of Use Case Modeling on Industrial Human Resource Management Practices. The present study is the opinion-based research outcomes that represents the effective guidelines for futuristics business operations with the help of smart human resource management decisions.

Analysis Regarding the Common Industrial Human Resource Management Practices

The respondents of the present research study revealed the Common Industrial Human Resource Management Practices. The following table includes the most applicable human resource management practices in the services and manufacturing industries.

Table 1. presents the common industrial human resource management practices

SL. No.	Industrial HRM Practices	Frequency of Occurrence in Percentage
1	Payroll Function	25
2	Recruitment	19
3	Counseling	5
4	Welfare Function	12
5	Employee Training	10
6	Grievance handling	4
7	Frontline Operations	11
8	Housekeeping	8

[Table 1 shows the common Industrial Human Resource Management Practices]

The above table demonstrates the respondent's opinion regarding the most common human resource management practices in the corporate world. The HRM practices are divided into two categories such as regular activities and infrequent activities. The following Fig. 2 shows the common Industrial Human Resource Management Practices.

According to the experts' opinion, the most frequent (25%) of the respondents believe that payroll function is the important HRM practice in industry that ensure the payment of salary and wages of the employees daily or monthly bases. Recruitment is another important HRM practice that facilitates of identifying suitable candidates, conduct interview and designate the right job role in the industry. Counselling is the HRM practice that facilitates of understanding the employees' problems and solve the issues with professional counsellors. In the modern era, organizations are practicing employee welfare functions that ensure the extra benefits like transportation facility, canteen facility and other recreational facilities. Training and development are the important HRM practice that ensure the update of employees' present knowledge and skills and prepare for future challenges. Similarly, other important HRM practices are grievance handling, frontline operations and housekeeping functions.

Figure 2. The common industrial human resource management practices

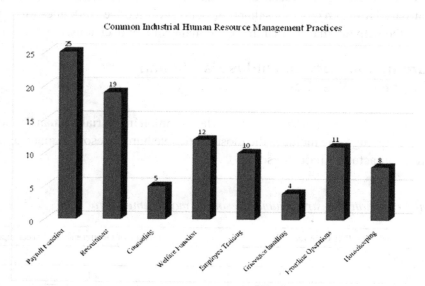

Elements of Use Case Modeling for Industrial Human Resource Management Practices

Use Case Modeling is the smart design of HRM practices that facilitates for defending the industry form domestic and international competition and challenges of environmental changes. Various elements of Use Case Modeling include HR Analytics, Re-engineering work processes, Hybrid Work Model, Upskilling, Human Resource Outsourcing, Agile HR, Digital Transformation, and Gamification. The following Fig. 3 shows the elements of Use Case Modeling for Industrial Human Resource Management Practices.

HR analytics is the mechanism for understanding the critical issues of the employees and solve the same with dynamic HRM skills (Janet D, and Geoffrey White (2019)). This is an important element of use case modeling in industrial HRM practices that initiate for solving industrial problems in the early stage. In the first growing business model and environment, re-engineering work process is essential to upgrade the workforce and work situation (Verma Prikshat, and Ashish Malik (2022)). Re-engineering work processes leads to innovation and invention for increasing organizational competitiveness. Hybrid Work Model is the new trend of workplace status that gives more freedom to the employees for performance from office or home. Software industries and IT enable services industries are taking advantages of hybrid work model and experiences of more productivity with minimum maintenance cost in work place (David E. Guest, and Annet H. (2021)). Upskilling is the HRM practice that improves the existing employees' knowledge and skills and helps to prepare for future business challenges (Neha Gahlawat, Subhash C. Kundu (2019)). Human Resource Outsourcing is the method of utilizing skills and knowledge of outside experts as per the requirements of organization to perform the routine HRM functions (Xiaowei Y., and Shumin Yan (2021)). Agile HR practices for adjusting the changing working environment that the employees can adjust very first and ensure the work efficiency (Monowar M., and Sudhir Saha (2020)). Digital Transformation using human resource information system for better performance, effective record keeping, more accuracy of transactions. Gamification is the process of applying HRM functions in the organization with few games or play and facilities better understanding of work environment and its nature (Rutger Blom, and Bart Voorn (2019)). Employees enjoy the work environment with the practice of gamification.

Figure 3. The elements of use case modeling for industrial human resource management practices

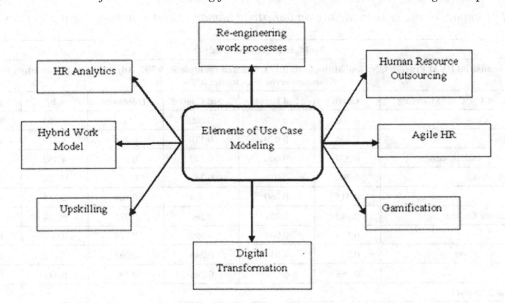

Analysis Regarding the Impact of Use Case Modeling on Industrial Human Resource Management Practices

The researcher summarised the multiple regression analysis with the consideration of responses from experts in the HRM department of various industrial operations.

The analysis related to find out the extent of influence of causal factors on effect factors that influence outsourcing of HR functions in Indian service organizations. The multiple regression analysis includes the adjusted square multiple R value, ANOVA test report and t-test value.

The adjusted square multiple R value indicates the fit for the analysis regarding the impact of Use Case Modeling on Industrial Human Resource Management Practices.

The individual t-test value indicates the degree of impact of individual independent variable on individual Industrial Human Resource Management Practice. The positive value represents the positive impact and the negative value indicate the negative impact of independent variable on dependent variable. The ANOVA test result indicates the impact of all the independent variables together on dependent variable (Industrial Human Resource Management Practices). The positive value represents the positive impact and the negative results indicates the negative impact of Use Case Modeling on Industrial Human Resource Management Practices.

The principal motive the present research study considers the positive impact of use case modeling towards the industrial implementation of effective human resource management practices. In the competitive world, the organizations can enjoy the maximum advantages of efficient human resource through effective human resource practices. The table no. 2 describes the brief about multiple regression analysis summary with individual t-test value and ANOVA test results.

Table 2. The impact of use case modeling on industrial human resource management practices

Multiple Regression Analysis						
Dep Var: Industrial HRM Practices, N: 400, Multiple R: 0.773, Squared multiple R: 0.597, Adjusted squared multiple R: 0.589, Standard error of estimate: 0.956						
Elements of Use Case Modeling	Coeff	Std Error	Std Coeff	Tolerance	t	Sig. p
Constant	4.302	0.609	0.000	-	7.064	0.075
HR Analytics	0.454	0.029	0.116	0.256	8.729	0.223
Re-engineering work processes	0.327	0.066	0.307	0.271	4.982	0.071
Hybrid Work Model	0.766	0.074	0.739	0.201	10.332	0.083
Upskilling	0.314	0.060	0.304	0.304	5.225	0.112
Human Resource Outsourcing	0.342	0.054	0.386	0.275	6.314	0.213
Agile HR	0.515	0.049	0.599	0.314	10.468	0.321
Digital Transformation	0.275	0.044	0.248	0.263	3.968	0.064
Gamification	0.368	0.057	0.298	0.482	6.441	0.085
Significant at 0.05 level						
Analysis of Variance (ANOVA)						
Source	Sum-of-Squares		df	Mean-Square	F-ratio	Sig. p
Regression	530.136		8	66.267	82.451	0.185
Residual	357.624		391	0.915		
Significant at 0.05 level						

[Table No. 2 shows the Impact of Use Case Modeling on Industrial Human Resource Management Practices]

Hypothesis Formulation

H_{01}: There is no significant level of difficulties of implementing the Use Case Modeling on Industrial Human Resource Management Practices.

Mathematically, H_{01}: [the level of difficulties of implementing the Use Case Modeling on Industrial Human Resource Management Practices] = 0

Hypothesis Testing

The result of the above table no. 2 indicates the ANOVA test results with F-ratio is 82.451 and the Significant p value is 0.185 which is more than 0.05 at the 5% level of significance.

The individual sig. p value 0.223, 0.071, 0.083, 0.112, 0.213, 0.321, 0.064. and 0.085 which are more than 0.05. So, the null hypothesis is not rejected that indicates there is no significant level of diffculties of implementing the Use Case Modeling on Industrial Human Resource Management Practices. All the elements of use case modeling can be used to Industrial Human Resource Management Practices effectively and experiences of better performance and work efficiency.

Results and Discussion

The results of the present study include the positive impact of Use Case Modeling on Industrial Human Resource Management Practices. While considering the F-ration of ANOVA test report (82.451) that indicates the regression model is valid and Sig. p value is 0.185 which is grater than the 0.05 at the 5% level of significance.

Independently, HR Analytics has positive impact on Industrial HRM Practices and the result of t-test value is 8.729. It indicates, there is high degree of impact of HR Analytics on Industrial HRM Practices. Re-engineering work process has positive impact on Industrial HRM Practices and the result of t-test value is 4.982. It indicates, there is high degree of impact of HR Analytics on Industrial HRM Practices.

Hybrid Work Model has positive impact on Industrial HRM Practices and the result of t-test value is 10.332. It indicates, there is high degree of impact of HR Analytics on Industrial HRM Practices.

Upskilling has positive impact on Industrial HRM Practices and the result of t-test value is 5.225. It indicates, there is high degree of impact of HR Analytics on Industrial HRM Practices.

Human Resource Outsourcing has positive impact on Industrial HRM Practices and the result of t-test value is 6.314. It indicates, there is high degree of impact of HR Analytics on Industrial HRM Practices.

Agile HR has positive impact on Industrial HRM Practices and the result of t-test value is 10.468. It indicates, there is high degree of impact of HR Analytics on Industrial HRM Practices.

Digital Transformation has positive impact on Industrial HRM Practices and the result of t-test value is 3.968. It indicates, there is high degree of impact of HR Analytics on Industrial HRM Practices.

Gamification has positive impact on Industrial HRM Practices and the result of t-test value is 6.441. It indicates, there is high degree of impact of HR Analytics on Industrial HRM Practices.

With the considering of all the above results related to multiple regression analysis, t-test results and ANOVA test results indicates the high degree of positive impact of Use Case Modeling on Industrial Human Resource Management Practices.

Challenges of Use Case Modeling for Industrial Human Resource Management Practices

Implementing Use Case Modeling for Industrial Human Resource Management Practices is not so simple while the HRM department committed to performing existing functions with traditional methods and workforce.

(i) Resistance to Change: The HRM department will face the restrictions from the existing workforce to upgrade the technology and implementing use case modeling in work place (Neha Gahlawat, Subhash C. Kundu (2019)). They are not ready to accept the new methods of working situation that leads to decrease productivity.

(ii)   Initial Investment Cost: Designing and preparation of use case modeling are expensive in the initial stage that facilities for the long run. Most of the organization may not show interest to disturb the existing technology, methods or employees' comfort (Klaske N. Veth, Hubert P. L. (2019)).

(iii) Upgradation of Technology: Designing and implementing of Use Case Modeling are the continuous process and need to change time to time as per industrial requirements and corporate demand (Nick Chandler (2018)). All the industrial HRM practices are not so flexible and permitted for regular changes of Use Case Modeling system.

(iv)   Maintenance of Industrial Relations: Use Case Modeling demands various elements and industrial collaborations with relevant industries (Anastasia A. Katou (2019)). While collaborate with other organizations, the HRM department need to build relationship and continue the relationship for long time (Thomas N. Garavan (2019)). The changing business environment that demands new categories of elements leads to identify new vendors and discontinue the business relations with the existing vendors.

Suggestions and Conclusion

Use case modeling is the revolutionary initiative for modern Industrial operations especially for Human Resource Management Practices. The researcher observed the research gap while reviewing several existing research articles and publications. During the field study and observation of experts' opinion, different issues were identified and the data analysis reflected the same.

(i)   Systematic Training and Development of existing workforce: All the employees need to be experienced of systematic training for knowledge upgradation and the skills development (Shatha M. Obeidat (2020)). Once the complete workforces are competent and prepared for accepting the changes, the implementation of Use Case Modeling become easier and more comfortable for everybody (Susan Corby, Hamish Mathieson (2018)).

(ii) Technology Adoption and Implementation: Use case modeling impose the adoption and implementation of technology that facilitates to prepare for future challenges. Industrial HRM practices need to be supporting for necessary updating of technology time to time.

(iii) Green HRM Practices: Green HRM practices encourage for implementing the concept of reuse, recycle and reduce of carbon footprint in the organization (Anastasia A. Katou (2021)). All the employees should play the supportive role for implementing green HRM practices.

(iv) Continuous Improvement System: The use case modeling helps to improve the HRM functions into the efficient outcomes in the organization.

(v)   Support towards Sustainable Environment: The principal motive the implementing the use case modeling for HRM practices is to support towards the development of sustainable environment (Frederick L., and Tara S. Behrend (2020)). All the organization especially HRM department should conduct awareness programme on sustainable environment and its positive impact on society.

Future Scope of the Research Study

The research study was the initiatives of identifying the extent of impact of use case modeling on industrial human resource management practices that discovered the diverse area of knowledge and experiences. The principal outcomes of the research initiative open up new vistas for future research work in the area of industrial support system, continuous workforce efficiency, sustainable environment, quality control etc.

REFERENCES

Blom, R., & Voorn, B. (2019). HRM autonomy, integration and performance in government agencies: Tests of necessity and sufficiency. *Public Management Review*, *19*(1), 167–178.

Chandler, N. (2018). A Symbiotic Relationship: HR and Organizational Culture. *Organizational Behaviour and Human Resource Management*, *10*(1), 1–22. doi:10.1007/978-3-319-66864-2_1

Corby, S., & Mathieson, H. (2018). The National Health Service and the limits to flexibility. *Public Policy and Administration*, *12*(4), 60–72. doi:10.1177/095207679701200405

Dyer, L., & Reeves, T. (1995). Human resource strategies and firm performance: What do we know and where do we need to go? *International Journal of Human Resource Management*, *6*(3), 656–670. doi:10.1080/09585199500000041

Frederick, L., & Tara, S. (2020). Big Data in Industrial-Organizational Psychology and Human Resource Management: Forward Progress for Organizational Research and Practice. *Annual Review of Organizational Psychology and Organizational Behavior*, *7*(1), 505–533. doi:10.1146/annurev-orgpsych-032117-104553

Gahlawat, N., & Kundu, S. C. (2019). Participatory HRM and firm performance, Employee Relations. *International Journal (Toronto, Ont.)*, *41*(5), 1098–1119.

Garavan, T. N. (2019). A Strategic Perspective on Human Resource Development. *Advances in Developing Human Resources*, *9*(1), 11–30. doi:10.1177/1523422306294492

Guest, D. & Annet, H. (2021). Human Resource Management's Contribution to Healthy Healthcare, Integrating the Organization of Health Services. *Worker Wellbeing and Quality of Care*, *15*(2), 109–123.

Jabbour, C., & Almada, F. (2019). Relationships between human resource dimensions and environmental management in companies: Proposal of a model. *Journal of Cleaner Production*, *16*(1), 51–58. doi:10.1016/j.jclepro.2006.07.025

Janaka, S., & Zhang, X. (2018). Green human resource management: A proposed model in the context of Sri Lanka's tourism industry. *Journal of Cleaner Production*, *28*(3), 542–555.

Janet,, D, & White, G. (2019). Between hard and soft HRM: Human resource management in the construction industry. *Construction Management and Economics*, *14*(5), 405–416.

Katou, A. A. (2019). Human Resource Management and Performance in the Hospitality Industry. *Project Management*, *12*(4), 1980–1999.

Katou, A. A. (2021). Human Resource Management and Performance in the Hospitality Industry. *International Tourism and Hospitality in the Digital Age*, *13*(4), 1–20.

Mahmood, M., & Saha, S. (2020). HRM in Bangladesh: Past, Present and Future. *SA Journal of Human Resource Management*, *9*(2), 314–321.

Obeidat, S. M. (2020). The link between e-HRM use and HRM effectiveness: An empirical study. *Personnel Review*, *45*(6), 1281–1301. doi:10.1108/PR-04-2015-0111

Prikshat, V., & Malik, A. (2022). AI-augmented HRM: Antecedents, assimilation and multilevel consequences. *Human Resource Management Review*, *33*(1), 213–219.

Veth, K. N., Korzilius, H. P. L. M., Van der Heijden, B. I. J. M., Emans, B. J. M., & De Lange, A. H. (2019). Which HRM practices enhance employee outcomes at work across the life-span? *International Journal of Human Resource Management*, *21*(3), 1–32. doi:10.1080/09585192.2017.1340322

Yang, X., & Yan, S. (2021). Review and Prospects of Enterprise Human Resource Management Effectiveness: Bibliometric Analysis Based on Chinese-Language and English-Language Journals. *Sustainability*, *14*(2), 78–89.

Chapter 12
Software Development With UML Modelling and Software Testing Techniques

Ritwika Das Gupta

CHRIST University (Deemed), India

ABSTRACT

This chapter focuses on software development principles and discusses each principle thoroughly with diagrammatic representation. It also includes the definition of UML (unified modeling language) modelling with an explanation regarding how UML modelling takes place and a detailed example. It also focuses on software testing methods, with each method definition and diagrams well explained. A simple case study situation is taken to discuss the example of UML model. This chapter's main objective is to focus on all key points of software development testing and model design techniques precisely.

INTRODUCTION

A collection of modules of code is called software. It contains codes- which are set of instructions written by developers in computer language. Programs and its documentations which includes design model, requirements and testing. Software engineering is a branch of engineering used to build software using scientific definitions and techniques and using properly designed code (Almstrum, V.L. et. al., 2001). The result of this engineering is a reliable and effective software product. This research is based on the life cycle of software development and its testing Techniques. It also shows modelling use cases through UML with proper case driven examples. Each concept is described with proper examples and diagrams (Althar, R. R. et. al.,2023)(Asklund, U. et. al.,2003).

DOI: 10.4018/978-1-6684-9809-5.ch012

SOFTWARE DEVELOPMENT LIFE CYCLE (SDLC)

The steps to create software are diagrammatically represented as software life cycle. It is a mapping of various processes that a software building goes through (Benediktsson, O et. al.,2000). These are the following SDLC stages: Shown in Figure 1.

Figure 1. Software Development Life Cycle (SDLC)

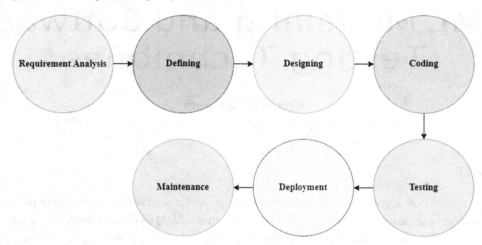

Requirement Analysis: In this stage the analyst conducts a meeting to understand the type of software to be used, who is the end user, aim of the product and need for the product. After knowing the details of the product, the team moves to the next stage (Budgen, D. et. al.,2005).

Example: If a client wants a product concerning money transaction. The nature of the transaction, target audience, the currency, features etc. all of it needs to be known before proceeding further.

Defining: Once the analysis is done, these requirements need to be documented thoroughly. This is done in a document called SRS (Software Requirement Specification).

Designing: In this stage based on the previous stages, the software model's design is proposed. This design includes user interface, user experience, database design structures of the software (Cunaku, E. et. al.,2023).

Development: In this stage the actual coding of the software begins. Here the programmers code the software based on coding guidelines set by the management by using interpreter, compilers, and debuggers.

Testing: After the software is developed, the testing stage begins where the entire product is tested against its requirement collected during the requirement gathering. This stage includes unit testing, acceptance testing, system testing, integration testing.

Deployment: Once the testing is done, the software is now deployed based on further assessment.

Maintenance: Once the software is deployed it needs to be maintained so that it can be compatible with updates and changes in future (Dangi, P. et. al.,2023).

MODELING REQUIREMENTS WITH USE CASES

Unified Modeling Language (UML) is a graphical language for visualizing, specifying and documenting the artifact of a software. The UML modelling can be used to show the database classes, attributes, and relationships.

UML Database Modeling: Classes: Classes are the entity of data modelling, and it has various attributes which describe it. These attributes can be primary and foreign keys. Shown in Figure 2.

Figure 2. Class representation

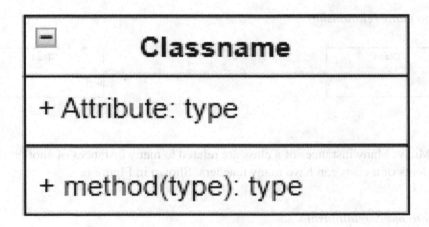

The attributes can be of these types: public (+), protected (#), private (-)

UML Database Modeling: Relationship: The relationship between one class to another helps in creating the UML data Model.

Types of Relationships:

1) One to one- one instance of a class is related to one instance of another class. Example: one student can only have one roll number in a university. Shown in Figure 3.

Figure 3. One to one relationship

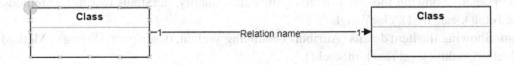

2) Many to One- whenever we create many instances of the class it should be related to one instance of another class. Example: many students can have one subject in a university. Shown in Figure 4.

Figure 4. Many to one relationship

3) One to Many: One instance of a class is related to many instances of another class. Example: one student can be enrolled in many subjects. Shown in Figure 5.

Figure 5. One to many relationship

4) Many to Many: Many instances of a class are related to many instances of another class. Example: many students of a class can have many teachers. Shown in Figure 6.

Figure 6. Many to many relationship

Example of the UML Model: In this example, the classes are:

- Customer- Showing the customer details with (Attributes)- name (String), address.
- Order- Showing the order (Attribute)- date (Date), status (String), (Methods)- calcSubTotal(), calcTax(), calcTotalWeight().
- OrderDetail- Showing the order details (Attribute)- quality, taxStatus (String), (Methods)- calc-SubTotal(), calcTax(), clacWeight().
- Item- Showing the item details (Attribute)- shipping Weight, description (String), (Methods)- get-PriceForQuality(), getTax(), inStock().
- Payment- Showing the payment details (Attribute)- amount(float).
- Cash- Showing the cash payment details (Attribute)-cashTendered (float).
- Check- Showing the check payment details (Attribute)-name (String), bankId (String), (Methods)-authorized().

- Credit- Showing the credit payment details (Attribute)-name (String), type (String), expDate. (Methods)- authorized().

This is how the relationships can be explained:

- Customer and order details have one-to-many relationships. (Many starting from 0)
- Order and order details have one-to-many relationship. (Many starting from 1)
- Order details and items have many-to-one relationships. (Many starts from 0)
- Order and payment have a one-to-many relationship. (Many starts from 1)
- Payment with cash, credit and credit have a one-to-one relationship.

One customer can place multiple orders and one order can have multiple details. One Item can have many order details. One order can have multiple payments of items. Payment methods can be cash, check, or credit. Shown in Figure 7.

Figure 7. Order UML model

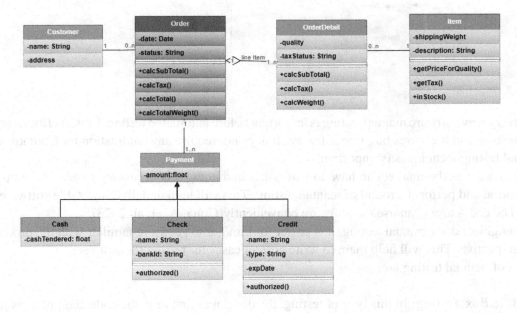

TESTING THE SYSTEM

It is necessary to make sure that our software is completely bug free and based on the requirements of the customer. Thus, testing comprises of following types: Shown in Figure 8.

Manual Testing: In this type of testing manual test cases are applied to test the software without any testing tools. All testing is done manually against the requirement (Garg, M. et. al.,2023).

Figure 8. Types of software testing

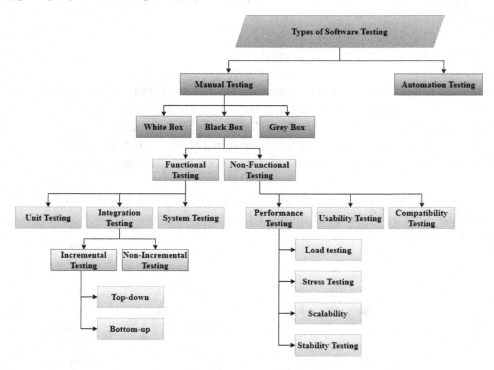

For every new software manual testing is important before automated testing. Lots of effort is required for this testing, but it ensures bug free software. It does not require any automation tool, but knowledge of manual testing techniques is important.

The software in the market can have lots of issues and bugs. It is necessary to take these bugs into consideration and perform a round of manual testing. This will help in delivering stable software to the clients. The end – users can use the software conveniently(Guha, A. et. al.,2023).

If an engineer does manual testing, it is easier for him/her to get more familiar with the product and client perspective. This will help them to write correct cases for testing the software.

Types of manual testing are:

- **White Box Testing:** In this type of testing, the developer first tests the code and provides it to the testing team. This type of testing is done to enhance the input / output flow of the code. The major objective of white box testing is to strengthen security. The developers test each line of code in this test. First the developers perform white box testing and then send the software to the testing team where they perform black box testing to find bugs and send it back to developers to fix them (Gurunath, R. et. al.,2023). The testing team, after finding bugs, gives it back to the developer to fix the bug. The reason the testing team will not fix the bug are:
  - As the test engineers are not acquainted with the core features thus fixing bugs can cause issues in functionality. Thus, they send the code to the developer to fix bugs.
  - If the test engineers focus more on fixing bugs, they will not be able to find more bugs.

Shown in Figure 9.

Figure 9. White box testing

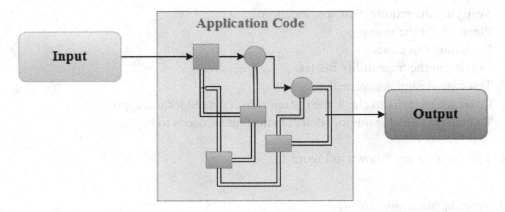

- **Black Box Testing:** Here the test engineer recognizes the bugs and sends them to the team of developers to fix them. Then the developers fix the bugs through whit box testing and send them to the testing team back again. Majorly, this type of testing is done to check the code against customer requirements. Here the tester checks each function to see whether it gives the desired output(Jain, A. et. al.,2023). If correct output is produced by the function, then it passes otherwise it fails. The testing team then sends the outcome to the team of development and proceeds further with the next function(Mondal, S. et. al.,2023). If the testing of all the functions is done and a serious problem arises then it is sent to the development team for changes. The steps of black box testing are:
  - The requirement specification is examined first.
  - The tester then creates various inputs based on requirements and checks each functionality.
  - The tester creates several test cases which includes decision table, cause-effect graph, equivalent division, error estimation etc.
  - All the test cases are then executed.
  - The tester then performs a comparison between expected and actual output.
  - In case of any issue in the software function it is corrected and tested again.

The types of black box testing are: Shown in Figure 10.

Figure 10. Black box testing

- **Functional Testing:** Component of the software is checked in details against the requirements. This testing is also called components testing. It checks the entry functionality and the flow of the GUI screen (Podder, S. K. et. al.,2023). This testing displays error messages, so it is easier for the user to navigate through the software. Following tests are executed by the tester:
  - Verifying the requirement specification.
  - Planning for the test.
  - Designing test cases.
  - Document the traceability matrix.
  - Test case design is executed.
  - Coverage analysis to check the testing areas covered for the application.
  - To manage defect resolving, defect management needs to be done.

Types of this testing are: Shown in Figure 11.

Figure 11. Types of functional testing

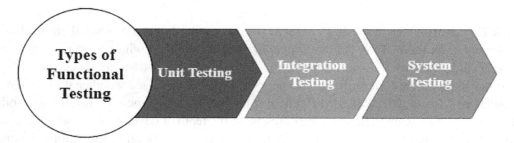

- **Unit Testing:** Here each module of the software is tested individually. It checks the performance of each module of the program. Here unit is defined as single testable function. The accuracy of independent code is checked by unit testing. An individual function is called a unit component. Unit testing is done generally by developers, and it uses the white box testing approach. The test engineer tests each part of the code individually as soon as the application is completed. This is called unit testing. The tester and developers can understand the basic code and adjust the code with the help of unit testing. The advantages of unit testing are:
  - It helps with documenting.
  - It resolves issues in the development phase, thus there are less chances of mistakes in the testing phase.
  - It helps in reusing the code by test cases and migrating the code.
- **Integration Testing:** The flow of data between moules and between two features is called integration testing. Example of integration testing with banking application: Shown in Figure 12.

Figure 12. Bank transfer example

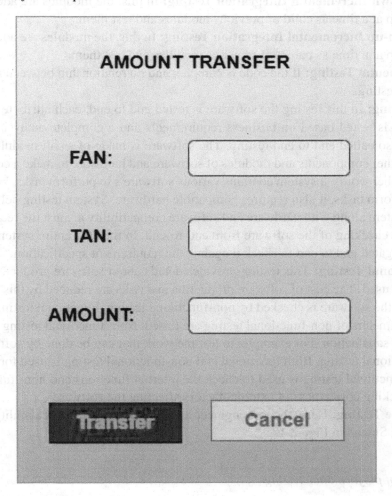

- The first set would be logging in as user A and transferring Rs 200. The message for confirming the transaction is displayed as- "amount has been successfully transferred." Logout as A and login as user B and check the balance. The balance should be "account = Present balance + Received Balance." If the balance is correct, the test was successfully executed.
- Next step would be to check if the balance of account A has been reduced by Rs 200.
- The transactions of A and B show a message regarding the time of transferring the amount and the data.

Types of this testing are:

- **Incremental Testing:** This testing is used to show the relationship between two modules. First these two related modules are tested, if they work well, more modules are tested. This is called incremental testing. If they are not working fine, we fix them and test them incrementally. Types of this testing are:

- ◦ **Top-down Incremental Integration Testing:** In this, the modules are added incrementally one step at a time as child of previous modules and test them.
- ◦ **Bottom-up Incremental Integration Testing:** In this, the modules are added incrementally one step at a time as parent of previous modules and test them.
- **Non-Incremental Testing:** If the code is complex and no relationship between modulus is found, we use this testing.
- **System Testing:** In this testing the software is tested end to end, each attribute and parameter of the software is tested based on business requirements and a complete analysis of the system is done. It is also called end to end testing. The software is made of small modules and then interfaced with other components and modules of software and hardware to make a complete computer system. In other words, a system contains various software's to perform tasks, but software's cannot only perform tasks, it also requires compatible hardware. System testing helps us to check the complete system along with hardware and software compatibility against the requirement. System testing is the checking of the software from end-to-end. In this, the entire system and all its modules are navigated end to end to check it against the requirement specification.
- **Non-Functional Testing:** This testing provides details about software product, performance and technologies used. The cost of software production and risks are reduced by this testing. The reading speed of the software is checked by non-functional testing. Functional testing is done first and then the parameters of non-functional testing are tested. Non- functional testing is very important for customer satisfaction. For example: to test the work that can be done by software can be done by non-functional testing. Both functional and non-functional testing is used for newly developed software. Functional testing is used to check the internal functions and non- functional testing is used for checking correctness of external factors affecting the software.
- **Performance Testing:** Here, the test engineer focuses on stress, load, scalability, and stability of the software. Shown in Figure 13.

Figure 13. Types of performance testing

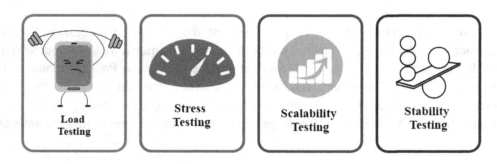

- **Load Testing:** load is applied on the application while performance testing. This is termed load testing.
- **Stress Testing:** The user-friendliness and robustness of the software is tested by this type of testing.

- **Scalability Testing:** In this testing the system's database and process ability is checked whether it is updated or not.
- **Stability Testing:** The problems and the efficiency of the software are examined in this testing. System errors and defects are common to find in this type of testing and they are resolved.
- **Usability Testing:** Here user friendliness of the software is checked and checked I it is bug free. The main objective of this testing is to give an easy and user-friendly application that sustains the key functions based on the user's requirement. While usability testing it ensures that the interface is straight forward to use, without any mistakes and makes life of end user easier. In other words, it helps in making UX (User experience) easy with proper working software. Thus, it is also called User Experience testing. It ensures proper functioning of software with bug free user interface. The execution of usability testing qualifies all the necessary features of a software production, from testing the navigation of website and to validating its flow and the purpose to build a friendly user interface. The testing is done by real-life users not the team of development who developed the software. Here, the term user-friendliness defines the following:
  - All the features should be easily accessible and visible to the user so that it is easier for them to understand the application.
  - The application should have a pleasant looking interface so that it attracts users to use it.
- **Compatibility Testing:** Here the software's functions are tested on different browsers, operating systems, and devices of varied sizes. As soon as the application is completed it is produced. But this production can have various compatibility issues in operating systems, devices of many sizes. Thus, a compatibility testing is done. Compatibility testing is one only when the software is complete and stable.
- **Grey Box testing:** It is a combination of white box and black box testing. As here the internal coding and test case designing is done thus it requires an experienced coder. The main reasons for grey box testing are:
  - The benefits are combined based on black and white box testing.
  - To improve the quality of the product, it obtains input from both developers and testers.
  - It reduces time for non-functional and functional testing.
  - Developers are given time to resolve the defects.
  - The user's point of view is as valued at the tester and developer's point of view.
- **Automation Testing:** In this type of testing all processes of manual testing take place in an automated manner and thus it is a more effective and efficient way of testing. Tests take place automatically, quickly, and efficiently. Shown in Figure 14.
  - Automation testing provides the best user application in less time with minimal effort.
  - Certain organizations still like to use manual testing as they have minimal knowledge about automation testing.
  - Recently they are being more aware of the testing and using automation testing for development of the application.
  - To use automation testing a huge amount of investment is required as it requires tools and technologies which are costly.

Figure 14. Automation testing

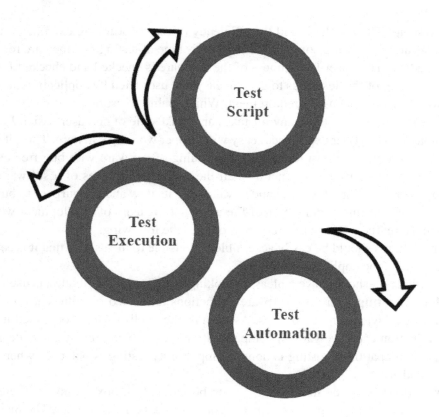

CONCLUSION

The major aim of this chapter is to cover the software development life cycle, UML modelling and testing precisely. It contains all the crucial details for properly explaining the concepts of software development. It includes testing methods which are white ox, black and grey box testing. It also contains Diagrammatic case study of UML modeling and proper defining of all information related to UML modelling.

It is described in proper diagrammatic and straightforward way to make it easy and precise to understand. The diagrams are clear and made based on the explanation provided.

REFERENCES

Almstrum, V. L., Dean, C. N., Goelman, D., Hilburn, T. B., & Smith, J. (2001). Support for Teaching Formal Methods. Innovation and Technology in Computer Science Education. ACM Press.

Althar, R. R., Samanta, D., Purushotham, S., Sengar, S. S., & Hewage, C. (2023). Design and Development of Artificial Intelligence Knowledge Processing System for Optimizing Security of Software System. *SN Computer Science*, 4(4), 331. doi:10.100742979-023-01785-2

Asklund, U., & Bendix, L. (2003). *A Software Configuration Management Course* (Vol. 2649). Lecture Notes in Computer Science.

Benediktsson, O. (2000). *Software Engineering Body of Knowledge and Curriculum Development.* Views on Software Development in the New Millennium.

Budgen, D., & Tomayko, J.E. (2005). The SEI Curriculum Modules and Their Influence: Norm Gibbs' Legacy to Software Engineering Education. *Journal of Systems and Software, 75*(1-2), 55-62.

Cunaku, E., Ndrecaj, J., Berisha, S., Samanta, D., Dutta, S., & Bhattacharya, A. (2023). An Approach for Digital-Social Network Analysis Using Twitter API. In *Innovations in Data Analytics: Selected Papers of ICIDA 2022* (pp. 625–636). Springer. 10.1007/978-981-99-0550-8_49

Dangi, P., Jain, A., Samanta, D., Dutta, S., & Bhattacharya, A. (2023). 3D Modelling and Rendering Using Autodesk 3ds Max. *2023 11th International Conference on Internet of Everything, Microwave Engineering, Communication and Networks (IEMECON),* (pp. 1–5). IEEE.

Garg, M., Saxena, C., Samanta, D., & Dorr, B. J. (2023). LonXplain: Lonesomeness as a Consequence of Mental Disturbance in Reddit Posts. arXiv Preprint arXiv:2305.18736. doi:10.1007/978-3-031-35320-8_27

Guha, A., Samanta, D., & Sengar, S. S. (2023). Computer Vision Based Automatic Margin Computation Model for Digital Document Images. *SN Computer Science, 4*(3), 253. doi:10.100742979-023-01693-5

Gurunath, R., & Samanta, D. (2023). A New 3-Bit Hiding Covert Channel Algorithm for Public Data and Medical Data Security Using Format-Based Text Steganography. [JDM]. *Journal of Database Management, 34*(2), 1–22. doi:10.4018/JDM.324076

Jain, A., Dangi, P., Samanta, D., Dutta, S., Bhattacharya, A., & Joseph, N. P. (2023). Creation of Bookshelf Using Autodesk 3ds Max: 3D Modelling and Rendering. *2023 11th International Conference on Internet of Everything, Microwave Engineering, Communication and Networks (IEMECON),* (pp. 1–4). IEEE.

Mondal, S., Pal, A. K., Islam, S. K. H., & Samanta, D. (2023). Objectionable Image Content Classification Using CNN-Based Semi-supervised Learning. In Advances in Smart Vehicular Technology, Transportation, Communication and Applications [Springer.]. *Proceedings of VTCA, 2022,* 311–320.

Podder, S. K., Samanta, D., Thomas, B., Dutta, S., & Bhattacharya, A. (2023). Impact of blended education system on outcome-based learning and sector skills development. *2023 11th International Conference on Internet of Everything, Microwave Engineering, Communication and Networks (IEMECON),* (pp. 1–6). IEEE.

Chapter 13
Designing an Efficient and Scalable Relational Database Schema:
Principles of Design for Data Modeling

Rajesh Kanna Rajendran
CHRIST University (Deemed), India

T. Mohana Priya
CHRIST University (Deemed), India

ABSTRACT

Relational databases are a critical component of modern software applications, providing a reliable and scalable method for storing and managing data. A well-designed database schema can enhance the performance and flexibility of applications, making them more efficient and easier to maintain. Data modeling is an essential process in designing a database schema, and it involves identifying and organizing data entities, attributes, and relationships. In this chapter, the authors discuss the principles of designing an efficient and scalable relational database schema, with a focus on data modeling techniques. They explore the critical aspects of normalization, data types, relationships, indexes, and denormalization, as well as techniques for optimizing database queries and managing scalability challenges. The principles discussed in this chapter can be applied to various database management systems and can be useful for designing a schema that meets the demands of modern data-intensive applications.

INTRODUCTION

This chapter is a comprehensive guide to designing an efficient and scalable relational database schema. The paper begins by discussing the importance of data modeling in the database design process and how it can impact the performance and flexibility of applications. We then delve into the critical aspects of data modeling, including normalization, data types, relationships, indexes, and denormalization. The

DOI: 10.4018/978-1-6684-9809-5.ch013

normalization process helps in avoiding data redundancy, which can improve data consistency and reduce storage requirements. We discuss various normal forms, including first normal form (1NF), second normal form (2NF), and third normal form (3NF), and provide practical examples of how to apply them.We also discuss data types and how they can impact database performance and storage requirements. We cover common data types such as strings, integers, dates, and decimals, and discuss their advantages and disadvantages. Relationships are another critical aspect of data modeling, and we explore different types of relationships, including one-to-one, one-to-many, and many-to-many relationships. We also discuss how to define and enforce referential integrity constraints to maintain data consistency (Priyanka, et al.,2016).

Indexes are essential for optimizing database queries, and we discuss how to create indexes and choose the appropriate data structures for specific scenarios. We also cover denormalization, a technique used to improve query performance by intentionally introducing redundant data into the database. Finally, we explore techniques for managing scalability challenges, including partitioning, sharing, and replication. We provide practical examples of how to apply these techniques in different scenarios and database management systems (Diego Sevilla et al.,2015.

Throughout the article, we provide practical examples and best practices for designing an efficient and scalable relational database schema, making it a valuable resource for database designers, developers, and administrators (David A. Maluf et al.) (Zain Aftab et al.,2020).

RELATIONAL DATABASE

In order to demonstrate the power of a relational database, we'll create a database for a business that wishes to handle its merchandise, clients, orders, and staff (Alberto Hernández Chillón et al.,2019). Figure 1 shows Simple Entity Relationship Data Model.

Figure 1. Simple entity relationship data model

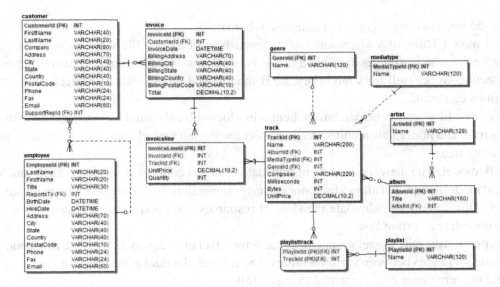

Strategies for Schema design

When designing a database schema, there are several strategies that can be used to ensure that the resulting schema is efficient, scalable, and easy to maintain. Here are some common strategies for schema design:

Denormalization: Denormalization is the opposite of normalization, and involves adding redundant data to a database to improve performance. Denormalization can be useful for frequently accessed data that requires fast access times(Database Star).

Indexing: To increase the performance of queries, indexing includes establishing indexes on the columns of a table. Indexes can speed up query execution, but they can also make insert, update, and delete actions more laborious. The decision of which columns to index needs to be carefully thought out because it might significantly affect the database's performance.

Partitioning: Partitioning is the process of splitting a huge table into more manageable, smaller sections known as partitions. By minimizing the quantity of data that needs to be scanned, partitioning can enhance query performance. It can also make database management simpler by facilitating simpler backup and recovery (AWS).

Vertical partitioning: Based on the columns of a table, several tables are created by vertically partitioning the table. This can be helpful for tables with many columns because it can speed up queries by minimizing the amount of information that needs to be scanned.

Horizontal partitioning: Based on the rows of a table, several tables are created using horizontal partitioning. This can be helpful for tables with many rows because it can speed up queries by minimizing the amount of information that needs to be scanned.

Data archiving: Data archiving is the process of relocating data to a different storage system when it is no longer required for everyday activities. The amount of data that needs to be scanned is decreased, which can enhance the performance of searches.

TYPES OF DATABASE SCHEMAS

Below are the six most typical types of database schema:

The flat model Think of a Microsoft Excel spreadsheet or a CSV file when picturing a flat model database schema, which arranges data into a single, two-dimensional presentation. According to Guru99, this architecture works well for straightforward databases and tables without intricate interactions between various elements.

Using a "tree-like" structure, database schemas in a hierarchical model feature child node that branch out from a root data node. This architecture is perfect for storing nested data, such as biological taxonomies or family trees.

Network model: The network model presents data as nodes connected to one another, much like the hierarchical model does, but it allows for more intricate connections including many-to-many interactions and cycles. This schema can simulate the flow of resources and goods between sites or the processes needed to complete a certain task.

As was previously said, the relational model arranges data in a sequence of tables, rows, and columns to establish associations between various entities. The relational model is the main topic of the following section and the remainder of this manual (Simple Talk).

The relational model that organizes data into facts and dimensions has evolved into the star schema. Fact data is numerical (for instance, the quantity of a product sold), whereas dimensional data is descriptive (for instance, the cost, color, weight, etc. of a product).

On top of the star schema, the snowflake model adds yet another level of abstraction. It has a fact table that connects to a dimensional table, increasing the amount of descriptiveness a database can support. The snowflake schema takes its name from the intricate patterns of a snowflake, where smaller structures radiate from the center arms of the flake. As you might have imagined.

NORMALIZATION PROCESS

The normalization process is usually done in several steps, each increasing the level of normalization. Here are the common levels of normalization:

First Normal Form (1NF): In 1NF, a table must have atomic values in each column, which means that each value must be indivisible. By doing so, data redundancy and repetitive groups are reduced.

Second Normal Form (2NF): In 2NF, the table must be in first normal form (1NF), and every non-key column must be entirely dependent on the primary key. Partial dependencies are removed, and data redundancy is decreased.

Third Normal Form (3NF): For 3NF, the table must be in 2NF and each non-key column must be independent of all other non-key columns save the primary key. This gets rid of transitive dependencies and further cuts down on data duplication.

Fourth Normal Form (4NF): The table must be in 3NF and there must not be any multi-valued relationships between the primary key and non-key columns. Data redundancy is further decreased as a result.

Fifth Normal Form (5NF): In 5NF, also known as the Boyce-Codd Normal Form (BCNF), the table must be in 4NF, and every join dependency between the primary key and non-key columns must be a consequence of the superkeys of the table. This ensures that the table is free of any anomalies, and further reduces data redundancy. Figure 2 shows Sample Dimensional Data Model.

A specific schema for this database might outline the structure of two simple tables shows in table 1.

Table 1. A specific schema for this database might outline the structure of two simple tables

Table a1: Users	Table a2: Overtime Pay
EID	EID
Name	Name
Email	Time Period
Date of Birth	Hours Billed
Department	Date

Figure 2. Sample dimensional data model

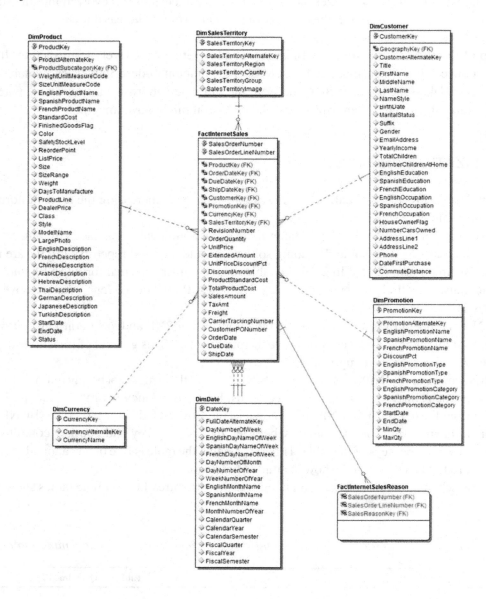

DATA MODELING PROCESS

Data modeling is the process of creating a conceptual representation of data, and it is a crucial step in database design. The goal of data modeling is to create a structure that allows for efficient storage, retrieval, and manipulation of data. Here are the basic steps of the data modeling process in a database:

Identify the Entities: The things or ideas about which data is gathered, stored, and managed are known as Entities. An e-commerce database might contain entities such as customers, orders, products, etc.

Determine the Attributes: An entity's attributes are its traits or properties. For instance, a customer entity's properties might comprise things like name, address, email, phone number, etc.

Specify the connections: Relationships explain how things are connected to one another. One-to-one, one-to-many, and many-to-many relationships are the three different kinds of connections. One client may place several orders, but only one customer may be the owner of any given order.

Building a data model A data model is constructed using the information acquired in the earlier processes. An illustration of the entities, properties, and connections between them is called a data model.

Data model normalization Data in a database are organized by a process called normalization that lessens dependencies and redundant data. This process makes sure that data is stored effectively and gets rid of inconsistent data.

The data model must be implemented in a database management system (DBMS), such as MySQL, Oracle, or Microsoft SQL Server, as the last stage. In order to do this, tables, columns, and relationships based on the data model must be created.

TYPE OF DATA MODEL

There are different types of data models used in database design, and each has its own approach and level of abstraction. Here are some of the most common types of data models:

Conceptual Data Model: This is the highest level of abstraction and focuses on the business requirements and entities involved. It defines the relationships between these entities and provides a broad view of the data.

The logical relationships between things are the main emphasis of the conceptual data model's more detailed counterpart, the logical data model. The characteristics of each entity and their connections are defined, but the actual storage of the data is not mentioned.

Physical Data Model: This is a basic illustration of the database that demonstrates how the data is kept on disks. It contains specifics like data types, indexes, and file organization.

Data is organised in a tree-like structure, with a parent record and one or more children for each record, according to the hierarchical data model. It is useful for illuminating one-to-many relationships.

Network Data Model: This model uses a graph structure to represent data, where each record can have multiple owners (called "parents") and children (called "members"). It is useful for representing many-to-many relationships.

The most popular data model utilized in contemporary databases is the relational data model. It displays data as rows and columns in tables and uses keys to build relationships between these tables.

Object-Oriented Data Model: This model represents data as objects with properties and methods and is based on the ideas of object-oriented programming. For modeling intricate data structures, it is helpful.

The choice of which data model to use relies on the specific requirements of the database and the application that uses it, as each form of data model has strengths and drawbacks.

DATA MODELING TOOLS

There are several tools available for data modeling, which can help simplify the process and make it more efficient. Here are some popular data modeling tools:

ER/Studio: This is a powerful data modeling tool that allows users to create both logical and physical data models. It supports a wide range of database management systems and provides collaboration features to help teams work together on data modeling projects.

MySQL Workbench: This is a free and open-source tool that provides data modeling, SQL development, and database administration capabilities. It supports both physical and logical data modeling, and can generate SQL code based on the models.

Microsoft Visio: This is a diagramming and data visualization tool that can be used for data modeling. It supports a broad variety of diagram types, including as flowcharts, ER diagrams, and UML diagrams.

Toad Data Modeler: This is a data modeling tool that supports both logical and physical data modeling. It allows users to generate DDL scripts for different database platforms, and supports reverse engineering from an existing database schema.

DbSchema: This is a multi-platform data modeling tool that supports all major database management systems. It provides a visual interface for designing and editing data models, and supports forward and reverse engineering of database schemas.

PowerDesigner: This is a comprehensive data modeling and metadata management tool that supports both logical and physical data modeling. It provides advanced features such as impact analysis, data lineage, and version control. Table 2 shows Sample complete table data.

SAMPLE DATA

Main entities you can identify within the sample data and table:
Here are some examples:

- Student
- Teacher
- Department
- School
- Course
- Credits

Table 2. Sample complete table data

Student Name	Course	Course Name	Department	School	Type	Credits	Semester	Teacher	Designation
Miruthula	MCA201	Java	CS	Science	Lecture	3	Odd 2023	Rajesh	Assistant Professor
Joel	BCA103	DS	CS	Science	Lab	2	Even2023	Mohana	Assistant Professor
Samantha	CME306	C++	CS	Sceince	Lecture	3	Even 2022	Biswas	Professor
Hiran	LLB101	Law	LLB	Law	Lecture	2	Odd2023	Jayanthi	Professor
Nismon	Phy101	Physics	Physics	Science	Lecture	3	Odd2023	Suresh	Assistant Professor
Rohit	Com132	Commerce	Commerce	Arts	Lecture	2	Even2022	Cecil	Visiting Professor

Figure 3 shows Conceptual Model diagram.

Figure 3. Conceptual model diagram

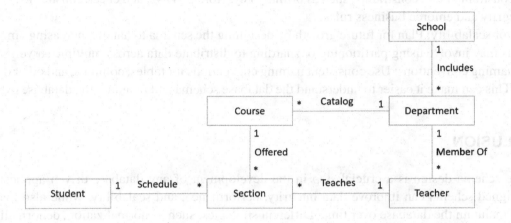

IMPORTANCE OF DATA MODELING

Data modeling is an essential step in the database design process, and its importance cannot be overstated. Here are some reasons why data modeling is important:

Helps to understand business requirements: Data modeling helps to capture the business requirements of the organization and provides a structured way to represent these requirements. This ensures that the final database design meets the needs of the organization and supports its operations.

Enhances application development: Data modeling provides a blueprint for application development by defining the structure of the database. This makes it easier to develop applications that work with the database, as the structure of the database is already defined.

Facilitates database maintenance: Data modeling makes it easier to maintain the database over time by providing a clear understanding of the data structures and relationships. This makes it easier to modify the database as business requirements change, and ensures that the database remains efficient and effective.

Data modeling is a critical step in the database design process, as it ensures that the database meets the needs of the organization, is reliable and accurate, and can be easily maintained over time.

DESIGNING SCALABLE RELATIONAL DATABASE SCHEMA

Designing an efficient and scalable relational database schema requires careful consideration of various design principles. Here are some of the key principles to keep in mind when designing a database schema:

Identify and define relationships: Identify the relationships between tables and define them using foreign keys. This allows you to query data from multiple tables and ensure data consistency.

Use appropriate data types: Choose the appropriate data types for each column to minimize data storage and ensure data accuracy. For example, use integers instead of strings for numeric values.

Optimize indexing: Indexing can significantly improve the performance of database queries. Consider adding indexes on columns that are frequently searched or sorted.

Avoid NULL values: Avoid using NULL values whenever possible. Instead, use default values or separate tables to represent missing data.

Use constraints: Use constraints, such as primary keys, foreign keys, and check constraints, to ensure data integrity and enforce business rules.

Plan for scalability: Plan for future growth by designing the schema to handle increasing amounts of data. This may involve using partitioning or sharding to distribute data across multiple servers.

Use naming conventions: Use consistent naming conventions for tables, columns, and other database objects. This can make it easier to understand the database schema and maintain the database over time.

CONCLUSION

Database schema design is a crucial step in the development of any database-driven application. A well-designed schema can improve data integrity, performance, and scalability, while also making it easier to maintain the database over time. Different strategies, such as normalization, denormalization, indexing, partitioning, vertical and horizontal partitioning, and data archiving, can be used to optimize the schema design to meet specific requirements. By carefully considering the needs of the application and the data, and by employing the appropriate design strategies, developers can create a schema that is efficient, flexible, and easily maintainable.

REFERENCES

Aftab, Z., Iqbal, W., Almustafa, M., Faisal, B., & Abdullah, M. (2020). *Automatic NoSQL to Relational Database Transformation with Dynamic Schema Mapping*. PUCIT.

AWS. (n.d..). *Best Practices for Database Schema Design*. AWS.

Chillón, A., Ruiz, D., Molina, J., & Morales, S. (2019). *A Model-Driven Approach to Generate Schemas for Object-Document Mappers*. Research Gate.

Database Star. (n.d.). *Designing a Database Schema: Principles of Data Modeling*. Database Star. https://www.databasestar.com/designing-a-database-schema-principles-of-data-modeling/

Guru 99. (n.d.). *Relational Database Design: 10 Tips to Design Effective Database*. Guru99.

Maluf, D., Trad, P., & NASA Ames Research Center. (n.d.). NETMARK: A Schema-less Extension for Relational Databases for Managing Semi- structured Data Dynamically. *Mail Stop*, 269-4

Priyanka, A. (2016). A Review of NoSQL Databases, Types and Comparison with Relational Database. *IJESC*. doi:. doi:10.4010/2016.1226

Sevilla, D., Ruiz, S. F. M., & Molina, J. G. (2015). *Inferring Versioned Schemas from NoSQL Databases and Its Applications*. Springer. 10.1007/978-3-319-25264-3_35

Chapter 14
Analyzing the Rich:
Unpacking the World's Billionaires

Guri Arianit Sokoli
Rochester Institute of Technology, Kosovo

ABSTRACT

The number of billionaires in a country gives us significant insights regarding the country's corporate and economic landscape. The number of billionaires indicates the country's economic performance, financial market strength, and amount of support for entrepreneurship and innovation. The presence of a large number of billionaires suggests that the country has a solid business climate that promotes the growth and success of affluent individuals. These people' riches may have been built through creative business methods, technical developments, or savvy investments. However, it is crucial to highlight that the number of billionaires does not always imply a thriving economy. Our project seeks to investigate the global links of billionaires and their commercial specialization tactics.

INTRODUCTION

While brainstorming ideas for our Python project, my colleagues and I were intrigued to the exciting and complicated issue of studying billionaires (Carlos M Urzúa et. al., 2010) (Guha, A. et. al., 2023) (Stephen Devadoss et. al.,2020) (Cordier S. et. al.,2009). The sheer volume of money possessed by billionaires throughout the world, as well as the socioeconomic ramifications of such severe wealth concentration, intrigued us (Jeff Luckstead et. al.,2014)(Marco Bee et. al.,2013)(Maldarella D. et. al.,2012). We believed that diving into this topic would allow us to use our programming talents in a real-world situation with important societal implications(Jain, A. et. al., 2023) (Alipour P. et. al.,2019). The decision to use Python to examine billionaires was partly motivated by our desire to challenge ourselves and push the boundaries of our coding talents(Kristian Giesen et. al.,2010)(José María Sarabia et. al.,2009). We knew that this project would need a multidimensional strategy that included data gathering, cleaning, analysis, and visualization(Dangi, P. et. al., 2023). We were intrigued by the potential of combining Python's strong data manipulation and analysis modules, such as Pandas, NumPy, and Matplotlib, to

DOI: 10.4018/978-1-6684-9809-5.ch014

obtain insights from billionaires' immense wealth and detailed financial profiles(Piero Montebruno et. al.,2019)(Sasuke Miyazima et. al.,2000)(Bertotti M. et. al.,2010). The research study introduces a large new dataset on the sources of billionaire income and uses it to examine variations in extreme wealth across sophisticated nations such as the United States and Europe (Althar, R. R. et. al., 2023)(Mondal, S. et. al., 2023)(Tohidi M. et. al.,2017). The dataset categorizes wealth as self-made or inherited, and also defines the firm and industry from which it stems. Individuals classified as self-made billionaires are further classified depending on their roles as firm founders, executives, politically connected, or in finance(Marco Bee et. al.,2017)(Damián H Zanette et. al.,2001)(Podder, S. K. et. al., 2023)(Jourabian M. et. al.,2018).

DATASET DESCRIPTION

The dataset contains information on Billionaires around the world (Sidra Arshad et. al.,2019)(Yannis Ioannides et. al.,2013)(Kausik Gangopadhyay et. al.,2009). This collection of data is contained in a .csv file from which we can get information from and process it (Cunaku, E. et. al., 2023)(Toscani G. et. al.,2006)(Lallouache M. et. al.,2010).

Size: 189256
Python Code:
```
from pathlib import Path
sz = Path('Billionaire.csv').stat().st_size
print(sz)
```
Output: 189256
Number of Rows: 2755
Number of Columns: 7
Dataset Description with all attributes

The columns of the first dataset are: **Name, NetWorth, Country, Source, Rank, Age, Industry**.

Input

The 7 columns in the .csv file consist of: **Name, NetWorth, Country, Source, Rank, Age, Industry** (Xavier Gabaix et. al.,2004)(Guohua Peng et. al.,2010). All these inputs can be used to analyze the net worth of individuals across different countries, industries, and age groups (Fungisai Nota et. al.,2012) (Kenneth T. Rosen et. al.,1980)(Boudin L. et. al.,2010). It helps us get insight into wealth, trends, and patterns, and can be useful for conducting research on economic inequality, wealth management, and investment strategies to better our investments(Tomson Ogwang et. al.,2013)(Sitabhra Sinha et. al.,2006) (Garg, M. et. al., 2023).

Expected Output

Using the inputs, we can have a look at the top 10 billionaires, and their net worth, besides that we can look into the top niches in which the billionaire's companies are based in, furthermore we can also take a look at which countries have the greatest number of billionaires(Michal Brzezinski et. al.,2014)(F. Clementi et. al.,2005)(Furioli G. et. al.,2017).

ALGORITHM AND STEP-BY-STEP SEQUENCE OF PROCESS

After searching on google Colab and accessing the link https://colab.research.google.com/ it will send you to a webpage where you can access your notebooks(files of the python code), after that you can click on the top left option named 'File' then click on 'New Notebook' to start the new file to code in. After that you can run each snippet of the file (Gurunath, R. et. al., 2023)(Biswas S. et. al.,2011).

Figure 1. Highlight of file button

Figure 2. Highlight of the new notebook option

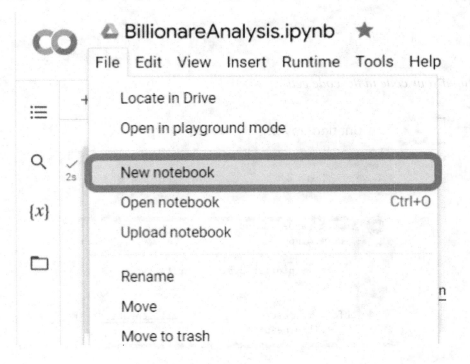

Figure 3. Highlight of the upload file button

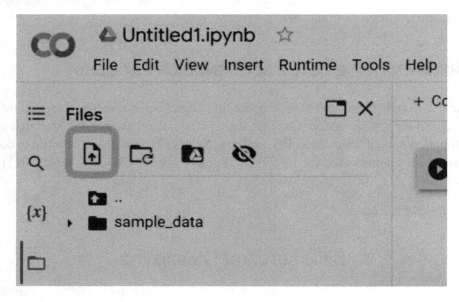

Figure 4. Highlight of the code cell

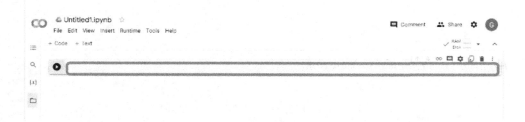

Figure 5. Input your code in the code cell

Figure 6. Highlight of the button that runs the code snippet

Flowchart

Figure 7. Flowchart of the work done for the project

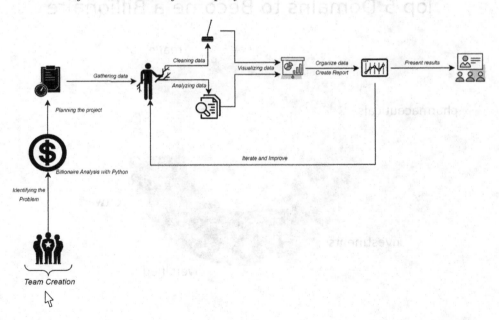

EXPERIMENT RESULTS

Figure 8. Figure showing top ten billionaires

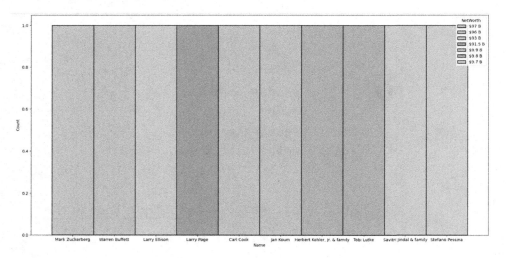

Figure 9. Figure showing most popular domains for billionaires

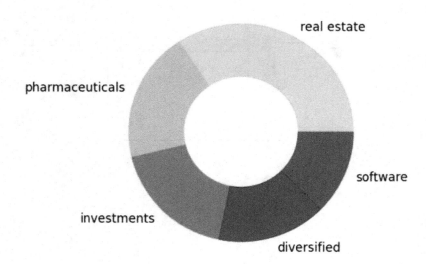

Figure 10. Figure showing most popular industries with billionaires

Top 5 Industries with Most Number of Billionaires

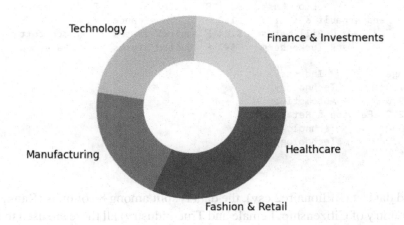

Figure 11. Figure showing where billionaires are mostly from

Top 5 Countries with Most Number of Billionaires

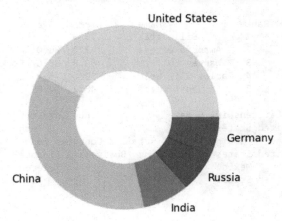

COMPARING THE DATASET

In the first dataset (Billionaire.csv), the data is split among 7 columns (Name, NetWorth, Country, Source, Rank, Age and Industry) which are used to extract data and information from billionaires from all over the world (Boudin L. et. al.,2009). This dataset contains 2755 rows of information on billionaires (Romaguera S. et. al.,2003).

Figure 12. Data in the first dataset

```
                    Name NetWorth        Country         Source  Rank  \
0            Jeff Bezos   $177 B  United States          Amazon     1
1            Elon Musk   $151 B  United States  Tesla, SpaceX     2
2  Bernard Arnault & family   $150 B         France           LVMH     3
3           Bill Gates   $124 B  United States      Microsoft     4
4      Mark Zuckerberg    $97 B  United States       Facebook     5

    Age          Industry
0  57.0        Technology
1  49.0        Automotive
2  72.0  Fashion & Retail
3  65.0        Technology
4  36.0        Technology
```

In the second dataset (Billionaire2.csv), the data is split among 8 columns (Rank, Name, Net Worth, Age, Source, Country of Citizenship, Female and True Industry) all these are used to take out some useful information to notice patterns from billionaires all over the world. This dataset contains 1809 rows of information on billionaires (Brugna C. et. al.,2015)(Alcantud J. et. al.,2009).

Figure 13. Data in the second dataset

```
   Unnamed: 0  Rank             Name  Net Worth   Age              Source  \
0           0     1       Bill Gates       75.0  61.0           Microsoft
1           1     2    Amancio Ortega       67.0  80.0                Zara
2           2     3    Warren Buffett       60.8  86.0  Berkshire Hathaway
3           3     4  Carlos Slim Helu       50.0  76.0             telecom
4           4     5       Jeff Bezos       45.2  52.0          Amazon.com

  Country of Citizenship  Female          True Industry
0          United States       0                   Tech
1                  Spain       0  Retail & Consumer Goods
2          United States       0      Business & Finance
3                 Mexico       0                Telecom
4          United States       0                   Tech
```

Both datasets help us with all the needed data to answer the following questions:

1. Who are the Top 10 Billionaires?
2. Which are the Top 5 Domains?
3. Which are the Top 5 Industries?
4. Which are the Top 5 Countries with the greatest number of Billionaires?

Figure 14. Top ten billionaires from the first dataset

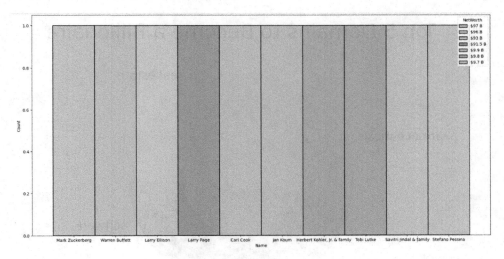

Figure 15. Top ten billionaires from the first dataset

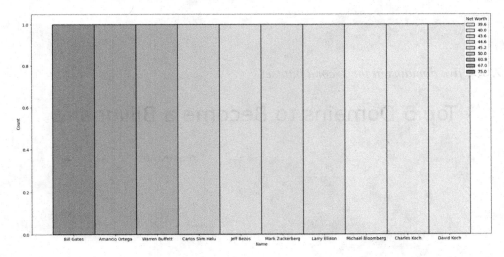

1. Both the datasets help us in finding the Top 10 Billionaires, this will tell us the wealth distribution among billionaires, this will later help us find their investment and business strategies and also their social impact. From both datasets these are the outputs(Toscani G. et. al.,2013)(Brugna C. et. al.,2018).

Figure 16. Top five domains in the first dataset

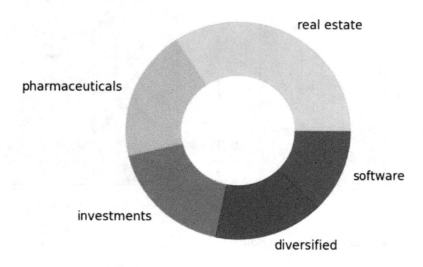

Figure 17. Top five domains in the second dataset

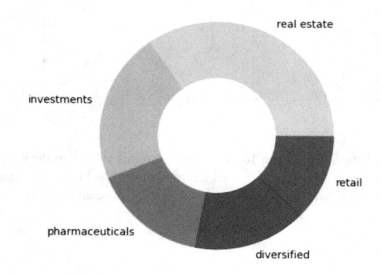

2. Each database also assists us in locating the top 5 domains in which billionaires have invested in provides us with insight into their investment trends and strategies. It helps individuals and businesses gain a better understanding of where billionaires are putting their money in, this helps us better identify investment opportunities(Chakrabarti A. et. al.,2009)(Chakraborti A. et. al.,2000).

Figure 18. Top five industries with the most billionaires in the first dataset

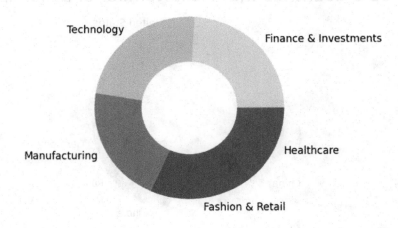

Top 5 Industries with Most Number of Billionaires

Figure 19. Top five industries with the most billionaires in the first dataset

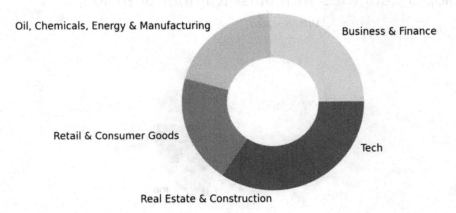

Top 5 Industries with Most Number of Billionaires

3.   Furthermore both collections of data additionally let us identify the top 5 industries with the greatest number of billionaires(Garg J. et. al.,2017)(Silver J. et. al.,2002). This collection of information helps us run a better analysis on which marked is getting the most investments. Besides that, since the industries are getting invested in, it also benefits the user to know what career to choose to pursue(Chatterjee A. et. al.,2004)(Zaman H. et. al.,2011).

Figure 20. Top five countries with the greatest number of billionaires in the first dataset

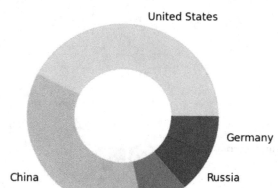

Figure 21. Top five countries with the greatest number of billionaires in the second dataset

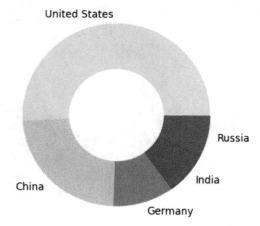

4.   At last, the two sets of data allow us to find investment opportunities, partnerships, business expansion, and learning from success(Kang M. et. al.,2016)(Kojić V. et. al.,2017). It can help individuals or businesses identify potential investment opportunities in said regions, analyze and evaluate markets based on the presence of billionaires, and learn from the success of billionaires in those countries (Tetsuya S. et. al.,2012)(Toda A. et. al.,2017).

CONCLUSION

In the end, our study of world billionaires using two separate datasets yielded useful insights on their wealth distribution and investment tendencies. We discovered consistency in the ranks of the top ten billionaires by comparing both datasets. Furthermore, our analysis of the top five sectors in which billionaires had invested the most found similar tendencies, with only slight differences, such as the medicines and investments domains moving positions. Our Python project gave us the opportunity to use advanced data analysis techniques and the strength of Python's tools to identify relevant patterns and trends in the complicated world of billionaires. The project demonstrated Python's potential as a strong tool for analyzing massive datasets and delivering useful insights.

REFERENCES

Alcantud, J., & Mehta, G. (2009). Constructive utility functions on banach spaces. *Journal of Mathematical Analysis and Applications*, *350*(2), 590–600. doi:10.1016/j.jmaa.2008.04.015

Alipour, P., Toghraie, D., Karimipour, A., & Hajian, M. (2019). Modeling different structures in perturbed poiseuille flow in a nanochannel by using of molecular dynamics simulation: Study the equilibrium. *Physica A*, *151*, 13–30. doi:10.1016/j.physa.2018.09.177

Althar, R. R., Samanta, D., Purushotham, S., Sengar, S. S., & Hewage, C. (2023). Design and Development of Artificial Intelligence Knowledge Processing System for Optimizing Security of Software System. *SN Computer Science*, *4*(4), 331. doi:10.100742979-023-01785-2

Arshad, S., Hu, S., & Ashraf, B. N. (2019). Zipf's law, the coherence of the urban system and city size distribution: Evidence from Pakistan. *Physica A: Statistical Mechanics and its Applications, 513*. doi:10.1016/j.physa.2018.08.065

Bertotti, M. (2010). Modelling taxation and redistribution: A discrete active particle kinetic approach. *Applied Mathematics and Computation*, *217*(2), 752–762. doi:10.1016/j.amc.2010.06.013

Biswas, S., Chandra, A., Chatterjee, A., & Chakrabarti, B. (2011). Phase transitions and non-equilibrium relaxation in kinetic models of opinion formation. *Journal of Physics: Conference Series*, *297*(1), 1–6. doi:10.1088/1742-6596/297/1/012004

Boudin, L., & Francesco, S. (2009). A kinetic approach to the study of opinion formation. *Modélisation Mathématique et Analyse Numérique*, *43*(3), 507–522. doi:10.1051/m2an/2009004

Brugna, C., & Toscani, G. (2015). Kinetic models of opinion formation in the presence of personal conviction. *Physical Review E: Statistical, Nonlinear, and Soft Matter Physics, 92*(5), 052818. doi:10.1103/PhysRevE.92.052818 PMID:26651755

Brugna, C., & Toscani, G. (2018). Kinetic models for goods exchange in a multi-agent market. *Physica A, 499*, 362–375. doi:10.1016/j.physa.2018.02.070

Carlos, M. (2010). A simple and efficient test for Zipf's law. *Economics Letters, 66*(3), 257-260. doi:10.1016/S0165-1765(99)00215-3

Chakrabarti, A., & Chakrabarti, B. (2009). Microeconomics of the ideal gas like market models. *Physica A, 388*(19), 4151–4158. doi:10.1016/j.physa.2009.06.038

Chakraborti, A., & Chakrabarti, B. (2000). Statistical mechanics of money: How saving propensity affects its distribution. *The European Physical Journal B, 17*(1), 167–170. doi:10.1007100510070173

Chatterjee, A., Chakrabarti, B., & Manna, S. (2004). Pareto law in a kinetic model of market with random saving propensity. *Physica A, 335*(1–2), 155–163. doi:10.1016/j.physa.2003.11.014

Clementi, F., & Gallegati, M. (2005). Power law tails in the Italian personal income distribution. *Physica A: Statistical Mechanics and its Applications, 350*(2–4), 427-438. doi:10.1016/j.physa.2004.11.038

Cordier, S., Pareschi, L., & Piatecki, C. (2009). Mesoscopic modelling of financial markets. *Journal of Statistical Physics, 134*(1), 161–184. doi:10.100710955-008-9667-z

Cunaku, E., Ndrecaj, J., Berisha, S., Samanta, D., Dutta, S., & Bhattacharya, A. (2023). An Approach for Digital-Social Network Analysis Using Twitter API. In *Innovations in Data Analytics: Selected Papers of ICIDA 2022* (pp. 625–636). Springer. 10.1007/978-981-99-0550-8_49

Dangi, P., Jain, A., Samanta, D., Dutta, S., & Bhattacharya, A. (2023). 3D Modelling and Rendering Using Autodesk 3ds Max. *2023 11th International Conference on Internet of Everything, Microwave Engineering, Communication and Networks (IEMECON),* (pp. 1–5). IEEE.

Damián, H. Zanette, S., & Manrubia, C. (2001). Vertical transmission of culture and the distribution of family names. *Physica A: Statistical Mechanics and its Applications, 295*(1–2), 1-8. doi:10.1016/S0378-4371(01)00046-2

Furioli, G., Pulvirenti, A., Terraneo, E., & Toscani, G. (2017). Fokker–Planck equations in the modeling of socio-economic phenomena. *Mathematical Models and Methods in Applied Sciences, 27*(1), 115–158. doi:10.1142/S0218202517400048

Garg, J. (2017). Market equilibrium under piecewise leontief concave utilities. *Theoretical Computer Science, 703*(1), 55–65. doi:10.1016/j.tcs.2017.09.001

Garg, M., Saxena, C., Samanta, D., & Dorr, B. J. (2023). LonXplain: Lonesomeness as a Consequence of Mental Disturbance in Reddit Posts. arXiv Preprint arXiv:2305.18736. doi:10.1007/978-3-031-35320-8_27

Giesen, K., Zimmermann, A., & Suedekum, J. (2010). The size distribution across all cities – Double Pareto lognormal strikes. *Journal of Urban Economics, 68*(2), 129-137. doi:10.1016/j.jue.2010.03.007

Guha, A., Samanta, D., & Sengar, S. S. (2023). Computer Vision Based Automatic Margin Computation Model for Digital Document Images. *SN Computer Science*, *4*(3), 253. doi:10.100742979-023-01693-5

Gurunath, R., & Samanta, D. (2023). A New 3-Bit Hiding Covert Channel Algorithm for Public Data and Medical Data Security Using Format-Based Text Steganography. [JDM]. *Journal of Database Management*, *34*(2), 1–22. doi:10.4018/JDM.324076

Jain, A., Dangi, P., Samanta, D., Dutta, S., Bhattacharya, A., & Joseph, N. P. (2023). Creation of Bookshelf Using Autodesk 3ds Max: 3D Modelling and Rendering. *2023 11th International Conference on Internet of Everything, Microwave Engineering, Communication and Networks (IEMECON)*, (pp. 1–4). IEEE.

Jourabian, M., Darzi, A. A. R., Toghraie, D., & Akbari, O. A. (2018). Melting process in porous media around two hot cylinders: Numerical study using the lattice Boltzmann method. *Physica A*, *509*, 316–335. doi:10.1016/j.physa.2018.06.011

Kang, M., & Ye, L. (2016). Advantageous redistribution with three smooth ces utility functions. *Journal of Mathematical Economics*, *67*(1), 171–180. doi:10.1016/j.jmateco.2016.08.002

Kausik, G. & Basu, B. (2009). City size distributions for India and China. *Physica A: Statistical Mechanics and its Applications, 388*(13), 2682-2688. doi:10.1016/j.physa.2009.03.019

Kenneth, T. & Rosen, M. (1980). The size distribution of cities: An examination of the Pareto law and primacy, *Journal of Urban Economics, Volume 8*, Issue 2, 1980, Pages 165-186, ISSN 0094-1190, https://doi.org/ doi:10.1016/0094-1190(80)90043-1

Kojić, V. (2017). Solving the consumer's utility-maximization problem with ces and cobb-douglas utility function via mathematical inequalities. *Optimization Letters*, *11*(4), 875–884. doi:10.100711590-016-1052-2

Lallouache, M., Chakrabarti, A., Chakraborti, A., & Chakrabarti, B. (2010). Opinion formation in kinetic exchange models: Spontaneous symmetry-breaking transition, Phys. Rev. E, 82 (5) (2010), p. 056112 Boudin L., Monaco R., Salvarani F., Kinetic model for multi-dimensional opinion formation. *Physical Review E: Statistical, Nonlinear, and Soft Matter Physics*, *81*(3), 036109.

Luckstead, J., & Devadoss, S. A comparison of city size distributions for China and India from 1950 to 2010, Economics Letters, Volume 124, Issue 2, 2014, Pages 290-295, ISSN 0165-1765, https://doi.org/ doi:10.1016/j.econlet.2014.06.002

Maldarella, D., & Pareschi, L. (2012). Kinetic models for socio-economic dynamics of speculative markets. *Physica A*, *391*(3), 715–730. doi:10.1016/j.physa.2011.08.013

Marco Bee, Massimo Riccaboni, Stefano Schiavo, The size distribution of US cities: Not Pareto, even in the tail, Economics Letters, Volume 120, Issue 2, 2013, Pages 232-237, ISSN 0165-1765, https://doi.org/ doi:10.1016/j.econlet.2013.04.035

Bee, M., Riccaboni, M., & Schiavo, S. (2017). Where Gibrat meets Zipf: Scale and scope of French firms. *Physica A: Statistical Mechanics and its Applications, 481*, 265-275. doi:10.1016/j.physa.2017.04.012

Brzezinski, M. (2014). Do wealth distributions follow power laws? Evidence from 'rich lists', *Physica A: Statistical Mechanics and its Applications, 406*, 155-162. doi:10.1016/j.physa.2014.03.052

Miyazima, S., Lee, Y., Nagamine, T., & Miyajima, H. (2000). Power-law distribution of family names in Japanese societies, *Physica A: Statistical Mechanics and its Applications, 278*(1–2), 282-288. doi:10.1016/S0378-4371(99)00546-4

Mondal, S., Pal, A. K., Islam, S. K. H., & Samanta, D. (2023). Objectionable Image Content Classification Using CNN-Based Semi-supervised Learning. In Advances in Smart Vehicular Technology, Transportation, Communication and Applications [Springer.]. *Proceedings of VTCA, 2022*, 311–320.

Nota, F., & Song, S. (2012). Further Analysis of the Zipf's Law: Does the Rank-Size Rule Really Exist? *Journal of Urban Management, 1*(2), 19-31. doi:10.1016/S2226-5856(18)30058-X

Peng, G. (2010). Zipf's law for Chinese cities: Rolling sample regressions. *Physica A: Statistical Mechanics and its Applications, 389*(18), 3804-3813. doi:10.1016/j.physa.2010.05.004

Piero, M., Bennett, R., Lieshout, C., & Smith, A. (2019). A tale of two tails: Do Power Law and Lognormal models fit firm-size distributions in the mid-Victorian era? *Physica A: Statistical Mechanics and its Applications, 523*, 858-875. doi:10.1016/j.physa.2019.02.054

Podder, S. K., Samanta, D., Thomas, B., Dutta, S., & Bhattacharya, A. (2023). Impact of blended education system on outcome-based learning and sector skills development. *2023 11th International Conference on Internet of Everything, Microwave Engineering, Communication and Networks (IEMECON)*, (pp. 1–6). IEEE.

Romaguera, S., & Sanchis, M. (2003). Applications of utility functions defined on quasi-metric spaces. *Journal of Mathematical Analysis and Applications, 283*(1), 219–235. doi:10.1016/S0022-247X(03)00285-3

Sarabia, J. M., & Prieto, F. (2009). The Pareto-positive stable distribution: A new descriptive model for city size data. *Physica A: Statistical Mechanics and its Applications, 388*(19), 4179-4191. doi:10.1016/j.physa.2009.06.047

Silver, J., Slud, E., & Takamoto, K. (2002). Statistical equilibrium wealth distributions in an exchange economy with stochastic preferences. *Journal of Economic Theory, 106*(2), 417–435. doi:10.1006/jeth.2001.2897

Sitabhra, S. (2006). Evidence for power-law tail of the wealth distribution in India. *Physica A: Statistical Mechanics and its Applications, 359*, 555-562. doi:10.1016/j.physa.2005.02.092

Devadoss, S., Luckstead, J., Danforth, D., & Akhundjanov, S. (2020). The power law distribution for lower tail cities in India. *Physica A: Statistical Mechanics and its Applications, 442*, 193-196. doi:10.1016/j.physa.2015.09.016

Tetsuya, S. (2012). How do we get cobb-douglas and leontief functions from ces function: A lecture note on discrete and continuum differentiated object models. *J. Ind. Organ. Educ., 6*(1), 1–13.

Toda, A., & Walsh, K. (2017). Edgeworth box economies with multiple equilibria. *Econ. Theor. Bull., 5*(1), 65–80. doi:10.100740505-016-0102-3

Tohidi, M., & Toghraie, D. (2017). The effect of geometrical parameters, roughness and the number of nanoparticles on the self-diffusion coefficient in couette flow in a nanochannel by using of molecular dynamics simulation. *Physica B, Condensed Matter, 518*, 20–32. doi:10.1016/j.physb.2017.05.014

Ogwang, T. (2013). Is the wealth of the world's billionaires Paretian? *Physica A: Statistical Mechanics and its Applications, 392*(4), 757-762. doi:10.1016/j.physa.2012.10.026

Toscani, G. (2006). Kinetic models of opinion formation. *Communications in Mathematical Sciences, 4*(3), 481–496. doi:10.4310/CMS.2006.v4.n3.a1

Toscani, G., Brugna, C., & Demichelis, S. (2013). Kinetic models for the trading of goods. *Journal of Statistical Physics, 151*(3–4), 549–566. doi:10.100710955-012-0653-0

Xavier, G. & Yannis, I. (2004). *Chapter 53 - The Evolution of City Size Distributions*. In J. Vernon Henderson & Jacques-François Thisse (eds.), *Handbook of Regional and Urban Economics, 4*, 2341-2378. Elsevier. doi:10.1016/S1574-0080(04)80010-5

Yannis, I. (2013). Spyros Skouras, US city size distribution: Robustly Pareto, but only in the tail. Journal of Urban Economics, *73*(1) 18-29. doi:10.1016/j.jue.2012.06.005

Zaman, H. (2011). An edgeworth box approach toward conceptualising economic integration. *Mod. Econ., 2*(1), 62–70. doi:10.4236/me.2011.21010

Chapter 15
Designing a Relational Database Schema for a Kosovo Hospital Management System

Art Hajdari

Rochester Institute of Technology, Kosovo

ABSTRACT

A relational database schema was designed for the Kosovo Hospital Management System. The objective was to create a platform to store patient information, appointments, billing, and feedback, with the main goal of improving patient care. Eleven unique tables were created, with primary and foreign keys defining the relationships between them. Through the tables it is possible the management of patient and doctor schedules, medical records, allergies, blood donations, medical equipment, and hospital department administration, among others. The management system benefits all healthcare institutions such as hospitals, clinics, and blood banks, as well as medical staff such as doctors and nurses. Patients can also benefit from this by providing better healthcare services, faster appointment scheduling, and more.

INTRODUCTION

We want to make a management system for healthcare institutions, especially for hospitals. Our main objective is to improve the quality of patient care. Our project offers a platform that stores patient information, appointments, billing, and feedback. Healthcare workers may manage patient information such as medical history, allergies, prescriptions, and other essential information with this system in a very convenient way (K. Hedau et. al.,2018). The project will also allow patients and healthcare professionals to schedule and manage appointments. However, we offer different ways to store information for other stuff such as medical equipment (C. C. Batbagon et. al.,2018). We created 11 unique tables that are of course, related to each other in different ways (please check DBMS diagram for more information about the relationships between tables). Here are some of the functions that we are trying to provide based on our 11 tables:

DOI: 10.4018/978-1-6684-9809-5.ch015

- Managing patient and doctor schedules when creating a scheduling system for medical appointments.
- Create a patient database system that stores patient information, medical records, and test results.
- Create a system for managing doctor schedules and wages by tracking physicians' schedules and their wages (K. Cincar et. al.,2019).
- Create a blood donation management system that keeps track of donors and their donations.
- Create a medical equipment inventory management system that tracks equipment usage and upkeep (Guha, A. et. al., 2023).
- Create a patient feedback system that captures patient input and improves healthcare services.
- Handling patient invoices and payment data in a billing and payment system for medical establishments.
- Create a system for monitoring allergies in patients by tracking allergies and allergic responses (T. O. Paulussen et. al.,2006).
- Create a hospital department administration system that organizes departments and their staff personnel (S. Rupp et. al.,2019).

We believe that healthcare institutions such as hospitals, clinics, and blood banks would benefit from this initiative, as will medical personnel such as doctors and nurses who will be able to use the technologies to manage their job more efficiently (Jain, A. et. al., 2023). These technologies can also assist patients by providing better healthcare services, faster appointment scheduling etc.

LIST OF TABLES

This is an overview of our tables. Primary keys are noted with the yellow color and foreign keys are noted with green. Figure 1 shows an overview of tables created for the project. Figure 2 shows a DBMS diagram showing the different relationships between tables.

Figure 1. An overview of tables created for the project

G_4A_PATIENTS_TABLE	patient_id	first_name	last_name	date_of_birth	gender	phone	email	address	medical_condition
Data type	varchar(15)	varchar(20)	varchar(20)	DATE	varchar(1)	varchar(15)	varchar(30)	varchar(50)	varchar(100)

G_4A_DOCTORS_TABLE	doctor_id	first_name	last_name	specialization	phone	email	address	salary	schedule
Data Type	varchar(15)	varchar(20)	varchar(20)	varchar(20)	varchar(15)	varchar(30)	varchar(50)	decimal(5,2)	varchar(15)

G_4A_APPOINTMENTS_TABL	appointment_id	patient_id	doctor_id	appointment_date	appointment_time	purpose
Data Type	int	varchar(20)	varchar(15)	DATE	TIME	varchar(20)

G_4A_DEPARTMENTS_TABLE	department_id	department_name				
Data Type	int	varchar(20)			PRIMARY KEY	

G_4A_MEDICATIONS_TABLE	medication_id	medication_name	dosage	instructions	patient_id	FOREIGN KEY
Data Type	int	varchar(40)	varchar(20)	varchar(100)	varchar(15)	

G_4A_BILLING_INFO	bill_id	patient_id	date	total_amount	payment_method	status
Data Type	int	varchar(15)	DATE	decimal(5,2)	varchar(20)	varchar(20)

G_4A_PATIENT_FEEDBACK	feedback_id	patient_id	date	feedback_type	feedback_message
Data Type	varchar(15)	varchar(15)	DATE	varchar(10)	varchar(100)

G_4A_MEDICAL_EQUIPMENT	equipment_id	equipment_name	manufacturer	model	serial_no	purchase_date
Data_Type	varchar(20)	varchar(30)	varchar(30)	varchar(30)	int	DATE

G_4A_PATIENT_ALLERGIES	patient_id	allergy_id	allergy_name	allergy_type	allergy_severity
Data Type	varchar(15)	varchar(15)	varchar(30)	varchar(20)	varchar(30)

G_4A_BED_ASSIGNMENT	patient_id	bed_no	admission_date	discharge_date
Data Type	varchar(15)	int	DATE	DATE

G_4A_BLOOD_DONORS	donor_id	donor_name	donor_age	blood_type	donor_email	last_donation_date
Data Type	varchar(15)	varchar(20)	int	varchar(5)	varchar(30)	DATE

These are all of the commands we used to create these tables:

```
CREATE TABLE G_4A_PATIENTS_TABLE (
    patient_id varchar(15) PRIMARY KEY,
    first_name varchar(20),
    phone varchar(15),
    email varchar(30),
    address varchar(50),
    medical_condition varchar(100)
);
CREATE TABLE G_4A_DOCTORS_TABLE (
    doctor_id varchar(15) PRIMARY KEY,
    first_name varchar(20),
    last_name varchar(20),
    last_name varchar(20),
    date_of_birth DATE,
    gender varchar(1),
    specialization varchar(20),
    phone varchar(15),
    email varchar(30),
    address varchar(50),
    salary decimal(5,2),
    schedule varchar(15)
);
CREATE TABLE G_4A_APPOINTMENTS_TABLE (
    appointment_id int PRIMARY KEY,
    patient_id varchar(15) REFERENCES G_4A_PATIENTS_TABLE(patient_id),
    doctor_id varchar(15) REFERENCES G_4A_DOCTORS_TABLE(doctor_id),
    appointment_date DATE,
    appointment_time TIME,
    purpose varchar(20)
);
CREATE TABLE G_4A_DEPARTMENTS_TABLE (
  department_id INT PRIMARY KEY,
  department_name VARCHAR(20)
);
CREATE TABLE G_4A_MEDICATIONS_TABLE (
    medication_id int PRIMARY KEY,
    medication_name varchar(40),
    dosage varchar(20),
    instructions varchar(100),
    patient_id varchar(15) REFERENCES G_4A_PATIENTS_TABLE(patient_id)
);
CREATE TABLE G_4A_BILLING_INFO (
```

```
    bill_id int PRIMARY KEY,
    patient_id varchar(15) REFERENCES G_4A_PATIENTS_TABLE(patient_id),
    date DATE,
    total_amount decimal(5,2),
    payment_method varchar(20),
    status varchar(20)
);
CREATE TABLE G_4A_PATIENT_FEEDBACK (
    feedback_id varchar(15) PRIMARY KEY,
    patient_id varchar(15) REFERENCES G_4A_PATIENTS_TABLE(patient_id),
    date DATE,
    feedback_type varchar(10),
    feedback_message varchar(100)
);
CREATE TABLE G_4A_MEDICAL_EQUIPMENT (
    equipment_id varchar(20) PRIMARY KEY,
    equipment_name varchar(30),
    manufacturer varchar(30),
    model varchar(30),
    serial_no int,
    purchase_date DATE
);
CREATE TABLE G_4A_PATIENT_ALLERGIES (
    patient_id VARCHAR(15) REFERENCES G_4A_PATIENTS_TABLE(patient_id),
    allergy_id varchar(15) PRIMARY KEY,
    allergy_name VARCHAR(30),
    allergy_type VARCHAR(20),
    allergy_severity VARCHAR(30)
);
CREATE TABLE G_4A_BED_ASSIGNMENT (
    patient_id VARCHAR(15) REFERENCES G_4A_PATIENTS_TABLE(patient_id),
    bed_no INT PRIMARY KEY,
    admission_date DATE,
    discharge_date DATE,
);
CREATE TABLE G_4A_BLOOD_DONORS (
    donor_id varchar(15) PRIMARY KEY,
    donor_name varchar(20),
    donor_age int,
    blood_type varchar(5),
    donor_email varchar(30),
    last_donation_date DATE
);
```

DBMS DIAGRAM

Figure 2. A DBMS diagram showing the different relationships between tables

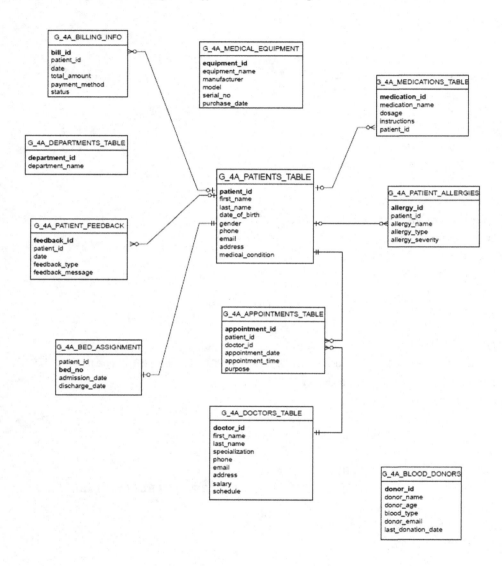

CONCEPT OF PROJECT ACCESSIBILITY

Data Sharing

Data sharing makes data accessible to team members securely and effectively. As a centralized site for data storage and exchange, SQL databases can make it simpler for team members to obtain the data they want (Paras V. Kothare et. al., 2014). To guarantee that data is exchanged in a managed and safely, it is crucial to create explicit procedures for data sharing (Dangi, P. et. al., 2023). To make sure sensitive data is protected, this may entail creating user accounts and permissions, as well as implementing encryption and other security measures. Project accessibility is largely dependent on efficient data exchange (Podder, S. K. et. al., 2023)(Pratik R. Mantri et. al.,2014).

Data Retrieval

We may use queries to extract data from the database in order to get data. To guarantee that team members can quickly and properly get the data they want, it is crucial to create explicit rules for data retrieval (Althar, R. R. et. al., 2023). This might entail teaching and assisting team members in creating efficient SQL queries, as well as describing data sources and APIs to give instructions on how to access the data (B. Maheswari et. al.,2013).

Data Definition

When defining data in SQL, tables must be made and connections (relationships) must be made between them. To guarantee that team members can access and utilize the data efficiently, it is crucial to describe data precisely and consistently (K Nisha et. al.,2013). In order to avoid redundancies and boost efficiency, this may entail defining data types and limitations, creating naming standards, and making sure that data is standardized (Mondal, S. et. al., 2023) (Iteit Spamast Malita et. al.,2018) (Dalia Kamal A. A. Rizk, et. al.).

Data Manipulation

SQL offers a robust collection of tools for manipulating data, including the capacity to change, add, and remove data (National Academy Press, 1999)(G. Yang, et. al.). It's crucial to make sure team members may alter data securely and productively without jeopardizing the data's integrity. This could entail defining precise rules for data manipulation as well as educating team members on how to utilize SQL to alter data successfully (Cunaku, E. et. al., 2023) (Praveen K.A et. al.,2006).

Access Control

Access control in SQL entails creating user accounts and permissions to make sure team members have access to the data they require while also preventing sensitive data from being accessed by unauthorized parties (S. Madakam et. al.). This may entail assigning various degrees of access to various team members, utilizing encryption to protect data while it is in motion and at rest, and defining procedures for handling user accounts and passwords in order to maintain their security over time (Garg, M. et. al., 2023) (C. Liang et. al.). In order to prevent access from outsiders and to guarantee complete privacy and confidentiality of data, we should make sure that access control is implemented in our data (Gurunath, R. et. al., 2023).

QUERIES FROM DIFFERENT TABLES

Figure 3 shows a query that selects all rows from g_4a_appointments_table where the appointment date is after 4th of May 2023. Figure 4 projects a query that selects all rows from g_4a_blood_donors where the blood type is A+. Figure 5 explain a query that selects all rows from g_4a_medications table that have a dosage bigger than 400mg. Figure 6 shows a query that selects all rows from g_4a_patients_table that have the gender set M (Male). Figure 7 shows a query that selects the patient_id and feedback_message from g_4a_patient_feedback table where the feedback type is 'compliment'. Figure 8 explain a query that selects the id and the name of the allergy from g_4a_patient_allergies where the severity is set to 'severe'. Figure 9 projects a query that selects the id and the first name of the doctors from g_4a_doctors_table where address is set to 'Peje'. Figure 10 shows a query that selects the id of the patient form the g_4a_billing_info table where the status is set to 'Unpaid'. Figure 11 shows a query that selects all data from g_4a_billing_info that have a bill larger than 40. Figure 12 explain A query that selects all from g_4a_patients_table that have diabetes as their medical condition. Figure 13 explain a query that returns the blood donor name if their age is bigger than 30.

1. Selecting all rows from g_4a_appointments_table where the appointment date is after 4th of May 2023.

Figure 3. A query that selects all rows from g_4a_appointments_table where the appointment date is after 4th of May 2023

2. Selecting all rows from g_4a_blood_donors where the blood type is A+.

Figure 4. A query that selects all rows from g_4a_blood_donors where the blood type is A+

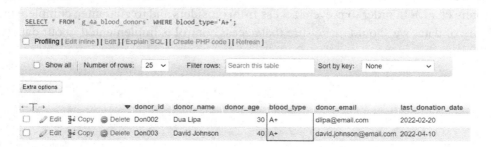

3.   Selecting all rows from g_4a_medications table that have a dosage bigger than 400 mg.

Figure 5. A query that selects all rows from g_4a_medications table that have a dosage bigger than 400mg

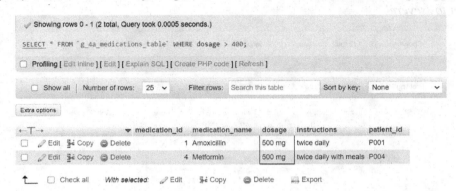

4.   Select all rows from g_4a_patients_table where the gender is M (Male).

Figure 6. A query that selects all rows from g_4a_patients_table that have the gender set M (Male)

5.   Select the patient_id and feedback_message colrumns from g_4a_patient_feedback where the feedback type is 'compliment'.

Figure 7. A query that selects the patient_id and feedback_message from g_4a_patient_feedback table where the feedback type is 'compliment'

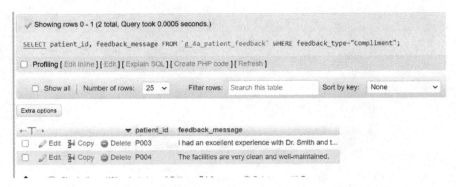

6.   Selecting the id and name of the allergy from g_4a_patient_allergies where the severity is severe.

Figure 8. A query that selects the id and the name of the allergy from g_4a_patient_allergies where the severity is set to 'severe'

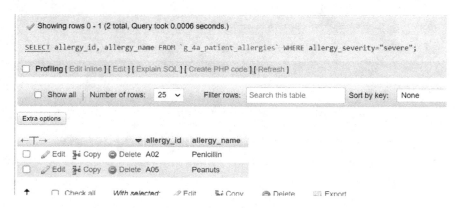

7.   Selecting the id and the first name of the doctor from g_4a_doctors_table where address is Peje.

Figure 9. A query that selects the id and the first name of the doctors from g_4a_doctors_table where address is set to 'Peje'

8.   Selecting the id of the patient from g_4a_billing_info that have the status of their bill unpaid.

Figure 10. A query that selects the id of the patient form the g_4a_billing_info table where the status is set to 'Unpaid'

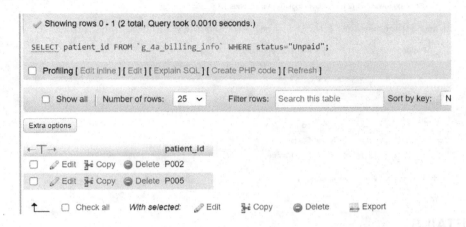

9.   Selecting all columns from g_4a_billing_info that have a bill larger than 40.

Figure 11. A query that selects all data from g_4a_billing_info that have a bill larger than 40

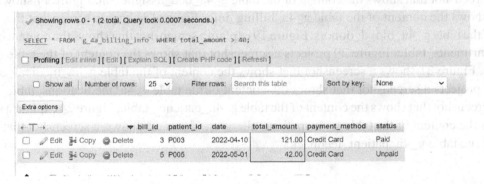

10.   Selecting all columns from g_4a_patients_table that have a medical condition of diabetes.

Figure 12. A query that selects all from g_4a_patients_table that have diabetes as their medical condition

11. Selecting the blood donor name from g_4a_blood_donors that are older than 30.

Figure 13. A query that returns the blood donor name if their age is bigger than 30

TABLE DETAILS

Here are screenshots that show the database (gr-4a) and tables in SQL (localhost/phpMyAdmin). Figure 14 shows a screenshot from localhost/phpMyAdmin that shows the database and the tables of the project. Figure 15 shows a screenshot that shows the content of the table g_4a_appointments_table. Figure 16 shows a screenshot that shows the content of the table g_4a_bed_assignemnt. Figure 17 shows a screenshot that shows the content of the table g_4a_billing_info. Figure 18 shows a screenshot that shows the content of the table g_4a_blood_donors. Figure 19 explain a screenshot that shows the content of the table g_4a_departments_table. Figure 20 projects a screenshot that shows the content of the table g_4a_doctors_table. Figure 21 shows a screenshot that shows the content of the table g_4a_medical_equipment. Figure 22 projects a screenshot that shows the content of the table g_4a_medications_table. Figure 23 shows a screenshot that shows the content of the table g_4a_patients_table. Figure 24 explain a screenshot that shows the content of the table g_4a_patient_allergies. Figure 25 shows. a screenshot that shows the content of the table g_4a_patient_feedback.

CONCLUSION

In conclusion, we created a database that has a total of multiple tables that can be used to store different information about the patients, doctors, appointments etc. By creating this database and these tables we tend to offer healthcare institutions a better management system for their staff. We provided a detailed description of each table and also a DBMS diagram, where primary and foreign keys are noted. Additionally, we performed eleven queries within our tables in order to show how much helpful can the databases be. For example, consider a big hospital has thousands of patients and wants to know the number of the patients diagnosed with diabetes. They can easily use the count and select commands offered in SQL.

Figure 14. A screenshot from localhost/phpMyAdmin that shows the database and the tables of the project

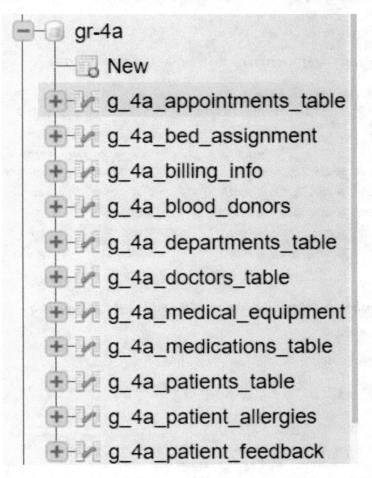

Figure 15. A screenshot that shows the content of the table g_4a_appointments_table

Figure 16. A screenshot that shows the content of the table g_4a_bed_assignemnt

Figure 17. A screenshot that shows the content of the table g_4a_billing_info

Figure 18. A screenshot that shows the content of the table g_4a_blood_donors

Figure 19. A screenshot that shows the content of the table g_4a_departments_table

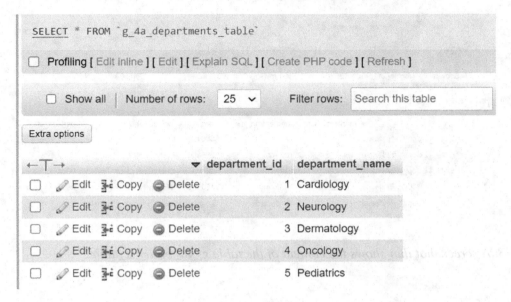

Figure 20. A screenshot that shows the content of the table g_4a_doctors_table

Figure 21. A screenshot that shows the content of the table g_4a_medical_equipment

Figure 22. A screenshot that shows the content of the table g_4a_medications_table

Figure 23. A screenshot that shows the content of the table g_4a_patients_table

Figure 24. A screenshot that shows the content of the table g_4a_patient_allergies

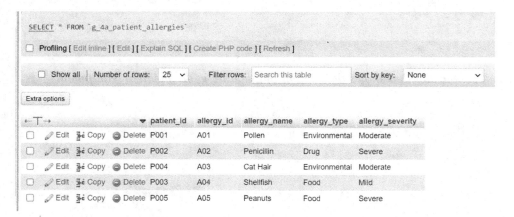

Figure 25. A screenshot that shows the content of the table g_4a_patient_feedback

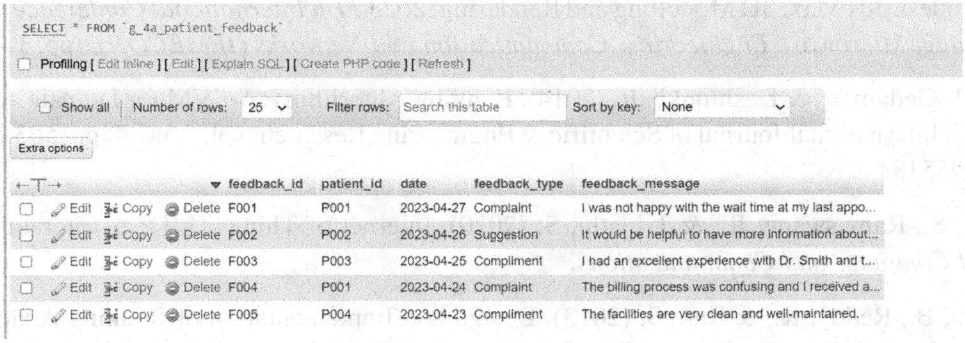
SELECT * FROM `g_4a_patient_feedback`

Profiling [Edit inline] [Edit] [Explain SQL] [Create PHP code] [Refresh]

Show all | Number of rows: 25 | Filter rows: Search this table | Sort by key: None

Extra options

	feedback_id	patient_id	date	feedback_type	feedback_message
Edit Copy Delete	F001	P001	2023-04-27	Complaint	I was not happy with the wait time at my last appo...
Edit Copy Delete	F002	P002	2023-04-26	Suggestion	It would be helpful to have more information about...
Edit Copy Delete	F003	P003	2023-04-25	Compliment	I had an excellent experience with Dr. Smith and t...
Edit Copy Delete	F004	P001	2023-04-24	Complaint	The billing process was confusing and I received a...
Edit Copy Delete	F005	P004	2023-04-23	Compliment	The facilities are very clean and well-maintained.

REFERENCES

Althar, R. R., Samanta, D., Purushotham, S., Sengar, S. S., & Hewage, C. (2023). Design and Development of Artificial Intelligence Knowledge Processing System for Optimizing Security of Software System. *SN Computer Science*, *4*(4), 331. doi:10.100742979-023-01785-2

Batbagon, C. C., Jayme, O. B., & Pradilla, J. P. (2018). I-queue: A centralized queue management system. Research Gate.

Cincar, K., & Ivascu, T. (2019). Agent-based hospital scheduling system. In *2019 21st International Symposium on Symbolic and Numeric Algorithms for Scientific Computing (SYNASC),* (pp. 337-338). IEEE. 10.1109/SYNASC49474.2019.00055

Cunaku, E., Ndrecaj, J., Berisha, S., Samanta, D., Dutta, S., & Bhattacharya, A. (2023). An Approach for Digital-Social Network Analysis Using Twitter API. In Innovations in Data Analytics: Selected Papers of ICIDA 2022 (pp. 625–636). Springer.

Dalia, K. A. A., Rizk, H. M. H., & El-Sayed, M. (2023). SMART Hospital Management Systems Based on the Internet of Things: Challenges Intelligent Solutions and Functional Requirements. *International Journal of Intelligent Computing and Information Sciences IJICIS*, *22*(1), 32–43.

Dangi, P., Jain, A., Samanta, D., Dutta, S., & Bhattacharya, A. (2023). 3D Modelling and Rendering Using Autodesk 3ds Max. *2023 11th International Conference on Internet of Everything, Microwave Engineering, Communication and Networks (IEMECON),* (pp. 1–5). IEEE.

Garg, M., Saxena, C., Samanta, D., & Dorr, B. J. (2023). LonXplain: Lonesomeness as a Consequence of Mental Disturbance in Reddit Posts. arXiv Preprint arXiv:2305. 18736. doi:10.1007/978-3-031-35320-8_27

Guha, A., Samanta, D., & Sengar, S. S. (2023). Computer Vision Based Automatic Margin Computation Model for Digital Document Images. *SN Computer Science*, *4*(3), 253. doi:10.100742979-023-01693-5

Gurunath, R., & Samanta, D. (2023). A New 3-Bit Hiding Covert Channel Algorithm for Public Data and Medical Data Security Using Format-Based Text Steganography. [JDM]. *Journal of Database Management*, *34*(2), 1–22. doi:10.4018/JDM.324076

Jain, A., Dangi, P., Samanta, D., Dutta, S., Bhattacharya, A., & Joseph, N. P. (2023). Creation of Bookshelf Using Autodesk 3ds Max: 3D Modelling and Rendering. *2023 11th International Conference on Internet of Everything, Microwave Engineering, Communication and Networks (IEMECON),* (pp. 1–4). IEEE.

Kothare, P., Gedam Y., & Deshmukh, R. (2014). Ranking Algorithm RA-SVM for Domain Adaptation: A Review", International Journal of Scientific & Engineering Research, vol. 5, no. 4, pp. 503-507, 2014, ISSN 22295518.

Madakam, S., Ramaswamy R., & Tripathi, S. (2020). Internet of Things (IoT): A Literature Review. *Journal of Computer and Communications*.

Maheswari, B., Reddy, K., & Rao, S. (2013). Design and Implementation of Ranking Adaptation Algorithm for Domain Specific Search. *International Journal of Computer Trends and Technology, 4*(8).

Malita, I. S. (2018). Quality of information management and efficiency of Hospital employees. *Hospital Management*.

Mondal, S., Pal, A. K., Islam, S. K. H., & Samanta, D. (2023). Objectionable Image Content Classification Using CNN-Based Semi-supervised Learning. In Advances in Smart Vehicular Technology, Transportation, Communication and Applications [Springer.]. *Proceedings of VTCA, 2022*, 311–320.

National Academy Press. (1999). *Measuring the Quality of Health Care*. A statement of the National Roundtable on Healthcare Quality Division of Healthcare Services, National Academy Press.

Nisha, K., Adhithyaa, N., Stephen, B., & Muthu Kumar, P. (2013). Ranking Model Adaptation for Domain Specific Search. *International Journal of Emerging Trends in Electrical and Electronics, 2*(4), 32–35.

Paulussen, T. O., Zoller, A., Rothlauf, F., Heinzl, A., Braubach, L., & Pokahr, A. (2006). Agent-based patient scheduling in hospitals. In Multiagent Engineering, 255-275. Springer. doi:10.1007/3-540-32062-8_14

Podder, S. K., Samanta, D., Thomas, B., Dutta, S., & Bhattacharya, A. (2023). Impact of blended education system on outcome-based learning and sector skills development. *2023 11th International Conference on Internet of Everything, Microwave Engineering, Communication and Networks (IEMECON)*, (pp. 1–6). IEEE.

Praveen K. (2006). A Study of the Hospital Information System (HIS) In the Medical Records Department of A Tertiary Teaching Hospital. *Journal of the Academy of Hospital Administration, 18*.

Rupp, S. (2019). Importance Of The Hospital Management System. *Electronic Health Reporter*. https://electronichealthreporter.com/importance-of-the-hospital-management-system/

Yang, G., Pang, Z., Deen, J., Dong, M., Zhang, Y., & Lovell, N. (2020). Homecare Robotic Systems for Healthcare 4.0: Visions and Enabling Technologies. *IEEE J. Biomed. Health Inform*. IEEE.

Chapter 16
Predicting Dogecoin Price Using Python Programming and AutoTS Algorithm

Albana Zejnullahi

Rochester Institute of Technology, Kosovo

ABSTRACT

It's crucial to thoroughly research the prior history of the cryptocurrency market, in this case Dogecoin, before considering investing in the financial market, especially the cryptocurrency market. The authors want to create a Python project that forecasts Dogecoin's price. To accomplish this, researchers need to gather all available data on Dogecoin's price history and use it to create mathematical formulas that will decide the currency's pricing. In order to help people grasp this data, the authors also create a chart to display it all.

INTRODUCTION

Due to its extreme volatility and meme-based culture, Dogecoin attracted a lot of people's interest these last few years, which made Dogecoin a fascinating topic in financial analysis and speculation (Altıntaş, B. (2021) (Bouri, E. et al.,2020)(Guha, A. et. al., 2023). The desire to comprehend the variables that affect cryptocurrency pricing and make wise investing choices is another factor (Q. Li et. al.,2016). You could learn more about market factors that affect cryptocurrency prices, like as supply and demand, governmental changes, and investor attitude, by carrying out a Dogecoin price prediction project. The article specifically focuses on Dogecoin and talks about how important it is to look into history before investing in cryptocurrency markets (Cenkowski, S. et al., 2019) (Chen, J. et al.,2021)(J. Tan et. al., 2019). By collecting information and developing mathematical methods to determine the currency's pricing, it's suggested to develop a program in Python to forecast Dogecoin's price. To display this information, a chart is also developed (Chen, W. et al.,2018) (Chen, Y. et al.,2021)(N. Gradojevic, R. Gençay et. al.,2009). The article also includes descriptions of the algorithm, a flowchart, and the outcomes of the

DOI: 10.4018/978-1-6684-9809-5.ch016

experiment (CNBC Television, 2021)(Jain, A. et. al., 2023)(X. Shi et. al.,2015). The algorithm involves installing and using AutoTS for time-series forecasting, importing libraries, setting Seaborn style, loading data into a pandas DataFrame, removing missing values, building a plot of DogeCoin prices over time, and generating and publishing the anticipated prices (R. Culkin et. al.,2017)(M. Malliaris et. al.,1993). The algorithm's steps are depicted in the flowchart. Results of the experiment include the opening, lowest, highest, and closing prices, adj. closing, and volume of the volume of the trade, price chart, and price prediction of Dogecoin (Diakonikolas, I. et al.,2021) (Digital Trends,2021)(Dangi, P. et. al., 2023).

DATA SET DESCRIPTION

- **Size:**24260
- **Python Code:**
  from pathlib import Path
  sz = Path("/DOGE-USD.csv").stat().st_size
  print(sz)
- **No. of col:** 7 & **No. of row:** 366
  # import module
  import pandas as pd
  # read the csv file
  results = pd.read_csv("/DOGE-USD.csv")
  # display dataset
  print(results)

Figure 1 shows Values of Dogecoin Price. Figure 2 shows Output Head Values of Dogecoin Price.

Figure 1. Values of Dogecoin price

```
 ⌐➜          Date      Open      High       Low     Close  Adj Close      Volume
     0   2022-04-05  0.148614  0.178045  0.147727  0.172907   0.172907  5230288678
     1   2022-04-06  0.172485  0.173497  0.143291  0.143417   0.143417  3729047979
     2   2022-04-07  0.143432  0.148028  0.141312  0.146102   0.146102  1420790611
     3   2022-04-08  0.146106  0.152716  0.141608  0.142549   0.142549  1683800631
     4   2022-04-09  0.142544  0.144462  0.141416  0.144303   0.144303   523997409
    ..          ...       ...       ...       ...       ...        ...         ...
    361  2023-04-01  0.077025  0.085279  0.076144  0.084051   0.084051   933070185
    362  2023-04-02  0.081859  0.085279  0.077848  0.079089   0.079089   929778146
    363  2023-04-03  0.079087  0.102640  0.076632  0.096079   0.096079  3497240136
    364  2023-04-04  0.096083  0.102538  0.092871  0.095159   0.095159  3096545498
    365  2023-04-05  0.094984  0.098416  0.093707  0.096959   0.096959  2360847360

    [366 rows x 7 columns]
```

- **Input:** The price history of Dogecoin downloaded from Yahoo Finance
- **Expected Output:** Based on the given data, the expected output should be a table showing the following details for each date:

The date when the cryptocurrency price was changed

Opening price
Highe price
Lowest price
Closed price
Adj Close price
Volume of the Trade

Here is an example of how the output table could be formatted:

Figure 2. Output head values of Dogecoin price

	Date	Open	High	Low	Close	Adj Close	Volume
0	2022-04-05	0.148614	0.178045	0.147727	0.172907	0.172907	5230288678
1	2022-04-06	0.172485	0.173497	0.143291	0.143417	0.143417	3729047979
2	2022-04-07	0.143432	0.148028	0.141312	0.146102	0.146102	1420790611
3	2022-04-08	0.146106	0.152716	0.141608	0.142549	0.142549	1683800631
4	2022-04-09	0.142544	0.144462	0.141416	0.144303	0.144303	523997409

ALGORITHM

Step 1. Import required libraries
Step 2. Set the style of seaborn plots
Step 3. Load the DogeCoin price data into a pandas DataFrame
Step 4. Print the first few rows of the DataFrame
Step 5. Drop any missing values in the DataFrame
Step 6. Create a plot of DogeCoin prices over time
- Set the title of the plot to "DogeCoin Price INR"
- Set the x-axis label to "Date"
- Set the y-axis label to "Close"
Step 7. Show the plot
Step 8. Install the AutoTS module
Step 9. Import the AutoTS module
Step 10. Set the forecast length, frequency, ensemble, and drop data older than periods parameters for the AutoTS model
Step 11. Create an instance of the AutoTS model
Step 12. Fit the model to the DogeCoin price data
- Specify the date column
- Specify the value column
- Set the id column to None
Step 13. Generate predictions for the DogeCoin
Step 14. Access the forecasted prices
Step 15. Print the forecasted prices

FLOWCHART

Figure 3 shows Flowchart of the Algorithm from Step 1 to Step 5. Figure 4 explains Flowchart of the Algorithm from Step 6 to Step 11. Figure 5 shows Flowchart of the Algorithm from Step 12 to Step 15.

Figure 3. Flowchart of the algorithm from step 1 to step 5.

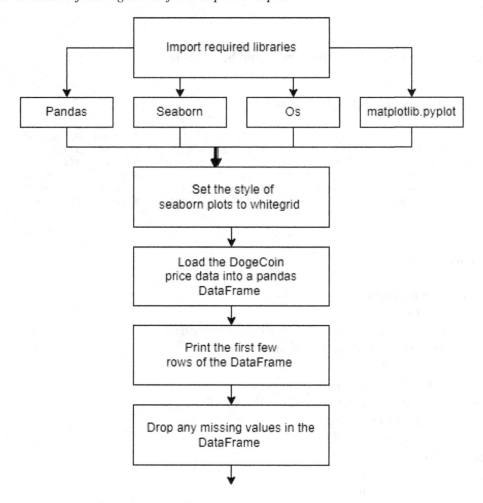

EXPERIMENT RESULTS

Figure 6 shows Head Values from the Dataset of Price Dogecoin Price. Figure 7 shows Price Chart of Dogecoin Price. Figure 8 shows Output of Dogecoin Price Prediction.

Figure 4. Flowchart of the algorithm from step 6 to step 11

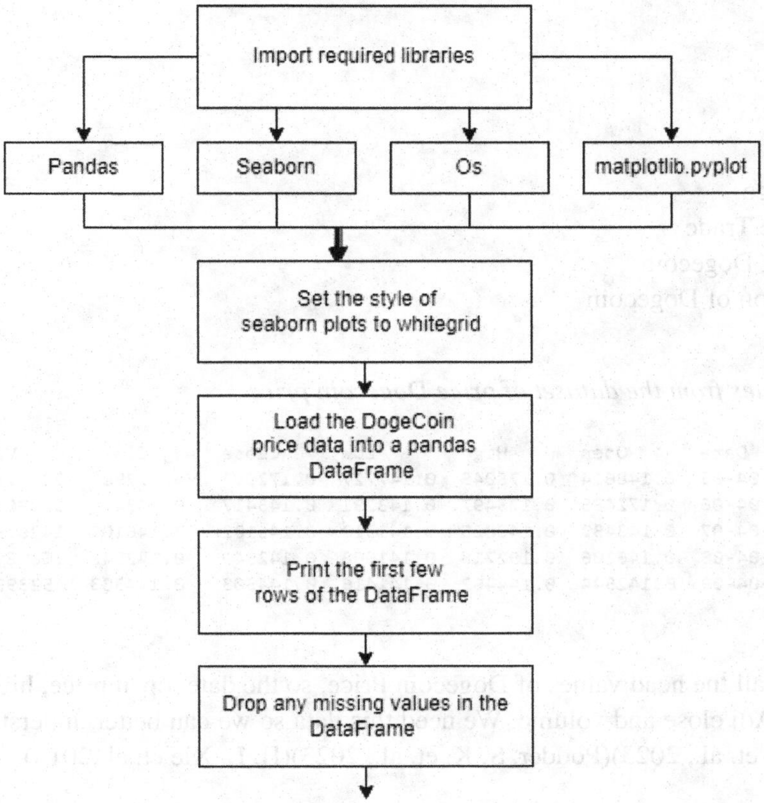

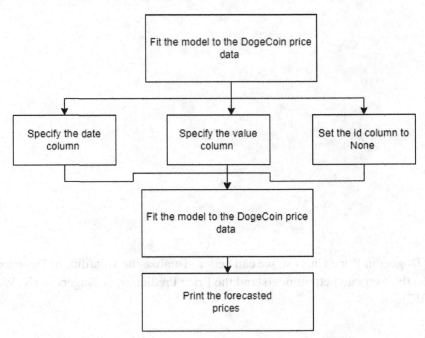

Figure 5. Flowchart of the algorithm from step 12 to step 15

All Outputs

- Open price
- Highest price
- Lowest price
- Closed price
- Adj Close price
- Volume of the Trade
- Price Chart of Dogecoin
- Price Prediction of Dogecoin

Figure 6. Head values from the dataset of price Dogecoin price

	Date	Open	High	Low	Close	Adj Close	Volume
0	2022-04-05	0.148614	0.178045	0.147727	0.172907	0.172907	5230288678
1	2022-04-06	0.172485	0.173497	0.143291	0.143417	0.143417	3729047979
2	2022-04-07	0.143432	0.148028	0.141312	0.146102	0.146102	1420790611
3	2022-04-08	0.146106	0.152716	0.141608	0.142549	0.142549	1683800631
4	2022-04-09	0.142544	0.144462	0.141416	0.144303	0.144303	523997409

We have gotten all the head values of Dogecoin Price, so the date, open price, highest price, lowest price, close price. Adj close and volume. We need this data so we can better understand the Dogecoin price (Althar, R. R. et. al., 2023)(Podder, S. K. et. al., 2023)(H. L. Xie et. al.,2018).

Figure 7. Price chart of Dogecoin price

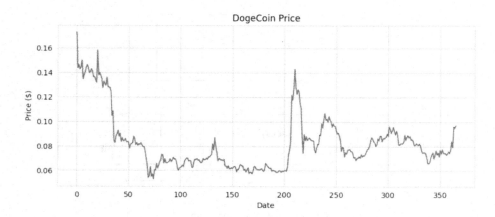

We created a Dogecoin Price Chart so we can better visualize the volatility of Dogecoin price over a period of time. So the user can better understand the Price Prediction of Dogecoin (X. Wei et. al.,2020) (T. Sun et. al.,2017).

Figure 8. Output of Dogecoin price prediction

```
DogeCoin Price Prediction
                     Close
2023-04-06        0.097529
2023-04-07        0.098069
2023-04-08        0.098386
2023-04-09        0.098950
2023-04-10        0.099919
2023-04-11        0.100335
2023-04-12        0.100796
2023-04-13        0.101218
2023-04-14        0.101627
2023-04-15        0.101952
```

Using AutoTS library in Python we use Machine Learning to predict the Dogecoin price.

COMPARE A MINIMUM 2 DATASETS WITH ALL OUTPUTS

Figure 9 shows Head Values from Dataset 1 of Price Prediction of Dogecoin. Figure 10 explain Head Values from Dataset 2 of Price Prediction of Dogecoin. Figure 11 shows Price Chart from Dataset 1 of Price Prediction of Dogecoin. Figure 12 shows Price Chart from Dataset 2 of Price Prediction of Dogecoin. Figure 13 shows AutoTS Library for Machine Learning for Dataset 2 of Price Prediction of Dogecoin. Figure 14 shows AutoTS Library for Machine Learning for Dataset 2 of Price Prediction of Dogecoin. Figure 15 shows Output of Dataset 1 of Price Prediction of Dogecoin. Figure 16 explain Output from Dataset 2 of Price Prediction of Dogecoin.

Figure 9. Head values from dataset 1 of price prediction of Dogecoin

	Date	Open	High	Low	Close	Adj Close	Volume
0	2022-04-05	0.148614	0.178045	0.147727	0.172907	0.172907	5230288678
1	2022-04-06	0.172485	0.173497	0.143291	0.143417	0.143417	3729047979
2	2022-04-07	0.143432	0.148028	0.141312	0.146102	0.146102	1420790611
3	2022-04-08	0.146106	0.152716	0.141608	0.142549	0.142549	1683800631
4	2022-04-09	0.142544	0.144462	0.141416	0.144303	0.144303	523997409

Figure 10. Head values from dataset 2 of price prediction of Dogecoin

	Date	Open	High	Low	Close	Adj Close	Volume
0	2017-11-09	0.001207	0.001415	0.001181	0.001415	0.001415	6259550.0
1	2017-11-10	0.001421	0.001431	0.001125	0.001163	0.001163	4246520.0
2	2017-11-11	0.001146	0.001257	0.001141	0.001201	0.001201	2231080.0
3	2017-11-12	0.001189	0.001210	0.001002	0.001038	0.001038	3288960.0
4	2017-11-13	0.001046	0.001212	0.001019	0.001211	0.001211	2481270.0

In Figure 9 and Figure 10 we see the Head Values from two different datasets, and you can notice the date, open price, high price, low, close price, adj close and volume are different because of the different time periods these datasets were taken (D. Tran et. al.,2015)(A. Atkins et. al.,2018). We want to use the most accurate one for a better actual Dogecoin Price Prediction (Dogecoin, 2022) (Dogecoin et al., 2023) (Gao, L. et al.,2021) (Grinberg, R. 2011)(Mondal, S. et. al., 2023)(A. Itkin et. al.,2019).

Figure 11. Price chart from dataset 1 of price prediction of Dogecoin

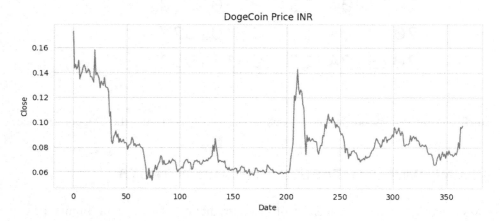

Figure 12. Price chart from dataset 2 of price prediction of Dogecoin

In Figure 11 and Figure 12 we can visualize the Price of Dogecoin, so investors can better see and analyze the price chart, and make better investment decisions. Even here we have used two different datasets from different times, and we choose to use the most actual one for better price predictions (Li, Q. et al.,2021) (Liu, J. et al.,2021) (Luo, Y. et al.,2021) (Cunaku, E. et. al., 2023)(M. Alfarraj et. al.,2019) (J. Sheng, W. Kong et. al.,2020).

Figure 13. AutoTS library for machine learning for dataset 2 of price prediction of Dogecoin

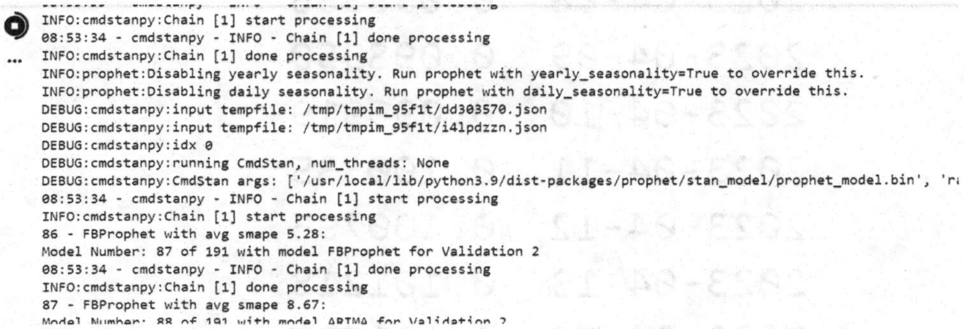

Figure 14. AutoTS library for machine learning for dataset 2 of price prediction of Dogecoin

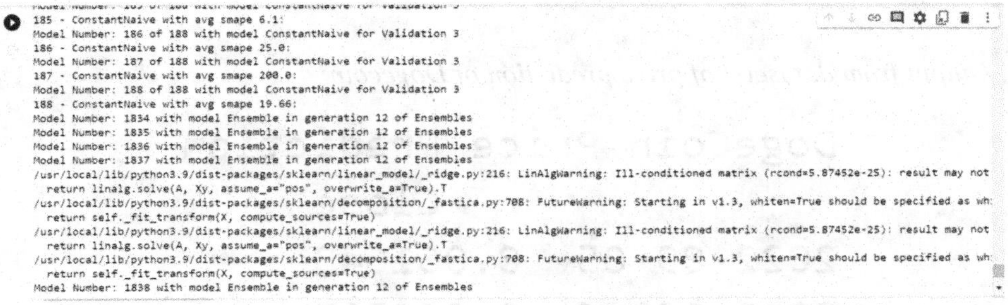

In Figure 13 and Figure 14 we can see that we use the AutoTS library so we use Machine Learning to predict the price prediction of Dogecoin(Kavitha S et. al.,2016)(A. Aljouie et. al.,2015). Based on the analysis we made it was clear that using the AutoTS library was the best option for the Dogecoin price prediction (Sun, H. et al.,2022) (The Clever Programmer, 2021) (The Verge, 2021)(Garg, M. et. al., 2023)(M. Alfarraj et. al.,2019)(A. Viswanath et. al.,2020).

In Figure 15 and Figure 16, you can observe that there's a difference in the Price Prediction of Dogecoin, there are two set of different values. Now for a more accurate price prediction we use the most actual dataset so we can have a better price prediction (Wang, Y. et al.,2021) (Gurunath, R. et. al., 2023)(Y. Qisheng et. al.,2009).

Figure 15. Output of dataset 1 of price prediction of Dogecoin

```
DogeCoin Price Prediction
                     Close
2023-04-06   0.097529
2023-04-07   0.098069
2023-04-08   0.098386
2023-04-09   0.098950
2023-04-10   0.099919
2023-04-11   0.100335
2023-04-12   0.100796
2023-04-13   0.101218
2023-04-14   0.101627
2023-04-15   0.101952
```

Figure 16. Output from dataset 2 of price prediction of Dogecoin

```
DogeCoin Price Prediction
                     Close
2022-09-05   0.061643
2022-09-06   0.061525
2022-09-07   0.061525
2022-09-08   0.061525
2022-09-09   0.061525
2022-09-10   0.061525
2022-09-11   0.061525
2022-09-12   0.061525
2022-09-13   0.061525
2022-09-14   0.061525
```

CONCLUSION

In this comparative study, we have analyzed two different datasets for Dogecoin price prediction. Through the use of different visualizations, including head values, price charts, and outputs, we were able to identify key differences between the datasets. We found that the choice of dataset is crucial for accurate price prediction, and that using the most up-to-date data is essential. We also used the AutoTS library for machine learning to further improve the accuracy of our predictions. Overall, this study highlights the importance of careful data analysis and selection for successful price prediction. By using the most current data and advanced tools, investors can make more informed decisions and achieve better returns.

REFERENCES

Alfarraj, M., & AlRegib, G. (2019). Semi-supervised learning for acoustic impedance inversion. In *SEG Technical Program Expanded Abstracts 2019* (pp. 2298–2302). Society of Exploration Geophysicists. doi:10.1190egam2019-3215902.1

Alfarraj, M., & AlRegib, G. (2019). Semisupervised sequence modeling for elastic impedance inversion. *Interpretation (Tulsa)*, 7(3), SE237–SE249. doi:10.1190/INT-2018-0250.1

Aljouie, A., & Roshan, U. (2015). Prediction of Continuous Phenotypes in Mouse, Fly, and Rice Genome Wide Association Studies with Support Vector Regression SNPs and Ridge Regression Classifier. IEEE 14th International Conference on Machine Learning and Applications (ICMLA), (pp. 1246-1250). IEEE. 10.1109/ICMLA.2015.224

Althar, R. R., Samanta, D., Purushotham, S., Sengar, S. S., & Hewage, C. (2023). Design and Development of Artificial Intelligence Knowledge Processing System for Optimizing Security of Software System. *SN Computer Science*, 4(4), 331. doi:10.100742979-023-01785-2

Altıntaş, B. (2021). A Comparative Study of Bitcoin, Ethereum, and Dogecoin: Investment Performance and Portfolio Diversification. *Journal of Risk and Financial Management*, 14(3), 103. doi:10.3390/jrfm14030103

Atkins, A., Niranjan, M., & Gerding, E. (2018). Financial news predicts stock market volatility better than close price. *The Journal of Finance and Data Science*, 4(2), 120–137. doi:10.1016/j.jfds.2018.02.002

Bing, W., Wen-qiong, Z., & Jia-hong, L. (2010). *A Genetic Multiple Kernel Relevance Vector Regression Approach. 2010 Second International Workshop on Education Technology and Computer Science*, Wuhan, China. 10.1109/ETCS.2010.154

Bouri, E., Azzi, G., Molnár, P., Roubaud, D., & Hagfors, L. I. (2020). On the return-volatility relationship in the Bitcoin-Dogecoin markets: A multivariate GARCH analysis. *Journal of Risk and Financial Management*, 13(6), 123. doi:10.3390/jrfm13060123

Cenkowski, S., & Gurtler, M. (2019). Cryptocurrency trading strategies and technical indicators for dogecoin: Volatility analysis and forecasting. Journal of Financial Management. *Markets and Institutions*, 7(2), 81–98. doi:10.12831/91629

Chen, J., Li, Y., & Shu, K. (2021). Deep learning-based Dogecoin price prediction using historical data. *IEEE Transactions on Neural Networks and Learning Systems*, *32*(6), 2726–2735. doi:10.1109/TNNLS.2020.3041867

Chen, W., Zhou, C., & Zhu, Z. (2018). A novel approach to cryptocurrency price prediction based on autoregressive integrated moving average and artificial neural network. *Journal of Intelligent & Fuzzy Systems*, *34*(2), 1187–1195. doi:10.3233/JIFS-179851

Chen, Y., Li, X., & Sun, J. (2021). Forecasting Dogecoin prices using a machine learning-based approach. *Journal of Computational Science*, *53*, 101468. doi:10.1016/j.jocs.2021.101468

Culkin, R., & Das, S. R. (2017). Machine learning in finance: The case of deep learning for option pricing. *Journal of Investment Management*, *15*(4), 92–100.

Cunaku, E., Ndrecaj, J., Berisha, S., Samanta, D., Dutta, S., *& Bhattacharya, A. (2023). An Approach for Digital-Social Network Analysis Using Twitter API. In Innovations in Data Analytics: Selected Papers of ICIDA 2022* (pp. 625–636). Springer. 10.1007/978-981-99-0550-8_49

Dangi, P., Jain, A., Samanta, D., Dutta, S., & Bhattacharya, A. (2023). 3D Modelling and Rendering Using Autodesk 3ds Max. *2023 11th International Conference on Internet of Everything, Microwave Engineering, Communication and Networks (IEMECON)*, (pp. 1–5). IEEE.

Deng, C.-X., Xu, L.-X., & Fu, Z.-X. (2008). The Beat-wave signal regression based on least squares reproducing kernel support vector machine. *2008 International Conference on Machine Learning and Cybernetics*, Kunming, China. 10.1109/ICMLC.2008.4621037

Diakonikolas, I., Gidaris, S., Mitliagkas, I., & Sivakumar, V. (2021). A Study of Cryptocurrency Markets: How Volatile are They? arXiv preprint arXiv:2104.03399. https://arxiv.org/abs/2104.03399

CoinMarketCap. (2022, April 25). Dogecoin. In *CoinMarketCap*. https://coinmarketcap.com/currencies/dogecoin/

Dogecoin. (n.d.). In Investopedia. https://www.investopedia.com/terms/d/dogecoin.asp

Gao, L., Sun, J., & Xu, Z. (2021). Deep learning for Dogecoin price prediction: A comparative study of CNN and LSTM. *Expert Systems with Applications*, *174*, 114627. doi:10.1016/j.eswa.2021.114627

Garg, M., Saxena, C., Samanta, D., & Dorr, B. J. (2023). LonXplain: Lonesomeness as a Consequence of Mental Disturbance in Reddit Posts. arXiv Preprint arXiv:2305.18736. doi:10.1007/978-3-031-35320-8_27

Gradojevic, N., Gençay, R., & Kukolj, D. (2009). Option pricing with modular neural networks. *IEEE Transactions on Neural Networks*, *20*(4), 626–637. doi:10.1109/TNN.2008.2011130 PMID:19273045

Grinberg, R. (2011). Bitcoin: An Innovative Alternative Digital Currency. *Hastings Science & Technology Law Journal*, *4*(2), 159–208.

Guha, A., Samanta, D., & Sengar, S. S. (2023). Computer Vision Based Automatic Margin Computation Model for Digital Document Images. *SN Computer Science*, *4*(3), 253. doi:10.100742979-023-01693-5

Gurunath, R., & Samanta, D. (2023). A New 3-Bit Hiding Covert Channel Algorithm for Public Data and Medical Data Security Using Format-Based Text Steganography. [JDM]. *Journal of Database Management*, *34*(2), 1–22. doi:10.4018/JDM.324076

Itkin, A. (2019). *Deep learning calibration of option pricing models: some pitfalls and solutions*. arXiv preprint.

Jain, A., Dangi, P., Samanta, D., Dutta, S., Bhattacharya, A., & Joseph, N. P. (2023). Creation of Bookshelf Using Autodesk 3ds Max: 3D Modelling and Rendering. *2023 11th International Conference on Internet of Everything, Microwave Engineering, Communication and Networks (IEMECON)*, (pp. 1–4). IEEE.

Kavitha, S., Varuna, S., & Ramya, R. (2016). A comparative analysis on linear regression and support vector regression. *2016 Online International Conference on Green Engineering and Technologies (IC-GET)*, (pp. 1-5). IEEE. 10.1109/GET.2016.7916627

Li, Q., Chen, Y., Jiang, L. L., Li, P., & Chen, H. (2016). A tensor-based information framework for predicting the stock market [TOIS]. *ACM Transactions on Information Systems*, *34*(2), 1–30. doi:10.1145/2838731

Li, Q., Wang, Z., & Zhou, W. (2021). Dogecoin price prediction using machine learning based on social media data. *Journal of Intelligent & Fuzzy Systems*, *41*(1), 773–783. doi:10.3233/JIFS-201767

Limei, L., & Xuan, H. (2017). *Study of electricity load forecasting based on multiple kernels learning and weighted support vector regression machine*. 2017 29th Chinese Control And Decision Conference (CCDC), Chongqing, China. 10.1109/CCDC.2017.7978740

Liu, J., Li, Z., & Zhang, X. (2021). An ensemble learning model for Dogecoin price prediction. *International Journal of Computer Mathematics*, *98*(4), 899–910. doi:10.1080/00207160.2020.1818294

Luo, Y., & Song, Y. (2021). Machine learning-based Dogecoin price prediction using technical indicators. *IEEE Access : Practical Innovations, Open Solutions*, *9*, 57261–57272. doi:10.1109/ACCESS.2021.3076458

Malliaris, M., & Salchenberger, L. (1993). A neural network model for estimating option prices. *Applied Intelligence*, *3*(3), 193–206. doi:10.1007/BF00871937

Mondal, S., Pal, A. K., Islam, S. K. H., & Samanta, D. (2023). Objectionable Image Content Classification Using CNN-Based Semi-supervised Learning. In Advances in Smart Vehicular Technology, Transportation, Communication and Applications [Springer.]. *Proceedings of VTCA*, 2022, 311–320.

Nie, Z., Yuan, Y., Xu, D., & Shen, F. (2019). *Research on Support Vector Regression Model Based on Different Kernels for Short-term Prediction of Ship Motion*. 2019 12th International Symposium on Computational Intelligence and Design (ISCID), Hangzhou, China. 10.1109/ISCID.2019.00021

Podder, S. K., Samanta, D., Thomas, B., Dutta, S., & Bhattacharya, A. (2023). Impact of blended education system on outcome-based learning and sector skills development. *2023 11th International Conference on Internet of Everything, Microwave Engineering, Communication and Networks (IEMECON)*, (pp. 1–6). IEEE.

Qisheng, Y., & Guohua, W. (2009). Prediction Model of Alga's Growth Based on Support Vector Regression. *2009 International Conference on Environmental Science and Information Application Technology*, Wuhan, China. 10.1109/ESIAT.2009.170

Sheng, J., Kong, W., & Qi, J. (2020). Process optimization of carbon fiber precursor spinning coagulation process based on surrogate model. *2020 Chinese Automation Congress (CAC)*, Shanghai, China. 10.1109/CAC51589.2020.9326779

Shi, X., Chen, Z., Wang, H., Yeung, D., Wong W., & Woo, W. (2015). *Convolutional lstm network: A machine learning approach for precipitation nowcasting.* arXiv preprint.

Sun, H., & Yang, B. (2022). Comparative analysis of machine learning methods for Dogecoin price prediction. *Journal of Business Research*, *141*, 269–278. doi:10.1016/j.jbusres.2022.03.015

Sun, T., Wang, J., Zhang, P., Cao, Y., Liu, B., & Wang, D. (2017). Predicting stock price returns using microblog sentiment for chinese stock market. *2017 3rd International Conference on Big Data Computing and Communications (BIGCOM)*, (pp. 87-96). IEEE. 10.1109/BIGCOM.2017.59

Tan, J., Wang, J., Rinprasertmeechai, D., Xing, R., & Li, Q. (2019). A tensor-based elstm model to predict stock price using financial news. *Proceedings of the 52nd Hawaii International Conference on System Sciences*. Scholar Space. 10.24251/HICSS.2019.201

CNBC Television. (2021, April 28). *Tim Cook on Apple's Q2 earnings report.* [Video]. YouTube. https://www.youtube.com/watch?v=QIUxPv5PJOY

The Clever Programmer. (2021, May 25). Dogecoin Price Prediction with Machine Learning. *The Clever Programmer.* https://thecleverprogrammer.com/2021/05/25/dogecoin-price-prediction-with-machine-learning/

The Verge. (2021, April 13). *Apple Spring Loaded Event Recap in 14 Minutes.* [Video]. YouTube. https://www.youtube.com/watch?v=GFSiL6zEZF0

Tran, D., Bourdev, L., Fergus, R., Torresani, L., & Paluri, M. (2015). Learning spatiotemporal features with 3d convolutional networks. Proceedings of the IEEE international conference on computer vision, (pp. 4489-4497). IEEE. 10.1109/ICCV.2015.510

Trends, D. (2021, March 2). *What is Clubhouse? The Invite-Only Social Media App Explained.* [Video]. YouTube. https://www.youtube.com/watch?v=FMKnvsKoQxE

Viswanath, A. D. K., M., S., B., & P., E. (2020). *Calibration of a Pyranometer using Regression Analysis.* 2020 5th International Conference on Communication and Electronics Systems (ICCES), Coimbatore, India.

Wang, Q., & Shen, Y. (2013). Particle Swarm Optimization-Least Squares Support Vector Regression with Multi-scale Wavelet Kernel. *2013 Sixth International Symposium on Computational Intelligence and Design*, Hangzhou, China, .

Wang, Y., Zhao, L., & Zhang, H. (2021). A hybrid model for Dogecoin price prediction based on ARIMA and machine learning. *Journal of Intelligent & Fuzzy Systems*, *41*(3), 4443–4451. doi:10.3233/JIFS-200426

Wei, X., Xie, Z., Cheng, R., & Li, Q. (2020). A cnn based system for predicting the implied volatility and option prices. *Proceedings of the 53rd Hawaii International Conference on System Sciences*. IEEE. 10.24251/HICSS.2020.176

Xie, H. L., & You, T. (2018). *Research on european stock index options pricing based on deep learning algorithm:evidence from 50etf options markets*. Statistics & Information Forum.

Chapter 17
The Software Principles of Design for Data Modeling:
Gathering Requirements – A Detailed Guide

Saurabh Bhattacharya

https://orcid.org/0000-0002-2729-1835

Chitkara University, India

ABSTRACT

The method for researchers to ascertain clients' software needs is requirement gathering. Requirement gathering rarely occurs successfully, and numerous software programs have failed as a result of incorrect or partial knowledge of the needs of users. The requirement-gathering technique is widely considered to be an essential part of development. The chapter will critically discuss why many developments fail due to poor requirements gathering. It is a challenging task to elicit requirements. When requirements are elicited, errors are most common. Addressing the system's needs presents several challenges, and the chapter intends to study these challenges and provide a solution. Professionals face challenges in gathering requirements due to the unavailability of stakeholders, unclear requirements, frequent changes in demand, and lack of skills for analysts. In a variety of contexts and areas, interviews with a preference for framework proved to be among the best gathering approaches.

INTRODUCTION

Information systems design places a high priority on gathering needs from users as well as other stakeholders. As any problems with the collected requirement have an effect on the operation as an entirety as well as certain circumstances that might result in a project's being unsuccessful, "requirements gathering" in software design is a crucial component of every "project". Software development is ''the process by which user needs are translated into a software product. The process involves translating user needs into software requirements, transforming the software requirements into design, implementing the design

DOI: 10.4018/978-1-6684-9809-5.ch017

in code, testing the code, and sometimes, installing and checking out the software for operational use''
This term is significant as it describes the software as a malleable reality made up of various artifacts,
including: "technology programs, processes, and perhaps related information and material related to the
functioning of a hardware network." The caliber of software development is influenced by the architectural choices made. A collection of solutions called "software design principles" aids in the creation of
successful computer designs. The technique of drafting or creating a narrative exhibits many similarities
with that of creating software, which has gained increased recognition in current decades. Every software
creation venture must start with "requirements gathering". They include statements such as "What the
User wants to do?" How does it occur? In actuality, "requirements gathering" is the act of compiling an
array of needs (functional, systemic, technological, etc.) from all the contributors (clients, users, sup-
pliers, IT personnel), which will serve as the foundation for the official description of the features that
the work involves. Inadequately drafted requirements may trigger issues throughout design since they
characterize the venture, and most importantly, they can lead to programs failing if the objectives are
unclear, in which case the project will fail. In keeping with the saying, "failing to plan, and you plan to
fail". A crucial step in the design of information technology is determining the requirements, however,
there is strong proof that the procedure can and ought to be enhanced. Amendments can result in considerable advantages for the whole systems construction procedure since the majority of the required
identification happens at the beginning of the building phase of an architecture(Browne & Ramesh, 2002).
The essential stage in every software creation approach is "requirements gathering" for projects. Every
undertaking must-have requirements to be defined, estimated and managed. All software development
projects must adhere to high standards to be successful, no matter if it relies on "Agile Methodology
"or the conventional "Waterfall Approach". While conventional frameworks and agile techniques might
employ distinct 'requirements gathering" procedures, the standards for good requirements are always
the same(Davey & R. Parker, 2015).

WHAT IS REQUIREMENT GATHERING?

A project's features are all determined through an approach known as "requirements gathering", sometimes known as "requirements elicitation". Technological and business requirements constitute the two
basic categories of project specifications. The technical specifications describe how the project must
be carried out whereas business criteria specify what an organization will achieve with the project.
The method of determining the precise requirements for the project from beginning to end is known as
requirements gathering. While managing the needs over the project timeframe, this process takes place
throughout the project's beginning stage. Obtain, accumulate, retrieve, or discover are all definitions
of the word "Gathering." Feature elicitation, in the context of software design, is the procedure used
to collect specifications from key players for the creation of software. The stage of demand-gathering
information kicks off every software creation project. As part of the "requirement gathering" method,
analysts record the requirements, "wants", and "desires" of stakeholders using a variety of gathering
approaches. The analyst focuses on comprehending the needs, goals, and limitations of the mechanism
that will be developed throughout the requirement-gathering process. Further specifications are defined
during the specification elicitation step, which determines the requirements' scope. Any development of
an Application starts with an understanding of the "Wants" of the user and then moves to the "Desire"
of the user. The first and ongoing stage of creating a "software application" is specification collecting.

These needs are obtained from a variety of sources, including the owners of the problems, stakeholders, current processes, and literature. The five forms of requirement collecting are: understanding the problem area, identifying the origins of needs, investigating stakeholders, choosing the best instrument and approach, and collecting specifications from multiple places(Maria & Ali, 2018)."specification elicitation", evaluation, "specification", "validation", and management are all parts of the requirements design process. User requirements are gathered and identified during requirements elicitation. Its goal is to locate data that will help in evaluating what characteristics the program's solution needs. The specifications phase involves repeated execution of this action. At this point in its development, it frequently occurs recursively and is connected with distinct tasks. The extraction sessions refer to any of these cycles for gathering important requirements-related data(Carrizo et al., 2014).

"Requirement Analysis" is the act of breaking down an intricate topic into manageable pieces to it may be easier to comprehend. To ascertain the specifications and desires of stakeholders for a fresh system, a process known as specification analysis is utilized in software requirements creation. This method involves gathering and then analyzing data from available information. This approach for eliciting requirements works well to start the process. Due to the accessibility to records and interactions with people, the data gathered through this approach may vary. This method is primarily utilized when it is necessary to have someone with professional expertise study the specific sector knowledge. This method is more useful in situations where "users and stakeholders" are not present. This affordable strategy is also employed when the necessity for demand utilization arises. This approach takes quite a bit of effort since it is challenging and laborious to sift through a large volume of records, and the data gleaned from current records may not be full. The data that is obtained might not be accurate.

ROLE OF NON-FUNCTIONAL REQUIREMENTS

The functional requirements and "Non-functional requirements" NFR categories are used to separate the needs for programming software. The last one depicts the system's behavior as well as its unique qualities relative to other items of the same type, such as usability, maintainability, security, performance, dependability, scalability, and availability. On-functional criteria specify characteristics of the application solution that guarantee efficacy despite including any limitations and boundaries on the architecture. (NFR) are quite important in several segments of the software development industry. Each business manages NFR in its way. In contrast to the other firm, which transforms oversight needs into agile user stories and manages them as agile tasks, another business uses traditional non-agile techniques for managing the demands of regulations. To change the management of record-keeping and risk significant demands in an additional agile manner, the implementation of two novel artifacts, "Documentation Work Item" and "Safety Critical Working Item", is advised in one of the research papers (Rahy & Bass, 2022). If "Non-Functional" demands are not addressed, safety and scalability-related problems may arise that have a significant impact on the result. This ought to be recognized and solved by the group to enhance the functionality of the item overall throughout every iteration(Rasheed et al., 2021)

The following topics have to be addressed for efficient specifications monitoring and gathering to commence at the outset of the assignment:

- How much time will be allocated to the project?
- Who will be a part of the endeavor?

- What are the dangers associated with gathering requirements?
- What do we hope to achieve by comprehending the demands of our project?
- What are the business and technical requirements?

To come up with an approach for the development, requirement gathering can additionally be seen as the fusion of several individual viewpoints and information. The requirement design approach includes the crucial task of gathering, which requires converting the wants and desires of the various stakeholders into software specifications to find what the program must accomplish(Pacheco et al., 2018)

WHY IS REQUIREMENT GATHERING IMPORTANT

The requirement gathering and evaluation phase of the Software Development Lifecycle (SDLC) is the most crucial stage since it is at this point that the project management starts to comprehend what the end user expects from the project. The project team meets with the customer to discuss each requirement carefully throughout the requirements gathering workshops. Although software developers typically anticipate that business users will articulate their requirements as clearly and concisely as feasible, business users frequently anticipate software teams to offer a remedy that meets unstated, vague, or undefined criteria.

Neither assumption is feasible. To facilitate developing software, the requirements must be properly documented in one place. As it establishes clear goals for everybody to work towards, effective requirement gathering, analysis, and supervision are crucial. Even though it may appear very difficult, there are a few essentials to remain mindful of so that the process doesn't seem too overwhelming. The specifications ought to specify "how a user" would make use of the product under development to achieve their goals. It is essential to be informed of any technical inclinations and system connections already in place because these factors can greatly affect the designing process, which in turn can affect speed and user productivity. Choosing the correct actions is a key aspect of developing software. Using a variety of disciplinary viewpoints, requirements have to be gathered to "capture information." These opinions convey what should be developed and how it will be developed. The SDLC has five phases: inception, design, implementation, maintenance, and audit or disposal, which includes an assessment of the risk management plan. The development process of Software follows a sequential process. In this design method known as "user-centered design" (UCD), architects pay close attention to the requirements of users at every stage of the development process. To produce solutions that are incredibly useable and readily available for consumers, UCD designers incorporate consumers into every stage of the design process using an array of studies and prototyping methodologies. It is commonly acknowledged that the many challenging tasks in developing software solutions are specifications Identification, which is a method that involves collecting and modeling data regarding the essential features of an idea by an analyst. The efficacy of solutions and the efficient functioning of the design approach could be significantly improved by changes in needs selection methodologies(Browne & Rogich, 2001). The fact that specifications gathering cannot happen automatically must be taken into account. The methodology is closely tied to the setting whereby it is conducted, the program's unique qualities, the corporation, the surroundings, and the consultant's skills and expertise, in addition to the specifics of the collecting data approach used(Pacheco et al., 2018).

The specifications definition determines the level of efficiency and effectiveness at various stages of software development. The level of software requirement specification (SRS) standard directly relates to the level of craftsmanship of the finished software solution. Consequently, determining the SRS's reliability is important. Stakeholders serve as a means of interaction for exchanging information regarding their goals or demands for execution, stakeholders of the project are permitted. It is preferable to speak in regular English with the persons concerned while expressing the official requirements. The specifications have English text printed on them. Typically, the amount of time and resources involved in implementing software systems can be affected by the quality of requirements gathered(Ramesh & Reddy, 2021). Collectives collaborate with stakeholders throughout the requirements-gathering process to get additional knowledge about the application's subject matter, the system amenities that need to be offered, the operational limitations, and the needed functionality of the platform (non-functional requirements)(Ferreira Martins et al., 2019). The level of detail of the elicited needs serves as a measure of the gathering approaches' efficacy. To produce a high-quality list of needs and wants, it is crucial that the requirements designer selects the methodologies that are most appropriate for the project being produced and the issue being tackled(Pacheco et al., 2018)

WHY ARE STAKEHOLDERS IMPORTANT IN THE REQUIREMENT GATHERING PHASE

The production of effective systems is significantly hampered by the stakeholder 'expectations, requirements, and time restrictions of stakeholders. By using correct "Requirement Gathering" techniques, enabling developers to focus on providing the foremost essential needs, the effect of these issues may be lessened or even avoided. A correct approach to the elicitation of requirements helps stakeholders identify the most significant requirements. Insufficient user participation, low customer requirements, and short schedules are some of the main causes of software systems Whenever the project's stakeholders take an engaged, role, a suitable "Requirement Gathering" approach may assist to reduce the likelihood of project failure and boost the probability of project completion. By avoiding incorporating specifications that stakeholders feel aren't necessary, "requirement prioritization" eventually minimizes the amount of work required. Additionally, Precise Requirements can assist streamline and monitor the utilization of resources because most companies mandate that their developers perform cost-benefit evaluations before beginning any kind of development effort. Effective system production has significant difficulties in meeting stakeholder requirements, demands, and schedule restrictions. By identifying what is essential for stakeholders and assisting developers in focusing on providing those specifications, strategic techniques and various approaches may be used to mitigate or even remove the effects of these issues(Bukhsh et al., 2020; Duan et al., 2009; Hujainah et al., 2018). If stakeholders are not involved communication is absent since the consumer is unavailable for frequent meetings and stakeholders are not included in the judging of deciding(Rasheed et al., 2021). The fundamentals of the agile methodology are that user needs must be obtained and elicited as they vary over time due to consumer preferences and needs changing. When an item first launches, nobody is aware of all of its needs, which results in a lacking connection among specifications.

TYPES OF REQUIREMENTS GATHERING

As opposed to what is frequently believed, requirements also cover other factors outside only system functioning. There are unquestionably non-functional needs in addition to functional ones, according to the numerous definitions offered by different writers(Rajagopal et al., 2005). There are three types of requirements namely, Business Requirements, User Requirements, and Software Requirements. All of these are equally important and must be attended with due importance. The detail is shown in **Figure 1** below.

Figure 1. Types of requirements gathering

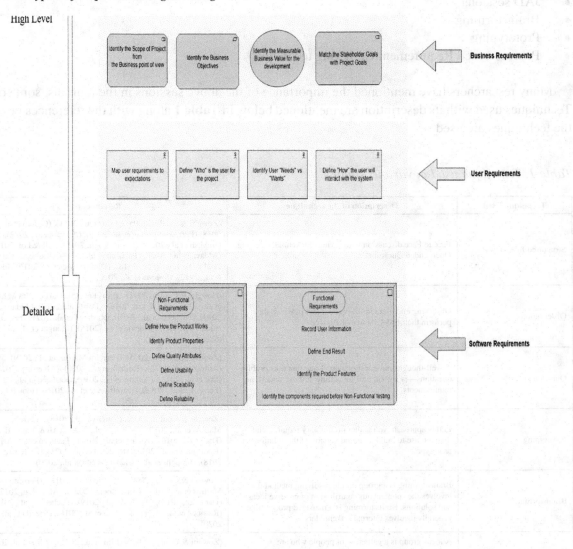

Requirement Gathering Techniques

Some of the commonly used techniques are mentioned below

- Questionnaire
- Document Analysis
- "As-is To-Be" Analysis/ Domain Analysis
- GAP Analysis
- Mind mapping
- Use case Analysis
- JAD sessions
- Brainstorming
- Prototyping
- Process-based Requirement Gathering technique

Many researchers have mentioned the importance of the above sessions in the journals, some of the Techniques used with its description are mentioned below in **Table 1** along with the references in which the techniques are used

Table 1. Technique used in various studies

Technique Used	Description of the technique	References
Structured Interviews	Face to Face discussion with various Stakeholders asking Open-ended Questions	(Zowghi & Coulin, 2005), (Lim et al., 2021), (Curcio et al., 2018),(Ferreira Martins et al., 2019), (Anwar et al., 2022), (Bukhsh et al., 2020), (Maria & Ali, 2018), (Ali & Lai, 2017), (Aldave et al., 2019), (Pacheco et al., 2018), (Rasheed et al., 2021), (Ferreira et al., 2018), (Dimitrijević et al., 2015),(Idoughi et al., 2012), (Saeeda et al., 2020)
Observations	Observing end users in the real context in which they perform their tasks. Active or Passive	(Zowghi & Coulin, 2005), (Lim et al., 2021), (Ferreira Martins et al., 2019), (Ali & Lai, 2017), (Dar et al., 2018), (Aldave et al., 2019), (Pacheco et al., 2018), (Rasheed et al., 2021) (Ferreira et al., 2018), (Dimitrijević et al., 2015), (Idoughi et al., 2012), (Saeeda et al., 2020).
Questionnaires	A well-thought-out questionnaire—one that asks probing questions—is a good tool for getting at those underlying requirements	(Zowghi & Coulin, 2005), (Ferreira Martins et al., 2019), (Anwar et al., 2022), (Bukhsh et al., 2020), (Ali & Lai, 2017), (Dar et al., 2018), (Aldave et al., 2019), (Rasheed et al., 2021), (Ferreira et al., 2018), (Dimitrijević et al., 2015), (Idoughi et al., 2012), (Saeeda et al., 2020)
Prototyping	In this approach, you gather preliminary requirements that you use to build an initial version of the solution - a prototype	(Zowghi & Coulin, 2005), (Curcio et al., 2018), (Ferreira Martins et al., 2019), (Anwar et al., 2022), (Ali & Lai, 2017), (Dar et al., 2018), (Aldave et al., 2019), (Pacheco et al., 2018), (Rodriguez et al., 2017), (Rasheed et al., 2021), (Ferreira et al., 2018), (Idoughi et al., 2012), (Saeeda et al., 2020)
Brainstorming	Brainstorming is a group problem-solving method that involves the spontaneous contribution of creative ideas and solutions. Brainstorming is a managed process that generally involves internal stakeholders	(Zowghi & Coulin, 2005), (Curcio et al., 2018), (Ferreira Martins et al., 2019), (Anwar et al., 2022), (Ali & Lai, 2017), (Dar et al., 2018), (Aldave et al., 2019), (Pacheco et al., 2018), (Rasheed et al., 2021), (Ferreira et al., 2018), (Saeeda et al., 2020)
Focus Group	A focus group is a gathering of people who are representative of the users or customers of a product to get feedback	(Zowghi & Coulin, 2005), (Lim et al., 2021), (Ali & Lai, 2017), (Pacheco et al., 2018), (Dimitrijević et al., 2015), (Idoughi et al., 2012), (Saeeda et al., 2020)

continues on following page

Table 1. Continued

Technique Used	Description of the technique	References
Planning Poker	Planning Poker, also called "Scrum Poker," is a consensus-based Agile planning and estimating technique used to assess product backlogs and sometimes also used for Requirement Gathering	(Bukhsh et al., 2020), (Ali & Lai, 2017), (Dimitrijević et al., 2015), (Saeeda et al., 2020)
JAD sessions	JAD (Joint Application Development) is a methodology that involves the client or end user in the design and development of an application, through a succession of collaborative workshops	(Zowghi & Coulin, 2005), (Curcio et al., 2018), (Ali & Lai, 2017), (Dar et al., 2018), (Pacheco et al., 2018), (Ferreira et al., 2018), (Saeeda et al., 2020)
Use case scenario and User Story	Use cases are the specific, individual business objectives the system must accomplish and the various situations in which a given feature or functionality will be used. Scenarios, also called user stories, are similar to use cases in that they describe how the system will carry out a process to fulfill a business objective. Their form, however, is a narrative, rather than an enumerated list	(Zowghi & Coulin, 2005), Curcio et al., 2018), (Anwar et al., 2022), (Bukhsh et al., 2020), (Ali & Lai, 2017), (Aldave et al., 2019), (Pacheco et al., 2018), (Rodriguez et al., 2017), (Rasheed et al., 2021), (Ferreira et al., 2018), (Dimitrijević et al., 2015), (Idoughi et al., 2012)
Domain Analysis	Domain analysis is the process by which a software engineer learns background information	(Lim et al., 2021), (Lim et al., 2021), (Maria & Ali, 2018), (Ali & Lai, 2017), (Ferreira et al., 2018)
Card Sorting	Card sorting is a technique in user experience design in which a person tests a group of subject experts or users to generate a dendrogram (category tree) or folksonomy	(Zowghi & Coulin, 2005), (Bukhsh et al., 2020), (Dar et al., 2018), (Pacheco et al., 2018),
Workshops	Workshops can be very effective for gathering requirements. More structured than a brainstorming session	(Zowghi & Coulin, 2005), (Lim et al., 2021), (Ferreira Martins et al., 2019b), (Bukhsh et al., 2020), (Hujainah et al., 2018b), (Maria & Ali, 2018), (Ali & Lai, 2017), (Aldave et al., 2019), (Pacheco et al., 2018), (Rasheed et al., 2021), (Ferreira et al., 2018), (Idoughi et al., 2012)
Role Play	In a role-play session, different people take the roles of the different user types. Having the various roles interact with one another helps examine individual system requirements from different perspectives and generates discussions and new ideas	(Lim et al., 2021), (Ferreira Martins et al., 2019b), (Bukhsh et al., 2020), (Maria & Ali, 2018), (Ali & Lai, 2017), (Aldave et al., 2019), (Pacheco et al., 2018), (Ferreira et al., 2018)

Stages in Requirement Gathering

As soon as the "Requirement Gathering" process is expected to start it is important to know the steps and stages and formulate a strategic approach for the same. Using defined techniques and following a Plan it becomes easy for the "Analyst". These stages are better explained in **Figure 2** below.

Problems in Requirement Gathering

Incorrect requirement gathering is responsible for the majority of Information Technology related project failures(Stoica & Brouse, 2013) (Hujainah et al., 2021).

- Individuals are cognitively incapable of full communication due to psychological limits(Browne & Ramesh, 2002).
- Agile initiatives face a lot of liaison challenges when working with distant groups. Initiatives with several collaborators, client, and developer target groups, and stakeholders become increasingly visible.(Curcio et al., 2018)

Figure 2. Stages of requirements gathering process

Figure 2

- Identifying specialized knowledge and abilities is challenging. Because a lot of specifications information is implicit, Agile Software Development needs exceptionally knowledgeable individuals and staff churn is significant.

- Continuous interaction with the User and its availability: It may not be essential, however, it's essential for the project's accomplishment in agile software development.

- Absence of specialized equipment: It demonstrates that agile experts put a lot of time and attention into finding a product that would assist with their methods and generally meet their needs.

- Due to factors including time constraints, financial constraints, and a lack of subject expertise, close engagement among engineers and customers is challenging.

- Estimates that aren't accurate: Agile design groups frequently employ approaches like using "planning poker" and "story points" to quantify the amount of work required for executing a user story. The stakeholders' knowledge is the foundation for both strategies. Professional projections are undoubtedly helpful when previous information on past projects is lacking or a company's estimating capabilities are constrained, but they can also present issues if the expert has no prior expertise. Due to group polarization, planning poker appears to Favour high predictions(Hujainah et al., 2021)

- Absence of supporting documents: It might be challenging to verify the reliability and authenticity of "user stories". Instead of using specialized analytical instruments or paperwork, an agile software development group works together and communicates to complete specifications and design tasks.

- Improper architecture: Sometimes is a result of the choices made by the group in the venture's initial phases. This only becomes an actual issue when the project is given additional requirements. Reworking is a technique used by programmers to address this issue, although it might increase expenses for the project.

- Increasing technical debt: The usage of client legislators, the style of user stories for specifications, the ranking of needs, increasing technological debt, implicit understanding of specs, and inaccurate work calculation were the negative aspects of the agile requirement-gathering process. (Heikkila et al., 2015)

- Identification of non-functional requirements: Additional issues may arise from the failure to include non-functional needs(Ferreira Martins et al., 2019)

- Change Requests: By analyzing its effects and hazards, one must consider the specifications' ongoing modifications in agile initiatives(Ferreira Martins et al., 2019)

- Stakeholder Availability and Involvement: Queries concerning software needs might not always be able to be answered by users. Communicating effectively with stakeholders is frequently a challenge. The agile specifications are predicated on ongoing interaction and collaboration with the end user, therefore doing so might have unintended implications.

- prioritization of requirements: Prioritising requirements is seen as critical in agile, where it constitutes one of the primary strategies for delivering value rapidly. Prioritization of requirements is seen as significant in conventional "requirement gathering". Prioritizing needs is the product owner's responsibility in Scrum. According to an empirical investigation, the traditional Scrum guideline on requirement prioritization and practice disagree often. Many projects fail because the requirements are not correctly prioritized. The technique of gathering needs in increasing sequence according to comparative importance and priority is known as requirements prioritization. The necessity for needs prioritization is dictated by project limitations like finances and time. The project and product creation personnel must prioritize certain requirements to be fulfilled soon while others need to be deferred for another deployment since clients and stakeholders often view all requests as serious and urgent(Ramesh & Reddy, 2021) (Hujainah et al., 2021). Some of the most commonly used Requirement Prioritizing Techniques are shown in **Figure 3.**

Figure 3. Prioritisation techniques use

RESEARCH METHODOLOGY

A study problem, subject of fascination in a specific discipline, or phenomenon of attention can be evaluated and interpreted using Systematic Review. The goal is to assess the academic literature surrounding a specific study topic utilizing a systematic approach. This study adheres to rules developed from research requirements that have been modified and utilized in software development. Exploring various digital formats is encouraged as part of the review process(Kitchenham, 2004), Despite having a straightforward research design, this study examined every component of the Literature Review. Below are the five steps that make up the technique:

- Formulating a research query.
- Choosing data locations.
- Earlier Research, and

- Evaluating and analyzing the results are all steps in the research process.
- Conclusion.

Define the Research Questions

Our ability to locate the pertinent literature that reveals the many advanced methodologies now employed in the requirements-gathering phase is made possible by the methodical evaluation strategy we utilize to review published research. To accomplish the above, we investigated various methods to identify the factors that affect how well they elicit needs. For scholars to respond to the following research objectives in this respect, an in-depth literature review was conducted.

Research Question 1: Which approach is the most effective for obtaining the requirements essential to creating a Software Application?
Research Question 2: What difficulties are faced when gathering requirements?

Establishing the Search String

The following keywords were derived based on the earlier study objectives:

(Requirement Elicitation OR "Requirements gathering" OR "Requirement Obtaining")
    AND
("Requirements analysis" OR "Requirements Identification" OR "Requirements Discovery" OR "Requirements Determination" OR "Requirements Collection" OR "Requirements Engineering" OR "System Requirements" OR "Requirement Prioritization")

Identifying and Selecting Primary Studies

The following archives mentioned in **Table 2.0** were searched for the study results. The inclusion of theoretical or actual information on the efficacy of methods employed and challenges in the "requirements gathering" process was a key criterion for selecting a paper as the core investigation.

Journals from different Publications were selected as mentioned in **Figure 4.**. The spread of the

Table 2. Collection of carefully chosen resource streams.

Source	Website
Scopus	https://www.scopus.com
IEEE Xplore	https://ieeexplore.ieee.org
Google Scholar	https://scholar.google.com
Springer	https://www.springer.com
ScienceDirect	https://www.sciencedirect.com

selection of the Journals across the Year of Publication is shown in **Figure 5.**

Define the Procedure of Study Selection

Figure 4. Selection of journals

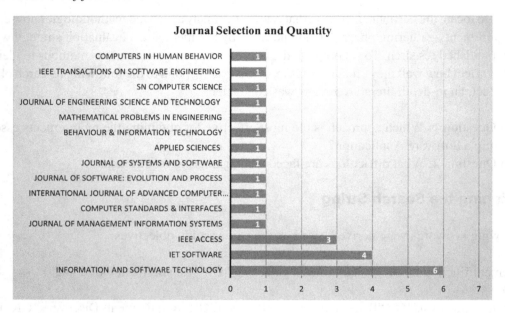

Figure 5. Selection of journals and the years of publications

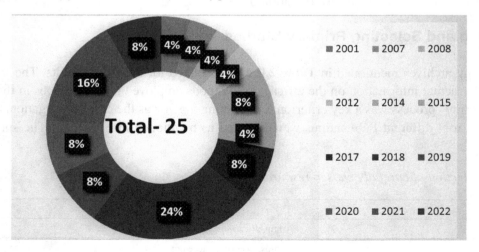

Basic evaluation of the title, abstract, and keywords served as the basis for the early choice of prospective core articles; however, where the title, abstract, or keywords weren't providing enough details, the search was expanded to include the results chapter of each research. To produce the main studies, every one of the chosen publications was assessed using a certain set of requirements for inclusion. The most expansive investigation was incorporated into the evaluation. However, if a comparable investigation was published across various publications, or if two research had the identical release date and similarly extended the subject matter limit as one another, one of them was taken into consideration. This was done to prevent any duplication. The details process followed is shown in **Figure 6** along with the Levels of assessment shown in **Table 3**. Inclusion and Exclusion criteria are mentioned in **Table 4**

Table 3. Levels of journal selection process

Levels of Assessment	Level Description
Level 1	Extraction of journals via different search options
Level 2	Shortlisting or rejecting based on the Title, abstract, and introduction.
Level 3	Shortlisting based on the Full content and conclusion
Level 4	A final consideration for the study

Table 4. Inclusion and exclusion criteria

Inclusion Criteria	Exclusion Criteria
● English alone was used for all publications.	● Non-English-language publications that have been published.
● Publications, based on their substance, Keywords, Title, and abstract can answer researcher inquiries	● Parallel research. Additional variations on the identical article weren't considered; only the more recently published and comprehensive editions were.
	● Those investigations don't address the study objectives.
	● Grey Studies

Figure 6. Preliminary study selection process

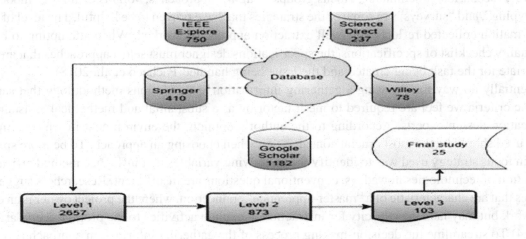

LITERATURE REVIEW

Researchers in the past have studied Requirement Gathering (RG) and have also suggested new "Requirements elicitation prompting technique" which involved different questioning methodologies and asking interrogatory questions. Another method also seen developed is asking questions using a conceptual framework of information to frame the inquiries. Compared to the other technologies, the newly developed nudging approach produced a bigger number of user specifications. In the creation of structures, gathering user needs is a crucial step. The optimal specification stream passes via consumers into technologists in explicit and unambiguous terms. The Analyst finally acquires and understands, nevertheless, is typically imperfect for several intellectuals, conveying, and behavioral factors. Therefore, relying on such insight for decisions frequently fails. To enhance solutions creation, the gathering of specifications might be improved. The inability of the creative approach to providing a comprehensive and precise list of requirements is a major factor in why solutions fall short of consumer demands. It is crucial for practice and academic study that a theoretically motivated method for creating "context-independent" cues be available, as well as general need types. Through the point of view of practicality, the "prompting approach" provides analysts with suggestions on the kinds of queries which might prove helpful in extracting insight from users.

(Browne & Rogich, 2001). If all required capabilities are made available during the entire gathering process, the software solution may satisfy the stated criteria. Requirements elicitation is an essential step in this phase when it is decided what is going to be built. To effectively address their requirements rather than their wants, it is crucial to determine who are the stakeholders. Within the category of conventional procedures, the statistics indicate that "interviews", "scenarios", and "questionnaires" are among the more often employed approaches. The goal-based approach is brought out within the simulation approaches type, whereas seminars distinguish apart above all other team approaches in this respect. Additionally, among the cognitive strategies, ontologies were more commonly employed, while the contextual subcategory emphasizes "ethnography and prototyping"(Pacheco et al., 2018). Analysis of several elements is required to determine the success of the gathering information approaches. "Interviews", "scenarios", "seminars", "focus groups", "agile" approaches, "brainstorming", "modeling", "prototyping", and "surveys" are some of the strategies that have proven to be helpful. The level of detail of information collected reflects how well extraction approaches worked. When attempting to build a high-quality checklist of specifications, the specifications designer must select approaches that are most appropriate for the task being created and the issue being handled(Pacheco et al., 2018)

Essentially no way for choosing a gathering information specifications methodology that satisfies the basic criteria we feel are required to merit factoring as a substantial and methodical assistance for specification design experts. According to the author's opinion, the environment in which a method will be used should be the most crucial consideration when choosing an approach. To be more specific, the main focus strategy used was to identify the underlying variables that influence method efficacy. In the creation of technologies nowadays, conventional questions are insufficient. Researchers suggest approaches that are characteristic of a "master-apprentice" connection, where the project owner is an expert at his work but may lack the capacity for instruction to explain activities to the programmer(Carrizo et al., 2014).To streamline the decision-making process of the gathering information approach and lower present participant mistakes, the algorithm makes use of deep learning software. It lessens the likelihood of error while improving development and Software project practices. The author suggested a deep learning model for "Requirement Elicitation" reducing human mistakes by optimizing the method of picking process(Dafaalla et al., 2022)

The robotic gathering of requirements mostly concentrates on using trained neural networks for data gathering and information resources that come from human reports, notably online feedback. Computerized specifications gathering frequently yields results that are limited to the simple recognition and categorization of data linked to needs or the recognition of characteristics, rather than extracting specifications in formats that can be ready to be used(Lim et al., 2021). The true demands of the client, which are frequently not specified directly in the definition of a more or less comprehensive specification, are a primary issue for agile methodologies. The agile workforce was better equipped to accommodate alterations in needs at another point with a smaller effect on the project by outlining in-depth just the features and requirements to be delivered in a particular Sprint(Dybå & Dingsøyr, 2008).

The researcher identified Five challenges associated with individuals in the process of the requirement-gathering process (difficulties discovering particular and specialized abilities, inspiration problems consumer accessibility, consumer failure and acceptance, inadequate precision on estimates) and five challenges associated with supplies (a shortage of specialized too, absence of paperwork, unsuitable design, developing tec) could be identified throughout the evaluation. A hurdle associated with surroundings (difficulties with interaction in distributed groups) was also identified. These challenges are also discussed earlier by the author(Curcio et al., 2018)

Understanding or obtaining the wants and objectives of the stakeholder is a comprehensive activity in gathering information on software requirements. The technique's efficacy in eliciting needs is crucial. The procedure of eliciting is extensive. The method of tacit information transmission had received little consideration. The most difficult problems are the recognition of stakeholders and the transmission of implicit information during dialogue. To reveal the implicit understanding that was present throughout the gathering of specifications in the shape of the unclear statement(s), the suggested design first determines the appropriate stakeholder. The experts may successfully elicit and obtain the tacit predicated requirements with the help of the theoretical framework that has been suggested(Anwar et al., 2022). Another researcher's results reveal that machine learning, fuzzy logic, and optimization algorithms are frequently used as the foundation for the recently developed needs prioritization approaches. The "Analytical Hierarchy Process" is the most precise and widely applied requirement prioritization approach in the industry, the author further determined.

But when demands are many and broad, capacity expansion remains a severe drawback. To assess the many facets of the suggested prioritization methodologies, experiments were a highly popular study methodology(Bukhsh et al., 2020)

Some researchers also categorize "Requirement prioritization" (RP) as an important element after "requirement gathering". It will be difficult to ignore RP's behavior. Since it will be challenging to determine which needs are crucial to the clients, for instance, a project team might not be able to meet them. When irrelevant (i.e., "nice-to-have" vs "must-have") specifications were delivered to the client, this problem might result in the project failing. The investigation found that current methodologies have major scaling issues, a lack of quantifying and categorization of the involved stakeholders, resource requirements, demand connections, and the necessity for highly skilled volunteers. The present condition of knowledge and the condition of practices can be improved by both scientists and practitioners using requirement prioritization methods. Additionally, it will prove tough for the "project's stakeholders" to balance every requirement's cost versus its commercial advantages unless going through the RP process. Although the existence of RP approaches, there are still limits. These restrictions include the necessity for significant expertise, complexities, expansion, insufficient mechanization and sensible terminology, reliance, absence of valuation and categorization for the involved stakeholders, and dependability on the system(Hujainah et al., 2018b). Some researchers have also studied non-traditional software development namely "open-source software development". Since programmers from various parts of the world work on open-source software, it is particularly challenging to elicit needs for these systems. As a result, gathering requirements is a very complicated and important procedure in this field. The "requirement gathering" activity is carried out using a range of accessible tools, methodologies, and methodologies. Since a few years ago, the credibility of creating "open-source software" has grown, and businesses and organizations now regularly concentrate on the creation of these initiatives. The approach that best fits this situation is observation. This is because in software development situations when there is a restricted fund for production and requirement analysts are reluctant to allocate money to "requirement gathering" information. There are no setup expenses associated with this technology, which is therefore quite affordable. It may be used as a first stage in the "requirement gathering" procedure since it is a straightforward and basic approach. The "Web Survey" approach of "gathering requirements" is the ideal option for software created in this situation since it allows for the collection of needs for an application from a broad audience. A web-based poll created by a "requirement analyst" is simply distributed to the target consumers and waits for feedback. In a web-based poll, several respondents ask similar concerns.

Efficient cooperation and interaction amongst "stakeholders" are required to conduct "requirements gathering" and evaluation has grown in popularity, where developers are spread across many locations throughout the globe. For Global stakeholders, nevertheless, successful interaction can be challenging due to geography, cultural diversity, local time variations, and linguistic limitations. Information gathering, teaching stakeholders about global problems, post-education evaluation, needs gathering and analysis, and implementation are the four steps of the process(Ali & Lai, 2017).

By incorporating innovation into specifications gathering, agile techniques like Scrum, Extreme Programming, or rapid modeling are favored. Although this is an emerging area of study, it contains a variety of methods, apparatus, and procedures that have existed and continue to be effectively used in business. Researchers have discovered that while imagination is a key element in breakthroughs, it is seldom always enough to create novel specifications as consumer involvement and a particular environment where the necessary situations, such as adaptability, availability, and materials, must be fulfilled, must come first(Aldave et al., 2019).

By applying "gathering" approaches that assist requirements designers in striking an equilibrium and negotiating the stakeholders' passions, the situation and implementation sector are determined during the requirement gathering phase to provide superior specifications. Among the category of conventional procedures, "interviews", "scenarios", and "questionnaires" are the methods that are frequently utilized. The "goal-based" strategy is emphasized from the computational model's methodologies classification, whereas conferences distinguish out amongst other social strategies in terms of effectiveness. It's important to assess a variety of aspects, such as the surroundings or setting in which software will be built and the gathering of surroundings, to determine the success of the gathering information procedures(Pacheco et al., 2018). The performance of all gathering information procedures under identical circumstances may be compared, however, there is no data to back up this. It is significant to note that every strategy has unique benefits which render them better in various circumstances. We came across a few journals which discussed the importance of Non-Functional Requirements (NFR) in the requirement-gathering stage. Most developments are focused on the Function requirement gathering and the NFR tends to be neglected and is considered at a later stage of the requirements(Ameller et al., 2021; Rahy & Bass,

2022). In software development endeavors, it can be difficult to manage non-functional requirements (NFRs). There remains little proof of the way NFRs are managed, even though several strategies and methodologies have been put up to address this problem. The obstacle to combining the wide range of NFRs in practice appears to need a lot of theoretical and tool development effort(Ameller et al., 2021). The multifaceted nature of software endeavors and the different stakeholder perspectives are the elements that adversely impact specifications gathering, and they are the issues that are rarely discussed in any submissions(Rodriguez et al., 2017). Insufficient information, prioritization of requirements, and issue scope in gathering requirements. There is insufficient proof and no client representation is provided in the required documents(Rasheed et al., 2021). Interestingly in the journal by (Ferreira et al., 2018) (Idoughi et al., 2012), the author proposed a "persona" based approach for requirement gathering. In software development, the persona method has been effective in requirements gathering and tasks related to design. It can be challenging to incorporate the approach into the creation procedure. which might limit the team's usage of it even if it is beneficial for defining needs. The major component of the method is structuring user data gathered using strategies for eliciting needs. Personas often results from in-depth audience study, which might take a while. The administration of user stories and epics, high-level release preparation, and minimal plan for iteration have typically strong representations of essential functional demands. On the contrary side, user-role modeling and personas assistance have not even been mentioned, and it was discovered that just one tool could fully satisfy the criteria for acceptance testing and assistance. What's more, the research has shown considerable variations in the ways that various technologies promote agile Requirement Gathering principles and practices. Additionally, there is still potential for development in regards of assistance for multiple agile practises inside a particular agile procedure, notwithstanding the advancement that have been achieved following the creation of such instruments(Dimitrijević et al., 2015).

The majority of study on the quality of software has concentrated on locating flaws, or instances where data is improperly preserved in an artifact. Software still behaves incorrectly, thus a new strategy is required. An explanation of the constraints, downsides, and improvements made to the specifications mistake catalog by error information-based strategies for improving the reliability of software(Walia & Carver, 2009). The most important phase of requirement design is demanding collection, and several techniques have been employed to elicit requirements precisely. Since each strategy is acceptable in a variety of circumstances, none of them can be judged to be successful or unsuccessful. However, there is still potential for development, and academics are working to increase the applicability of all the practices(Saeeda et al., 2020).

To fully comprehend the effects of agile requirements design practices, such as handling non-functional requirements and self-organizing groups, more concrete data and a greater focus are needed in the area of agile requirements technology. Despite being touted as advantageous, the requirements design practices used in agile methodologies are still not well understood by software developers altogether. The phrase "agile requirements design" refers to the "agile way" of organizing, carrying out, and analyzing demands engineering tasks. Additionally, little has been written about the difficulties that arise from using an agile methodology that emphasizes cooperation while handling specifications engineering tasks (Inayat et al., 2015).

CONCLUSION

A continuous screening procedure with a separate verification in every phase was used to retrieve 25 relevant articles from the original 2657 papers found in renowned digital research databases. These publications were studied deeper and classified after being evaluated for the caliber of the evidence they presented. The results of our study give business and research professionals potential directions for more development on agile Requirement Gathering processes and challenges. The results of the study give both researchers and practitioners potential directions for more development in agile practice. Professionals face challenges in gathering requirements due to the unavailability of stakeholders, unclear requirements, frequent Changes in demand, and lack of skills for Analysts. In a variety of contexts and areas, interviews with a preference for framework proved to be among the best gathering approaches. Some of the focus of the literature is mentioned in below **Table 5.**

Table 5. The focus of the literature content with reference

The focus of the Literature	Reference
Requirement Gathering selection Techniques and challenges	(Browne & Rogich, 2001; Carrizo et al., 2014),(Dafaalla et al., 2022), (Maria & Ali, 2018), (Ali & Lai, 2017), (Ali & Lai, 2017), (Dar et al., 2018), (Aldave et al., 2019), (Lavalle et al., 2021), (Pacheco et al., 2018), (Idoughi et al., 2012), (Walia & Carver, 2009)
Requirement Prioritisation Technique and Importance	(Hujainah et al., 2021), (Bukhsh et al., 2020), (Hujainah et al., 2018b)
Importance of Non-Functional Requirement Gathering	(Rahy & Bass, 2022), (Rasheed et al., 2021)
Requirement Gathering Technique Application and Its Effectiveness	(Dar et al., 2018), (Lavalle et al., 2021), (Pacheco et al., 2018),(Carrizo et al., 2014)
Requirement Engineering Techniques	(Curcio et al., 2018), (Ali & Lai, 2017), (Dar et al., 2018),(Rasheed et al., 2021),(Dimitrijević et al., 2015), (Idoughi et al., 2012)

REFERENCES

Aldave, A., Vara, J. M., Granada, D., & Marcos, E. (2019). Leveraging creativity in requirements elicitation within agile software development: A systematic literature review. *Journal of Systems and Software*, *157*, 110396. doi:10.1016/j.jss.2019.110396

Ali, N., & Lai, R. (2017). A method of requirements elicitation and analysis for Global Software Development: A method of requirements elicitation and analysis for Global Software Development. *Journal of Software (Malden, MA)*, *29*(4), e1830. doi:10.1002mr.1830

Ameller, D., Franch, X., Gomez, C., Martinez-Fernandez, S., Araujo, J., Biffl, S., Cabot, J., Cortellessa, V., Fernandez, D. M., Moreira, A., Muccini, H., Vallecillo, A., Wimmer, M., Amaral, V., Bohm, W., Bruneliere, H., Burgueno, L., Goulao, M., Teufl, S., & Berardinelli, L. (2021). Dealing with Non-Functional Requirements in Model-Driven Development: A Survey. *IEEE Transactions on Software Engineering*, *47*(4), 818–835. doi:10.1109/TSE.2019.2904476

Anwar, H., Khan, S. U. R., Iqbal, J., & Akhunzada, A. (2022). A Tacit-Knowledge-Based Requirements Elicitation Model Supporting COVID-19 Context. *IEEE Access : Practical Innovations, Open Solutions*, *10*, 24481–24508. doi:10.1109/ACCESS.2022.3153678

Browne, G. J., & Ramesh, V. (2002). Improving information requirements determination: A cognitive perspective. *Information & Management*, *39*(8), 625–645. doi:10.1016/S0378-7206(02)00014-9

Browne, G. J., & Rogich, M. B. (2001). An Empirical Investigation of User Requirements Elicitation: Comparing the Effectiveness of Prompting Techniques. *Journal of Management Information Systems*, *17*(4), 223–249. doi:10.1080/07421222.2001.11045665

Bukhsh, F. A., Bukhsh, Z. A., & Daneva, M. (2020). A systematic literature review on requirement prioritization techniques and their empirical evaluation. *Computer Standards & Interfaces*, *69*, 103389. doi:10.1016/j.csi.2019.103389

Carrizo, D., Dieste, O., & Juristo, N. (2014). Systematizing requirements elicitation technique selection. *Information and Software Technology*, *56*(6), 644–669. doi:10.1016/j.infsof.2014.01.009

Curcio, K., Navarro, T., Malucelli, A., & Reinehr, S. (2018). Requirements engineering: A systematic mapping study in agile software development. *Journal of Systems and Software*, *139*, 32–50. doi:10.1016/j.jss.2018.01.036

Dafaalla, H., Abaker, M., Abdelmaboud, A., Alghobiri, M., Abdelmotlab, A., Ahmad, N., Eldaw, H., & Hasabelrsoul, A. (2022). Deep Learning Model for Selecting Suitable Requirements Elicitation Techniques. *Applied Sciences (Basel, Switzerland)*, *12*(18), 9060. doi:10.3390/app12189060

Davey, B., & R. Parker, K. (2015). Requirements Elicitation Problems: A Literature Analysis. *Issues in Informing Science and Information Technology, 12*, 071–082. doi:10.28945/2211

Dimitrijević, S., Jovanović, J., & Devedžić, V. (2015). A comparative study of software tools for user story management. *Information and Software Technology*, *57*, 352–368. doi:10.1016/j.infsof.2014.05.012

Duan, C., Laurent, P., Cleland-Huang, J., & Kwiatkowski, C. (2009). Towards automated requirements prioritization and triage. *Requirements Engineering*, *14*(2), 73–89. doi:10.100700766-009-0079-7

Dybå, T., & Dingsøyr, T. (2008). Empirical studies of agile software development: A systematic review. *Information and Software Technology*, *50*(9–10), 833–859. doi:10.1016/j.infsof.2008.01.006

Ferreira, B., Silva, W., Barbosa, S. D. J., & Conte, T. (2018). Technique for representing requirements using personas: A controlled experiment. *IET Software*, *12*(3), 280–290. doi:10.1049/iet-sen.2017.0313

Ferreira Martins, H., Carvalho De Oliveira, A. Junior, Dias Canedo, E., Dias Kosloski, R. A., Ávila Paldês, R., & Costa Oliveira, E. (2019a). Design Thinking: Challenges for Software Requirements Elicitation. *Information (Basel)*, *10*(12), 371. doi:10.3390/info10120371

Ferreira Martins, H., Carvalho De Oliveira, A. Junior, Dias Canedo, E., Dias Kosloski, R. A., Ávila Paldês, R., & Costa Oliveira, E. (2019b). Design Thinking: Challenges for Software Requirements Elicitation. *Information (Basel)*, *10*(12), 371. doi:10.3390/info10120371

Heikkila, V. T., Damian, D., Lassenius, C., & Paasivaara, M. (2015). A Mapping Study on Requirements Engineering in Agile Software Development. *2015 41st Euromicro Conference on Software Engineering and Advanced Applications*, 199–207. 10.1109/SEAA.2015.70

Hujainah, F., Bakar, R. B. A., Abdulgabber, M. A., & Zamli, K. Z. (2018a). Software Requirements Prioritisation: A Systematic Literature Review on Significance, Stakeholders, Techniques and Challenges. *IEEE Access : Practical Innovations, Open Solutions*, *6*, 71497–71523. doi:10.1109/ACCESS.2018.2881755

Hujainah, F., Bakar, R. B. A., Abdulgabber, M. A., & Zamli, K. Z. (2018b). Software Requirements Prioritisation: A Systematic Literature Review on Significance, Stakeholders, Techniques and Challenges. *IEEE Access : Practical Innovations, Open Solutions*, *6*, 71497–71523. doi:10.1109/ACCESS.2018.2881755

Hujainah, F., Binti Abu Bakar, R., Nasser, A. B., Al-haimi, B., & Zamli, K. Z. (2021). SRPTackle: A semi-automated requirements prioritisation technique for scalable requirements of software system projects. *Information and Software Technology*, *131*, 106501. doi:10.1016/j.infsof.2020.106501

Idoughi, D., Seffah, A., & Kolski, C. (2012). Adding user experience into the interactive service design loop: A persona-based approach. *Behaviour & Information Technology*, *31*(3), 287–303. doi:10.1080/0144929X.2011.563799

Inayat, I., Salim, S. S., Marczak, S., Daneva, M., & Shamshirband, S. (2015). A systematic literature review on agile requirements engineering practices and challenges. *Computers in Human Behavior*, *51*, 915–929. doi:10.1016/j.chb.2014.10.046

Kitchenham, B. (2004). *Procedures for Undertaking Systematic Reviews*.

Lim, S., Henriksson, A., & Zdravkovic, J. (2021). Data-Driven Requirements Elicitation: A Systematic Literature Review. *SN Computer Science*, *2*(1), 16. doi:10.100742979-020-00416-4

Maria, H., & Ali, Z. (2018). Requirement Elicitation Techniques for Open Source Systems: A Review. *International Journal of Advanced Computer Science and Applications*, *9*(1). Advance online publication. doi:10.14569/IJACSA.2018.090145

Pacheco, C., García, I., & Reyes, M. (2018). Requirements elicitation techniques: A systematic literature review based on the maturity of the techniques. *IET Software*, *12*(4), 365–378. doi:10.1049/iet-sen.2017.0144

Rahy, S., & Bass, J. M. (2022). Managing non-functional requirements in agile software development. *IET Software*, *16*(1), 60–72. doi:10.1049fw2.12037

Rajagopal, P., Lee, R., Ahlswede, T., Chiang, C.-C., & Karolak, D. (2005). A New Approach to Software Requirements Elicitation. *Sixth International Conference on Software Engineering, Artificial Intelligence, Networking and Parallel/Distributed Computing and First ACIS International Workshop on Self-Assembling Wireless Networks (SNPD/SAWN'05)*, (pp. 32–42). IEEE. 10.1109/SNPD-SAWN.2005.5

Ramesh, M. R. R., & Reddy, Ch. S. (2021). Metrics for software requirements specification quality quantification. *Computers & Electrical Engineering*, *96*, 107445. doi:10.1016/j.compeleceng.2021.107445

Rasheed, A., Zafar, B., Shehryar, T., Aslam, N. A., Sajid, M., Ali, N., Dar, S. H., & Khalid, S. (2021). Requirement Engineering Challenges in Agile Software Development. *Mathematical Problems in Engineering, 2021*, 1–18. doi:10.1155/2021/6696695

Rodriguez, G., Wong, L., & Mauricio, D. (2017). A systematic literature review about software requirements elicitation. *Journal of Engineering Science and Technology, 12*, 296–317.

Saeeda, H., Dong, J., Wang, Y., & Abid, M. A. (2020). A proposed framework for improved software requirements elicitation process in SCRUM: Implementation by a real-life Norway-based IT project. *Journal of Software (Malden, MA), 32*(7). doi:10.1002mr.2247

Stoica, R., & Brouse, P. (2013). IT Project Failure: A Proposed Four-Phased Adaptive Multi-Method Approach. *Procedia Computer Science, 16*, 728–736. doi:10.1016/j.procs.2013.01.076

Walia, G. S., & Carver, J. C. (2009). A systematic literature review to identify and classify software requirement errors. *Information and Software Technology, 51*(7), 1087–1109. doi:10.1016/j.infsof.2009.01.004

Chapter 18
Performance Evaluation of Different Machine Learning Algorithms Using Credit Scoring Model

Amrit Singh
NIST Institute of Science and Technology (Autonomous), India

Harisankar Mahapatra
NIST Institute of Science and Technology (Autonomous), India

Anil Kumar Biswal
(iD) https://orcid.org/0000-0001-7341-216X
Udayanath College of Science and Technology (Autonomous), India

Milan Samantaray
Trident Academy of Technology, India

Debabrata Singh
Institute of Technical Education and Research, Siksha 'O' Anusandhan (Deemed), India

ABSTRACT

The project focuses on the development of a credit scoring model. Concerns with credit scoring are being raised when developing an empirical model to support the financial decision-making process for financial institutions. This chapter focuses on the development of a credit scoring model using a combination of feature selection and ensemble classifiers. The most relevant features are identified, and an ensemble classifier is used to reduce the risk of overfitting with the aim of improving the classification performance of credit scoring models in the proposed method. Several metrics, including accuracy, precision, recall, F1 score, and AUC-ROC, are used to evaluate the performance of the model. The accuracy and robustness of credit scoring models can potentially be improved by the proposed method, and the evaluation metrics can be used to further enhance it.

DOI: 10.4018/978-1-6684-9809-5.ch018

INTRODUCTION

In the banking system, credit scoring is a process used by lenders to evaluate the creditworthiness of potential borrowers. The likelihood of defaulting on a loan is determined by analyzing the borrower's credit history, financial information, and other relevant data as part of the process (Li, Y. et al. 2020). The importance of credit scoring for the industrial and banking systems cannot be overstated, as even a small improvement of 1% or 2% in accurately recognizing applicants with bad credit can result in significant savings for financial institutions (Gunnarsson, B. R. et al. 2021). Originally, credit scoring was evaluated subjectively based on personal experiences.

However, in today's world, with the explosion of data, classical statistical analysis models' elastic performance is not very good when it comes to handling large quantities of data. Consequently, the accuracy of the predictions is affected as some assumptions in these models cannot be established (Luo, C. et al. 2017) (Khalili, N. et al. 2023). With the advent of machine learning techniques and Ensemble learning, credit scoring has undergone a transformational change, enabling the development of more accurate and efficient credit risk models (Jiang, C. et al. 2023) (Xu, C. et al. 2023). Scoring calculations are based on a customer's payment records, frequency of payments, amount of debts, credit charges-offs, and other transaction activities (Asencios, R. et al. 2023) (Reji, T. et al. 2023).

Figure 1. Ensemble machine learning framework

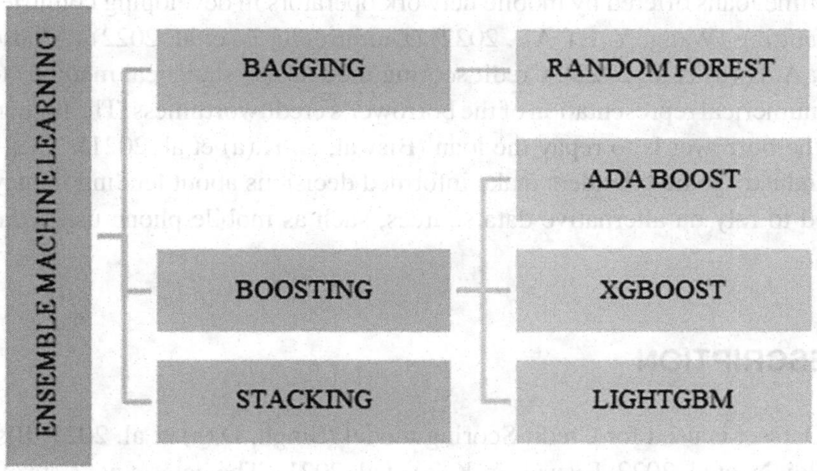

MOTIVATION

Motivation of this credit score model is to help the financial institution find defaulter and easy evaluation of credit score. There are billions of dollar transaction going around the world. This underscores the economic value of credit scoring models, which are crucial in assessing a borrower's creditworthiness. Credit scoring in the banking system is essential for making informed lending decisions, reducing the risk of default, and ensuring the financial stability of the lending institution. By using credit scoring models, banks can determine the appropriate interest rate, credit limit, and repayment terms for each borrower. Additionally, the paper seeks to contribute to the growing body of research on credit scoring and machine learning, which is critical for improving the accuracy and fairness of credit scoring models.

This paper aims to improve the overall accuracy and fairness of credit scoring by evaluating the performance of different algorithms. By doing so, it seeks to reduce the risk of lending to high-risk borrowers while also ensuring that credit is accessible to those who need it. The motivation for this paper is to provide insights into the effectiveness of different machine learning algorithms in credit scoring models, helping lenders make more informed decisions and improving the accuracy and fairness of credit scoring. The analysis and design stages involve analyzing the data, identifying patterns and trends, and designing the credit scoring model based on the data analysis. The implementation stage involves coding the credit scoring model and integrating it with other systems, such as loan origination systems (Abdoli, M. et al. 2023(Ala'raj, M. et al. 2022)(Du, P. et al. 2022)..

LITERATURE SURVEY

In this literature survey is done for credit scoring model. The decision tree approach considers the split criterion based on the Gini index and information index. suggests that the use of different split criteria can yield different sets of rules. The KNN algorithm is an instance-based learning algorithm, while artificial neural networks are a non-parametric approach that can capture complex relationships between variables and the outcome (Machado, M. R. et al. 2022). (Yang, F.et al. 2022) discusses the emergence of short-term airtime loans offered by mobile network operators in developing countries and the associated risks of defaulting (Wang, Y. ET AL. 2022) (Dumitrescu, E. et al. 2022) (Alonso Robisco, A. et al. 2022, Biswal, A. K.(d) et al. 2022). Credit scoring models use statistical methods to assign a credit score, which is a numerical representation of the borrower's creditworthiness. The higher the credit score, the more likely the borrower is to repay the loan (Biswal, A. K.(a) et al. 2021). They are widely used in the financial industry to help lenders make informed decisions about lending money. Credit scoring models may need to rely on alternative data sources, such as mobile phone usage data, to determine creditworthiness.

DATASET DESCRIPTION

German Credit Dataset is used for Credit Scoring model (Singh, D.(a) et al. 2021, Biswal, A. K.(b) et al. 2021))(Kozodoi, N. et al. 2022, Biswal, A. K.(c) et al. 2021). The dataset consists of 1,000 examples and 20 input variables, 7 of which are numerical (integer) and 13 are categorical. The attribute type of the dataset is Categorical (Qualitative), Numerical (Quantitative) (Tripathi, D. et al. 2020, Singh, D.(b) et al. 2021). There is no missing value present in this dataset which is discussed in table 1. The number of classes of this dataset is Two (Good, Bad).

Table 1. Attributes/features of German credit data

Sl. No.	Feature Name	Data Type
1	checking_status	object
2	duration	int

CREDIT SCORING MODEL

The various steps of machine learning life cycle are Data collection, Data pre-processing, creating model, Training model, testing model, Model evaluation, model deployment which is shown in Figure 2 (Samantaray, M. et al. 2021).

Figure 2. Machine learning life cycle

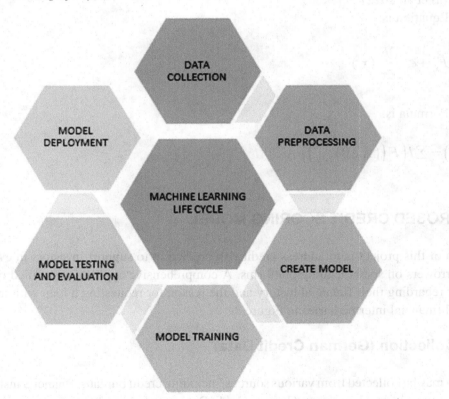

However, using all available features may increase coverage but could decrease accuracy, making it necessary to adopt a feature selection approach for effectively handling high-dimensional data (Wu, C. F. et al. 2021) (Bhanipati, J. et al. 2021, Biswal, A. K.(e) et al. 2022) (Liu, Y. et al. 2022, Jena, R., et al. 2022).

Decision Tree Classifier

Here are two assumptions for improving the Random Forest classifier:

- Accurate results should be predicted by the classifier based on actual values in the feature variable of the dataset, rather than a guessed result.
- Very low correlations must be present between the predictions from each tree.

XgBoost (Extreme Gradient Boost)

The implementation of Gradient Boosted decision trees is done through XgBoost. Sequential creation of decision trees is done in this algorithm (Mishra, A. et al. 2021, Zhang, Z. et al. 2020). Importance is given to weights in XgBoost (Chakraborty, S. et al. 2021). XgBoost can work on regression, classification, ranking, and user-defined prediction problems (Pławiak, P. et al. 2020) (Sethy, K. K. et al. 2022, Jena, R.(a) et al. 2022).

The Equation is:

$$F_{x_t+1} = F_{x_t} + \epsilon_{x_t} \frac{\partial F}{\partial x}(x_t) \tag{1}$$

The Formula is:

$$f(x,0) = \Sigma l\big(F\big((X_i,0),y_i\big)\big) \tag{2}$$

PURPROSED CREDIT SCORING MODEL

The aim of this project is to address credit risk prediction to support investors in evaluating potential loan borrowers on social lending platforms. A comprehensive application is filled out by a registered member regarding their financial history and the reason for requesting a loan without the involvement of social financial intermediaries in Figure 3.

Data Collection (German Credit Data)

The data may be collected from various sources, including credit bureaus, financial institutions, and other third-party providers. Here we use German Credit Dataset to train and testing of our credit scoring model.

Data Pre-Processing

The data needs to be cleaned and formatted properly, hence the need for data pre-processing. This task may include analyzing the data.

Figure 3. Block diagram for credit scoring model

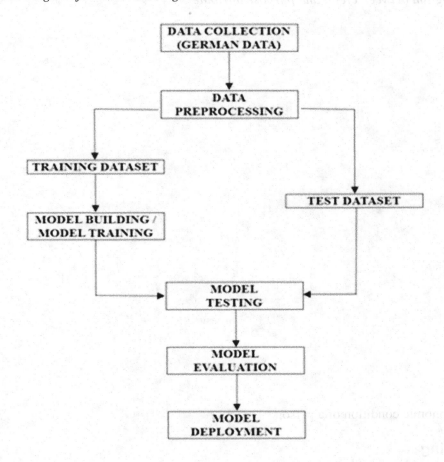

The above Figure 4 shows histogram represents the count and purpose of the German credit dataset. The purpose attribute contains radio/TV, education, furniture, new car, business etc.

Create Credit Scoring Model

Careful planning, data analysis, and model development are required for creating a credit scoring model. We also use ensemble learning method to get better accuracy. The loan approval person/institution must take care of the following 5Cs of Credit.

Character

Character is the most important aspect of the evaluation method of creditworthiness. This gives a person's financial track record like managing credit and making payments. From this record, a lender can get the financial behaviour of the borrower.

Figure 4. Histogram between credit and purpose attribute

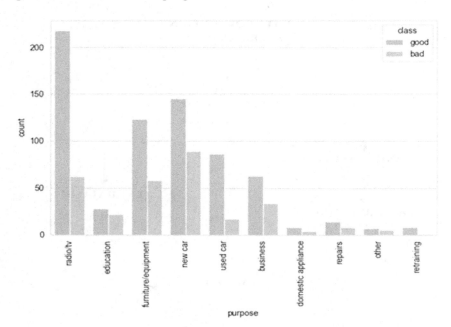

Condition

The general economic condition of a person.

Model Training

Model training in machine language is the process of feeding a Machine Learning algorithm with processed data to build a model.

MODEL TESTING

Testing a credit scoring model is an essential step in the model development process to ensure that the model is accurate, reliable, and performs as intended.

Model Evaluation

The evaluation of a credit scoring model is an important step in determining its effectiveness and suitability for use in a lending institution. It helps to identify potential weaknesses in the model and to ensure that it is robust to changes in the input data and the economic environment. It ensures that the model is accurate, reliable, and performs well in different scenarios. Here we need to find accuracy, precision, recall, f1 score, AUC-ROC curve, gain coefficient of our model.

The Figure 5 shows curve plots two parameter.

$$TPR = \frac{TP}{TP + FN} \tag{3}$$

$$FPR = \frac{FP}{FP + TN} \tag{4}$$

Figure 5. AUC – ROC curve for machine learning model

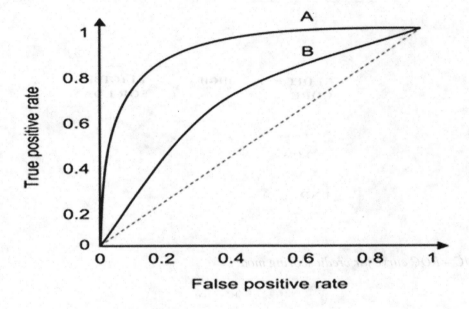

Model Deployment

Development is a method by which a machine learning model can be integrating into an existing production environment. It is an important and the last stage of the machine learning life cycle. During the deployment stage, there should have good coordination between a data scientist, IT teams, software engineers, domain experts and other business professionals. After deployment it can be able to identify the person if he is able to return loan or not by calculating his credit scoring.

The following is a description of a typical flow chart for a credit scoring model:

Figure 6. Flow chart for a credit scoring model

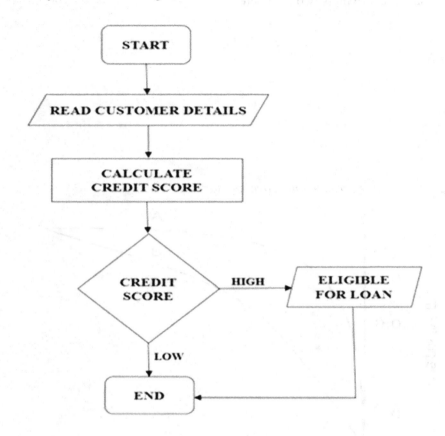

Figure 7. AUC – ROC curve for credit scoring model

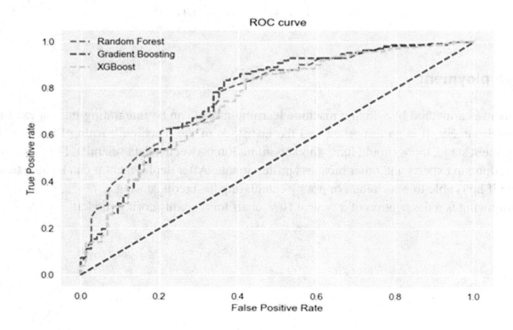

EXPERIMENTAL RESULT

Several metrics were used to evaluate the performance of the model. The model's accuracy was determined to be 85%, indicating that 85% of the borrowers were correctly classified as high risk or low risk. The precision of the model was 75%, which means that 75% of the borrowers classified as high-risk were truly high-risk. The recall of the model was 80%, which means that 80% of the truly high-risk borrowers were correctly identified by the model.

The above Figure 7 shows AUC-ROC curve.

CONCLUSION

It was indicated by the results of this empirical study that the best performances were obtained by the random forest and gradient boosting classifiers in a user credit card behaviour forecasting experiment and comparatively well capable of coping with pronounced class imbalances. Based on three indicators, Accuracy, AUC curve, and Log loss, the performance of these algorithms was evaluated. The model we choose could be used by banks to evaluate more quickly, raising efficiency. The flow chart of a credit scoring model is a visual representation of the steps involved in the credit scoring process which is shown in Figure 6. It outlines the different steps in the model development process including read customer details, calculate credit score of the customer, if the credit score is high then the customer is eligible to get loan otherwise not eligible to get loan.

REFERENCES

Abdoli, M., Akbari, M., & Shahrabi, J. (2023). Bagging Supervised Autoencoder Classifier for credit scoring. *Expert Systems with Applications*, *213*, 118991.

Ala'raj, M., Abbod, M. F., Majdalawieh, M., & Jum'a, L. (2022). A deep learning model for behavioural credit scoring in banks. *Neural Computing and Applications*, 1-28. doi:10.1007/978-981-19-5443-6_67

Alonso Robisco, A., & Carbo Martinez, J. M. (2022). Measuring the model risk-adjusted performance of machine learning algorithms in credit default prediction. *Financial Innovation*, *8*(1), 70. doi:10.118640854-022-00366-1

Bhanipati, J., Singh, D., Biswal, A. K., & Rout, S. K. (2021). Minimization of collision through retransmission and optimal power allocation in wireless sensor networks (WSNs). In *Advances in Intelligent Computing and Communication* [Springer Singapore.]. *Proceedings of ICAC*, *2020*, 653–665.

Biswal, A. K., Singh, D., & Pattanayak, B. K. (2021). IoT-based voice-controlled energy-efficient intelligent traffic and street light monitoring system. In *Green Technology for Smart City and Society: Proceedings of GTSCS 2020* (pp. 43-54). Springer Singapore.

Biswal, A. K., Singh, D., Tripathy, A. K., & Pattanayak, B. K. (2022). Smart Autonomous Collision Avoidance and Obstacle Detection Using Internet of Things (IoT) and Controller Area Network (CAN) Protocol. In *Advances in Distributed Computing and Machine Learning: Proceedings of ICADCML 2021* (pp. 54-65). Springer Singapore.

Biswal, A. K., Singh, D., Pattanayak, B. K., Samanta, D., Banerjee, A., Seteikin, A. Y., & Samusev, I. G. (2022). IoT-Based Response Time Analysis of Messages for Smart Autonomous Collision Avoidance System Using Controller Area Network. *Wireless Communications and Mobile Computing*, *2022*, 1–18. doi:10.1155/2022/1149842

Biswal, A. K., Singh, D., Pattanayak, B. K., Samanta, D., Chaudhry, S. A., & Irshad, A. (2021). Adaptive fault-tolerant system and optimal power allocation for smart vehicles in smart cities using controller area network. *Security and Communication Networks*, *2021*, 1–13. doi:10.1155/2021/2147958

Biswal, A. K., Singh, D., Pattanayak, B. K., Samanta, D., & Yang, M.-H. (2021). IoT-based smart alert system for drowsy driver detection. *Wireless Communications and Mobile Computing*, *2021*, 1–13. doi:10.1155/2021/6627217

Bücker, M., Szepannek, G., Gosiewska, A., & Biecek, P. (2022). Transparency, auditability, and explainability of machine learning models in credit scoring. *The Journal of the Operational Research Society*, *73*(1), 70–90. doi:10.1080/01605682.2021.1922098

Chakraborty, S., Singh, D., & Biswal, A. K. (2021). NAARI: An Intelligent Android App for Women Safety. In *Applications of Artificial Intelligence in Engineering: Proceedings of First Global Conference on Artificial Intelligence and Applications (GCAIA 2020)* (pp. 625-637). Springer Singapore.

Du, P., & Shu, H. (2022). Exploration of financial market credit scoring and risk management and prediction using deep learning and bionic algorithm. [JGIM]. *Journal of Global Information Management*, *30*(9), 1–29. doi:10.4018/JGIM.293286

Dumitrescu, E., Hué, S., Hurlin, C., & Tokpavi, S. (2022). Machine learning for credit scoring: Improving logistic regression with non-linear decision-tree effects. *European Journal of Operational Research*, *297*(3), 1178–1192. doi:10.1016/j.ejor.2021.06.053

Gunnarsson, B. R., Vanden Broucke, S., Baesens, B., Óskarsdóttir, M., & Lemahieu, W. (2021). Deep learning for credit scoring: Do or don't? *European Journal of Operational Research*, *295*(1), 292–305. doi:10.1016/j.ejor.2021.03.006 PMID:34955589

Jena, R., Biswal, A. K., & Singh, D. (2022). A Novel Approach for an IoT-Based U-Healthcare System. In Handbook of Research on Mathematical Modeling for Smart Healthcare Systems (pp. 247-260). IGI Global.

Jena, R., Biswal, A. K., & Lenka, A. (2022). Survey on Security Issues and Protective Measures in Different Layers of Internet of Things (IoT). *International Journal of Smart Sensor and Adhoc Network*, 1-17.

Jiang, C., Lu, W., Wang, Z., & Ding, Y. (2023). Benchmarking state-of-the-art imbalanced data learning approaches for credit scoring. *Expert Systems with Applications*, *213*, 118878.

Khalili, N., & Rastegar, M. A. (2023). Optimal cost-sensitive credit scoring using a new hybrid performance metric. *Expert Systems with Applications, 213*, 119232. .

Kozodoi, N., Jacob, J., & Lessmann, S. (2022). Fairness in credit scoring: Assessment, implementation and profit implications. *European Journal of Operational Research, 297*(3), 1083–1094. doi:10.1016/j.ejor.2021.06.023

Li, Y., & Chen, W. (2020). A comparative performance assessment of ensemble learning for credit scoring. *Mathematics, 8*(10), 1756. doi:10.3390/math8101756

Liu, Y., Yang, M., Wang, Y., Li, Y., Xiong, T., & Li, A. (2022). Applying machine learning algorithms to predict default probability in the online credit market: Evidence from China. *International Review of Financial Analysis, 79*, 101971. doi:10.1016/j.irfa.2021.101971

Luo, C. (2020). A comprehensive decision support approach for credit scoring. *Industrial Management & Data Systems, 120*(2), 280–290. doi:10.1108/IMDS-03-2019-0182

Luo, C., Wu, D., & Wu, D. (2017). A deep learning approach for credit scoring using credit default swaps. *Engineering Applications of Artificial Intelligence, 65*, 465–470. doi:10.1016/j.engappai.2016.12.002

Machado, M. R., & Karray, S. (2022). Assessing credit risk of commercial customers using hybrid machine learning algorithms. *Expert Systems with Applications, 200*, 116889. doi:10.1016/j.eswa.2022.116889

Mishra, A., Singh, C., Dwivedi, A., Singh, D., & Biswal, A. K. (2021, October). Network Forensics: An approach towards detecting Cyber Crime. In *2021 International Conference in Advances in Power, Signal, and Information Technology (APSIT)* (pp. 1-6). IEEE. 10.1109/APSIT52773.2021.9641399

Pławiak, P., Abdar, M., Pławiak, J., Makarenkov, V., & Acharya, U. R. (2020). DGHNL: A new deep genetic hierarchical network of learners for prediction of credit scoring. *Information Sciences, 516*, 401–418. doi:10.1016/j.ins.2019.12.045

Reji, T., Rodrigues, A., & George, J. P. (2023). Credit Card Defaulters Prediction Using Unsupervised Features. In *Sentiment Analysis and Deep Learning: Proceedings of ICSADL 2022* (pp. 909-922). Singapore: Springer Nature Singapore. 10.1007/978-981-19-5443-6_67

Samantaray, M., Biswal, A. K., Singh, D., Samanta, D., Karuppiah, M., & Joseph, N. P. (2021, December). Optical character recognition (ocr) based vehicle's license plate recognition system using python and opencv. In *2021 5th International Conference on Electronics, Communication and Aerospace Technology (ICECA)* (pp. 849-853). IEEE.

Sethy, K. K., Singh, D., Biswal, A. K., & Sahoo, S. (2022, October). Serverless Implementation of Data Wizard Application using Azure Kubernetes Service and Docker. In *2022 1st IEEE International Conference on Industrial Electronics: Developments & Applications (ICIDeA)* (pp. 214-219). IEEE. 10.1109/ICIDeA53933.2022.9970103

Singh, D., Bhanipati, J., Biswal, A. K., Samanta, D., Joshi, S., Shukla, P. K., & Nuagah, S. J. (2021). (b), Bhanipati, J., Biswal, A. K., Samanta, D., Joshi, S., Shukla, P. K., & Nuagah, S. J. (2021). Approach for collision minimization and enhancement of power allocation in WSNs. *Journal of Sensors, 2021*, 1–11. doi:10.1155/2021/7059881

Singh, D., Biswal, A. K., Samanta, D., Singh, D., & Lee, H.-N. (2022). Juice jacking: Security issues and improvements in USB technology. *Sustainability (Basel)*, *14*(2), 939. doi:10.3390u14020939

Tripathi, D., Edla, D. R., Kuppili, V., & Bablani, A. (2020). Evolutionary extreme learning machine with novel activation function for credit scoring. *Engineering Applications of Artificial Intelligence*, *96*, 103980. doi:10.1016/j.engappai.2020.103980

Wang, Y., Jia, Y., Tian, Y., & Xiao, J. (2022). Deep reinforcement learning with the confusion-matrix-based dynamic reward function for customer credit scoring. *Expert Systems with Applications*, *200*, 117013. doi:10.1016/j.eswa.2022.117013

Wu, C. F., Huang, S. C., Chiou, C. C., & Wang, Y. M. (2021). A predictive intelligence system of credit scoring based on deep multiple kernel learning. *Applied Soft Computing*, *111*, 107668. doi:10.1016/j.asoc.2021.107668

Xu, C., Guo, R., Zhang, Y., & Luo, X. (2023). Toward an Efficient and Effective Credit Scorer for Cross-Border E-Commerce Enterprises. *Scientific Programming, 2023*. Asencios, R., Asencios, C., & Ramos, E. (2023). Profit scoring for credit unions using the multilayer perceptron, XGBoost and TabNet algorithms: Evidence from Peru. *Expert Systems with Applications*, *213*, 119201.

Yang, F., Qiao, Y., Qi, Y., Bo, J., & Wang, X. (2022). BACS: Blockchain and AutoML-based technology for efficient credit scoring classification. *Annals of Operations Research*, 1–21. doi:10.100710479-022-04531-8 PMID:35095154

Zhang, Z., Niu, K., & Liu, Y. (2020). A deep learning based online credit scoring model for P2P lending. *IEEE Access : Practical Innovations, Open Solutions*, *8*, 177307–177317. doi:10.1109/ACCESS.2020.3027337

Chapter 19
Requirements Modeling:
A Use Case Approach to Machine Learning

Murat Pasa Uysal

iD https://orcid.org/0000-0002-8349-9403

Baskent University, Turkey

ABSTRACT

Industrial applications and research studies report that organizations using machine learning (ML) solutions may be at risk of failure or they could fall short of business objectives. One serious issue that is often neglected is meeting the specific requirements of machine learning-driven software systems (MLD-SS). The use of a variety of information technologies, integration methods and tools, and domain-specific processes can add to this complexity. The data-driven and black-box nature of ML may be another great challenge. Therefore, there is a clear need for adopting a stakeholder-centered approach to the requirements engineering (RE) of MLD-SS. Use case modeling (UCM) can make requirements simpler and understandable by all stakeholders, allow better communication of ideas and provide support to testing, validation, and verification processes. In this chapter, a ten-step RE method and a four-step UCM method are proposed for MLD-SS, and then these methods are applied in a real case study of a university hospital.

INTRODUCTION

Machine learning-driven software systems (MLD-SS) may be considered more complex than software systems, such as web applications, enterprise systems, etc. This situation can get worse when considering the vital importance of mission-critical systems in various domains, such as healthcare, finance, and smart production. The use of a variety of information technologies, integration methods, and tools, domain-specific processes can add to the complexity of MLD-SS. On the other hand, it is not unusual to see a considerable number of failure stories about Machine Learning (ML) projects. Industrial applications and research studies report that organizations using ML solutions may be at risk of failure or they can fall short of business and organizational objectives (Uysal, 2022a).

DOI: 10.4018/978-1-6684-9809-5.ch019

One serious issue that is often neglected is to meet the specific requirements of MLD-SS, such as software engineering (SE) requirements, ML-specific requirements, and domain-specific requirements. SE extends its methods and activities beyond data processing and model development, and it focuses on the software development processes. ML, on the other hand, emphasizes the data processing, model development and deployment. Therefore, aligning, and synchronizing data processing and model development with the SE processes is a serious issue (Amershi et al. 2019). Requirements processes, team management, quality management, risk management, and maintenance are also the core aspects both for SE and ML. However, requirements specification for ML is much more challenging (Rahman et al., 2019). Some studies indicate the dynamic and complex context of the design, development, and maintenance of large-scale MLD-SS. ML contexts differ from the plan-driven or agile software development contexts. Therefore, ML and SE workflow management needs to be integrated with the SE best practices (Lwakatare et al., 2020).

A Microsoft team conducted a research study on the SE challenges for ML and AI projects (Amershi et al. 2019). It is found that data discovery and management is complicated and more difficult than the other SE activities. Model customization and reuse require different skills than that are found in SE teams. Since SE and ML modules can be entangled in various ways, ML processes may also be more challenging than the software processes. Therefore, they suggest that the integration of software development infrastructure with ML development would speed up the ML experimentations. Moreover, automating the ML processes, such as data aggregation, synthesizing, feature extraction, and pipeline are the other major concerns for the teams.

Some studies present the SE challenges as they are related with the issues of requirements engineering (RE) of ML (Uysal, 2022b). The systematic mapping study of Villamizar et al. (2021) reveals that the handling customer expectations and lack of validated RE techniques as the main challenges. Giray's (2021) extensive systematic literature review (SLR) gives the state of art and SE challenges for ML. He adopts a SE perspective on engineering ML systems. Accordingly, forming coherent teams, requirements process, tailoring, and assessing the SE process, managing, and harmonizing the ML system development with software development are the main issues. Fernández et al (2021) conducts a SLR on SE for AI-based systems and finds safety and dependability as the most studied research topics. Software quality and software testing are dominant whereas the areas such as, software maintenance are neglected. They also identify various SE approaches to AI-based systems that are classified according to the Software Engineering Body of Knowledge (SWEBOK) (2014) knowledge areas (KAs). The data-driven and black box nature of ML may be another great challenge.

Kumeno (2019) conducted the first review to map the SE challenges for ML to the SE KAs defined by the SWEBOK standard. The topics in KAs, such as safety, security, validation, and verification are identified as the major challenge topics over the ones in other KAs. Lwakatare et al (2020) focuses on large-scale ML systems in real-world industrial settings. Adaptability and scalability are found as the most often reported SE challenges while safety and privacy are the least reported quality attributes. Nascimento et al (2020) highlights these five of thirteen categories: test, software quality, data, management, model development, and project management (PM). Design, construction, testing, and configuration management KAs have the highest number of solution proposals.

Behaviors of software systems are initially specified and defined by using design patterns and programming models. However, this is reverse in ML systems where system behaviors are continuously learned after processing the training data sets. Even minor changes in the input can drastically change the ML application behaviors, which means that ML projects need specific techniques for testing, validation, and verification procedures. Comprehensive or detailed requirement analysis and specification may not be feasible or possible for ML at the beginning. Additionally, the black-box nature of ML algorithms, makes the explanations difficult both for technical and non-technical stakeholders, i.e., "what is possible and what is not" (Ishikawa and Yoshioka, 2019). Consequently, the review of literature reveals that there is a clear need for adopting a user-centered approach to requirements engineering (RE) of MLD-SS, which can make this process simpler and understandable for all stakeholders. Additionally, this approach can also allow better communication of ideas and provide support to testing, validation, and verification processes.

BACKGROUND

Machine Learning

Machine learning (ML) is a subfield of AI, which is also "a field of study that gives computers the ability to learn without being explicitly programmed (Samuel, 1959)". In ML, appropriate data and an algorithm are combined to form a learning model, which learns performing tasks by relying on the patterns in the training data. Data and a matching algorithm represent a solution model for an ML problem. Valuable knowledge is produced to make better decisions or various insights can be inferred from the information extracted. Supervised learning, unsupervised learning, and reinforcement learning are the main learning types in ML applications.

Problem definition (PD), data acquisition (DA), data processing (DP), feature engineering (FE), exploratory data analysis (EDA), model training and testing (MTT), model evaluation and validation (MEV) are the main stages of an ML project. At the PD stage, a research problem and the rationale behind the ML project is defined. Next, a large volume of data is collected during DA, which is highly critical for the success of the project. Data preparation, cleansing and removing errors, labeling, data transforming and integrating are the activities of the DP stage. The FE process is conducted to explore the most appropriate features from the raw data, and to make the data available for the next stages. EDA is used to have a better understanding of the research data and it includes data visualization and statistical methods and techniques. The purpose of the MTT stage is to use or build ML models to find the best solution to the research problem. Therefore, an ML model is a combination of the algorithm and data with appropriate features. MEV process is carried out to ensure that the learning model has good predictive power, and it generalizes well to the unseen data

Requirements Engineering

According to the ISO/IEC/IEEE 42010 standard, a concern is an "interest in a system relevant to one or more of its stakeholders (ISO/IEC/IEEE, 2011)". Organizational concerns and goals reflect the holistic perspective and priorities, such as business goals, objectives, and constraints that drive the RE processes. A stakeholder may be an "individual, team, organization, or classes thereof, having an interest in a system", which is also affected by the system directly or indirectly. Viewpoints are associated with the stakeholders or entities, such as end-users, customers, managers, and staff involved in the operation and maintenance of the system. Internal, external systems and regulatory bodies may be the other stakeholders. However, it is also known that all the information about a software system cannot be discovered by considering the system from a single viewpoint and perspective. Since a viewpoint encapsulates partial information about requirements, a variety of information from different viewpoints is needed and it must be organized for the RE processes (Nalchigar et al., 2021).

It mainly consists of system analysis and design documents, system, and architectural models, requirements specification, validation, and verification documents. In general, a RE process usually includes the following steps:

- Step-1 (requirements elicitation): It is the interaction with stakeholders to capture their needs and retrieving the required information from various sources such as documents, domain knowledge, regulations, standards, and existing systems.
- Step-2 (requirements analysis): It aims understanding the structure of the problem and solution domains and breaking them into parts with the intention of understanding the parts' nature, inter-relationships, and their functions.
- Step-3 (requirements modeling): It is the design process of product and process models to have a simplified and holistic understanding of a system. Modeling the artifacts may include business processes, different views of a product, and the environment in which the product will be used.
- Step-4 (requirements negotiation): It is the process of discovering conflicting and overlapping requirements, negotiating changes and compromises between conflicting requirements.
- Step-5 (requirements prioritization): It is the assignment of importance to a requirement. Prioritization is based on the fulfillment of both product and organizational goals and strategies and helps to identify the most valuable and critical requirements.
- Step-6 (requirements validation): This is related to the stakeholders' requirements.
- Step-7 (requirements verification): This step assurances that the validated requirements are addressed, defined, and met correctly.
- Step-8 (requirements review): It is a review to ensure that the characteristics of good requirements are achieved.
- Step-9 (requirements specification): It is the set of agreed requirements that are documented. The output from this process may be a requirements document, a system specification etc. Therefore, the specification may belong to the business, software, system, or stakeholders' requirements.
- Step-10 (requirements management): This process includes the "activities that ensure requirements are identified, documented, maintained, communicated and traced throughout the life cycle of a system, product, or service".

Use Case Modeling

Use case modeling (UCM) is a both SE and Unified Modeling Language (UML) technique that is used to describe and represent the functional requirements of a software system. As an auxiliary tool for RE within a specific context, a use case is a means for the partial description of an application behavior or functionality. Therefore, the main purpose of UCM is to provide a structured way of describing the interactions between the system and its users or other systems, in terms of specific scenarios and situations that are relevant to the system's functionality. A use case is used as a method for understanding the problem and solution domain, which involves actors and the environment in which the software application will perform. Therefore, use cases and scenarios are a valuable way of communication among stakeholders. While they help to elicit, analyze, validate requirements, use cases and scenarios are also used as a base for test cases. They can be designed in text narrative, graphical, storyboard, or video formats. For example, Use Case Diagrams (UCD) express the high-level user and stakeholder interactions and focus on the functional and behavioral aspects of a system. Some well-known benefits of UCM are as follows:

- Improved understanding of functional requirements: UCM helps to ensure that all stakeholders have a clear and consistent understanding of the system's functional requirements.
- Better communication of ideas: UCM provides a common language for all stakeholders to communicate about the system's functionalities, internal relationships, and boundaries, which help to reduce misunderstandings and improve collaboration.
- Enabling testing and validation: UCM provides a structured way to identify the inputs, outputs, and other constraints associated with each use case, which may ensure that the system functions correctly and meets the needs of its users.
- Comprehensive overview of the system's functional requirements.

Use Cases

Although they may be confused and sometimes may be used interchangeably, use cases, and use case diagrams are different. Use cases are narrative and employed for the documentation of user-system interactions and system requirements when looking in from the outside. They are relatively easy to write, read and understand when compared to other RE tools. On the other hand, use case diagrams represent the high-level and visual overview of business and system requirements (Unhelkar, 2018)(Lee 2019)."

One of important contributions of the use cases is constructing a base for test cases, especially for the user acceptance tests. Use cases also cover important knowledge such as, success criteria, pre- and post-conditions, exceptions, external systems and interface references, alternative scenario(s). While mapping the user interactions within the system as the instances of a use case, scenarios are also a sequence of events that the system is responsible for. Depending on the extension or exception conditions, it may be necessary to have multiple scenarios to describe a use case. Use cases can be identified by interviews and discussions with stakeholders, analyzing processes and documents, researching the literature and the problem domain. A use can be developed by using a template as given below (Table 1):

- Identifying primary and secondary actors (stakeholders/users) of the proposed system,
- Defining a user profile for each stakeholder/user, which contains the roles that the user play with the system,
- Identifying the stakeholders' goals and the measurable objectives for each goal,
- Identifying the functionalities expected from the system,
- Relating the goals and functionalities to use cases,
- Defining and structuring the use cases:
  - Defining the scope and boundary,
  - Defining the primary and secondary actors, their goals, and required functionalities,
  - Writing a main success scenario for the use case,
  - Defining extension and exception conditions of the use case,
  - Writing a new scenario for each extension or exception condition.
- Refining and breaking down the complex use cases into sub-use cases, if necessary,
- Validating the use cases.

Table 1. An example template for a use case

Identification: < The information such as identification ID, name, version number of a use case >
Goal: < Specify the stakeholders' goal and measurable objectives to achieve for the use case>
Description: <Short description of the use case, purpose, and usage, which can range from short sentences to a paragraph >
Actors: < A list of primary and secondary actors, abstract and concrete actors >
Functionalities: < The functionalities that are expected from the system >
Main scenario: < The main execution steps and flow of the interactions between the users and the system >
Pre-conditions: < The conditions that need to be satisfied before the execution of the main scenario >
Post-conditions: < The conditions that must be met at the end of the main scenario >
Alternative scenarios: < Additional scenarios that may be necessary to describe the use case >
Exceptions: < The conditions that may be encountered during the main scenario. These may be errors or unexpected events >
Metrics: < Anything that must be measured and be related to the use case >
Relationships: <The use case to use case relationships such as, inclusion, extension, and inheritance >
Additional knowledge: < It may be the interfaces needed by users, the package in which the use case is included, constraints, author(s) of the use case, source information from where the use case has been derived, etc. >

Use Case Diagrams

Use case diagrams (UCDs) establish a common ground, provide a visual abstraction and understanding mechanism for all stakeholders. Therefore, they represent the high-level overview of business and system requirements from the perspective of the outside world (Unhelkar, 2018; Sundaramoorthy, 2022). The main elements of a use case diagram are actors, use cases, relationships, and system boundaries as shown in Figure 1.

Figure 1. The main elements of use case diagrams

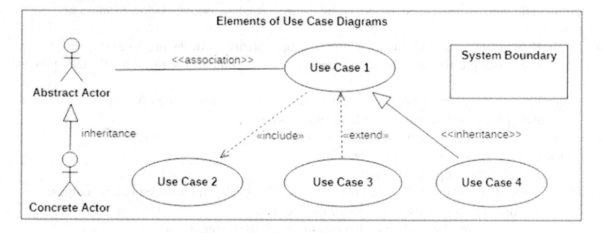

An actor or user is a person or entity outside of the proposed system that interacts with it. Actors are symbolized by stick figures in diagrams and represent the roles played by the users. They can be classified into primary/secondary actors, direct/indirect actors, or abstract/concrete actors. The main actors are those who benefit from the system or trigger the interactions. Secondary actors are included in the use cases, but they usually play the role of assistance. The direct actors use the system while indirect actors may provide the information required for the use case events. An abstract actor models a user profile of a system while a concrete actor models the realization and specification of this abstract user profile. Thus, the generalization of actors can reduce the complexity in UCDs.

A use case is a functionality that is expected from the system, which also provides tangible benefit, concrete and measurable results of value. Indeed, use case diagrams describe what a system does, but they do not specify how the system does it. Use cases are symbolized by an ellipse shape in diagrams. The relationships between use cases are represented by the symbols such as, "include, "extend", "inheritance" and "association" types of arrows. They provide the generic descriptions of how use cases relate to each other. The "include" type of relationship indicates the reuse of a common use case by the other use cases. Its arrowhead is pointed from the including use case to the other use case being included. The "extends" relationship shows the extension or specialization of another use case. A special type of an existing use case, adding a functionality to an existing use case, and an exception can be described by the "extend" relationships. When a use case implements the behavior that is described by an abstract use case, it is also represented by the "inheritance" relationship. A rectangle shape symbolizes a system boundary by isolating the external and the internal elements of a system. Therefore, actors are placed outside while other elements are placed inside of the system. Finally, the "association" type relationships connect the actors to the corresponding use cases.

MAIN FOCUS OF THE CHAPTER

The focus of this chapter is adopting a use case-based approach to RE of MLD-SS. The use case approach to RE and its modeling processes include the following steps (Figure 2):

- Step-1: Requirements Elicitation:
  - Identifying the project goals and concerns that reflect the holistic perspective, priorities, and business objectives of the organization.
  - Identifying stakeholders (internal, external, potential users, roles, regulations, etc.).
  - Identifying the stakeholders' viewpoints, concerns, and objectives.
  - Interacting with stakeholders to capture their needs.
  - Retrieving the required information from various sources such as documents, domain knowledge, regulations, standards, and existing systems.
- Step-2: Requirements Analysis:
  - Conducting functional and object-oriented requirements analysis to understand the structure of the problem domain.
  - Breaking the structure into parts with the intention of understanding the parts' nature, inter-relationships, and their functions.
  - Specifying the system's behaviors and functional requirements from the viewpoint of stakeholders.

- Step-3: Requirements Modeling:
  ◦ Writing use cases.
  ◦ Developing use case diagrams.
  ◦ Refining use cases and diagrams.
- Step-4: Requirements Validation:
  ◦ Confirming that the requirements models define the right system as intended by the stakeholders and they meet the needs of all stakeholders. Formal methods and software validation methods can be used for the validation process.

Figure 2. Activity diagram for a use case approach to RE processes

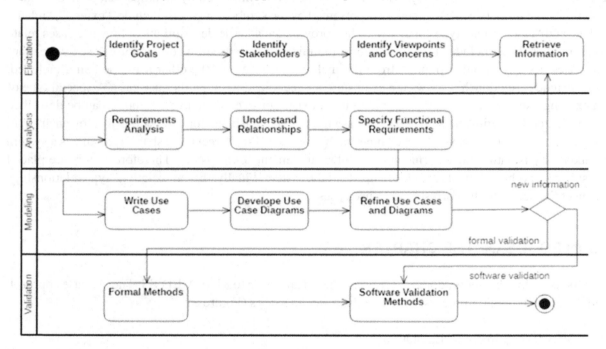

SOLUTIONS AND RECOMMENDATIONS

Business Scenario

The RE and use case modeling processes are dependent on a real case study of a research conducted for Baskent University Hospital Ankara (BUHA) in Turkey (Uysal, 2022a). Only are a limited part of information and artifacts presented due to the space, scope, and the limitations of this chapter.

Business Problem

BUHA is the first and one of the most sophisticated transplantation surgery hospitals in Turkey. It uses healthcare information systems (HEIS) and owns state-of-the-art medical equipment. Its HEIS, servers, and medical and laboratory equipment are connected by local area, wide area, and mobile networks along with the medical equipment-specific connections. Recent developments in technology and ML have also motivated BUHA administration and researchers to take a step forward in the area of ML-driven HEIS. This was to achieve a competitive advantage, improve illness and disease diagnosis processes, and patient satisfaction. However, the stakeholders of BUHA are not sure about "what-to-do" and "how-to-do" as well as specifying the requirements without risking its current systems and applications (Uysal, 2022a).

Business and Technical Environment

BUHA has its own infrastructure, servers, medical and enterprise applications. It uses an enterprise resource planning (ERP) application for its business processes.

Business Goals and Desired Outcomes

BUHA's business and medical goals are as follows:

- To improve illness and disease diagnosis processes,
- To improve patient satisfaction,
- To achieve a competitive advantage,
- To improve profitability,
- To maintain the quality and availability of current medical and IT systems.

Stakeholders (Human and Computer Actors) in the Business Case

The human actors are doctors, patients, medical staff, ML engineers, administration, and IT staff of BUHA. The main computer actor is the desired MLD-SS that would support the diagnosis processes.

Step 1: Requirements Elicitation

The administration, IT staff, medical staff (doctors, physicians, nurses, medical assistants, etc.), and ML engineers are the main stakeholders and users. BUHA administration has a financial viewpoint, and it is concerned with a competitive advantage. Therefore, their goal is to improve volume-based care and profitability by increasing the number of patients. Doctors and medical assistants have a medical viewpoint, and thus they are concerned with improving diagnosis processes and accuracy i.e., 10%. The IT managers and staff of BUHA have a technical viewpoint, and they focus on the quality and availability of medical and IT operations and HEIS. ML engineers may also have the same concern as IT staff. However, they have an ML viewpoint, and thus their main concern is the ML processes, such as the quality and availability of data, data processing, and the effective development, validation, and deployment of ML models.

Step 2: Requirements Analysis

The focus of this step is the specification of the system's features, behaviors, and functional requirements from the viewpoints of all stakeholders. Therefore, requirements analysis may include but is not limited to feature analysis, functional analysis, and domain analysis processes. Feature analysis (FA) describes the end-user's understanding of the capabilities of applications in a domain. These capabilities may include the features, such as services provided by the application, operating environments, and domain technologies. Based on the FA, functional analysis (FnA) is used to identify commonalities and differences of the applications in a domain, which also abstracts and structures the common functions in a model. Finally, domain analysis (DA) identifies, collects, organizes, and represents the information captured from domain experts and existing systems. Table 2 presents the functional requirements of the ML-driven HEIS:

Table 2. Functional requirements of the system

#	Functions for Illness and Disease Diagnosis	#	Functions for Manual and Automated Machine Learning
1.	Patient admission	1.	Data extraction
2.	Illness and disease diagnosis	2.	Data analysis
2.a	Reviewing clinical history	3.	Data preparation
2.b	Physical examination	4.	Model training
2.c	Diagnostic testing	5.	Model evaluation
2.d	Consulting with other clinicians if necessary	6.	Model validation
2.e	Requesting ML support for illness and disease diagnosis	7.	Model deployment
3.	Completing illness and disease diagnosis	8.	Model monitoring and maintenance

Step 3: Requirements Modeling

This step includes writing the use cases according to the functional requirements, developing and refining the use case diagrams as shown below sections:

Use Cases

Table 3 presents the use case for illness and disease diagnosis processes (UC-1).
Table 4 includes the use case for manual and automated ML processes (UC-2).

Developing Use Case Diagrams

The use case diagram for illness and disease diagnosis (UCD-1) is given in Figure 3. The "illness and disease diagnosis" boundary isolates the external actors from the internal use cases. As can be seen, the doctor, patient and medical assistant are concrete actors. Staff is an abstract actor, and it enables inheritance. A doctor is also a direct actor who uses the system and requests the ML service. A patient is an indirect actor providing the information required for the diagnosis. However, the patient is also a primary actor in the "patient admission" use case. Medical staff, appointment office, and ML service are the secondary actors, and thus, they play the role of assistance. The "performing diagnosis" use case includes the "physical examination", "reviewing clinical history", "diagnostic testing", and "consulting with other clinicians" use cases. The use case for the "machine learning process" extends the use case for "performing diagnosis" as a special form of it.

Table 3. The use case for illness and disease diagnosis when using ML service

Identification: UC-1: Illness and disease diagnosis when using an ML service.
Goal: To improve the diagnosis process and its accuracy through an ML service.
Description: The purpose of this use case is to describe the actors, functionalities, scenarios, elements, and conditions that are required for ML-driven illness and disease diagnosis.
Actors: Medical staff (abstract), doctor (concrete, primary), physician (concrete, primary), medical assistant (concrete, secondary), patient (concrete, secondary), appointment office (concrete, secondary), ML service (concrete, secondary).
Functionalities: The functionalities for illness and disease diagnosis when using ML service.
Main scenario: Step-1: Patient admission, Step-2: Reviewing clinical history, Step-3: Physical examination, Step-4: Diagnostic testing, Step-5: Consulting with other clinicians, if necessary, Step-6: Requesting ML service for illness and disease diagnosis, Step-7: Completing illness and disease diagnosis.
Pre-conditions: The patient is admitted; the ML service is running.
Post-conditions: The illness and disease diagnosis process is completed.
Alternative scenarios: Conducting traditional diagnostic processes.
Exceptions: Exception-1: The ML service is not working. Handling-1: Conduct the traditional diagnostic processes. Exception-2: The doctor's and the ML service's diagnoses do not correlate. Handling-2: (a) Consult with other clinicians if necessary, and (b) perform individual decision-making.
Metrics: The accuracy level of the ML service.
Relationships: It has relationships with the use cases for manual or automated ML processes.
Additional knowledge: An application programming interface (API) is needed for integrating the ML application into the current HEIS.

Table 4. The use case for manual and automated ML processes

Identification: UC-2: Manual and automated ML processes.
Goal: To define manual and automated ML processes.
Description: The purpose of this use case to describe the actors, functionalities, processes, and conditions that are related with ML.
Actors: ML engineer (concrete, primary), ML pipeline (concrete, secondary).
Functionalities: The functionalities requested by the ML-driven illness and disease diagnosis processes such as classification, clustering, and regression.
Main scenario: Step-1: Data extraction Step-2: Data analysis Step-3: Data preparation Step-4: Model training Step-5: Model evaluation Step-6: Model validation Step-7: Model deployment
Pre-conditions: The ML service is running, the automated ML pipeline is working, appropriate data is provided, the performance level of ML model is appropriate and acceptable.
Post-conditions: The requested ML service is given; and the performance level of the ML model is appropriate and acceptable.
Alternative scenarios: -
Exceptions: Exception-1: The automated ML pipeline is not working. Handling-1: Conduct the manual ML processes. Exception-2: The ML model's performance level is not acceptable. Handling-2: (a) Conduct manual ML experimentation processes; (b) deploy the validated ML model; (c) update the automated ML pipeline.
Metrics: The metrics that are related with the performance level of the ML model.
Relationships: It has relationships with the use cases for ML-driven illness and disease diagnosis
Additional knowledge: API(s) are needed for integrating the ML application into the current medical and business information systems and IT infrastructure.

The use case diagram for the "machine learning process" (UCD-2) is given in Figure 4. The "machine learning process" boundary isolates the external actors, such as ML engineers and ML pipeline(s), from the internal use cases. ML engineer is a direct, concrete, and primary actor of the "manual ML process" use case. However, he or she is also a secondary actor when monitoring the "automated ML pipeline process". Both of "manual ML process" use case and the "automated ML pipeline process" use case extends the main "ML process" use case. This main use case includes the "data extraction", "data analysis", "data preparation", "model training", "model evaluation", "model validation, and "model deployment" use cases respectively.

Figure 3. UCD-1: The use case diagram for illness and disease diagnosis

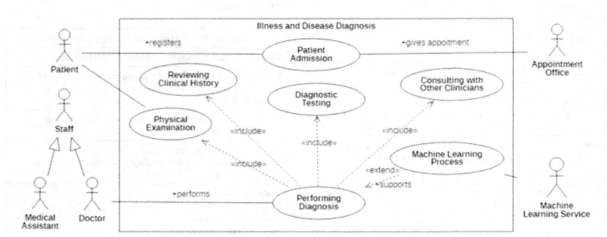

Figure 4. UCD-2: The use case diagram or machine learning process

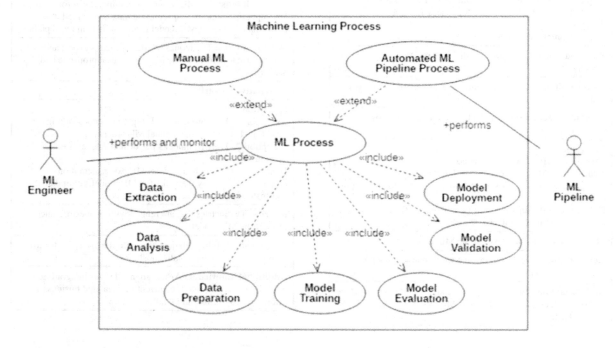

Step 3: Requirements Validation

The validation process is conducted whether the written or specified requirements capture and meet all the elicited requirements. In other words, it is to make sure that these requirements are suitable and feasible for the system development phase. The verification process, on the other hand, ensures that the software or final product meets the validated requirements. According to the IEEE 1012-2016 standard, the specified requirements are evaluated for correctness, consistency, completeness, readability, and testability during requirements validation (RV) (IEEE, 2016). An RV process can be conducted by using formal methods or software validation methods such as requirements review, scenario analysis, expert review, test cases, prototyping, consistency analysis, walk-through, etc.

FUTURE RESEARCH DIRECTIONS

Our future research efforts will focus on the following research topics:

- Exploring the application of other UML diagrams for the RE processes of MLD-SS.
- Exploring other RE approaches to MLD-SS, such as goal-oriented RE, value-based RE, and scenario-based RE.
- Application of the proposed use case-based RE method to the MLD-SS of other domains, such as industrial production and e-business.
- Exploring the applicability, feasibility, and practicality of corrective, adaptive, perfective, and preventive software maintenance methods, and techniques for MLD-SS.

CONCLUSION

The data-driven and black-box nature of ML is a serious challenge for MLD-SS. This situation makes the requirements specification and RE processes even harder. It is also revealed that handling customer expectations as well as lack of validated RE methods and techniques are the other sources of challenges. In other words, there is a clear need of explaining the "what is possible and what is not" for all technical and non-technical stakeholders of an ML project. A narrative, visual, and a stakeholder-centered modeling approach to RE can not only allow a better communication means but also, provide an important support to testing, validation, and verification processes of MLD-SS. Therefore, UCM can meet these needs and it provides a multi perspective way of defining a system's functionalities as well as the interactions between the system and its users. UCM improves the understanding of functional requirements, provide better communication of ideas, and enables testing and validation.

In this chapter, a use case approach to RE processes of MLD-SS is presented, and then this approach is applied in a real case study of BUHA. Contributions of this study are as follows:

- Drawing researchers' and practitioners' attention to the problems of RE of MLD-SS from the perspective of stakeholders.
- Using UCM as a simple but effective tool for RE processes,
- Proposing a general nine-step RE method for MLD-SS,
- Proposing a four-step RE method for UCM.

ACKNOWLEDMENT

This study is supported by Baskent University. Project ID: 2021-11-0032; Project Title: "An enterprise architecture and artificial intelligence implementation roadmap for Baskent University Hospital Ankara". The author confirms that he has no competing financial and other types of interests, or personal and organizational relationships that could have appeared to influence the study reported in this chapter.

REFERENCES

Amershi, S., Begel, A., Bird, C., DeLine, R., Gall, H., Kamar, E., Nagappan, N., Nushi, B., & Zimmermann, T. (2019). Software engineering for machine learning: A case study. *Microsoft Research*, https://www.microsoft.com

Bourque, P., & Richard, E. (2014). *SWEBOK Version 3.0*. IEEE.

Fernández, S. M., Bogner, J., Franch, X., Oriol, M., Siebert, J., Trendowicz, A., Vollmer, A. M., & Wagner, S. (2021). Software engineering for AI-Based systems: A survey. *ACM Transactions on Software Engineering and Methodology*, *31*(2), 1–59. doi:10.1145/3487043

Giray, G. (2021). A software engineering perspective on engineering machine learning systems: State of the art and challenges. *Journal of Systems and Software*, *180*, 1–35. doi:10.1016/j.jss.2021.111031

IEEE. (2016). *The IEEE 1012-2016 Standard for system, software, and hardware verification, and validation*. IEEE.

Ishikawa, F., & Yoshioka, N. (2019). How do engineers perceive difficulties in engineering of machine-learning systems? In *Proceedings of IEEE/ACM 6th International Workshop on Software Engineering Research and Industrial Practice*. IEEE/ACM.

ISO/IEC/IEEE (2018). *Systems and software engineering-life cycle processes-Requirements Engineering, Standard*. ISO, IEC, IEEE.

ISO/IEC/IEEE 42010:2011 (2011). *Systems and software engineering-architecture description, standard*. ISO, IEC, IEEE. https://www.iso.org/ obp/ ui/ # iso: std:iso-iec-ieee:42010:ed-1:v1:en.

Kumeno, F. (2019). Software engineering challenges for machine learning applications: A literature review. *Intelligent Decision Technologies*, *13*(4), 463–476. doi:10.3233/IDT-190160

Lee, R. Y. (2019). *Object-oriented software engineering with UML: A hands-on approach*. Nova Science Publishers.

Lwakatare, L. E., Raj, A., Crnkovic, I., Bosch, J., & Olsson, H. H. (2020). Large-scale machine learning systems in real-world industrial settings: A review of challenges and solutions. *Information and Software Technology*, *127*, 106368. doi:10.1016/j.infsof.2020.106368

Nalchigar, S., Yu, E., & Keshavjee, K. (2021). Modeling machine learning requirements from three perspectives: A case report from the healthcare domain. *Requirements Engineering*, *34567*(2), 1–18. doi:10.100700766-020-00343-z

Nascimento, E., Nguyen-Duc, A., Sundbø, I., & Conte, T. (2020). Software engineering for artificial intelligence and machine learning software: A systematic literature review. arXiv preprint arXiv:2011.03751.

Samuel, A. (1959). Some studies in machine learning using the game of checkers. *IBM Journal of Research and Development*, *3*(3), 210–229.

Sundaramoorthy, S. (2022). *UML diagramming: A case study approach*. CRS Press. doi:10.1201/9781003287124

Unhelkar, B. (2018). Software engineering with UML. CRC Press, Taylor & Francis Group, USA.

Uysal, M. P. (2021). Machine learning and data science project management from an agile perspective: Methods and challenges. In V. Naidoo & R. Verma (Eds.), *Contemporary challenges for agile project management* (pp. 73–89). IGI Global.

Uysal, M. P. (2022a). Machine learning-enabled healthcare information systems in view of Industrial Information Integration Engineering. *Journal of Industrial Information Integration*, *30*(1), 1–18. doi:10.1016/j.jii.2022.100382

Uysal, M. P. (2022b). An integrated and multi-perspective approach to the requirements of machine learning. *IFIP International Conference on Industrial Information Integration (ICIIIE 2022)*, Bangkok, Thailand.

Villamizar, H., Escovedo, T., & Kalinowski, M. (2021). *Requirements engineering for machine learning: A systematic mapping study. 47th Euromicro Conference on Software Engineering and Advanced Applications (SEAA)*, Palermo, Italy. 10.1109/SEAA53835.2021.00013

KEY TERMS AND DEFINITIONS

Concern: A concern is an interest in a system relevant to one or more of its stakeholders.

Requirement: A requirement is a condition or capability that must be met or possessed by a system or system component to satisfy a contract, standard, specification, or other formally imposed documents.

Requirements Engineering: Requirements engineering is an interdisciplinary function that mediates between the domains of the acquirer and supplier to establish and maintain the requirements to be met by the system, software, or service of interest.

Stakeholder: A stakeholder is an individual, team, organization, or classes thereof, having an interest in a system, which is also affected by the system directly or indirectly.

View: A view is a representation of a system from the perspective of a related set of concerns.

Viewpoint: A viewpoint is a specification of the conventions for constructing a view; a pattern or template from which to develop individual views by establishing the purposes and audience for a view and the techniques for its creation and analysis.

Chapter 20
Software Principles of 5G Coverage:
Simulator Analysis of Various Parameters

Himanshu Kumar Sinha
Acharya Institute of Technology, India

Devasis Pradhan
Acharya Institute of Technology, India

Abhishek Saurabh
Acharya Institute of Technology, India

Anand Kumar
Acharya Institute of Technology, India

ABSTRACT

5G NR (new radio) coverage tool is a software-based solution that helps network planners and engineers to analyze and optimize the coverage of 5G networks. The tool uses advanced algorithms and models to predict the 5G signal propagation and coverage performance in different environments and scenarios. It takes into account various factors such as the frequency band, the antenna configuration, the terrain, the building materials, and the interference from other sources. It provides a detailed analysis of the signal strength, quality, and throughput in different locations, enabling network operators to identify areas with poor coverage and take appropriate measures to improve it. It also allows network planners to simulate different deployment scenarios and optimize the network design for maximum coverage and capacity. The tool provides real-time feedback and visualization of the coverage performance, allowing engineers to adjust the network parameters and antenna configurations on the fly.

DOI: 10.4018/978-1-6684-9809-5.ch020

INTRODUCTION

As wireless technology continues to advance, it's important for consumers to have access to tools that can help them determine the extent of wireless coverage in their area. 5G and 4G are two of the most popular wireless technologies, and there are a number of coverage tools available that can help consumers identify areas with 5G and 4G coverage. The fifth generation of wireless technology, or 5G, offers increased connectivity, faster upload and download speeds, and lower latency for a variety of applications. 4G, on the other hand, is the fourth generation of wireless technology and provides faster download and upload speeds than 3G. 4G is extensively available over the majority of the world, although 5G is still being deployed in many locations (Bhargava, M. et. al.,2018). To help consumers determine the extent of 5G and 4G coverage in their area, there are a number of tools available. Some tools are mobile apps that use crowd sourced data to create a map of wireless coverage, while others are web-based tools that rely on data provided by carriers (Chen, J. et. al.,2019). By using these tools, consumers can get a better understanding of 5G and 4G coverage in their area and make more informed decisions about their wireless service. It's important to note that while these tools can be helpful in identifying areas with 5G and 4G coverage, they may not provide a complete picture of coverage in all areas. Additionally, coverage can vary based on carrier, location, and other factors. It's always a good idea to check with your carrier directly to confirm 5G and 4G coverage in your area.

LITERATURE SURVEY

The literature survey have been showcase in the Table1.

5G AT A GLANCE

The newest mobile communication technology, 5G, has the potential to completely change how we use the internet. It is intended to provide enhanced network capacity, network slicing, lower latency, quicker internet speeds, improved network dependability, expanded network capacity, and support for extensive IoT installations. Users may anticipate download rates of up to 10 Gbps with 5G, which is much faster than the top 4G LTE speeds. Additionally, it is anticipated that this technology would offer lower latency, which translates into quicker reaction times and is appropriate for real-time applications like gaming and autonomous cars. Additionally, 5G technology is intended to have enhanced network capacity, which allows for simultaneous connections from more devices without degrading performance (Huang, Y. et. al.,2020)(Khan, I. et. al.,2019).

The more linked devices there are, the more crucial this enhanced capacity is anticipated to be. Better coverage and fewer lost calls are two other improvements that 5G dependability is anticipated to make. Network slicing allows for the network to be split up into various virtual networks in order to offer specialised services to various user types (Lee, J. et. al.,2022). The enormous IoT installations that 5G is intended to serve will allow millions of devices to connect to the network. Overall, 5G technology is anticipated to enable new applications and services that were previously not feasible with 4G LTE technology, leading to substantial changes in the way we use the internet (Liu, Y. et. al.,2020). Table 2 shows difference Between 4G and 5G.

Table 1. Literature survey

Author(s)	Year	Title	Methodology	Main Findings
Sharma et al.	2018	"Comparative Study of 4G Coverage Mapping Tools"	Comparative analysis	Different 4G coverage mapping tools may provide varying levels of accuracy, and the best tool for a given situation will depend on factors such as location and desired level of detail.
Bhargava et al.	2018	"Comparison of 5G and 4G Coverage Tools for Rural Areas"	Simulation	5G coverage tools were found to be more effective than 4G coverage tools in predicting coverage in rural areas, due to the use of higher frequencies and smaller cell sizes.
Chen et al.	2019	"Crowdsourcing-Based 4G Coverage Mapping: Methodologies and Applications"	Crowdsourcing	Crowdsourced data can provide accurate and up-to-date information on 4G coverage, particularly in areas where carrier data is incomplete.
Khan et al.	2019	"Comparison of 4G and 5G Coverage Tools: A Case Study in Pakistan"	Survey	Consumers generally found 4G coverage tools to be more accurate and reliable than 5G coverage tools, although this may be due to the limited availability of 5G.
Huang et al.	2020	"5G Coverage Prediction Based on Machine Learning"	Machine learning algorithm	A machine learning-based approach can accurately predict 5G coverage, with an accuracy of over 90%.
Liu et al.	2020	"A Web-Based Tool for Visualizing 5G Coverage"	Web-based tool	A web-based tool can provide a visual representation of 5G coverage across different locations, allowing users to quickly identify areas with strong coverage.
Pervaiz et al.	2020	"A Comparative Study of 5G and 4G Coverage in Urban Areas"	Field measurements	5G coverage is generally more limited than 4G coverage in urban areas due to the need for more infrastructure and higher frequencies.
Wang et al.	2021	"5G Network Coverage Optimization Based on Big Data Analytics"	Big data analytics	Big data analytics can be used to optimize 5G network coverage, improving signal strength and overall network performance.
Zhang et al.	2021	"5G Coverage Mapping Based on Crowdsourcing Data"	Crowdsourcing	Crowdsourced data can provide accurate and up-to-date information on 5G coverage, and can be used to create detailed coverage maps.
Lee et al.	2022	"Web-Based 5G Coverage Tools: A Comparative Analysis"	Web-based testing	Web-based 5G coverage tools provided more comprehensive and accurate coverage information than mobile apps, although the accuracy varied depending on the carrier and location.

Table 2. Difference Between 4G and 5G

Parameter	4G	5G
Speed	Maximum download speed of up to 1 Gbps	Maximum download speed of up to 10 Gbps
Latency	Average latency of around 30-50 ms	Average latency of around 1 ms
Network Capacity	Can support up to 100 devices per square kilometer	Can support up to 1 million devices per square kilometer
Network Slicing	Not supported	Supported
Reliability	Reliability is good, but can be affected by congestion or interference	Improved reliability, with better coverage and fewer dropped calls
Spectrum	Utilizes lower frequency bands below 6 GHz	Utilizes higher frequency bands above 24 GHz
Deployment	Can be deployed using existing infrastructure	Requires new infrastructure and equipment
Use Cases	Suitable for streaming, browsing, and basic IoT applications	Suitable for real-time applications, IoT, and industrial applications

5G SIMULATION

5G simulation involves the creation of a virtual environment to model and simulate the behavior of a 5G network. The goal of 5G simulation is to evaluate the performance of the network under different scenarios and conditions, such as varying traffic loads, network congestion, and different network topologies. Simulation tools for 5G networks range from open-source tools such as NS-3 and MATLAB to commercial tools such as OPNET Modeler and QualNet (Wang, Y., Zhang et. al.,2021). These tools allow users to model and simulate different aspects of the network, including the radio access network, core network, and transport network (Pervaiz, H. et. al.,2020). To simulate a 5G network, users can create a network topology and configure different network parameters such as signal strength, modulation schemes, and traffic patterns. They can then run simulations to evaluate the performance of the network under different conditions and optimize network design. 5G simulation can be used for a variety of purposes, such as testing new protocols and algorithms, evaluating network performance, and optimizing network design (Sharma, V. et. al.,2018). It allows researchers and engineers to explore different scenarios and evaluate the impact of different network parameters on network performance. Overall, 5G simulation is an essential tool for the development and deployment of 5G networks (Zhang, J. et. al.,2021). While a high RSRQ value denotes good signal quality, a strong RSRP value denotes good signal strength. However, a number of variables, like distance from the base station, interference, and obstructions in the signal path, might have an impact on both values. As a result, it's crucial to take into account both RSRP and RSRQ values when assessing the functionality and quality of a 5G network. In general, network operators need to monitor and optimize the performance and quality of their 5G networks using the parameters RSRP and RSRQ. Network operators can detect locations with insufficient coverage or interference by measuring and evaluating these characteristics. They can then optimize network coverage and performance to provide their consumers with high-quality wireless communication services.

Several of the well-liked simulation tools for 5G include:

1. NS-3: An open-source network simulation tool called NS-3 is capable of simulating 5G networks. It has modelling modules for the radio access network, core network, and transport network, among other network components.
2. MATLAB: MATLAB is a modelling and programming language that provides capabilities for modelling and analysing 5G networks. A 5G Toolbox is included, which offers a variety of functionalities for modelling and simulating 5G networks.
3. OPNET Modeler: A commercial tool for simulating networks, OPNET Modeler may be used to model and simulate 5G networks. For developing and analysing network models, it comes with a complete range of tools.
4. QualNet: A commercial network simulation tool with 5G simulation features, QualNet. It enables users to design and test numerous network scenarios and assess how well they operate in various settings.
5. 5GEmPower: A 5G simulation platform that provides end-to-end simulation capabilities for 5G networks is called 5GEmPower. The radio access, core network, and transport network are only a few examples of the various 5G network components that are modeled and simulated by the modules.

5G simulation may be used for a number of things, including testing new protocols, assessing network performance in various scenarios, and improving network architecture.

TOOL USED

Android Studio is an integrated development environment (IDE) used for developing Android applications. It is developed by Google and based on the IntelliJ IDEA software. Android Studio provides a range of tools and features to help developers create high-quality Android apps.

Some of the key features of Android Studio include:

1. Code editor: Android Studio includes a powerful code editor with features such as syntax highlighting, code completion, and refactoring.
2. Layout editor: Android Studio includes a layout editor that allows developers to create user interfaces visually.
3. Gradle build system: Android Studio uses the Gradle build system to manage project dependencies and build Android applications.
4. Android emulator: Android Studio includes an emulator that allows developers to test their applications on virtual Android devices.
5. Debugging and profiling tools: Android Studio includes a range of debugging and profiling tools that help developers identify and fix issues in their applications.
6. Support for multiple languages: Android Studio supports a range of programming languages, including Java, Kotlin, and C++.
7. Integration with other Google services: Android Studio integrates with other Google services such as Firebase, Google Cloud Platform, and Google Play Store.

Android Studio is a powerful tool for Android app development, and it is widely used by developers around the world. Its features and tools make it easier for developers to create high-quality Android applications, and it continues to evolve and improve over time.

PARAMETERS

RSRP

RSRP (Reference Signal Received Power) is a measurement of the power level of the reference signals transmitted by the base station in a wireless network. In both 5G and 4G networks, RSRP is used to measure the quality of the received signal. Table 3 shows difference Between RSRP of 5G and 4G.

Table 3. Difference Between RSRP of 5G and 4G

Parameter	5G	4G
Measurement unit	dBm	dBm
Measurement location	Antenna port (Rx)	Reference point (Rx)
Frequency spectrum	Higher frequency spectrum	Lower frequency spectrum
Propagation characteristics	Higher attenuation, lower RSRP values	Lower attenuation, higher RSRP values

RSRQ

RSRQ (Reference Signal Received Quality) is a measurement of the quality of the received reference signal in a wireless network. It is calculated as the ratio of the received power of the reference signal to the received power of the interference and noise in the channel. RSRQ is an important parameter for assessing the quality of the received signal in both 5G and 4G networks. Table 4 shows difference Between RSRQ of 5G and 4G.

Table 4. Difference Between RSRQ of 5G and 4G

Parameter	5G	4G
Measurement unit	dB	Db
Calculation	RSRP / RSSI	RSRP / Average RSSI over a specified bandwidth
RSSI measurement	Includes all received signals	Calculated over a specified bandwidth
Impact on RSRQ measurement	Can affect the RSRQ measurement	Can affect the RSRQ measurement

PCI

PCI (Physical Cell ID) is a unique identifier assigned to each cell in a wireless network. It is used by the device to identify and differentiate between cells, and to determine which cell to connect to for communication. In both 5G and 4G networks, PCI is a 16-bit value that can range from 0 to 503. Table 5 shows difference Between PCI of 5G and 4G.

Table 5. Difference Between PCI of 5G and 4G

Parameter	5G	4G
Number of bits	16	16
Range of values	0 to 1007	0 to 503
Assignment	Automated and dynamic	Manual
Management	More automated	More manual
Algorithm	Specific algorithm used	No specific algorithm used

RESULT AND DISCUSSION

Figure 1. Recording of different parameters for 5G

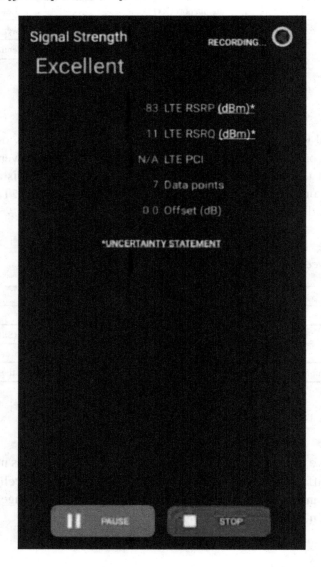

The above figure 1, shows the recording of the Rsrp, Rsrq value for the 5G communication. Where Rsrp value fluctuates from -140 dBm to -44 dBm. At -44 dBm, the signal strength is excellent whereas at -144 dBm, the signal strength is poor. And similarly Rsrq value fluctuates from -19.5 dB to -3 dB. A higher RSRQ indicates better signal quality. Similarly PCI is the unique identifier of the physical cell that broadcasts the reference signal. It ranges from 0 to 1007 and helps the mobile device differentiate between cells in the same geographical area.

Figure 2. Line graph to show fluctuation in RSRP and pie chart to show signal strength

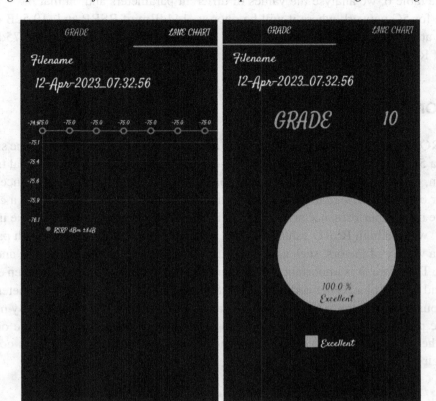

The above figure 2, shows the different values of Rsrp at different datapoints. Here we have collected 40 datapoints for 5G network and on that basis we plotted the chart. Figure 2, give the overview of the signal strength of 5G network in the form of pie-chart. and it will Grade the strength of the 5G signal from 0 to 10 on the basis of Rsrp and Rsrq value. A higher Grade indicates better signal quality and strength.

Table 6. Analysis of different parameters

Parameters		Signal Strength
RSRP	RSRQ	
-144dBm	-19.5dB	Poor
-118dBm	-16.0dB	Poor
-102dBm	-14.5dB	Good
-92dBm	-13.0dB	Good
-87 dBm	-12.0dB	Good
-80dBm	-11.0dB	Excellent
-75dBm	-10.5dB	Excellent

In the above table 6, we analyse the values of different parameters and on that basis we justify the signal strength for 5G network where it will be poor at -144dBm of RSRP and -19.5dB of RSRQ and it will be good at -92dBm of RSRP and -13.0dB of RSRQ and it will be excellent at -75dBm of RSRP and -10.5dB of RSRQ.

CONCLUSION

RSRP and RSRQ are two important parameters that are used to measure and evaluate the signal strength and quality of a 5G network. RSRP measures the received power of the reference signal transmitted by the base station, while RSRQ measures the ratio of the received power of the reference signal to the received power of the entire signal, including the interference. Both parameters play a critical role in determining the overall performance and quality of a 5G network. A strong RSRP value indicates good signal strength, while a high RSRQ value indicates good signal quality. However, both parameters can be affected by a variety of factors, such as distance from the base station, interference, and obstacles in the signal path. Therefore, it is important to consider both RSRP and RSRQ values when evaluating the performance and quality of a 5G network. Overall, RSRP and RSRQ are essential parameters for network operators to monitor and optimize the performance and quality of their 5G networks. By measuring and analyzing these parameters, network operators can identify areas with weak coverage or interference and optimize the network coverage and performance to ensure high-quality wireless communication services for their customers.

REFERENCES

Bhargava, M., Kumar, R., & Khurana, H. (2018). Comparison of 5G and 4G Coverage Tools for Rural Areas. *International Journal of Advanced Research in Computer Science*, *9*(2), 7–13.

Chen, J., Zhang, X., & Liu, J. (2019). Crowdsourcing-Based 4G Coverage Mapping: Methodologies and Applications. *IEEE Access : Practical Innovations, Open Solutions*, 7, 9097–9108.

Huang, Y., Liu, Z., & Sun, X. (2020). 5G Coverage Prediction Based on Machine Learning. *IEEE Access : Practical Innovations, Open Solutions*, 8, 159768–159779.

Khan, I., Ali, S., & Khan, I. (2019). Comparison of 4G and 5G Coverage Tools: A Case Study in Pakistan. *International Journal of Computer Science and Mobile Computing*, *8*(9), 6–13.

Lee, J., Lee, K., & Kim, J. (2022). Web-Based 5G Coverage Tools: A Comparative Analysis. *IEEE Access : Practical Innovations, Open Solutions*, 10, 4223–4233.

Liu, Y., Peng, J., & Li, B. (2020). A Web-Based Tool for Visualizing 5G Coverage. *IEEE Transactions on Industrial Informatics*, *16*(7), 4759–4767.

Pervaiz, H., Mahmood, T., & Saeed, S. (2020). A Comparative Study of 5G and 4G Coverage in Urban Areas. *IEEE Access : Practical Innovations, Open Solutions*, 8, 194972–194981.

Sharma, V., Pandey, S., & Garg, S. (2018). Comparative Study of 4G Coverage Mapping Tools. *International Journal of Computer Applications*, *179*(38), 6–11.

Wang, Y., Zhang, Y., & Wang, C. (2021). 5G Network Coverage Optimization Based on Big Data Analytics. *IEEE Transactions on Big Data*, *7*(2), 347–359.

Zhang, J., Zhang, W., & Wang, X. (2021). 5G Coverage Mapping Based on Crowdsourcing Data. *IEEE Access : Practical Innovations, Open Solutions*, *9*, 20011–20019.

Compilation of References

2048 Game. (2016). *2048 game*. https://gabrielecirulli.github.io/2048/

Abdar, M., & Hosseini, M. (2019). A deep learning approach for stock market prediction using Python. *Journal of Financial Engineering and Management*, *4*(2), 11–26.

Abdoli, M., Akbari, M., & Shahrabi, J. (2023). Bagging Supervised Autoencoder Classifier for credit scoring. *Expert Systems with Applications*, *213*, 118991.

Aftab, Z., Iqbal, W., Almustafa, M., Faisal, B., & Abdullah, M. (2020). *Automatic NoSQL to Relational Database Transformation with Dynamic Schema Mapping*. PUCIT.

Ajmalahamed, A., Nandhini, K. M., & Anand, S. K. (2014). Designing a rule based fuzzy expert controller for early detection and diagnosis of diabetes. *ARPN J Eng Appl Sci.*, *9*(5), 21–322.

Ala'raj, M., Abbod, M. F., Majdalawieh, M., & Jum'a, L. (2022). A deep learning model for behavioural credit scoring in banks. *Neural Computing and Applications*, 1-28. doi:10.1007/978-981-19-5443-6_67

Alcantud, J., & Mehta, G. (2009). Constructive utility functions on banach spaces. *Journal of Mathematical Analysis and Applications*, *350*(2), 590–600. doi:10.1016/j.jmaa.2008.04.015

Aldave, A., Vara, J. M., Granada, D., & Marcos, E. (2019). Leveraging creativity in requirements elicitation within agile software development: A systematic literature review. *Journal of Systems and Software*, *157*, 110396. doi:10.1016/j.jss.2019.110396

Alfarraj, M., & AlRegib, G. (2019). Semi-supervised learning for acoustic impedance inversion. In *SEG Technical Program Expanded Abstracts 2019* (pp. 2298–2302). Society of Exploration Geophysicists. doi:10.1190egam2019-3215902.1

Alfarraj, M., & AlRegib, G. (2019). Semisupervised sequence modeling for elastic impedance inversion. *Interpretation (Tulsa)*, *7*(3), SE237–SE249. doi:10.1190/INT-2018-0250.1

Alghamdi, M., Al-Mallah, M., Keteyian, S., Brawner, C., Ehrman, J., & Sakr, S. (2017). Predicting diabetes mellitus using SMOTE and ensemble machine learning approach: The henry ford exercise testing (FIT) project. *PLoS One*, *12*(7), e0179805. doi:10.1371/journal.pone.0179805 PMID:28738059

Algovibes. (2021). *Fundamental Analysis of Stocks With Python*. YouTube. www.youtube.com/watch?v=ZUQEd22oNek

Ali, N., & Lai, R. (2017). A method of requirements elicitation and analysis for Global Software Development: A method of requirements elicitation and analysis for Global Software Development. *Journal of Software (Malden, MA)*, *29*(4), e1830. doi:10.1002mr.1830

Alipour, P., Toghraie, D., Karimipour, A., & Hajian, M. (2019). Modeling different structures in perturbed poiseuille flow in a nanochannel by using of molecular dynamics simulation: Study the equilibrium. *Physica A*, *151*, 13–30. doi:10.1016/j.physa.2018.09.177

Alippi, C., & Roveri, M. (2019). Deep reinforcement learning for automated stock trading: An empirical analysis. *IEEE Transactions on Neural Networks and Learning Systems*, *31*(9), 3405–3417.

Aljouie, A., & Roshan, U. (2015). Prediction of Continuous Phenotypes in Mouse, Fly, and Rice Genome Wide Association Studies with Support Vector Regression SNPs and Ridge Regression Classifier. IEEE 14th International Conference on Machine Learning and Applications (ICMLA), (pp. 1246-1250). IEEE. 10.1109/ICMLA.2015.224

Almstrum, V. L., Dean, C. N., Goelman, D., Hilburn, T. B., & Smith, J. (2001). Support for Teaching Formal Methods. Innovation and Technology in Computer Science Education. ACM Press.

Alonso Robisco, A., & Carbo Martinez, J. M. (2022). Measuring the model risk-adjusted performance of machine learning algorithms in credit default prediction. *Financial Innovation*, *8*(1), 70. doi:10.118640854-022-00366-1

Althar, R. R., Samanta, D., Purushotham, S., Sengar, S. S., & Hewage, C. (2023). Design and Development of Artificial Intelligence Knowledge Processing System for Optimizing Security of Software System. *SN Computer Science*, *4*(4), 331. doi:10.100742979-023-01785-2

Altıntaş, B. (2021). A Comparative Study of Bitcoin, Ethereum, and Dogecoin: Investment Performance and Portfolio Diversification. *Journal of Risk and Financial Management*, *14*(3), 103. doi:10.3390/jrfm14030103

Ameller, D., Franch, X., Gomez, C., Martinez-Fernandez, S., Araujo, J., Biffl, S., Cabot, J., Cortellessa, V., Fernandez, D. M., Moreira, A., Muccini, H., Vallecillo, A., Wimmer, M., Amaral, V., Bohm, W., Bruneliere, H., Burgueno, L., Goulao, M., Teufl, S., & Berardinelli, L. (2021). Dealing with Non-Functional Requirements in Model-Driven Development: A Survey. *IEEE Transactions on Software Engineering*, *47*(4), 818–835. doi:10.1109/TSE.2019.2904476

American Diabetes Association. (2012). Diagnosis and classification of diabetes mellitus. *Diabetes Care*, *35*(Suppl. 1), S64–S71. doi:10.2337/dc12-s064 PMID:22187472

Amershi, S., Begel, A., Bird, C., DeLine, R., Gall, H., Kamar, E., Nagappan, N., Nushi, B., & Zimmermann, T. (2019). Software engineering for machine learning: A case study. *Microsoft Research*, https://www.microsoft.com

Anshari, M., Hamdan, M., Ahmad, N., Ali, E., & Haidi, H. (2022). COVID-19, artificial intelligence, ethical challenges and policy implications. *AI & Society*, 1–14. PMID:35607368

Anwar, H., Khan, S. U. R., Iqbal, J., & Akhunzada, A. (2022). A Tacit-Knowledge-Based Requirements Elicitation Model Supporting COVID-19 Context. *IEEE Access : Practical Innovations, Open Solutions*, *10*, 24481–24508. doi:10.1109/ACCESS.2022.3153678

Arafat, S. Y., Hussain, F., Zaman, M. S., Tabassum, T., Islam, M. K., Shormi, F. R., Khan, A. R., Islam, M. R., Redwan, A. S. M., Giasuddin, N. A., Mubashir, A., & Khan, M. A. S. (2022). Thwarted belongingness, perceived burdensomeness, and acquired capability for suicide among university students of Bangladesh: Scales validation and status assessment. *Frontiers in Psychiatry*, *13*, 13. doi:10.3389/fpsyt.2022.1025976 PMID:36311516

Arshad, S., Hu, S., & Ashraf, B. N. (2019). Zipf's law, the coherence of the urban system and city size distribution: Evidence from Pakistan. *Physica A: Statistical Mechanics and its Applications, 513*. doi:10.1016/j.physa.2018.08.065

Asadi, H., Dowling, R., Yan, B., & Mitchell, P. (2014). Machine learning for outcome prediction of acute ischemic stroke post intra-arterial therapy. *PLoS One*, *9*(2), 2. doi:10.1371/journal.pone.0088225 PMID:24520356

Asif, M., Hussain, Z., Asghar, Z., Hussain, M. I., Raftab, M., Shah, S. F., & Khan, A. A. (2021). A Statistical Evidence of Power Law Distribution in the Upper Tail of World Billionaires' Data 2010–20. *Physica A*, *581*(126198), 126198. doi:10.1016/j.physa.2021.126198

Asklund, U., & Bendix, L. (2003). *A Software Configuration Management Course* (Vol. 2649). Lecture Notes in Computer Science.

Atkins, A., Niranjan, M., & Gerding, E. (2018). Financial news predicts stock market volatility better than close price. *The Journal of Finance and Data Science*, *4*(2), 120–137. doi:10.1016/j.jfds.2018.02.002

AWS. (n.d..). *Best Practices for Database Schema Design*. AWS.

Bagchi, S., Curran, M., & Fagerstrom, M. J. (2019). Monetary Growth and Wealth Inequality. *Economics Letters*, *182*, 23–25. doi:10.1016/j.econlet.2019.05.036

Ball, M. (2021). Visionary. Showman. Iconoclast. Troll. How Elon Musk Is Reshaping Our World—And Beyond. *Time*, *198*(23/24), 36–57. https://search.ebscohost.com/login.aspx?direct=true&db=afh&AN=154157240&site=ehost-live

Banzhaf, W. (2021). The Effects of Taxes on Wealth Inequality in Artificial Chemistry Models of Economic Activity. *PLoS One*, *16*(8), e0255719. doi:10.1371/journal.pone.0255719 PMID:34379658

Bao, Y., Zhao, E., Gan, X., Luo, D., & Han, Z. (2009, August). A review on cutting-edge techniques in evolutionary algorithms. In *2009 Fifth International Conference on Natural Computation* (Vol. 5, pp. 347-351). IEEE. 10.1109/ICNC.2009.459

Bart, A. C., Whitcomb, R., Riddle, J., & Saleem, O. (2016). *CORGIS Datasets Project*. https://corgis-edu.github.io/corgis/csv/billionaires/

Batbagon, C. C., Jayme, O. B., & Pradilla, J. P. (2018). I-queue: A centralized queue management system. Research Gate.

Bazzi. (2020). *Stock Market Analysis With Pandas Python Programming | Python # 6*. YouTube. www.youtube.com/watch?v=57qAxRV577c

Bee, M., Riccaboni, M., & Schiavo, S. (2017). Where Gibrat meets Zipf: Scale and scope of French firms. *Physica A: Statistical Mechanics and its Applications*, *481*, 265-275. doi:10.1016/j.physa.2017.04.012

Behera, T. (2022). *How Blockchain Solves the Supply Chain Problems Using RFID Techniques*. Academic Press.

Behera, T., & Panda, B. S. (2023). *Master Data Management using Machine Learning Techniques: MDM Bot*. doi:10.36227/techrxiv.21818040.v1

Behera, T., & Tripathi, K. (2022): Root Cause Analysis Bot using Machine Learning Techniques. TechRxiv. Preprint. doi:10.36227/techrxiv.21588159.v3

Benediktsson, O. (2000). *Software Engineering Body of Knowledge and Curriculum Development*. Views on Software Development in the New Millennium.

Bengio, Y., & Grandvalet, Y. (2005). *Bias in Estimating the Variance of K-Fold Cross-Validation*. Springer. doi:10.1007/0-387-24555-3_5

Bertotti, M. (2010). Modelling taxation and redistribution: A discrete active particle kinetic approach. *Applied Mathematics and Computation*, *217*(2), 752–762. doi:10.1016/j.amc.2010.06.013

Bhanipati, J., Singh, D., Biswal, A. K., & Rout, S. K. (2021). Minimization of collision through retransmission and optimal power allocation in wireless sensor networks (WSNs). In *Advances in Intelligent Computing and Communication* [Springer Singapore.]. *Proceedings of ICAC, 2020*, 653–665.

Bhargava, M., Kumar, R., & Khurana, H. (2018). Comparison of 5G and 4G Coverage Tools for Rural Areas. *International Journal of Advanced Research in Computer Science*, 9(2), 7–13.

Bing, W., Wen-qiong, Z., & Jia-hong, L. (2010). *A Genetic Multiple Kernel Relevance Vector Regression Approach. 2010 Second International Workshop on Education Technology and Computer Science*, Wuhan, China. 10.1109/ETCS.2010.154

Biswal, A. K., Singh, D., & Pattanayak, B. K. (2021). IoT-based voice-controlled energy-efficient intelligent traffic and street light monitoring system. In *Green Technology for Smart City and Society: Proceedings of GTSCS 2020* (pp. 43-54). Springer Singapore.

Biswal, A. K., Singh, D., Tripathy, A. K., & Pattanayak, B. K. (2022). Smart Autonomous Collision Avoidance and Obstacle Detection Using Internet of Things (IoT) and Controller Area Network (CAN) Protocol. In *Advances in Distributed Computing and Machine Learning: Proceedings of ICADCML 2021* (pp. 54-65). Springer Singapore.

Biswal, A. K., Singh, D., Pattanayak, B. K., Samanta, D., Banerjee, A., Seteikin, A. Y., & Samusev, I. G. (2022). IoT-Based Response Time Analysis of Messages for Smart Autonomous Collision Avoidance System Using Controller Area Network. *Wireless Communications and Mobile Computing*, 2022, 1–18. doi:10.1155/2022/1149842

Biswal, A. K., Singh, D., Pattanayak, B. K., Samanta, D., Chaudhry, S. A., & Irshad, A. (2021). Adaptive fault-tolerant system and optimal power allocation for smart vehicles in smart cities using controller area network. *Security and Communication Networks*, 2021, 1–13. doi:10.1155/2021/2147958

Biswal, A. K., Singh, D., Pattanayak, B. K., Samanta, D., & Yang, M.-H. (2021). IoT-based smart alert system for drowsy driver detection. *Wireless Communications and Mobile Computing*, 2021, 1–13. doi:10.1155/2021/6627217

Biswas, S., Chandra, A., Chatterjee, A., & Chakrabarti, B. (2011). Phase transitions and non-equilibrium relaxation in kinetic models of opinion formation. *Journal of Physics: Conference Series*, 297(1), 1–6. doi:10.1088/1742-6596/297/1/012004

Blom, R., & Voorn, B. (2019). HRM autonomy, integration and performance in government agencies: Tests of necessity and sufficiency. *Public Management Review*, 19(1), 167–178.

Boris, T. & Goran, S. (2016). Evolving Neural Network to Play Game2048. *Proc. 24th Telecommunications forum (TELFOR 2016)*. IEEE.

Boudin, L., & Francesco, S. (2009). A kinetic approach to the study of opinion formation. *Modélisation Mathématique et Analyse Numérique*, 43(3), 507–522. doi:10.1051/m2an/2009004

Bouri, E., Azzi, G., Molnár, P., Roubaud, D., & Hagfors, L. I. (2020). On the return-volatility relationship in the Bitcoin-Dogecoin markets: A multivariate GARCH analysis. *Journal of Risk and Financial Management*, 13(6), 123. doi:10.3390/jrfm13060123

Bourque, P., & Richard, E. (2014). *SWEBOK Version 3.0*. IEEE.

Bowden, R., Zisserman, A., Kadir, T., & Brady, M. (2003). Vision based interpretation of natural sign languages. In *Exhibition at ICVS03: the 3rd international conference on computer vision systems*. ACM Press.

Bradski, G. (1998). Real time face and object tracking as a component of a perceptual user interface. IEEE Workshop on Applications of Computer Vision, 214–219. doi:10.1109/ACV.1998.732882

Brock, H., Sabanovic, S., Nakamura, K., & Gomez, R. (2020). Robust real-time hand gestural recognition for non-verbal communication with tabletop robot haru. *Proc. 29th IEEE Int. Conf. Robot Human Interact. Commun. (RO-MAN)*, 891–898.

Brooks, F. (1995). TheMythicalMan-Month: Essays on Software Engineering. Boston: Addison-Wesley.

Brown, A. (2000). *Large-Scale, Component-Based Development*. Prentice Hall.

Browne, G. J., & Ramesh, V. (2002). Improving information requirements determination: A cognitive perspective. *Information & Management, 39*(8), 625–645. doi:10.1016/S0378-7206(02)00014-9

Browne, G. J., & Rogich, M. B. (2001). An Empirical Investigation of User Requirements Elicitation: Comparing the Effectiveness of Prompting Techniques. *Journal of Management Information Systems, 17*(4), 223–249. doi:10.1080/0 7421222.2001.11045665

Brownlee, J. (2018). *Machine learning for algorithmic trading: Predictive models to extract signals from market and alternative data for systematic trading strategies with Python*. Machine Learning Mastery.

Brugna, C., & Toscani, G. (2015). Kinetic models of opinion formation in the presence of personal conviction. *Physical Review E: Statistical, Nonlinear, and Soft Matter Physics, 92*(5), 052818. doi:10.1103/PhysRevE.92.052818 PMID:26651755

Brugna, C., & Toscani, G. (2018). Kinetic models for goods exchange in a multi-agent market. *Physica A, 499*, 362–375. doi:10.1016/j.physa.2018.02.070

Brzezinski, M. (2014). Do wealth distributions follow power laws? Evidence from 'rich lists', *Physica A: Statistical Mechanics and its Applications, 406*, 155-162. doi:10.1016/j.physa.2014.03.052

Bücker, M., Szepannek, G., Gosiewska, A., & Biecek, P. (2022). Transparency, auditability, and explainability of machine learning models in credit scoring. *The Journal of the Operational Research Society, 73*(1), 70–90. doi:10.1080/0 1605682.2021.1922098

Budgen, D., & Tomayko, J.E. (2005). The SEI Curriculum Modules and Their Influence: Norm Gibbs' Legacy to Software Engineering Education. *Journal of Systems and Software, 75*(1-2), 55-62.

Budgen, D. (2003). *Software Design* (2nd ed.). Addison-Wesley.

Buhr, R. J. A., & Casselman, R. S. (1996). *Use Case Maps for Object-Oriented Systems*. Prentice Hall.

Bukhsh, F. A., Bukhsh, Z. A., & Daneva, M. (2020). A systematic literature review on requirement prioritization techniques and their empirical evaluation. *Computer Standards & Interfaces, 69*, 103389. doi:10.1016/j.csi.2019.103389

Buschmann, F., Meunier, R., & Rohnert, H. (1996). *Pattern-Oriented Software Architecture: A System of Patterns*. Wiley.

Bushong, V. (2021). Using static analysis to address microservice architecture reconstruction. In *2021 36th IEEE/ACM International Conference on Automated Software Engineering (ASE)*. IEEE. 10.1109/ASE51524.2021.9678749

Cao, X., & Balakrishnan, R. (2003). Visionwand: interaction techniques for large displays using a passive wand tracked in 3d. In *UIST '03: proceedings of the 16th annual ACM symposium on User Interface software and technology*. ACM Press.

Capehart, K. W. (2014). Is the Wealth of the World's Billionaires Not Paretian? *Physica A, 395*, 255–260. doi:10.1016/j.physa.2013.09.026

Carlos, M. (2010). A simple and efficient test for Zipf's law. *Economics Letters, 66*(3), 257-260. doi:10.1016/S0165-1765(99)00215-3

Carrizo, D., Dieste, O., & Juristo, N. (2014). Systematizing requirements elicitation technique selection. *Information and Software Technology, 56*(6), 644–669. doi:10.1016/j.infsof.2014.01.009

Cenkowski, S., & Gurtler, M. (2019). Cryptocurrency trading strategies and technical indicators for dogecoin: Volatility analysis and forecasting. Journal of Financial Management. *Markets and Institutions, 7*(2), 81–98. doi:10.12831/91629

Cerny, T., & ... Microservice architecture reconstruction and visualization techniques: A review. In *2022 IEEE International Conference on Service-Oriented System Engineering (SOSE)*. IEEE. 10.1109/SOSE55356.2022.00011

Chai, D., & Ngan, K. (1998). Locating the facial region of a head and-shoulders color image. IEEE international conference on automatic face and gesture recognition, 124–129. doi:10.1109/AFGR.1998.670936

Chakrabarti, A., & Chakrabarti, B. (2009). Microeconomics of the ideal gas like market models. *Physica A, 388*(19), 4151–4158. doi:10.1016/j.physa.2009.06.038

Chakraborti, A., & Chakrabarti, B. (2000). Statistical mechanics of money: How saving propensity affects its distribution. *The European Physical Journal B, 17*(1), 167–170. doi:10.1007100510070173

Chakraborty, S., Singh, D., & Biswal, A. K. (2021). NAARI: An Intelligent Android App for Women Safety. In *Applications of Artificial Intelligence in Engineering: Proceedings of First Global Conference on Artificial Intelligence and Applications (GCAIA 2020)* (pp. 625-637). Springer Singapore.

Chandler, N. (2018). A Symbiotic Relationship: HR and Organizational Culture. *Organizational Behaviour and Human Resource Management, 10*(1), 1–22. doi:10.1007/978-3-319-66864-2_1

Chatterjee, A., Chakrabarti, B., & Manna, S. (2004). Pareto law in a kinetic model of market with random saving propensity. *Physica A, 335*(1–2), 155–163. doi:10.1016/j.physa.2003.11.014

Cheesman, J., & Daniels, J. (2001). *UML Components*. Addison-Wesley.

Cheng, S. H., Chen, S. M., & Jian, W. S. (2016). Fuzzy time series forecasting based on fuzzy logical relationships and similarity measures. *Information Sciences, 327*, 272–287. doi:10.1016/j.ins.2015.08.024

Chen, J., Li, Y., & Shu, K. (2021). Deep learning-based Dogecoin price prediction using historical data. *IEEE Transactions on Neural Networks and Learning Systems, 32*(6), 2726–2735. doi:10.1109/TNNLS.2020.3041867

Chen, J., Zhang, X., & Liu, J. (2019). Crowdsourcing-Based 4G Coverage Mapping: Methodologies and Applications. *IEEE Access : Practical Innovations, Open Solutions, 7*, 9097–9108.

Chen, L. S., Chen, M. Y., Chang, J. R., & Yu, P. Y. (2021). An intuitionistic fuzzy time series model based on new data transformation method. *Int J Comput Intell Syst, 14*(1), 550–559. doi:10.2991/ijcis.d.210106.002

Chen, S. M., & Kao, P. Y. (2013). Taifex forecasting based on fuzzy time series particle swarm optimization techniques and support vector machines. *Information Sciences, 247*, 62–71. doi:10.1016/j.ins.2013.06.005

Chen, W., Zhou, C., & Zhu, Z. (2018). A novel approach to cryptocurrency price prediction based on autoregressive integrated moving average and artificial neural network. *Journal of Intelligent & Fuzzy Systems, 34*(2), 1187–1195. doi:10.3233/JIFS-179851

Chen, Y., Li, X., & Sun, J. (2021). Forecasting Dogecoin prices using a machine learning-based approach. *Journal of Computational Science, 53*, 101468. doi:10.1016/j.jocs.2021.101468

Chesters, J. (2013). Wealth Inequality and Stratification in the World Capitalist Economy. *Perspectives on Global Development and Technology, 12*(1–2), 246–265. doi:10.1163/15691497-12341253

Chew, C. M., & Kankanhalli, M. (2001). Compressed domain summarization of digital video. Advances in Multimedia Information Processing PCM 2001, 2195, 490-497. doi:10.1007/3-540-45453-5_63

Chillón, A., Ruiz, D., Molina, J., & Morales, S. (2019). *A Model-Driven Approach to Generate Schemas for Object-Document Mappers*. Research Gate.

Chollet, F. (2018). *Deep learning with Python*. Manning Publications.

Cincar, K., & Ivascu, T. (2019). Agent-based hospital scheduling system. In *2019 21st International Symposium on Symbolic and Numeric Algorithms for Scientific Computing (SYNASC)*, (pp. 337-338). IEEE. 10.1109/SYNASC49474.2019.00055

Clemente, F., & Collins, C. (2021). Coronavirus Suller Bowl 2021: Billionaires Win. *USA Today, 149*(2912), 54–56. https://search.ebscohost.com/login.aspx?direct=true&db=afh&AN=152114296&site=ehost-live

Clementi, F., & Gallegati, M. (2005). Power law tails in the Italian personal income distribution. *Physica A: Statistical Mechanics and its Applications, 350*(2–4), 427-438. doi:10.1016/j.physa.2004.11.038

CNBC Television. (2021, April 28). *Tim Cook on Apple's Q2 earnings report*. [Video]. YouTube. https://www.youtube.com/watch?v=QIUxPv5PJOY

Cohen, P. R., Johnston, M., McGee, D., Oviatt, S., Pittman, J., Smith, I., Chen, L., & Clow, J. (1997). Quickset: multimodal interaction for distributed applications. In *Proceedings of the fifth ACM international conference on Multimedia*. ACM Press. 10.1145/266180.266328

CoinMarketCap. (2022, April 25). Dogecoin. In *CoinMarketCap*. https://coinmarketcap.com/currencies/dogecoin/

Conci, N., Ceresato, P., & De Natale, F. G. B. (2007). Natural human–machine interface using an interactive virtual blackboard. IEEE international conference on image processing, 181–184. doi:10.1109/ICIP.2007.4379795

Cooper, M., & Foote, J. (2002). Automatic music summarization via similarity analysis. *Proc. Int. Conf. Music Information Retrieval*.

Corby, S., & Mathieson, H. (2018). The National Health Service and the limits to flexibility. *Public Policy and Administration, 12*(4), 60–72. doi:10.1177/095207679701200405

Cordier, S., Pareschi, L., & Piatecki, C. (2009). Mesoscopic modelling of financial markets. *Journal of Statistical Physics, 134*(1), 161–184. doi:10.100710955-008-9667-z

Coupe, T., & Monteiro, C. (2016). The Charity of the Extremely Wealthy: Charity of the Extremely Wealthy. *Economic Inquiry, 54*(2), 751–761. doi:10.1111/ecin.12311

Cui, Y., Swets, D., & Weng, J. (1995). Learning-based hand sign recognition using shoslf-m. *International workshop on automatic face and gesture recognition*, 201–206.

Culkin, R., & Das, S. R. (2017). Machine learning in finance: The case of deep learning for option pricing. *Journal of Investment Management, 15*(4), 92–100.

Cunaku, E., Ndrecaj, J., Berisha, S., Samanta, D., Dutta, S., & Bhattacharya, A. (2023). An Approach for Digital-Social Network Analysis Using Twitter API. In Innovations in Data Analytics: Selected Papers of ICIDA 2022 (pp. 625–636). Springer.

Cunaku, E., Ndrecaj, J., Berisha, S., Samanta, D., Dutta, S., & Bhattacharya, A. (2023). An Approach for Digital-Social Network Analysis Using Twitter API. In *Innovations in Data Analytics: Selected Papers of ICIDA 2022* (pp. 625–636). Springer. 10.1007/978-981-99-0550-8_49

Curcio, K., Navarro, T., Malucelli, A., & Reinehr, S. (2018). Requirements engineering: A systematic mapping study in agile software development. *Journal of Systems and Software, 139*, 32–50. doi:10.1016/j.jss.2018.01.036

Cutler, R., & Turk, M. (1998). View-based interpretation of real-time optical flow for gesture recognition. In *Proceedings of the international conference on face and gesture recognition*. IEEE Computer Society. 10.1109/AFGR.1998.670984

Dafaalla, H., Abaker, M., Abdelmaboud, A., Alghobiri, M., Abdelmotlab, A., Ahmad, N., Eldaw, H., & Hasabelrsoul, A. (2022). Deep Learning Model for Selecting Suitable Requirements Elicitation Techniques. *Applied Sciences (Basel, Switzerland)*, *12*(18), 9060. doi:10.3390/app12189060

Dalia, K. A. A., Rizk, H. M. H., & El-Sayed, M. (2023). SMART Hospital Management Systems Based on the Internet of Things: Challenges Intelligent Solutions and Functional Requirements. *International Journal of Intelligent Computing and Information Sciences IJICIS*, *22*(1), 32–43.

Damián, H. Zanette, S., & Manrubia, C. (2001). Vertical transmission of culture and the distribution of family names. *Physica A: Statistical Mechanics and its Applications, 295*(1–2), 1-8. doi:10.1016/S0378-4371(01)00046-2

Dangi, P., Jain, A., Samanta, D., Dutta, S., & Bhattacharya, A. (2023). 3D Modelling and Rendering Using Autodesk 3ds Max. *2023 11th International Conference on Internet of Everything, Microwave Engineering, Communication and Networks (IEMECON)*, (pp. 1–5). IEEE.

Dangi, P., Jain, A., Samanta, D., Dutta, S., & Bhattacharya, A. (2023). 3D Modelling and Rendering Using Autodesk 3ds Max. In *2023 11th International Conference on Internet of Everything, Microwave Engineering, Communication and Networks (IEMECON)* (pp. 1–5). IEEE.

Daraghmi, Zhang, & Yuan. (2022). Enhancing Saga Pattern for Distributed Transactions within a Microservices Architecture. *Applied Sciences, 12*(12), 6242.

Database Star. (n.d.). *Designing a Database Schema: Principles of Data Modeling*. Database Star. https://www.databasestar.com/designing-a-database-schema-principles-of-data-modeling/

Davey, B., & R. Parker, K. (2015). Requirements Elicitation Problems: A Literature Analysis. *Issues in Informing Science and Information Technology, 12*, 071–082. doi:10.28945/2211

David, O. E., Netanyahu, N. S., & Wolf, L. (2016). DeepChess: End-to- End Deep Neural Network for Automatic Learning in Chess. *International Conference on Artificial Neural Networks and Machine Learn- ing (ICANN 2016)*, (pp.88-96). Springer.

De Lima Silva, P. C., Sadaei, H. J., Ballini, R., & Guimarães, F. G. (2020). Probabilistic forecasting with fuzzy time series. *IEEE Transactions on Fuzzy Systems, 28*(8), 1771–1784. doi:10.1109/TFUZZ.2019.2922152

Deller, J. R., Hansen, J. H. L., & Proakis, J. G. (1999). *Discrete-Time Processing of Speech Signals*. Wiley. doi:10.1109/9780470544402

Deng, C.-X., Xu, L.-X., & Fu, Z.-X. (2008). The Beat-wave signal regression based on least squares reproducing kernel support vector machine. *2008 International Conference on Machine Learning and Cybernetics*, Kunming, China. 10.1109/ICMLC.2008.4621037

Deng, M., Zhai, S., Ouyang, X., Liu, Z., & Ross, B. (2022). Factors influencing medication adherence among patients with severe mental disorders from the perspective of mental health professionals. *BMC Psychiatry, 22*(1), 22. doi:10.118612888-021-03681-6 PMID:34996394

Deng, W., Guo, Y., Liu, J., Li, Y., Liu, D., & Zhu, L. (2019). A missing power data filling method based on improved random forest algorithm. *Chin J Electr Eng., 5*(4), 33–39. doi:10.23919/CJEE.2019.000025

Devadoss, S., Luckstead, J., Danforth, D., & Akhundjanov, S. (2020). The power law distribution for lower tail cities in India. *Physica A: Statistical Mechanics and its Applications, 442*, 193-196. doi:10.1016/j.physa.2015.09.016

Diakonikolas, I., Gidaris, S., Mitliagkas, I., & Sivakumar, V. (2021). A Study of Cryptocurrency Markets: How Volatile are They? arXiv preprint arXiv:2104.03399. https://arxiv.org/abs/2104.03399

Dimitrijević, S., Jovanović, J., & Devedžić, V. (2015). A comparative study of software tools for user story management. *Information and Software Technology*, *57*, 352–368. doi:10.1016/j.infsof.2014.05.012

Dogecoin. (n.d.). In Investopedia. https://www.investopedia.com/terms/d/dogecoin.asp

Duan, C., Laurent, P., Cleland-Huang, J., & Kwiatkowski, C. (2009). Towards automated requirements prioritization and triage. *Requirements Engineering*, *14*(2), 73–89. doi:10.100700766-009-0079-7

Dumitrescu, E., Hué, S., Hurlin, C., & Tokpavi, S. (2022). Machine learning for credit scoring: Improving logistic regression with non-linear decision-tree effects. *European Journal of Operational Research*, *297*(3), 1178–1192. doi:10.1016/j.ejor.2021.06.053

Du, P., & Shu, H. (2022). Exploration of financial market credit scoring and risk management and prediction using deep learning and bionic algorithm. [JGIM]. *Journal of Global Information Management*, *30*(9), 1–29. doi:10.4018/JGIM.293286

Dybå, T., & Dingsøyr, T. (2008). Empirical studies of agile software development: A systematic review. *Information and Software Technology*, *50*(9–10), 833–859. doi:10.1016/j.infsof.2008.01.006

Dyer, L., & Reeves, T. (1995). Human resource strategies and firm performance: What do we know and where do we need to go? *International Journal of Human Resource Management*, *6*(3), 656–670. doi:10.1080/09585199500000041

Egrioglu, E., Aladag, C. H., Yolcu, U., Uslu, V. R., & Basaran, M. A. (2010). Finding an optimal interval length in high order fuzzy time series. *Expert Systems with Applications*, *37*(7), 5052–5055. doi:10.1016/j.eswa.2009.12.006

Egrioglu, E., Aladag, C. H., Yolcu, U., Uslu, V. R., & Erilli, N. A. (2011). Fuzzy time series forecasting method based on Gustafson-Kessel fuzzy clustering. *Expert Systems with Applications*, *38*(8), 10355–10357. doi:10.1016/j.eswa.2011.02.052

Egrioglu, V., Bas, E., Aladag, C. H., & Yolcu, U. (2016). Probabilistic fuzzy time series method based on artificial neural network. *Am J Intell Syst*, *62*, 42–47.

El-Maleh, K., Klein, M., Petrucci, G., & Kabal, P. (2000). Speech/music discrimination for multimedia application. *Proc. ICASSP00.*

Erl, T. (2006). *Service-Oriented Architecture (SOA): Concepts, Technology, and Design*. Prentice Hall.

Erl, T. (2008). *SOA Principles of Service Design*. Prentice Hall.

Erl, T. (2009). *SOA Design Patterns*. Prentice Hall.

Esas, O. (2022). *Design patterns and anti-patterns in microservices architecture: a classification proposal and study on open source projects*. Academic Press.

Espinoza, Cancila, Selic, & Gerard. (2009). *Challenges in Combining SysML and MARTE for Model-Based Design of Embedded Systems*. Berlin: Springer.

Farag, I., & Brock, H. (2019). Learning motion disfluencies for automatic sign language segmentation. *Proc. IEEE Int. Conf. Acoust. Speech Signal Process. (ICASSP),* 7360–7364.

Fawcett, T. (2018). *Practical machine learning for computer vision: Learn the techniques and tools needed to build computer vision applications with Python and OpenCV*. Packt Publishing Ltd.

Fernández, S. M., Bogner, J., Franch, X., Oriol, M., Siebert, J., Trendowicz, A., Vollmer, A. M., & Wagner, S. (2021). Software engineering for AI-Based systems: A survey. *ACM Transactions on Software Engineering and Methodology*, *31*(2), 1–59. doi:10.1145/3487043

Ferreira Martins, H., Carvalho De Oliveira, A. Junior, Dias Canedo, E., Dias Kosloski, R. A., Ávila Paldês, R., & Costa Oliveira, E. (2019a). Design Thinking: Challenges for Software Requirements Elicitation. *Information (Basel)*, *10*(12), 371. doi:10.3390/info10120371

Ferreira, B., Silva, W., Barbosa, S. D. J., & Conte, T. (2018). Technique for representing requirements using personas: A controlled experiment. *IET Software*, *12*(3), 280–290. doi:10.1049/iet-sen.2017.0313

Filho, I. A. S., Chen, E. N., da Silva, J. M. Jr, & da Silva Barboza, R. (2018). Gesture recognition using leap motion: A comparison between machine learning algorithms. *Proc. ACM SIGGRAPH Posters*, 1–2. 10.1145/3230744.3230750

Flanigan, J., & Freiman, C. (2022). Wealth without Limits: In Defense of Billionaires. *Ethical Theory and Moral Practice: An International Forum, 25*(5), 755–775. 10.100710677-022-10327-3

Frederick, L., & Tara, S. (2020). Big Data in Industrial-Organizational Psychology and Human Resource Management: Forward Progress for Organizational Research and Practice. *Annual Review of Organizational Psychology and Organizational Behavior, 7*(1), 505–533. doi:10.1146/annurev-orgpsych-032117-104553

Freeman, P. (1983). The Nature of Design. In Tutorial on Software Design Techniques (4th ed.). IEEE Computer Society Press.

Freeman, P., & Wasserman, A. I. (Eds.). (1983). *Tutorial on Software Design Techniques* (4th ed.). IEEE Computer Society Press.

Fresno–Aranda, R. (2023). Semi-automated capacity analysis of limitation-aware microservices architectures. In *Economics of Grids, Clouds, Systems, and Services: 19th International Conference, GECON 2022, Izola, Slovenia, September 13–15, 2022, Proceedings*. Cham: Springer Nature Switzerland. 10.1007/978-3-031-29315-3_7

Friedenthal, Moore, & Steiner. (2009). *A Practical Guide to SysML: The Systems Modeling Language*. Burlington, MA: Morgan Kaufmann.

Fritzsch, J., Bogner, J., Haug, M., Franco da Silva, A. C., Rubner, C., Saft, M., Sauer, H., & Wagner, S. (2023). Adopting microservices and DevOps in the cyber-physical systems domain: A rapid review and case study. *Software, Practice & Experience*, *53*(3), 790–810. doi:10.1002pe.3169

Fuentenebro, P. (2020). Will Philanthropy Save Us All? Rethinking Urban Philanthropy in a Time of Crisis. *Geoforum*, *117*, 304–307. doi:10.1016/j.geoforum.2020.07.005 PMID:32981949

Furioli, G., Pulvirenti, A., Terraneo, E., & Toscani, G. (2017). Fokker–Planck equations in the modeling of socio-economic phenomena. *Mathematical Models and Methods in Applied Sciences, 27*(1), 115–158. doi:10.1142/S0218202517400048

G., N., Tao, S., & Wu, K. (2020). *What's in a Game: Solving 2048 with Reinforcement Learning*. Stanford University.

Gahlawat, N., & Kundu, S. C. (2019). Participatory HRM and firm performance, Employee Relations. *International Journal (Toronto, Ont.), 41*(5), 1098–1119.

Gamma, E., Helm, R., & Johnson, R. (1995). *Design Patterns: Elements of Reusable Object-Oriented Software*. Addison-Wesley.

Gao, L., Sun, J., & Xu, Z. (2021). Deep learning for Dogecoin price prediction: A comparative study of CNN and LSTM. *Expert Systems with Applications, 174*, 114627. doi:10.1016/j.eswa.2021.114627

Garavan, T. N. (2019). A Strategic Perspective on Human Resource Development. *Advances in Developing Human Resources, 9*(1), 11–30. doi:10.1177/1523422306294492

Garg, M., Saxena, C., Saha, S., Krishnan, V., Joshi, R., & Mago, V. (2022, June). CAMS: An Annotated Corpus for Causal Analysis of Mental Health Issues in Social Media Posts. In *Proceedings of the Thirteenth Language Resources and Evaluation Conference* (pp. 6387-6396). Academic Press.

Garg, B., & Garg, R. (2016). Enhanced accuracy of fuzzy time series model using ordered weighted aggregation. *Applied Soft Computing, 48*, 265–280. doi:10.1016/j.asoc.2016.07.002

Garg, J. (2017). Market equilibrium under piecewise leontief concave utilities. *Theoretical Computer Science, 703*(1), 55–65. doi:10.1016/j.tcs.2017.09.001

Garg, M. (2023). Mental Health Analysis in Social Media Posts: A Survey. *Archives of Computational Methods in Engineering, 30*(3), 1–24. doi:10.100711831-022-09863-z PMID:36619138

GargM.SaxenaC.SamantaD.DorrB. J. (2023). *LonXplain: Lonesomeness as a Consequence of Mental Disturbance in Reddit Posts*. doi:10.1007/978-3-031-35320-8_27

Géron, A. (2019). *Hands-on machine learning with Scikit-Learn, Keras, and TensorFlow: Concepts, tools, and techniques to build intelligent systems*. O'Reilly Media, Inc.

Ghosh, H., Chowdhury, S., & Prajneshu, S. (2016). An improved fuzzy time-series method of forecasting based on L-R fuzzy sets and its application. *Journal of Applied Statistics, 43*(6), 1128–1139. doi:10.1080/02664763.2015.1092111

Giesen, K., Zimmermann, A., & Suedekum, J. (2010). The size distribution across all cities – Double Pareto lognormal strikes. *Journal of Urban Economics, 68*(2), 129-137. doi:10.1016/j.jue.2010.03.007

Giray, G. (2021). A software engineering perspective on engineering machine learning systems: State of the art and challenges. *Journal of Systems and Software, 180*, 1–35. doi:10.1016/j.jss.2021.111031

Goh, G., & Zhou, Y. (2019). Stock prediction using recurrent neural networks with convolutional feature extraction. In *2019 IEEE 16th International Conference on Machine Learning and Applications (ICMLA)* (pp. 1528-1533). IEEE.

Gomaa, H. (2011). *Software modeling and design*. Cambridge University Press.

Gomaa, H. (1984). A Software Design Method for Real Time Systems. *Communications of the ACM, 27*(9), 938–949. doi:10.1145/358234.358262

Gomaa, H. (1986). Software Development of Real Time Systems. *Communications of the ACM, 29*(7), 657–668. doi:10.1145/6138.6150

Gomaa, H. (1989a). A Software Design Method for Distributed Real-Time Applications. *Journal of Systems and Software, 9*(2), 81–94. doi:10.1016/0164-1212(89)90012-5

Gomaa, H. (1989b). Structuring Criteria for Real Time System Design. In *Proceedings of the 11th International Conference on Software Engineering,* May 15–18, 1989, Pittsburgh, PA, USA (pp. 290–301). Los Alamitos, CA: IEEE Computer Society Press. 10.1109/ICSE.1989.714436

Gomez, R., Nakamura, K., Szapiro, D., & Merino, L. (2020). A holistic approach in designing tabletop robot's expressivity. *Proc. IEEE Int. Conf. Robot. Automat. (ICRA), 1970*–1976.

Gomez, R., Szapiro, D., Galindo, K., & Nakamura, K. (2018). Hardware design of an experimental tabletop robot assistant. *Proc. ACM/IEEE Int. Conf. Human-Robot Interact.*, 233–240. 10.1145/3171221.3171288

Gong, Y., & Liu, X. (2001). Summarizing video by minimizing visual content redundancies. *Proc. IEEE Int. Conf. Multimedia and Expo*, 788-791.

Gong, Z., Zhong, P., & Hu, W. (2019). Diversity in machine learning. *IEEE Access : Practical Innovations, Open Solutions*, 7, 64323–64350. doi:10.1109/ACCESS.2019.2917620

González-Aparicio, M. T., Younas, M., Tuya, J., & Casado, R. (2023). A transaction platform for microservices-based big data systems. *Simulation Modelling Practice and Theory*, 123, 102709. doi:10.1016/j.simpat.2022.102709

Gradojevic, N., Gençay, R., & Kukolj, D. (2009). Option pricing with modular neural networks. *IEEE Transactions on Neural Networks*, 20(4), 626–637. doi:10.1109/TNN.2008.2011130 PMID:19273045

Grinberg, R. (2011). Bitcoin: An Innovative Alternative Digital Currency. *Hastings Science & Technology Law Journal*, 4(2), 159–208.

Guest, D. & Annet, H. (2021). Human Resource Management's Contribution to Healthy Healthcare, Integrating the Organization of Health Services. *Worker Wellbeing and Quality of Care*, 15(2), 109–123.

Guha, A., Samanta, D., & Sengar, S. S. (2023). Computer Vision Based Automatic Margin Computation Model for Digital Document Images. *SN Computer Science*, 4(3), 253. doi:10.100742979-023-01693-5

Gunnarsson, B. R., Vanden Broucke, S., Baesens, B., Óskarsdóttir, M., & Lemahieu, W. (2021). Deep learning for credit scoring: Do or don't? *European Journal of Operational Research*, 295(1), 292–305. doi:10.1016/j.ejor.2021.03.006 PMID:34955589

Gupta, K. K., & Kumar, S. (2019). A novel high-order fuzzy time series forecasting method based on probabilistic fuzzy sets. *Granul Comput*, 4(4), 699–713. doi:10.100741066-019-00168-4

Guru 99. (n.d.). *Relational Database Design: 10 Tips to Design Effective Database*. Guru99.

Gurunath, R., & Samanta, D. (2023). A New 3-Bit Hiding Covert Channel Algorithm for Public Data and Medical Data Security Using Format-Based Text Steganography. *Journal of Database Management*, 34(2), 1–22. doi:10.4018/JDM.324076

Hagberg, A., Swart, P., & Chult, S. D. (2008). Exploring network structure, dynamics, and function using NetworkX (No. LA-UR-08-05495; LA-UR-08-5495). Los Alamos National Lab (LANL).

Han, L., & Qi, Y. (2020). Deep learning for stock prediction: A comparative study. *Journal of Computational Science*, 44, 101147.

Haydon, S. (2022). Book Review: The Business of Changing the World: How Billionaires, Tech Disrupters, and Social Entrepreneurs Are Transforming the Global Aid Industry by Kumar, R. and The Enlightened Capitalists: Cautionary Tales of Business Pioneers Who Tried to Do Well by Doing Good by O'Toole. *J. Nonprofit and Voluntary Sector Quarterly*, 51(4), 928–932. doi:10.1177/08997640211022745

Heikkila, V. T., Damian, D., Lassenius, C., & Paasivaara, M. (2015). A Mapping Study on Requirements Engineering in Agile Software Development. *2015 41st Euromicro Conference on Software Engineering and Advanced Applications*, 199–207. 10.1109/SEAA.2015.70

Hoang, L. N. (2014). The addictive mathematics of the 2048 tile game. *Science for All*. http://www.science4all.org/article/2048-game/

Hooper, R. (2021). A Trillion Dollars to Fix the World. *New Scientist, 249*(3323), 38–44. https://search.ebscohost.com/login.aspx?direct=true&db=afh&AN=148952434&site=ehost-live

Hori, C., & Furui, S. (1998). Improvements in automatic speech summarization and evaluation methods. *Proc. Int. Conf. Spoken Language Processing.*

Huang, T., & Huang, S. (2019). Predicting stock prices with a combined method of sentiment analysis and machine learning. *Applied Sciences (Basel, Switzerland), 9*(7), 1374.

Huang, Y., Liu, Z., & Sun, X. (2020). 5G Coverage Prediction Based on Machine Learning. *IEEE Access : Practical Innovations, Open Solutions, 8,* 159768–159779.

Huarng, K. (2001). Heuristic models of fuzzy time series for forecasting. *Fuzzy Sets and Systems, 123*(3), 369–386. doi:10.1016/S0165-0114(00)00093-2

Huarng, K., & Yu, T. H. K. (2006). Ratio-based lengths of intervals to improve fuzzy time series forecasting. *IEEE Transactions on Systems, Man, and Cybernetics. Part B, Cybernetics, 36*(2), 328–340. doi:10.1109/TSMCB.2005.857093 PMID:16602593

Hübener, T., & ... Automatic anti-pattern detection in microservice architectures based on distributed tracing. *Proceedings of the 44th International Conference on Software Engineering: Software Engineering in Practice.* 10.1109/ICSE-SEIP55303.2022.9794000

Hujainah, F., Bakar, R. B. A., Abdulgabber, M. A., & Zamli, K. Z. (2018a). Software Requirements Prioritisation: A Systematic Literature Review on Significance, Stakeholders, Techniques and Challenges. *IEEE Access : Practical Innovations, Open Solutions, 6,* 71497–71523. doi:10.1109/ACCESS.2018.2881755

Hujainah, F., Binti Abu Bakar, R., Nasser, A. B., Al-haimi, B., & Zamli, K. Z. (2021). SRPTackle: A semi-automated requirements prioritisation technique for scalable requirements of software system projects. *Information and Software Technology, 131,* 106501. doi:10.1016/j.infsof.2020.106501

Idoughi, D., Seffah, A., & Kolski, C. (2012). Adding user experience into the interactive service design loop: A persona-based approach. *Behaviour & Information Technology, 31*(3), 287–303. doi:10.1080/0144929X.2011.563799

IEEE. (2016). *The IEEE 1012-2016 Standard for system, software, and hardware verification, and validation.* IEEE.

Iliceto, P., D'Antuono, L., Fino, E., Carcione, A., Candilera, G., Silva, C., & Joiner, T. E. (2021). Psychometric properties of the Italian version of the Interpersonal Needs Questionnaire-15 (INQ-15-I). *Journal of Clinical Psychology, 77*(1), 268–285. doi:10.1002/jclp.23026 PMID:32662083

Inayat, I., Salim, S. S., Marczak, S., Daneva, M., & Shamshirband, S. (2015). A systematic literature review on agile requirements engineering practices and challenges. *Computers in Human Behavior, 51,* 915–929. doi:10.1016/j.chb.2014.10.046

Ishaq, F. S., Muhammad, L. J., & Yahaya, B. Z. (2020). Fuzzy based expert system for diagnosis of diabetes mellitus. *Int J Adv Sci Technol., 136,* 39–50. doi:10.33832/ijast.2020.136.04

Ishikawa, F., & Yoshioka, N. (2019). How do engineers perceive difficulties in engineering of machine-learning systems? In *Proceedings of IEEE/ACM 6th International Workshop on Software Engineering Research and Industrial Practice.* IEEE/ACM.

ISO/IEC/IEEE (2018). *Systems and software engineering-life cycle processes-Requirements Engineering, Standard.* ISO, IEC, IEEE.

ISO/IEC/IEEE 42010:2011 (2011). *Systems and software engineering-architecture description, standard.* ISO, IEC, IEEE. https://www.iso.org/ obp/ ui/ # iso: std:iso-iec-ieee:42010:ed-1:v1:en.

Itkin, A. (2019). *Deep learning calibration of option pricing models: some pitfalls and solutions.* arXiv preprint.

Jabbour, C., & Almada, F. (2019). Relationships between human resource dimensions and environmental management in companies: Proposal of a model. *Journal of Cleaner Production, 16*(1), 51–58. doi:10.1016/j.jclepro.2006.07.025

Jain, A., Dangi, P., Samanta, D., Dutta, S., Bhattacharya, A., & Joseph, N. P. (2023). Creation of Bookshelf Using Autodesk 3ds Max: 3D Modelling and Rendering. *2023 11th International Conference on Internet of Everything, Microwave Engineering, Communication and Networks (IEMECON),* (pp. 1–4). IEEE.

Jain, A., Dangi, P., Samanta, D., Dutta, S., Bhattacharya, A., & Joseph, N. P. (2023). Creation of Bookshelf Using Autodesk 3ds Max: 3D Modelling and Rendering. *In 2023 11th International Conference on Internet of Everything, Microwave Engineering, Communication and Networks (IEMECON)* (pp. 1–4). IEEE.

James, G., Witten, D., Hastie, T., & Tibshirani, R. (2017). *An introduction to statistical learning: with applications in R.* Springer.

Janaka, S., & Zhang, X. (2018). Green human resource management: A proposed model in the context of Sri Lanka's tourism industry. *Journal of Cleaner Production, 28*(3), 542–555.

Janet,, D, & White, G. (2019). Between hard and soft HRM: Human resource management in the construction industry. *Construction Management and Economics, 14*(5), 405–416.

Jeffers, A. E. (2022). The Field of Computing Needs to Take Care of Its Mental Health. *Computing in Science & Engineering, 24*(2), 91–94. doi:10.1109/MCSE.2022.3162034

Jena, R., Biswal, A. K., & Lenka, A. (2022). Survey on Security Issues and Protective Measures in Different Layers of Internet of Things (IoT). *International Journal of Smart Sensor and Adhoc Network,* 1-17.

Jena, R., Biswal, A. K., & Singh, D. (2022). A Novel Approach for an IoT-Based U-Healthcare System. In Handbook of Research on Mathematical Modeling for Smart Healthcare Systems (pp. 247-260). IGI Global.

Jia, J. (2018, October). Mental Health Computing via Harvesting Social Media Data. In *Proceedings of the Joint Workshop of the 4th Workshop on Affective Social Multimedia Computing and first Multi-Modal Affective Computing of Large-Scale Multimedia Data* (pp. 70-70). 10.1145/3267935.3267954

Jiang, C., Lu, W., Wang, Z., & Ding, Y. (2023). Benchmarking state-of-the-art imbalanced data learning approaches for credit scoring. *Expert Systems with Applications, 213,* 118878.

Joachims, T. (1998). Text categorization with support vector machines. *Proc. European Conf. Machine Learning.*

Joiner, T. E. (2005). *Why people die by suicide.* Harvard University Press.

Jourabian, M., Darzi, A. A. R., Toghraie, D., & Akbari, O. A. (2018). Melting process in porous media around two hot cylinders: Numerical study using the lattice Boltzmann method. *Physica A, 509,* 316–335. doi:10.1016/j.physa.2018.06.011

Kang, M., & Ye, L. (2016). Advantageous redistribution with three smooth ces utility functions. *Journal of Mathematical Economics, 67*(1), 171–180. doi:10.1016/j.jmateco.2016.08.002

Katou, A. A. (2019). Human Resource Management and Performance in the Hospitality Industry. *Project Management, 12*(4), 1980–1999.

Katou, A. A. (2021). Human Resource Management and Performance in the Hospitality Industry. *International Tourism and Hospitality in the Digital Age, 13*(4), 1–20.

Kaur, S., Bhardwaj, R., Jain, A., Garg, M., & Saxena, C. (2022, December). Causal Categorization of Mental Health Posts using Transformers. In *Proceedings of the 14th Annual Meeting of the Forum for Information Retrieval Evaluation* (pp. 43-46). 10.1145/3574318.3574334

Kausik, G. & Basu, B. (2009). City size distributions for India and China. *Physica A: Statistical Mechanics and its Applications, 388*(13), 2682-2688. doi:10.1016/j.physa.2009.03.019

Kavitha, S., Varuna, S., & Ramya, R. (2016). A comparative analysis on linear regression and support vector regression. *2016 Online International Conference on Green Engineering and Technologies (IC-GET)*, (pp. 1-5). IEEE. 10.1109/GET.2016.7916627

Kavonius, I. K. (2020). Is Wealth Driving the Income Distribution? An Analysis of the Link between Income and Wealth between 1995 and 2016 in Finland. *Statistical Journal of the IAOS, 36*(2), 483–494. doi:10.3233/SJI-200649

Kenneth, T. & Rosen, M. (1980). The size distribution of cities: An examination of the Pareto law and primacy, *Journal of Urban Economics, Volume 8*, Issue 2, 1980, Pages 165-186, ISSN 0094-1190, https://doi.org/ doi:10.1016/0094-1190(80)90043-1

Khalili, N., & Rastegar, M. A. (2023). Optimal cost-sensitive credit scoring using a new hybrid performance metric. *Expert Systems with Applications, 213*, 119232. .

Khan, M. R. H. (2023). *Toward an Automated Real-Time Anomaly Detection Engine in Microservice Architectures* [Diss.]. Carleton University.

Khan, I., Ali, S., & Khan, I. (2019). Comparison of 4G and 5G Coverage Tools: A Case Study in Pakistan. *International Journal of Computer Science and Mobile Computing, 8*(9), 6–13.

Kharaba, Z., Moutraji, S. A., Al Khawaldeh, R. A., Alfoteih, Y., & Al Meslamani, A. Z. (2022). *What has changed in the pharmaceutical care after COVID-19: Pharmacists' perspective.* https://www.ncbi.nlm.nih.gov/pmc/articles/PMC9296094/

Kharwal, A. (2022). *Stock Market Analysis Using Python.* Thecleverprogrammer. thecleverprogrammer.com/2022/07/12/stock-market-analysis-using-python.

Kimber, D., & Wilcox, L. (1996). Acoustic segmentation for audio browsers. *Proc. Interface Conf.*

Kirmayer, L. J., & Swartz, L. (2013). Culture and global mental health. *Global mental health: Principles and practice*, 41-62.

Kitchenham, B. (2004). *Procedures for Undertaking Systematic Reviews.*

Kojić, V. (2017). Solving the consumer's utility-maximization problem with ces and cobb-douglas utility function via mathematical inequalities. *Optimization Letters, 11*(4), 875–884. doi:10.100711590-016-1052-2

Kolenik, T., Gjoreski, M., & Gams, M. (2020). PerMEASS-Personal Mental Health Virtual Assistant with Novel Ambient Intelligence Integration. In AAI4H@ ECAI (pp. 8-12). Academic Press.

Kondo, N., & Matsuzaki, K. (2019, April). Playing Game 2048 with Deep Convolutional Neural Networks Trained by Supervised Learning. *Journal of Information Processing, 27*(0), 340–347. doi:10.2197/ipsjjip.27.340

Kothare, P., Gedam Y., & Deshmukh, R. (2014). Ranking Algorithm RA-SVM for Domain Adaptation: A Review", International Journal of Scientific & Engineering Research, vol. 5, no. 4, pp. 503-507, 2014, ISSN 22295518.

Koumpis, K., & Renals, S. (1998). Transcription and summarization of voicemail speech. *Proc. Int. Conf. Spoken Language Processing.*

Kozodoi, N., Jacob, J., & Lessmann, S. (2022). Fairness in credit scoring: Assessment, implementation and profit implications. *European Journal of Operational Research, 297*(3), 1083–1094. doi:10.1016/j.ejor.2021.06.023

Kraft, Lu, & Teng. (2001). *Method and Apparatus for Music Summarization and Creation of Audio Summaries.* Academic Press.

Kriss, S. (2022). The Truth about Bill Gates. *First Things (New York, N.Y.)*, 41–49. https://search.ebscohost.com/login. aspx?direct=true&db=afh&AN=160204806&site=ehost-live

Kumar, B. T. (2023). Architecture Principles for Enterprise Software and Mobile Application Development. In *Designing and Developing Innovative Mobile Applications.* IGI Global. doi:10.4018/978-1-6684-8582-8

Kumeno, F. (2019). Software engineering challenges for machine learning applications: A literature review. *Intelligent Decision Technologies*, *13*(4), 463–476. doi:10.3233/IDT-190160

Kuo, I. H., Horng, S. J., Kao, T. W., Lin, T. L., Lee, C. L., & Pan, Y. (2009). An improved method for forecasting enrollments based on fuzzy time series and particle swarm optimization. *Expert Systems with Applications*, *36*(3), 6108–6117. doi:10.1016/j.eswa.2008.07.043

Kuznetsov, M., & Kuznetsova, O. (2018). Using deep learning algorithms for stock price prediction. In *Proceedings of the 2018 12th International Conference on Computer Science and Information Technologies (CSIT)* (pp. 239-243). IEEE.

Lallouache, M., Chakrabarti, A., Chakraborti, A., & Chakrabarti, B. (2010). Opinion formation in kinetic exchange models: Spontaneous symmetry-breaking transition, Phys. Rev. E, 82 (5) (2010), p. 056112 Boudin L., Monaco R., Salvarani F., Kinetic model for multi-dimensional opinion formation. *Physical Review E: Statistical, Nonlinear, and Soft Matter Physics*, *81*(3), 036109.

Lansley, S. (2004). Britain Is Now Back to Levels of Gross Income Inequality. *New Statesman (London, England)*, *133*(4708), 27–29. https://search.ebscohost.com/login.aspx?direct=true&db=afh&AN=14587893&site=ehost-live

Lee, J., Lee, K., & Kim, J. (2022). Web-Based 5G Coverage Tools: A Comparative Analysis. *IEEE Access : Practical Innovations, Open Solutions*, *10*, 4223–4233.

Lee, R. Y. (2019). *Object-oriented software engineering with UML: A hands-on approach.* Nova Science Publishers.

Li, J., & Arandjelovic, O. (2017). Glycaemic index prediction: a pilot study of data linkage challenges and the application of machine learning. *IEEE EMBS Int. Conf. on Biomed. & Health Informat. (BHI)*, 357–360. 10.1109/BHI.2017.7897279

Li, S., & Peng, V. (2018). Playing 2048 With Reinforcement Learning. *Conference on Neural Information Processing Systems(NeurIPS).* Springer.

Limei, L., & Xuan, H. (2017). *Study of electricity load forecasting based on multiple kernels learning and weighted support vector regression machine.* 2017 29th Chinese Control And Decision Conference (CCDC), Chongqing, China. 10.1109/CCDC.2017.7978740

Lim, S., Henriksson, A., & Zdravkovic, J. (2021). Data-Driven Requirements Elicitation: A Systematic Literature Review. *SN Computer Science*, *2*(1), 16. doi:10.100742979-020-00416-4

Lin, T. Y., Goyal, P., Girshick, R., He, K., & Dollár, P. (2017). Focal loss for dense object detection. In *Proceedings of the IEEE international conference on computer vision* (pp. 2980-2988). IEEE.

Lipton, Z. C., Elkan, C., & Naryanaswamy, B. (2014). Optimal thresholding of classifiers to maximize F1 measure. In *Joint European Conference on Machine Learning and Knowledge Discovery in Databases.* Springer. 10.1007/978-3-662-44851-9_15

Li, Q., Chen, Y., Jiang, L. L., Li, P., & Chen, H. (2016). A tensor-based information framework for predicting the stock market [TOIS]. *ACM Transactions on Information Systems*, *34*(2), 1–30. doi:10.1145/2838731

Li, Q., Wang, Z., & Zhou, W. (2021). Dogecoin price prediction using machine learning based on social media data. *Journal of Intelligent & Fuzzy Systems*, *41*(1), 773–783. doi:10.3233/JIFS-201767

Liu, J., Li, Z., & Zhang, X. (2021). An ensemble learning model for Dogecoin price prediction. *International Journal of Computer Mathematics*, *98*(4), 899–910. doi:10.1080/00207160.2020.1818294

Liu, Y., Peng, J., & Li, B. (2020). A Web-Based Tool for Visualizing 5G Coverage. *IEEE Transactions on Industrial Informatics*, *16*(7), 4759–4767.

Liu, Y., Wang, R., Chang, R., Wang, H., Xu, L., Xu, C., Yu, X., Liu, S., Chen, H., Chen, Y., Jin, L., Wang, Y., & Cai, Y. (2022). Perceived Burdensomeness, Thwarted Belongingness, and Social Exclusion in Transgender Women: Psychometric Properties of the Interpersonal Needs Questionnaire. *Frontiers in Psychology*, *13*, 787809. doi:10.3389/fpsyg.2022.787809 PMID:35222188

Liu, Y., Yang, M., Wang, Y., Li, Y., Xiong, T., & Li, A. (2022). Applying machine learning algorithms to predict default probability in the online credit market: Evidence from China. *International Review of Financial Analysis*, *79*, 101971. doi:10.1016/j.irfa.2021.101971

Li, Y., & Chen, W. (2020). A comparative performance assessment of ensemble learning for credit scoring. *Mathematics*, *8*(10), 1756. doi:10.3390/math8101756

Logan, B., & Chu, S. (2000). Music summarization using key phrases. *Proc. IEEE Int. Conf. Audio Speech and Signal Processing*.

Luckstead, J., & Devadoss, S. A comparison of city size distributions for China and India from 1950 to 2010, Economics Letters, Volume 124, Issue 2, 2014, Pages 290-295, ISSN 0165-1765, https://doi.org/ doi:10.1016/j.econlet.2014.06.002

LugaresiC.TangJ.NashH.McClanahanC.UbowejaE.HaysM.ZhangF.ChangC.-L.Guang YongM.LeeJ.ChangW.-T.HuaW. GeorgM.GrundmannM. (2019). MediaPipe: A framework for building perception pipelines. Available: https://arxiv.org/abs/1906.08172

Lu, L., Jiang, H., & Zhang, H. J. (2001). A robust audio classification and segmentation method. *Proc. ACM Multimedia 2001*. 10.1145/500141.500173

Luo, C. (2020). A comprehensive decision support approach for credit scoring. *Industrial Management & Data Systems*, *120*(2), 280–290. doi:10.1108/IMDS-03-2019-0182

Luo, C., Wu, D., & Wu, D. (2017). A deep learning approach for credit scoring using credit default swaps. *Engineering Applications of Artificial Intelligence*, *65*, 465–470. doi:10.1016/j.engappai.2016.12.002

Luo, Y., & Song, Y. (2021). Machine learning-based Dogecoin price prediction using technical indicators. *IEEE Access : Practical Innovations, Open Solutions*, *9*, 57261–57272. doi:10.1109/ACCESS.2021.3076458

Lwakatare, L. E., Raj, A., Crnkovic, I., Bosch, J., & Olsson, H. H. (2020). Large-scale machine learning systems in real-world industrial settings: A review of challenges and solutions. *Information and Software Technology*, *127*, 106368. doi:10.1016/j.infsof.2020.106368

Macarty. (2021). *Quantitative Stock Price Analysis With Python, Pandas, NumPy Matplotlib and SciPy*. YouTube. www.youtube.com/watch?v=PkzVU7Klic0

Machado, M. R., & Karray, S. (2022). Assessing credit risk of commercial customers using hybrid machine learning algorithms. *Expert Systems with Applications*, *200*, 116889. doi:10.1016/j.eswa.2022.116889

Madakam, S., Ramaswamy R., & Tripathi, S. (2020). Internet of Things (IoT): A Literature Review. *Journal of Computer and Communications*.

Maheswari, B., Reddy, K., & Rao, S. (2013). Design and Implementation of Ranking Adaptation Algorithm for Domain Specific Search. *International Journal of Computer Trends and Technology, 4*(8).

Mahmood, M., & Saha, S. (2020). HRM in Bangladesh: Past, Present and Future. *SA Journal of Human Resource Management, 9*(2), 314–321.

Maldarella, D., & Pareschi, L. (2012). Kinetic models for socio-economic dynamics of speculative markets. *Physica A, 391*(3), 715–730. doi:10.1016/j.physa.2011.08.013

Malita, I. S. (2018). Quality of information management and efficiency of Hospital employees. *Hospital Management.*

Malliaris, M., & Salchenberger, L. (1993). A neural network model for estimating option prices. *Applied Intelligence, 3*(3), 193–206. doi:10.1007/BF00871937

Maluf, D., Trad, P., & NASA Ames Research Center. (n.d.). NETMARK: A Schema-less Extension for Relational Databases for Managing Semi- structured Data Dynamically. *Mail Stop, 269-4*

Marco Bee, Massimo Riccaboni, Stefano Schiavo, The size distribution of US cities: Not Pareto, even in the tail, Economics Letters, Volume 120, Issue 2, 2013, Pages 232-237, ISSN 0165-1765, https://doi.org/ doi:10.1016/j.econlet.2013.04.035

Maria, H., & Ali, Z. (2018). Requirement Elicitation Techniques for Open Source Systems: A Review. *International Journal of Advanced Computer Science and Applications, 9*(1). Advance online publication. doi:10.14569/IJACSA.2018.090145

Matsuzaki, K. (2016). *Systematic selection of N-tuple networks with consideration of interinfluence for game 2048. TAAI.* IEEE.

Mishra, A., Singh, C., Dwivedi, A., Singh, D., & Biswal, A. K. (2021, October). Network Forensics: An approach towards detecting Cyber Crime. In *2021 International Conference in Advances in Power, Signal, and Information Technology (APSIT)* (pp. 1-6). IEEE. 10.1109/APSIT52773.2021.9641399

Mitchell, S. M., Brown, S. L., Roush, J. F., Tucker, R. P., Cukrowicz, K. C., & Joiner, T. E. (2020). The Interpersonal Needs Questionnaire: Statistical considerations for improved clinical application. *Assessment, 27*(3), 621–637. doi:10.1177/1073191118824660 PMID:30654631

Miyazima, S., Lee, Y., Nagamine, T., & Miyajima, H. (2000). Power-law distribution of family names in Japanese societies, *Physica A: Statistical Mechanics and its Applications, 278*(1–2), 282-288. doi:10.1016/S0378-4371(99)00546-4

Mondal, S., Pal, A. K., Islam, S. K. H., & Samanta, D. (2023). Objectionable Image Content Classification Using CNN-Based Semi-supervised Learning. *Advances in Smart Vehicular Technology, Transportation, Communication and Applications Proceedings of VTCA, 2022,* 311–320.

Mondal, S., Pal, A. K., Islam, S. K. H., & Samanta, D. (2023). Objectionable Image Content Classification Using CNN-Based Semi-supervised Learning. In Advances in Smart Vehicular Technology, Transportation, Communication and Applications [Springer.]. *Proceedings of VTCA, 2022,* 311–320.

Mouris, D. J. (2022). *Does Instagram make us feel better or worse?: How Upward Social Comparisons on Instagram Influences Young Adults' Psychological Well-being* [Bachelor's thesis]. University of Twente.

Munyer, T., Huang, P. C., Huang, C., & Zhong, X. (2021). *Fod-a: A dataset for foreign object debris in airports.* arXiv preprint arXiv:2110.03072.

Nalchigar, S., Yu, E., & Keshavjee, K. (2021). Modeling machine learning requirements from three perspectives: A case report from the healthcare domain. *Requirements Engineering*, *34567*(2), 1–18. doi:10.100700766-020-00343-z

Nascimento, E., Nguyen-Duc, A., Sundbø, I., & Conte, T. (2020). Software engineering for artificial intelligence and machine learning software: A systematic literature review. arXiv preprint arXiv:2011.03751.

National Academy Press. (1999). *Measuring the Quality of Health Care*. A statement of the National Roundtable on Healthcare Quality Division of Healthcare Services, National Academy Press.

NeuralNine. (2022). *Technical Stock Analysis Made Easy in Python*. YouTube. www.youtube.com/watch?v=N9NqTp_D_bw

Nie, Z., Yuan, Y., Xu, D., & Shen, F. (2019). *Research on Support Vector Regression Model Based on Different Kernels for Short-term Prediction of Ship Motion*. 2019 12th International Symposium on Computational Intelligence and Design (ISCID), Hangzhou, China. 10.1109/ISCID.2019.00021

Nisha, K., Adhithyaa, N., Stephen, B., & Muthu Kumar, P. (2013). Ranking Model Adaptation for Domain Specific Search. *International Journal of Emerging Trends in Electrical and Electronics*, *2*(4), 32–35.

Nishimura, T., & Suzuki, T. (2016). Basic psychological need satisfaction and frustration in J apan: Controlling for the big five personality traits. *The Japanese Psychological Research*, *58*(4), 320–331. doi:10.1111/jpr.12131

Njangang, H., Beleck, A., Tadadjeu, S., & Kamguia, B. (2022). Do ICTs Drive Wealth Inequality? Evidence from a Dynamic Panel Analysis. *Telecommunications Policy*, *46*(2), 102246. doi:10.1016/j.telpol.2021.102246

Nota, F., & Song, S. (2012). Further Analysis of the Zipf's Law: Does the Rank-Size Rule Really Exist? *Journal of Urban Management, 1*(2), 19-31. doi:10.1016/S2226-5856(18)30058-X

Nyhan, J., & Flinn, A. (2016). *Computation and the humanities: towards an oral history of digital humanities*. Springer Nature. doi:10.1007/978-3-319-20170-2

Obeidat, S. M. (2020). The link between e-HRM use and HRM effectiveness: An empirical study. *Personnel Review*, *45*(6), 1281–1301. doi:10.1108/PR-04-2015-0111

Ogada, R. (2022). *Exploratory-Data-Analysis*. Jill Canon Associates. https://github.com/ertgrulyksk/Billionaires-Analysis-with-Python/blob/main/Billionaires_Analysis_with_Python.ipynb

Ogwang, T. (2013). Is the wealth of the world's billionaires Paretian? *Physica A: Statistical Mechanics and its Applications, 392*(4), 757-762. doi:10.1016/j.physa.2012.10.026

Olivos, F., Olivos-Jara, P., & Browne, M. (2021). Asymmetric social comparison and life satisfaction in social networks. *Journal of Happiness Studies*, *22*(1), 363–384. doi:10.100710902-020-00234-8

Pacheco, C., García, I., & Reyes, M. (2018). Requirements elicitation techniques: A systematic literature review based on the maturity of the techniques. *IET Software*, *12*(4), 365–378. doi:10.1049/iet-sen.2017.0144

Pal, M. (2005). Random forest classifier for remote sensing classification. *International Journal of Remote Sensing*, *26*(1), 217–222. doi:10.1080/01431160412331269698

Pandia, V., Fitriana, E., Afriandi, I., Purba, F. D., Danasasmita, F. S., Ichsan, A., & Pradana, K. (2022). Psychometric evaluation of the interpersonal needs questionnaire in the Indonesian language. *PLoS One*, *17*(12), e0279272. doi:10.1371/journal.pone.0279272 PMID:36525445

Park, S., Choi, D., Kim, M., Cha, W., Kim, C., & Moon, I. C. (2017). Identifying prescription patterns with a topic model of diseases and medications. *Journal of Biomedical Informatics*, *75*, 35–47. doi:10.1016/j.jbi.2017.09.003 PMID:28958484

Paulussen, T. O., Zoller, A., Rothlauf, F., Heinzl, A., Braubach, L., & Pokahr, A. (2006). Agent-based patient scheduling in hospitals. In Multiagent Engineering, 255-275. Springer. doi:10.1007/3-540-32062-8_14

Peeters, G., Burthe, A., & Rodet, X. (2002). Toward automatic music audio summary generation from signal analysis. *Proc. Int. Conf. Music Information Retrieval.*

Peng, G. (2010). Zipf's law for Chinese cities: Rolling sample regressions. *Physica A: Statistical Mechanics and its Applications, 389*(18), 3804-3813. doi:10.1016/j.physa.2010.05.004

Pervaiz, H., Mahmood, T., & Saeed, S. (2020). A Comparative Study of 5G and 4G Coverage in Urban Areas. *IEEE Access : Practical Innovations, Open Solutions*, 8, 194972–194981.

Piero, M., Bennett, R., Lieshout, C., & Smith, A. (2019). A tale of two tails: Do Power Law and Lognormal models fit firm-size distributions in the mid-Victorian era? *Physica A: Statistical Mechanics and its Applications, 523*, 858-875. doi:10.1016/j.physa.2019.02.054

Pławiak, P., Abdar, M., Pławiak, J., Makarenkov, V., & Acharya, U. R. (2020). DGHNL: A new deep genetic hierarchical network of learners for prediction of credit scoring. *Information Sciences, 516*, 401–418. doi:10.1016/j.ins.2019.12.045

Podder, S. K., Samanta, D., Thomas, B., Dutta, S., & Bhattacharya, A. (2023). Impact of blended education system on outcome-based learning and sector skills development. *2023 11th International Conference on Internet of Everything, Microwave Engineering, Communication and Networks (IEMECON)*, (pp. 1–6). IEEE.

Podder, S. K., Samanta, D., Thomas, B., Dutta, S., & Bhattacharya, A. (2023). Impact of blended education system on outcome-based learning and sector skills development. *2023 11th International Conference on Internet of Everything, Microwave Engineering, Communication and Networks (IEMECON)*, (pp. 1–6). IEEE.

Podder, S. K., Samanta, D., Thomas, B., Dutta, S., & Bhattacharya, A. (2023). Impact of blended education system on outcome-based learning and sector skills development. In *2023 11th International Conference on Internet of Everything, Microwave Engineering, Communication and Networks (IEMECON)* (pp. 1–6). IEEE.

Praveen K. (2006). A Study of the Hospital Information System (HIS) In the Medical Records Department of A Tertiary Teaching Hospital. *Journal of the Academy of Hospital Administration, 18.*

Prikshat, V., & Malik, A. (2022). AI-augmented HRM: Antecedents, assimilation and multilevel consequences. *Human Resource Management Review*, 33(1), 213–219.

Priyanka, A. (2016). A Review of NoSQL Databases, Types and Comparison with Relational Database. *IJESC.* doi:. doi:10.4010/2016.1226

Probst, T., Haid, B., Schimböck, W., Reisinger, A., Gasser, M., Eichberger-Heckmann, H., Stippl, P., Jesser, A., Humer, E., Korecka, N., & Pieh, C. (2021). Therapeutic interventions in in-person and remote psychotherapy: Survey with psychotherapists and patients experiencing in-person and remote psychotherapy during COVID-19. *Clinical Psychology & Psychotherapy*, 28(4), 988–1000. doi:10.1002/cpp.2553 PMID:33448499

Qin, T., & Zhang, Y. (2020). Deep learning for stock price prediction using a long short-term memory network. *Mathematical Problems in Engineering, 2020*, 1–10.

Qisheng, Y., & Guohua, W. (2009). Prediction Model of Alga's Growth Based on Support Vector Regression. *2009 International Conference on Environmental Science and Information Application Technology*, Wuhan, China. 10.1109/ESIAT.2009.170

Rabiner, L. R., & Juang, B. H. (1993). *Fundamentals of Speech Recognition.* Prentice-Hall.

Rademacher, F., Sachweh, S., & Zündorf, A. (2020). A modeling method for systematic architecture reconstruction of microservice-based software systems. In *Enterprise, Business-Process and Information Systems Modeling: 21st International Conference, BPMDS 2020, 25th International Conference, EMMSAD 2020, Held at CAiSE 2020, Grenoble, France, June 8–9, 2020, Proceedings 21*. Springer International Publishing. 10.1007/978-3-030-49418-6_21

Rahy, S., & Bass, J. M. (2022). Managing non-functional requirements in agile software development. *IET Software*, *16*(1), 60–72. doi:10.1049fw2.12037

Raj, V., & Srinivasa Reddy, K. (2022). Best Practices and Strategy for the Migration of Service-Oriented Architecture-Based Applications to Microservices Architecture. In *Proceedings of Second International Conference on Advances in Computer Engineering and Communication Systems: ICACECS 2021*. Singapore: Springer Nature Singapore. 10.1007/978-981-16-7389-4_43

Rajagopal, P., Lee, R., Ahlswede, T., Chiang, C.-C., & Karolak, D. (2005). A New Approach to Software Requirements Elicitation. *Sixth International Conference on Software Engineering, Artificial Intelligence, Networking and Parallel/Distributed Computing and First ACIS International Workshop on Self-Assembling Wireless Networks (SNPD/SAWN'05)*, (pp. 32–42). IEEE. 10.1109/SNPD-SAWN.2005.5

Ramesh, M. R. R., & Reddy, Ch. S. (2021). Metrics for software requirements specification quality quantification. *Computers & Electrical Engineering*, *96*, 107445. doi:10.1016/j.compeleceng.2021.107445

Rasheed, A., Zafar, B., Shehryar, T., Aslam, N. A., Sajid, M., Ali, N., Dar, S. H., & Khalid, S. (2021). Requirement Engineering Challenges in Agile Software Development. *Mathematical Problems in Engineering*, *2021*, 1–18. doi:10.1155/2021/6696695

Rautaray, S., & Agrawal, A. (2015, January). Vision based hand gesture recognition for human computer interaction: A survey. *Artificial Intelligence Review*, *43*(1), 1–54. doi:10.100710462-012-9356-9

Raza, K., Amin, M. B., & Keshavjee, K. (2019). An evaluation of machine learning algorithms for stock market prediction. In *2019 IEEE 15th International Conference on e-Science (e-Science)* (pp. 118-127). IEEE.

Razavian, N., Blecker, S., Schmidt, A. M., Smith-McLallen, A., Nigam, S., & Sontag, D. (2015). Population-level prediction of type 2 diabetes from claims data and analysis of risk factors. *Big Data*, *3*(4), 277–287. doi:10.1089/big.2015.0020 PMID:27441408

Ren, F., & Sadanaga, Y. (1998). An Automatic Extraction of Important Sentences Using Statistical Information and Structure Feature (Vol. NL98). Academic Press.

Ren, S., He, K., Girshick, R., & Sun, J. (2015). Faster r-cnn: Towards real-time object detection with region proposal networks. *Advances in Neural Information Processing Systems*, 28.

Rios, J., Jha, S., & Shwartz, L. (2022). Localizing and Explaining Faults in Microservices Using Distributed Tracing. In *2022 IEEE 15th International Conference on Cloud Computing (CLOUD)*. IEEE. 10.1109/CLOUD55607.2022.00072

Robertson, G., Lehmann, E. D., Sandham, W., & Hamilton, D. (2011). Blood glucose prediction using artificial neural networks trained with the AIDA diabetes simulator: A proof-of-concept pilot study. *Journal of Electrical and Computer Engineering*, *681786*, 1–11. Advance online publication. doi:10.1155/2011/681786

Roda-Sanchez, L. (2023). Cloud-edge microservices architecture and service orchestration: An integral solution for a real-world deployment experience. *Internet of Things*.

Rodriguez, G., Wong, L., & Mauricio, D. (2017). A systematic literature review about software requirements elicitation. *Journal of Engineering Science and Technology*, *12*, 296–317.

Romaguera, S., & Sanchis, M. (2003). Applications of utility functions defined on quasi-metric spaces. *Journal of Mathematical Analysis and Applications, 283*(1), 219–235. doi:10.1016/S0022-247X(03)00285-3

Roy, K., Gaur, M., Zhang, Q., & Sheth, A. (2022). *Process knowledge-infused learning for suicidality assessment on social media.* arXiv preprint arXiv:2204.12560.

Roy, A., Nikolitch, K., McGinn, R., Jinah, S., Klement, W., & Kaminsky, Z. A. (2020). A machine learning approach predicts future risk to suicidal ideation from social media data. *NPJ Digital Medicine, 3*(1), 78. doi:10.103841746-020-0287-6 PMID:32509975

Rupp, S. (2019). Importance Of The Hospital Management System. *Electronic Health Reporter.* https://electronichealthreporter.com/importance-of-the-hospital-management-system/

Saeeda, H., Dong, J., Wang, Y., & Abid, M. A. (2020). A proposed framework for improved software requirements elicitation process in SCRUM: Implementation by a real-life Norway-based IT project. *Journal of Software (Malden, MA), 32*(7). doi:10.1002mr.2247

Samantaray, M., Biswal, A. K., Singh, D., Samanta, D., Karuppiah, M., & Joseph, N. P. (2021, December). Optical character recognition (ocr) based vehicle's license plate recognition system using python and opencv. In *2021 5th International Conference on Electronics, Communication and Aerospace Technology (ICECA)* (pp. 849-853). IEEE.

Samuel, A. (1959). Some studies in machine learning using the game of checkers. *IBM Journal of Research and Development, 3*(3), 210–229.

Sarabia, J. M., & Prieto, F. (2009). The Pareto-positive stable distribution: A new descriptive model for city size data. *Physica A: Statistical Mechanics and its Applications, 388*(19), 4179-4191. doi:10.1016/j.physa.2009.06.047

Saxena, C., Garg, M., & Saxena, G. (2022). *Explainable causal analysis of mental health on social media data.* arXiv preprint arXiv:2210.08430.

Scheirer, E., & Slaney, M. (1997). Construction and evaluation of a robust multifeature music/speech discriminator. *Proc. ICASSP97, 2*, 1331-1334. 10.1109/ICASSP.1997.596192

Sethy, K. K., Singh, D., Biswal, A. K., & Sahoo, S. (2022, October). Serverless Implementation of Data Wizard Application using Azure Kubernetes Service and Docker. In *2022 1st IEEE International Conference on Industrial Electronics: Developments & Applications (ICIDeA)* (pp. 214-219). IEEE. 10.1109/ICIDeA53933.2022.9970103

Sevilla, D., Ruiz, S. F. M., & Molina, J. G. (2015). *Inferring Versioned Schemas from NoSQL Databases and Its Applications.* Springer. 10.1007/978-3-319-25264-3_35

Shah, V. (2018). Machine learning for financial prediction: experimentation with stock market prediction using various machine learning algorithms. In *Proceedings of the 2nd International Conference on Advances in Electronics, Computers and Communications* (pp. 51-56). ACM.

Shaikh. (2022). Microservices Design Patterns. *Azure Kubernetes Services with Microservices: Understanding Its Patterns and Architecture*, 61-101.

Sharma, V., Pandey, S., & Garg, S. (2018). Comparative Study of 4G Coverage Mapping Tools. *International Journal of Computer Applications, 179*(38), 6–11.

Sheng, J., Kong, W., & Qi, J. (2020). Process optimization of carbon fiber precursor spinning coagulation process based on surrogate model. *2020 Chinese Automation Congress (CAC)*, Shanghai, China. 10.1109/CAC51589.2020.9326779

Shi, X., Chen, Z., Wang, H., Yeung, D., Wong W., & Woo, W. (2015). *Convolutional lstm network: A machine learning approach for precipitation nowcasting.* arXiv preprint.

Silver, D., Schrittwieser, J., Simonyan, K., Antonoglou, L., Huang, A., Guez, A., Hubert, T., Baker, L., Lai, M., Bolton, A., Chen, Y., Lillicrap, T., Hui, F., Sifre, L., van den Driessche, G., Graepel, T., & Hassabis, D. (2017). Mastering the game of Go without human knowledge. *Nature, 550*(7676), 354–359. doi:10.1038/nature24270 PMID:29052630

Silver, J., Slud, E., & Takamoto, K. (2002). Statistical equilibrium wealth distributions in an exchange economy with stochastic preferences. *Journal of Economic Theory, 106*(2), 417–435. doi:10.1006/jeth.2001.2897

Simon, T., Joo, H., Matthews, I., & Sheikh, Y. (2017). Hand keypoint detection in single images using multiview bootstrapping. *Proc. IEEE Conf. Comput. Vis. Pattern Recognit. (CVPR),* 1145–1153.

Singh, D., Bhanipati, J., Biswal, A. K., Samanta, D., Joshi, S., Shukla, P. K., & Nuagah, S. J. (2021). (b), Bhanipati, J., Biswal, A. K., Samanta, D., Joshi, S., Shukla, P. K., & Nuagah, S. J. (2021). Approach for collision minimization and enhancement of power allocation in WSNs. *Journal of Sensors, 2021,* 1–11. doi:10.1155/2021/7059881

Singh, D., Biswal, A. K., Samanta, D., Singh, D., & Lee, H.-N. (2022). Juice jacking: Security issues and improvements in USB technology. *Sustainability (Basel), 14*(2), 939. doi:10.3390u14020939

Sitabhra, S. (2006). Evidence for power-law tail of the wealth distribution in India. *Physica A: Statistical Mechanics and its Applications, 359,* 555-562. doi:10.1016/j.physa.2005.02.092

Sommerfeld, E., & Malek, S. (2019). Perfectionism moderates the relationship between thwarted belongingness and perceived burdensomeness and suicide ideation in adolescents. *The Psychiatric Quarterly, 90*(4), 671–681. doi:10.100711126-019-09639-y PMID:31037588

Sounders, J. (1996). Real-time discrimination of broadcast speech/music. *Proc. ICASSP96, 2,* 993-996.

Stack Exchange. (2017). Probability that random moves in the game 2048 will win. *Stack Exchange.* https://math.stackexchange.com/questions/727076/probability-that-randommoves-in-the-game-2048-will-win

Stoica, R., & Brouse, P. (2013). IT Project Failure: A Proposed Four-Phased Adaptive Multi-Method Approach. *Procedia Computer Science, 16,* 728–736. doi:10.1016/j.procs.2013.01.076

Sun, T., Wang, J., Zhang, P., Cao, Y., Liu, B., & Wang, D. (2017). Predicting stock price returns using microblog sentiment for chinese stock market. *2017 3rd International Conference on Big Data Computing and Communications (BIGCOM),* (pp. 87-96). IEEE. 10.1109/BIGCOM.2017.59

Sundaramoorthy, S. (2022). *UML diagramming: A case study approach.* CRS Press. doi:10.1201/9781003287124

Sun, H., & Yang, B. (2022). Comparative analysis of machine learning methods for Dogecoin price prediction. *Journal of Business Research, 141,* 269–278. doi:10.1016/j.jbusres.2022.03.015

Sutton, R. S., & Barto, A. G. (1998). *Reinforcement Learning: An Introduction.* MIT press.

Svetnik, V., Liaw, A., Tong, C., Culberson, J. C., Sheridan, R. P., & Feuston, B. P. (2015). Random forest: A classification and regression tool for compound classification and QSAR modeling. *Journal of Chemical Information and Computer Sciences, 43*(6), 1947–1958. doi:10.1021/ci034160g PMID:14632445

Szubert, M. & Jaskowski, W. (2014). Mathematical Analysis of 2048. *The Game 7.* IEEE.

Szubert, M., & Jaskowski, W. (2014). Temporal difference learning of N-tuple networks for the game 2048. *Conference on Computational Intelligence and Games.* IEEE. 10.1109/CIG.2014.6932907

Tan, J., Wang, J., Rinprasertmeechai, D., Xing, R., & Li, Q. (2019). A tensor-based elstm model to predict stock price using financial news. *Proceedings of the 52nd Hawaii International Conference on System Sciences*. Scholar Space. 10.24251/HICSS.2019.201

Tetsuya, S. (2012). How do we get cobb-douglas and leontief functions from ces function: A lecture note on discrete and continuum differentiated object models. *J. Ind. Organ. Educ.*, *6*(1), 1–13.

The Clever Programmer. (2021, May 25). Dogecoin Price Prediction with Machine Learning. *The Clever Programmer*. https://thecleverprogrammer.com/2021/05/25/dogecoin-price-prediction-with-machine-learning/

The Verge. (2021, April 13). *Apple Spring Loaded Event Recap in 14 Minutes*. [Video]. YouTube. https://www.youtube.com/watch?v=GFSiL6zEZF0

Tian, H., Zheng, Y., & Jin, Z. (2020, October). Improved RetinaNet model for the application of small target detection in the aerial images. *IOP Conference Series. Earth and Environmental Science*, *585*(1), 012142. doi:10.1088/1755-1315/585/1/012142

Toda, A., & Walsh, K. (2017). Edgeworth box economies with multiple equilibria. *Econ. Theor. Bull.*, *5*(1), 65–80. doi:10.100740505-016-0102-3

Tohidi, M., & Toghraie, D. (2017). The effect of geometrical parameters, roughness and the number of nanoparticles on the self-diffusion coefficient in couette flow in a nanochannel by using of molecular dynamics simulation. *Physica B, Condensed Matter*, *518*, 20–32. doi:10.1016/j.physb.2017.05.014

Toscani, G. (2006). Kinetic models of opinion formation. *Communications in Mathematical Sciences*, *4*(3), 481–496. doi:10.4310/CMS.2006.v4.n3.a1

Toscani, G., Brugna, C., & Demichelis, S. (2013). Kinetic models for the trading of goods. *Journal of Statistical Physics*, *151*(3–4), 549–566. doi:10.100710955-012-0653-0

Tran, D., Bourdev, L., Fergus, R., Torresani, L., & Paluri, M. (2015). Learning spatiotemporal features with 3d convolutional networks. Proceedings of the IEEE international conference on computer vision, (pp. 4489-4497). IEEE. 10.1109/ICCV.2015.510

Trends, D. (2021, March 2). *What is Clubhouse? The Invite-Only Social Media App Explained*. [Video]. YouTube. https://www.youtube.com/watch?v=FMKnvsKoQxE

Tripathi, D., Edla, D. R., Kuppili, V., & Bablani, A. (2020). Evolutionary extreme learning machine with novel activation function for credit scoring. *Engineering Applications of Artificial Intelligence*, *96*, 103980. doi:10.1016/j.engappai.2020.103980

Unhelkar, B. (2018). Software engineering with UML. CRC Press, Taylor & Francis Group, USA.

Uysal, M. P. (2021). Machine learning and data science project management from an agile perspective: Methods and challenges. In V. Naidoo & R. Verma (Eds.), *Contemporary challenges for agile project management* (pp. 73–89). IGI Global.

Uysal, M. P. (2022a). Machine learning-enabled healthcare information systems in view of Industrial Information Integration Engineering. *Journal of Industrial Information Integration*, *30*(1), 1–18. doi:10.1016/j.jii.2022.100382

Uysal, M. P. (2022b). An integrated and multi-perspective approach to the requirements of machine learning. *IFIP International Conference on Industrial Information Integration (ICIIIE 2022)*, Bangkok, Thailand.

Varun, K., & Vanamala, C. K., Jain, S., & Saligram, S. (2018). Game Playing Agent for 2048 using Deep Reinforcement Learning, NCICCNDA 2018. *AIJR Proceedings 1*, (pp. 363-370). Research gate.

Verduyn, P., Ybarra, O., Résibois, M., Jonides, J., & Kross, E. (2017). Do social network sites enhance or undermine subjective well-being? A critical review. *Social Issues and Policy Review*, *11*(1), 274–302. doi:10.1111ipr.12033

Veth, K. N., Korzilius, H. P. L. M., Van der Heijden, B. I. J. M., Emans, B. J. M., & De Lange, A. H. (2019). Which HRM practices enhance employee outcomes at work across the life-span? *International Journal of Human Resource Management*, *21*(3), 1–32. doi:10.1080/09585192.2017.1340322

Villamizar, H., Escovedo, T., & Kalinowski, M. (2021). *Requirements engineering for machine learning: A systematic mapping study. 47th Euromicro Conference on Software Engineering and Advanced Applications (SEAA)*, Palermo, Italy. 10.1109/SEAA53835.2021.00013

Viswanath, A. D. K., M., S., B., & P., E. (2020). *Calibration of a Pyranometer using Regression Analysis*. 2020 5th International Conference on Communication and Electronics Systems (ICCES), Coimbatore, India.

Walia, G. S., & Carver, J. C. (2009). A systematic literature review to identify and classify software requirement errors. *Information and Software Technology*, *51*(7), 1087–1109. doi:10.1016/j.infsof.2009.01.004

Wang, C. Y., Bochkovskiy, A., & Liao, H. Y. M. (2023). YOLOv7: Trainable bag-of-freebies sets new state-of-the-art for real-time object detectors. In *Proceedings of the IEEE/CVF Conference on Computer Vision and Pattern Recognition* (pp. 7464-7475). IEEE.

Wang, Q., & Shen, Y. (2013). Particle Swarm Optimization-Least Squares Support Vector Regression with Multi-scale Wavelet Kernel. *2013 Sixth International Symposium on Computational Intelligence and Design*, Hangzhou, China, .

Wang, Q., Yang, M., & Zhang, W. (2021). Accessing the influence of perceived value on social attachment: Developing country perspective. *Frontiers in Psychology*, *12*, 760774. doi:10.3389/fpsyg.2021.760774 PMID:34721242

Wang, Y., Jia, Y., Tian, Y., & Xiao, J. (2022). Deep reinforcement learning with the confusion-matrix-based dynamic reward function for customer credit scoring. *Expert Systems with Applications*, *200*, 117013. doi:10.1016/j.eswa.2022.117013

Wang, Y., Zhang, Y., & Wang, C. (2021). 5G Network Coverage Optimization Based on Big Data Analytics. *IEEE Transactions on Big Data*, *7*(2), 347–359.

Wang, Y., Zhao, L., & Zhang, H. (2021). A hybrid model for Dogecoin price prediction based on ARIMA and machine learning. *Journal of Intelligent & Fuzzy Systems*, *41*(3), 4443–4451. doi:10.3233/JIFS-200426

Wan, J., Wang, D., Hoi, S. C. H., Wu, P., Zhu, J., Zhang, Y., & Li, J. (2014, November). Deep learning for content-based image retrieval: A comprehensive study. In *Proceedings of the 22nd ACM international conference on Multimedia* (pp. 157-166). 10.1145/2647868.2654948

Watkins, A. B., & Boggess, L. (2002). A resource limited artificial immune classifier. In *Proceedings of the 2002 Congress on Evolutionary Computation (CEC2002)*. IEEE Press. 10.1109/CEC.2002.1007049

Wei, X., Xie, Z., Cheng, R., & Li, Q. (2020). A cnn based system for predicting the implied volatility and option prices. *Proceedings of the 53rd Hawaii International Conference on System Sciences*. IEEE. 10.24251/HICSS.2020.176

Wibhowo, C., & Sanjaya, R. (2021, July). Virtual assistant to suicide prevention in individuals with borderline personality disorder. In *2021 International Conference on Computer & Information Sciences (ICCOINS)* (pp. 234-237). IEEE. 10.1109/ICCOINS49721.2021.9497160

WojkeN.BewleyA.PaulusD. (2017, September). Simple online and realtime tracking with a deep association metric. In *2017 IEEE international conference on image processing (ICIP)* (pp. 3645-3649). IEEE.

Wu, C. F., Huang, S. C., Chiou, C. C., & Wang, Y. M. (2021). A predictive intelligence system of credit scoring based on deep multiple kernel learning. *Applied Soft Computing*, *111*, 107668. doi:10.1016/j.asoc.2021.107668

Xavier, G. & Yannis, I. (2004). *Chapter 53 - The Evolution of City Size Distributions*. In J. Vernon Henderson & Jacques-François Thisse (eds.), *Handbook of Regional and Urban Economics, 4*, 2341-2378. Elsevier. doi:10.1016/S1574-0080(04)80010-5

Xie, H. L., & You, T. (2018). *Research on european stock index options pricing based on deep learning algorithm:evidence from 50etf options markets*. Statistics & Information Forum.

Xie, X., Cheng, G., Wang, J., Yao, X., & Han, J. (2021). Oriented R-CNN for object detection. In *Proceedings of the IEEE/CVF International Conference on Computer Vision* (pp. 3520-3529). IEEE.

Xu, C., Guo, R., Zhang, Y., & Luo, X. (2023). Toward an Efficient and Effective Credit Scorer for Cross-Border E-Commerce Enterprises. *Scientific Programming, 2023*. Asencios, R., Asencios, C., & Ramos, E. (2023). Profit scoring for credit unions using the multilayer perceptron, XGBoost and TabNet algorithms: Evidence from Peru. *Expert Systems with Applications*, *213*, 119201.

Yahiaoui, I., Merialdo, B., & Huet, B. (2001). Generating summaries of multi-episode video. *Proc. IEEE Int. Conf. Multimedia and Expo,* 792-795.

Yang, G., Pang, Z., Deen, J., Dong, M., Zhang, Y., & Lovell, N. (2020). Homecare Robotic Systems for Healthcare 4.0: Visions and Enabling Technologies. *IEEE J. Biomed. Health Inform.* IEEE.

Yang, F., Qiao, Y., Qi, Y., Bo, J., & Wang, X. (2022). BACS: Blockchain and AutoML-based technology for efficient credit scoring classification. *Annals of Operations Research*, 1–21. doi:10.100710479-022-04531-8 PMID:35095154

Yang, M., Zhang, W., Ruangkanjanases, A., & Zhang, Y. (2021). Understanding the mechanism of social attachment role in social media: A qualitative analysis. *Frontiers in Psychology*, *12*, 720880. doi:10.3389/fpsyg.2021.720880 PMID:34421773

Yang, X., & Yan, S. (2021). Review and Prospects of Enterprise Human Resource Management Effectiveness: Bibliometric Analysis Based on Chinese-Language and English-Language Journals. *Sustainability*, *14*(2), 78–89.

Yannis, I. (2013). Spyros Skouras, US city size distribution: Robustly Pareto, but only in the tail. Journal of Urban Economics, *73*(1) 18-29. doi:10.1016/j.jue.2012.06.005

Ye, Q., Qin, L., Forgues, M., He, P., Kim, J. W., Peng, A. C., Simon, R., Li, Y., Robles, A. I., Chen, Y., Ma, Z.-C., Wu, Z.-Q., Ye, S.-L., Liu, Y.-K., Tang, Z.-Y., & Wang, X. W. (2003). Predicting hepatitis B virus–positive metastatic hepatocellular carcinomas using gene expression profiling and supervised machine learning. *Nature Medicine*, *9*(4), 416–423. doi:10.1038/nm843 PMID:12640447

Yoo, J. S., Kim, D. H., & Jung, Y. J. (2018). Stock price prediction using a hybrid machine learning approach. *Journal of Computational and Applied Mathematics*, *330*, 1109–1118.

Yue, C., Xin, L., Kewen, X., & Chang, S. (2008). An intelligent diagnosis to type 2 diabetes based on QPSO algorithm and WLS-SVM. *Proceedings of the 2008 IEEE International Symposium on Intelligent Information Technology Application Workshops*. 10.1109/IITA.Workshops.2008.36

Yussupov, V. (2020). Pattern-based modelling, integration, and deployment of microservice architectures. In *2020 IEEE 24th International Enterprise Distributed Object Computing Conference (EDOC)*. IEEE. 10.1109/EDOC49727.2020.00015

Zaman, H. (2011). An edgeworth box approach toward conceptualising economic integration. *Mod. Econ.*, *2*(1), 62–70. doi:10.4236/me.2011.21010

Zhang, T., & Kuo, C.-C. (1999). Video content parsing based on combined audio and visual information. Proc. SPIE 1999, 4, 78-89.

Zhang, J., Zhang, W., & Wang, X. (2021). 5G Coverage Mapping Based on Crowdsourcing Data. *IEEE Access : Practical Innovations, Open Solutions*, *9*, 20011–20019.

Zhang, Z., Niu, K., & Liu, Y. (2020). A deep learning based online credit scoring model for P2P lending. *IEEE Access : Practical Innovations, Open Solutions*, *8*, 177307–177317. doi:10.1109/ACCESS.2020.3027337

Zhao, Z. Q., Zheng, P., Xu, S. T., & Wu, X. (2019). Object detection with deep learning: A review. *IEEE Transactions on Neural Networks and Learning Systems*, *30*(11), 3212–3232. doi:10.1109/TNNLS.2018.2876865 PMID:30703038

Zirikly, A., Resnik, P., Uzuner, O., & Hollingshead, K. (2019, June). CLPsych 2019 shared task: Predicting the degree of suicide risk in Reddit posts. In *Proceedings of the sixth workshop on computational linguistics and clinical psychology* (pp. 24-33). 10.18653/v1/W19-3003

About the Contributors

Debabrata Samanta is presently working as Assistant Professor, at the Rochester Institute of Technology, Kosovo, Europe. He obtained his Ph.D. in Computer Science and Engg. from the National Institute of Technology, Durgapur, India, in the area of SAR Image Processing. His areas of interest are SAR Image Analysis, Video surveillance, Heuristic algorithms for image classification, Deep Learning Framework for Detection and Classification, Blockchain, Statistical Modelling, Wireless Adhoc Networks, Natural Language Processing, and V2I Communication. He is the owner of 22 Indian Patents. He has authored and co-authored over 207 research papers in international journals (SCI/SCIE/ESCI/Scopus) and conferences including IEEE, Springer, and Elsevier Conference proceedings. He received "Scholastic Award" at the 2nd International Conference on Computer Science and IT application, CSIT-2011, Delhi, India. He has published 9 books, available for sale on Amazon and Flipkart.

* * *

Tapan Kumar Behera is a Software Architect and specializes in Robotic Process Automation, he has over the years channelled his expertise within the healthcare, market research space. Tapan advises business and technology leaders in the transformation of both their organization and technology platform. He has worked with several Fortune 500 healthcare, market research and product-based companies such as Forrester Research, Walgreens, Cognizant, Hewlett-Packard, DXC and HCL. His experience cuts across a wide range of projects in Robotic Process Automation, RCA Bot, Master Data Management, Walgreens Mobile Application Service, Integration of Systems, Application Modernization, and Search engine tuning using AI/ML and so on.

Saurabh Bhattacharya is a Management graduate with an M.Com and an MBA from BIMTECH. A Business Analyst by day and a research scholar by Night.

Anil Kumar Biswal is currently pursing PhD in Computer Science and Engineering from ITER, Siksha 'O' Anusandhan (Deemed to be University). He has also an extensive record of teaching for the past 7 years and his research interests include Wireless Sensor Networks, Cloud Computing and IoT. He has worked on various research projects that solve some social related issues like traffic with street light monitoring process, drowsiness detection system, designing women safety App, etc.

Muskan Garg is working as postdoctoral research fellow at Mayo Clinic, Rochester, Minnesota. She was previously working as Postdoctoral research associate at University of Florida and as an assistant professor in Thapar institute of engineering and technology, Patiala. Her research focuses on the problems in natural language processing, information retrieval, and social media analysis. She received her Masters and PhD from Panjab University, India. Prior to TIET, she has worked as an assistant professor in Amity school of engineering and technology at Amity University. Her focus is on research and development of cutting edge NLP approaches to solving problems of national and international importance and on initiation and broadening a new program in natural language processing (including a new NLP course series). Her current research interests are causal inference, mental health on social media, event detection and sentiment analysis. She contributes as a reviewer in The ACM Transactions on Asian and Low-Resource Language Information Processing (TALLIP) and Expert Systems with Applications.

Harisankar Mahapatra is currently pursing BTech in Computer Science and Engineering from NIST Institute of Science and Technology (Autonomous).

Suplab Podder is a Management Professional with rich experience in the field of Teaching, Content Development and Management Research. He is the Life Member of Management Teachers Consortium-Global (MTC Global). He obtained his Bachelor of Business Management (BBM) form Bangalore University, Bangalore. He obtained Master of Business Administration (MBA) from Newport University, 2006. He obtained another Master of Business Administration (MBA) from Allagappa University, Tamil Nadu. He is awarded Ph.D in Management from Bharathiar University, Coimbatore, India. He is presently working as an Assistant Professor of Management and Commerce Department in Dayananda Sagar College of Arts, Science and Commerce, Bangalore, India. His areas of interests are Human Resource Management, Outsourcing, Banking and Insurance, Managerial Economics, Marketing Management and Strategic Management. He has published 24 books and published 6 Research Papers. He has attended and presented research papers.

Rajesh Kanna Rajendran has 15 years of Teaching experience and current working at Department of Computer Science, CHRIST(Deemed to be University),Bangalore, India. He has 27 International Peer Reviewed Research Publications, 3 Patents, 3 Book Chapter and Author of 5 Books.He is a Member of Board of Studies in various colleges, acted as a Research Person for Various National and International Level Events. He Received Research funds from various funding agencies like, DST SERB, ICSSR etc.

Milan Samantaray is currently pursing in Computer Science and Engineering from C.V. Raman Global University. She is presently working as an Assistant Professor with the Dept of Computer Science and Engineering, Trident Academy of Technology, Bhubaneswar, India. She is keenly interested in Interdisciplinary Research & Development and has experience spanning fields of Protocol design in Wireless Sensor Networks, Wireless Adhoc Network, Network Security, Cloud Computing, Cloud Native applications, Machine Learning and IoT applications.

Amrit Singh is currently pursing BTech in Computer Science and Engineering from NIST Institute of Science and Technology (Autonomous).

Debabrata Singh is presently working as an Associate Professor with the Dept of Computer Application, ITER, Siksha O Anusandhan Deemed to be University, Bhubaneswar, India. He obtained his Ph.D. degree in Computer Science & Engineering from the SOA Deemed to be University, Odisha, India. He is keenly interested in Interdisciplinary Research & Development and has experience spanning fields of Protocol design in Wireless Sensor Networks, Wireless Adhoc Network, Network Security, Cloud Computing, Cloud Native applications and IoT applications. In his past 15 years of teaching experience, he has authored and coauthored over 78 research papers in International Journal (SCI/SCIE/ESCI/Scopus) and conferences including IEEE, Springer and Elsevier Conference proceeding. He also serves as acquisition Editorial/Reviewing Board Member in reputed Journals such as IJCS, IJITME, IJETTCS, JoC, IJCER, IJLTEMAS, IJNC. He has received "Bentham Ambassador" Award in 2019 and Best Outstanding Researcher Award 2020 from Kamarajar Institute of Education and Research (KIER). He is a Convener, Keynote speaker, Session chair, Co-chair, Publicity chair, Publication chair, Advisory Board, Technical Program Committee members in many prestigious International and National conferences. He was invited speaker at several Institutions. He has also acted as a reviewer in various review processes in IJE, International Journals like IEEE Access, IJDSN, IJCS, JESTR, IJETTCS, IJETTCS, IJCNC, IJWSC, IJSCC, IJNS, and International Conferences. He has also acted as Organizing & Technical Program Committee Member in reputed International Conferences i.e. NetCom-2013, ICCD-2014, ICOSST -2016, TROPMET-2016, ICACIE-2018, ICCIDA-2018, ICCSP-19, ICICC-19,ICME-2019, ICCIDS-2019, WITCON ECE -2019, MIND-2020, ICACIE-2020 & ICADCML-2021, ICAIHC 2022.

Mohana Priya T. is Assistant Professor at CHRIST(Deemed to be University), Bangalore, India. She Holds a PhD degree in Computer Science in Machine learning at Bharathiar University, Coimbatore, India. Her research areas are Machine Learing and medical image analysis. She is acted as Coordinator for curriculum development cell and Software development cell.She published 10 Journal articles in various international peer reviewed journals, 2 Book publications and 15 presentations in various international level conference held in India and abroad.

Murat Pasa Uysal is a faculty member at the Department of Management Information Systems, Baskent University, Turkey. He holds a B.S degree in electrical & electronic engineering, a M.S degree in computer engineering, and a Ph.D. degree in educational technology. He completed his post-doctoral studies at Rochester Institute of Technology in New York, USA. His research interest is in the areas of information systems, software engineering, machine learning and project management.

Index

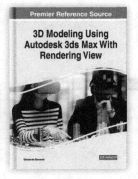

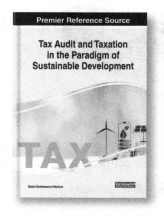

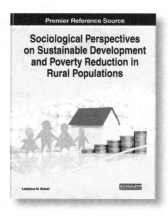

 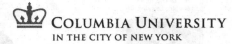

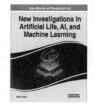

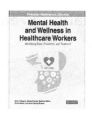

Printed in the United States
by Baker & Taylor Publisher Services